# Contents

# About the Author

Laura J. Hall, Ph.D., is a Professor at San Diego State University (SDSU) in the Department of Special Education. She has been working with individuals with autism spectrum disorders and their families for over 30 years and is responsible for the creation of the master's degree program with a specialization in autism at SDSU. Her current research interests focus on factors that facilitate the implementation of evidence-based practices by educators, and interventions that promote social interaction between learners with autism spectrum disorders and their peers. Dr. Hall's involvement with several boards of nonprofit organizations supporting autism is another way in which she is working to develop a solid community of practice in San Diego.

# Brief Contents

# Autism Spectrum Disorders

## From Theory to Practice

### Second Edition

DATE DUE

| | | | |
|---|---|---|---|
| 7/14 | | | |
| 28/16 | | | |

LAURA J. HALL

*San Diego State University*

PEARSON

Boston  Columbus  Indianapolis  New York  San Francisco  Upper Saddle River
Amsterdam  Cape Town  Dubai  London  Madrid  Milan  Munich  Paris  Montreal  Toronto
Delhi  Mexico City  Sao Paulo  Sydney  Hong Kong  Seoul  Singapore  Taipei  Tokyo

# Dedication

*Pat Krantz, Lynn McClannahan, and Sam Odom*
*Inspirational role models, mentors, and friends*

**Vice President and Editorial Director:** Jeffrey W. Johnston
**Executive Editor and Publisher:** Stephen D. Dragin
**Editorial Assistant:** Katherine Wiley
**Director of Marketing:** Margaret Waples
**Production Project Manager:** Elizabeth Gale Napolitano
**Image Permission Coordinator:** Mike Lackey

**Full-Service Project Management:** Pavithra Jayapaul, Jouve India
**Composition:** Jouve India
**Manager, Central Design:** Jayne Conte
**Cover Designer:** Bruce Kenselaar
**Cover Image:** © Papirazzi/Fotolia
**Printer/Binder/Cover Printer:** R. R. Donnelley & Sons/ Harrisonburg
**Text Font:** Palatino

Credits and acknowledgments borrowed from other sources and reproduced, with permission, in this textbook appear on the appropriate page within text.

**Library of Congress Cataloging-in-Publication Data**

Hall, Laura J.
Autism spectrum disorders : from theory to practice/Laura J. Hall. — 2nd ed.
  p. cm.
  Includes bibliographical references and indexes.
  ISBN-13: 978-0-13-265809-6
  ISBN-10: 0-13-265809-7
1. Autism in children. 2. Autistic children—Rehabilitation. I. Title.
  RJ506.A9H18 2012
  618.92'85882—dc23

                                        2012001265

10 9 8 7 6 5 4 3 2 1

ISBN 10: 0-13-265809-7
ISBN 13: 978-0-13-265809-6

# Preface

While researchers are trying to determine the currently unknown cause of autism spectrum disorders (ASD), there is a need for effective strategies to address the characteristics displayed by individuals with this classification. The need for knowledgeable and skilled educators who can identify and implement evidence-based practices is critical and is likely to remain so well into the future. *Autism Spectrum Disorders: From Theory to Practice* is a comprehensive text that provides information about ASD from up-to-date research on brain development and genetics to working with families to prepare adolescents and young adults for transition. Descriptions of common practices used by educators are organized by the theoretical perspective on which each practice is based. How to determine whether there is research support for a practice, or whether a practice is evidence-based, is explained. The research support, or lack thereof, is provided following each description of the approach, programs, and current practices.

## New to This Edition

The passing of the Combating Autism Act in 2006 and the increase in prevalence of ASD that continues to be reported by the Centers for Disease Control and Prevention has resulted in increased funding for research and increased attention by researchers. Each chapter in this revised edition has been updated to reflect the most current research outcomes. This edition also uses the results from several recent publications of literature reviews that have

identified evidence-based strategies and comprehensive programs (e.g., from the National Standards Project and the National Professional Development Center on Autism Spectrum Disorders) as the basis for reviewing common practices. The American Psychiatric Association has proposed new criteria for autism spectrum disorder for their revised diagnostic manual, which is planned for publication in 2013. This edition describes the criteria proposed in the DSM-5 and relates current research and practice to the newly proposed criteria. The following is a list of changes and updates in the second edition of *Autism Spectrum Disorders*:

- Literature reviews of all content areas have been updated, and description and emphasis on the identification of practices and strategies with sufficient research evidence, as determined by the National Standards Project and the National Professional Development Center on ASD, will provide state-of-the-art information about which practices are scientifically based.

- A chapter on Transition to Adulthood (Chapter 10) has been added. Content on preparing adolescents and young adults for post-secondary life will inform those working with this age range as well as those who wish to ensure that individuals with ASD are well prepared for adult life.

- Cultural and linguistic considerations are emphasized throughout the text, and especially so in the updated chapter on Cultural Approaches (Chapter 7), so that all practitioners are sensitive, knowledgeable, and aware of the influences of culture and language and can implement culturally responsive strategies.

■ The content on implementation of practices has been enhanced and moved to Chapter 3, where best practices in implementation science through the collaboration of stakeholders is discussed. Identification of evidence-based practices is only the first step; effective implementation is necessary for positive outcomes.

■ Each chapter contains suggestions for future research, and these updates take into account research questions that have been addressed in recent years and new questions that have arisen as a result of ongoing research. Students planning to conduct research will find the summaries of current research and recommendations for future research helpful in designing projects.

■ New contributors to the In Their Words features include, among others, leading professionals in the areas of parent-implemented programs for young children (Brooke Ingersoll) and family involvement during transition (Bonnie Kraemer); a teacher's perspective on implementing an evidence-based practice (Cindy Bolduc); and a young adult with ASD who provides excellent advice for preparing for, and gaining support during, post-secondary education (Erik Weber).

## Organization of the Book

The text is organized into three parts. Part I includes three introductory chapters. Chapter 1 focuses on the current approaches to determining the causes of autism spectrum disorders and provides a description of strategies used to address this disorder on a physiological level, such as through prescription medication, diet,

or activities to arouse or calm the sensory systems. Chapter 2 provides information regarding assessment that is organized by purpose (screening, diagnosis, educational planning). The emphasis in this chapter is on curriculum-based assessment that links assessment results to educational practice. The identification and effective implementation of evidence-based strategies are addressed in Chapter 3. This chapter is organized using *wh*-questions to discuss why, when, and where to intervene; who typically provides service; and what curriculum objectives are targeted. A description of the individualized education program (IEP) process is provided. The importance of working in collaboration with families and paraprofessionals is emphasized with recommendations for effective practice.

The following four chapters describe the programs and practices used to increase the skills of individuals with autism spectrum disorders and comprise Part II of the book. Each chapter is organized by theoretical perspective. Chapters 4 and 5 focus on programs and strategies based on applied behavior analysis. Programs and practices influenced by the developmental and social-relational theories are included in Chapter 6, and Chapter 7 focuses on the cultural approach to working with individuals with autism spectrum disorders. An emphasis on working collaboratively with families is discussed in all approaches, regardless of theoretical perspective. Each approach or program model includes a brief description of the theoretical perspective, an historical overview of strategies used by educators working with individuals with autism spectrum disorders, definitions and descriptions of key concepts of the approach, examples and illustrations of strategies based on key concepts, a description of a model program or classroom based on the approach, and a summary of the research evidence for the approach and practices.

Part III contains three chapters. The first two put together the information across the theoretical approaches described in Part II to address two areas that are frequently a focus for educators: communication (Chapter 8) and social relationships (Chapter 9). Chapter 10 focuses on preparing adolescents and young adults for transition. Best practices are summarized with examples of high-quality programs. Chapter 10 includes many resources for additional information and materials. This last chapter (and the book) concludes with a description of the major contributions to the field made by families and the importance of working in collaboration with families to influence policy, change systems, and build communities of practice.

## Features of the Text

### In Their Words

Boxes called In Their Words, found in each chapter, feature input and quotes from professionals and parents of individuals with autism spectrum disorders, and interviews with adults identified on the spectrum. These features augment the chapter content by enabling the reader to obtain the perspective of professionals using various theoretical approaches (e.g., Drs. Krantz and McClannahan, Dr. Mesibov, Dr. Wolfberg), from various disciplines such as speech-language pathology (Colleen Sparkman), occupational therapy (Janinne Karahalios), psychology (Dr. Natacha Akshoomoff, Dr. Brooke Ingersoll), and special education (Dr. Dean Fixsen, Dr. Bonnie Kraemer, Dr. Angela McIntosh, Sheila Wagner). Special education teachers (Cindy Bolduc, Penelope Bonggat), parents (Laura Wood, Juan and Sharon Leon) and adults with autism spectrum disorders (Eric, T. Lopez, Erik Weber) provide their perspective on employment, living independently with support, post-secondary education, and friendship and marriage.

### Evolution of Practices

The Evolution of Practices is a feature included in most chapters to reflect the development of approaches and practices over time and to capture the historical progression of events or strategy development. Educational practices with learners with autism spectrum disorders are far from static. These practices are influenced by changes in philosophy, policies, and research outcomes.

### Research Emphasis

The importance of research is emphasized throughout the text, including a review of the evidence for practices and suggestions for future research. This emphasis will be particularly helpful to master's degree and doctoral candidates, but it will provide direction for all practitioners who are working to further the field with information on the effectiveness of intervention strategies. Understanding the research evidence, or lack thereof, is important for all educators who are required to use only scientifically based practices.

### Chapter Objectives, Suggestions for Discussion, Resources

Each chapter begins with a list of chapter objectives for the information that can be learned by reading the chapter content. Chapters conclude with two features. The first is a list of suggestions for discussion that are focused on key points from the respective chapter. These suggestions for discussion include a suggestion for a debate (usually number 3 in the list) on a particular issue from the chapter. A list of resources (books and websites) provides additional information on various topics found in the respective chapter.

## New! CourseSmart eTextbook Available

CourseSmart is an exciting new choice for students looking to save money. As an alternative to purchasing the printed textbook, students can purchase an electronic version of the same content. With a CourseSmart eTextbook, students can search the text, make notes online, print out reading assignments that incorporate lecture notes, and bookmark important passages for later review. For more information or to purchase access to the CourseSmart eTextbook, visit www.coursesmart.com.

## Acknowledgments

This book would not have been possible without the education, professional guidance, and encouragement provided by my professional mentors Pat Krantz, Lynn McClannahan, Beth Sulzer-Azaroff, Gail McGee, and Sam Odom. I am also grateful to the individuals with autism spectrum disorders who taught me a great deal about how to address educational challenges with clarity, consistency, and humor. I am appreciative of the parents of the learners with ASD who have sought and supported my skills and have served as excellent partners. A special thank-you goes to my students, who have been exceptional research collaborators and who inspire me with the energy, enthusiasm, and affection that they bring to their work with learners and their families. I continue to learn from each of them.

This book would not have been possible without those at Pearson, such as Ann Castel Davis, who worked with me to actualize our vision for the text; Steve Dragin, who so clearly identified the book's strengths and areas that could be made stronger for the second edition; and Annette Joseph and Jamie Bushell, who responded to my many questions with speed and information. Much appreciation goes to Marianne L'Abbate from Jouve India who read every word in this book and offered valuable suggestions for clarity of the contents.

I would also like to thank the reviewers who provided excellent suggestions that contributed to the improvements in this second edition: Jonna L. Bobzien, Old Dominion University; Rita Brusca-Vega, Purdue University Calumet; Nilsa J. Thorsos, Azusa Pacific University; and Kathi Wilhite, East Carolina University. I would also like to express my gratitude to Cindy Bolduc and Amanda Romero for their help organizing the references, and to my family, especially my mother Phyllis Hall, who is an unequalled source of support and encouragement.

# CHAPTER ONE

# Classification and the Physiological Approach

The reader should be able to:

- Describe the deficits that are necessary for the diagnosis of autism spectrum disorder (ASD) according to the proposed DSM-5.
- Discuss the increase in reported prevalence rate and the factors that contribute to this finding.
- State the special diets that are used by children with ASD and briefly summarize the results of the double-blind research conducted on the GFCF diet.
- Provide a rationale used by occupational therapists for the use of sensory activities and discuss the implications for the lack of evidence to support these interventions.

The Autism Society of America (ASA) uses a ribbon of puzzle pieces as the symbol of autism spectrum disorders. This symbol is used because so much about autism spectrum disorders (ASD) remains unknown, or a puzzle.

Written on the About Autism page of the ASA website is the comment:

> Autism is defined by a certain set of behaviors and is a "spectrum disorder" that affects individuals differently and to varying degrees. There is no known single cause for autism, but increased awareness and funding can help families today. (Autism Society of America, 2011)

In this chapter the currently used classification systems of the *Diagnostic and Statistical Manual of Mental Disorders*, the *International Classification of Diseases*, and the classifications under the Individuals with Disabilities Education Act will be described. Each of these systems represents the consensus opinions of the authors at the time of publication, and all are revised as additional information about autism spectrum disorders is learned.

The evidence for a genetic influence on autism spectrum disorders and the current areas of focus in determining the cause will be explored. Much of the effort to find the cause focuses on the biology and physiology of individuals with ASD and their families. Interventions that address the biological or physiological aspects of an individual with autism spectrum disorder, such as the prescription of medication, recommendation for a special diet, and organizing activities that address arousal (calming or stimulating) such as sensory interventions, will be reviewed. In summary, this chapter includes a description of various classification systems for autism spectrum disorders; an explanation of the genetic, biological, and physiological areas under investigation to determine a cause; and descriptions of interventions aimed at changing the physiology of the individual.

## Classification Systems of Autism Spectrum Disorders

Classification of the characteristics associated with autism spectrum disorders (ASD) into a specific category occurred in the 1940s by Leo Kanner, a U.S. psychiatrist (1943), and Hans Asperger, a German pediatrician (1944). Influenced by adult psychiatry, the term **autistic** (derived from the Greek word *autos* for "self") was used as the description of negative symptoms when someone was entirely uninterested in the outside world (Houston & Frith, 2000). Kanner described a triad of impairments (social difficulties, communication problems, and repetitive and restricted activities) in his paper about 11 children from the Child Psychiatric Unit at Johns Hopkins University where he worked (Mesibov, Shea, & Adams, 2001).

Lorna Wing was one of the first people to use the term **spectrum** when describing a group of individuals displaying the characteristics of autism. In their project conducted in the 1970s (the Camberwell study), Wing and Gould (1978) found that individuals with autism varied in the degree of severity of their displayed characteristics, as well as in the form of differences and delays, leading the authors to begin to discuss this spectrum of disorders (Houston & Frith, 2000). Included in this spectrum were

individuals with no cognitive delays, referred to by the researchers as individuals with high-functioning autism, and individuals with Asperger syndrome (Wing, Leekam, Libby, Gould, & Larcombe, 2002). Wing was aware of Hans Asperger's work, and when she began to publish her research in the early 1980s she used the term **Asperger syndrome**, resulting in international awareness of this classification. Prior to this time, Asperger's work was not well known due to the fact that it was published only in German (Mesibov et al., 2001).

### Diagnostic and Statistical Manual of Mental Disorders

One of the main classification systems used internationally is the *Diagnostic and Statistical Manual of Mental Disorders* (DSM) published by the American Psychiatric Association (APA). Details of the characteristics that classify individuals with varying diagnoses are made by a group of psychiatrists, psychologists, and physicians with expertise in the area. The proposed criteria for the fifth edition of the manual are available for review on the APA website at www.dsm5 .org, and will be available in print form in 2013. The focus of the revised DSM version is on the variability in severity of characteristics that comprise autism spectrum disorders compared with the separate identification of Pervasive Developmental Disorders in the DSM-III and IV such as autistic disorder, Asperger syndrome, and pervasive developmental disorder not otherwise specified (PDD-NOS) (American Psychiatric Association, 1980; 1987; 1994, 2000).

The proposed criteria used for autism spectrum disorder include persistent deficits in (a) social communication and social interaction across contexts, and (b) restricted, repetitive patterns of behavior, interests, and activities with (c) symptoms that must be present in childhood that (d) limit and impair everyday functioning. Individuals must have deficits in all three subcategories of social communication and social interaction (deficits in [1] social-emotional reciprocity, [2] nonverbal communicative

**TABLE 1.1** Sample changes in diagnostic criteria for autism from the DSM

| DSM III-1980 | DSM IIIR-1987 | DSM IV-1994 and TR-2000 | Proposed DSM-5 2013 |
|---|---|---|---|
| Onset before 30 months | Onset before 36 months | Delays or abnormal functioning in one area (social interaction, language or play) before 36 months | Symptoms in early childhood |
| Gross deficits in language development | Qualitative impairment in both verbal and nonverbal communication | Qualitative impairment in communication | No separate impairments for communication |
| Pervasive lack of responsiveness to others | Qualitative impairment in reciprocal social interaction | Qualitative impairment in social interaction | Deficits in social-emotional reciprocity and social relationships |

behaviors, [3] developing and maintaining relationships) and two of four subcategories of restricted and repetitive patterns of behavior ([1] stereotyped or repetitive speech, motor movements or object use, [2] excessive adherence to routines, or ritualized patterns of verbal or nonverbal behavior, [3] highly restricted, fixated interests, [4] hyper- or hyporeactivity to sensory stimuli) to receive a diagnosis (http://www.dsm5.org/ProposedRevisions/Pages). Children with this diagnosis may have skill areas where they are functioning similar to typical peers or may even exceed the skills of peers in areas such as music, math, or reading.

The proposed criteria for the DSM-5 represent a change in the classification category as well as the sub criteria that comprise the symptoms compared with earlier versions of the manual (American Psychiatric Association, 1980, 1987, 1994, 2000). Table 1.1 shows some of the changes in language and age of onset for the versions between 1980 and 2011. It appears from the changes in diagnostic criteria over time that children can get a diagnosis if fewer characteristics appear later. Hyper- or hyposensitivity to sensory stimuli was included in early diagnostic versions (DSM III, 1980) and again in the latest proposed version (www.dsm5.org, 2011).

The proposed DSM-5 criteria were created under the assumption that deficits in communication and social interaction are inseparable and it is more accurate to consider them together and influenced by contextual and environmental variables. This decision was made based on literature reviews, expert consultation, and workgroup discussions (www.dsm5.org). Because distinctions among the disorders in previous versions of the manual were found to be inconsistent over time, and the use of diagnostic categories varied across sites, use of a single diagnostic category (autism spectrum disorder) was adopted in the latest version (www.dsm5.org). In the proposed DSM-5, it is recommended that the level of severity for social communication and restricted interests and repetitive behaviors is considered on a scale of 1 (requiring support) to 3 (requiring very substantial support).

### International Classification of Diseases

The *International Classification of Diseases*, published by the World Health Organization (WHO), is in its tenth version and is referred to as the ICD-10. The ICD-11 revision is in process and the target completion date is 2015 (http://www.who.int/classifications/icd/revision/en/index.html). This classification system is used widely in Europe as well as in other countries worldwide. Autism first appeared in the ICD in 1967, when it was listed as *infantile autism* under one of the subtypes of schizophrenia. In 1974, infantile autism was classified under behavior disorders of childhood, but without defining diagnostic criteria (Leekam, Libby, Wing, Gould, & Taylor, 2002). It is currently listed as *childhood autism* under pervasive developmental disorders (F84), with the following criteria for diagnosis: the presence of impaired or abnormal development before the age of 3 years and the characteristic abnormal functioning in the three areas of reciprocal social interaction; communication; and restricted, stereotyped, repetitive behavior (World Health Organization, 1992). Listed as common problems for individuals with this classification are phobias, sleep and eating disturbances, temper tantrums, and self-directed aggression.

Also listed in the ICD-10 is the category of *atypical autism*, defined as differing from autism in age of onset or in failing to fulfill all three sets of diagnostic criteria. Although similar in description to PDD-NOS from the DSM-IV-TR (American Psychiatric Association, 2000), it differs in the comments that atypical autism occurs most often with individuals having profound mental retardation or severe specific developmental disorder of receptive language (World Health Organization, 1992).

### Individuals with Disabilities Education Act (IDEA)

Autism was added as a separate category of disability that may require special education services in 1990 under PL 101–476, the Individuals with Disabilities Education Act (Knoblauch & Sorenson, 1998). To receive special education, (1) the child must have one or more of the disabilities from a list that includes autism and (2) must require special education and related services. Autism is defined by IDEA as a developmental disability significantly affecting verbal and nonverbal communication and social interaction, generally evident before age 3, that adversely affects a child's educational performance. Other characteristics often associated with autism are engagement in repetitive activities, stereotyped movements, resistance to

environmental change or change in daily routines, and unusual responses to sensory experiences. Individual states have their own criteria for eligibility of early intervention and special education services. It would be important for educators to be aware of what their own state requires for eligibility.

Classification systems are important in order to determine the outcomes of research. Replication is a hallmark of good science. If an intervention is demonstrated as helpful for a group of individuals classified with ASD, it will be important to replicate the intervention with a similar group prior to claiming effectiveness. Without a classification system, and the inherent definitions of characteristics, this replication would not be possible. Classification or diagnosis is also important for parents who are eager to understand the atypical behavior of their child.

## Prevalence

The **prevalence** is the number of cases of a condition that exists at a particular time in a defined population. The estimated prevalence rates following the creation of the classification category for autism in the 1940s was considered to be 4 or 5 in 10,000 for decades (Stevens et al., 2007). This estimate increased in the mid-1990s to 10 per 10,000 (1 in 1,000) for autism, and 22 per 10,000 for pervasive developmental disorder (PDD) (Mauk, Reber, & Batshaw, 1997). A review of 27 studies of prevalence completed internationally and published since 2000 places the current estimate at a rate of 1 in 143 for the spectrum of PDDs (Fombonne, Quirke & Hagen, 2011). The prevalence reported ranges by country, with the United Kingdom (1/86), the United States (1/110), and Japan (1/112) reporting higher rates, and Scandinavia (Finland and Denmark, 1/833; Iceland, 1/769) reporting lower rates (Grinker, Yeargin-Allsopp, & Boyle, 2011). However, different definitions and methods used in surveys make comparisons difficult (Fombonne et al., 2011). Many countries, especially low and middle-income countries, lack sufficient data to determine prevalence rates (Grinker et al., 2011).

Research indicates that regression, or loss of skills such as use of language, occurs in 1 in 4 children diagnosed with ASD and is associated with more severe symptoms (Fombonne et al., 2011). If regression occurs, it is likely to happen during the six months prior to age 2. Researchers have found that there is no difference on a range of outcome measures for children with or without regression (Ozonoff, Heung, & Thompson, 2011). The median percentage of individuals with autism spectrum disorders that have a co-occurring intellectual disability is 65% as calculated from 14 studies completed since 2000 (Dykens & Lense, 2011). It should be noted that estimates of how often intellectual disabilities occur with ASD varies widely and is influenced by definition and classification systems. Compared with the general population, epilepsy is 10 to 30 times more prevalent in individuals with ASD and occurs most often when there is a moderate to severe intellectual disability (Tuchman, 2011).

A report from the Centers for Disease Control and Prevention estimates the prevalence of autism spectrum disorders in the United States, or the number of cases identified, to be 1 in 110 (Rice, 2009). This information is based on data obtained across 14 states in the United States. Researchers in each of the states collected data from health and school records to determine the number of 8-year-olds diagnosed with ASD as well as the ethnic background of these students. The authors comment that the 14 states included in the study (Alabama, Arizona, Arkansas, Colorado, Georgia, Maryland, Missouri, New Jersey, North Carolina, Pennsylvania, South Carolina, Utah, West Virginia, and Wisconsin) are not representative of the nation and that the prevalence rates should be used with caution (Stevens et al., 2007). The prevalence rates vary among states, with an earlier study reporting lowest rates for Alabama and highest for New Jersey, and more recent analyses reveal lower rates for Florida and higher for Arizona and Missouri (Fombonne et al., 2011). Consistently

more boys than girls are classified with autism spectrum disorders, with a ratio of approximately 4 or 5 boys to 1 girl. Prevalence rates were reported to be about the same for White non-Hispanic and for Black non-Hispanic children, or for the two groups with large enough data to analyze. The median age of identification was 5.7 years, with Hispanic children being identified at later ages (Shattuck et al., 2009).

Whether the increase in prevalence rates represents a true increase in incidence of ASD has yet to be determined (Fombonne et al., 2011). The factors that may have contributed to the increase in prevalence include (1) an increased awareness by the public and by physicians and psychologists who make the diagnosis, (2) the broadening of the classification to include pervasive developmental disorder that requires minimum criteria for classification, (3) different methods for case finding, and (4) service availability (Fombonne et al., 2011). Epidemiologists also argue that ASD is a cultural phenomenon, and that how it is conceptualized influences both diagnosis and treatment; they explain ASD as an interplay of biological, cultural, and psychological phenomena (Grinker et al., 2011).

## What Causes Autism Spectrum Disorders?

### History of Attribution of Cause

Autism has long been considered a classification of a mental disorder. Early individuals with moderate to severe delays in language and social skills would have been placed in institutions to be "treated" by the medical establishment of the time. Kanner, a psychiatrist, first wrote about what was once called infantile autism and the associated symptoms in his paper in 1943. It is likely that individuals with autism who were high functioning were considered odd, loners who were not classified as needing intervention.

In the 1950s, psychiatrist Bruno Bettelheim attributed the symptoms of autism to uncaring and detached mothers who did not love their children enough. Treatment consisted of removing the children from these so-called **refrigerator mothers**; offering psychoanalysis or counseling to the mother; and providing play therapy to the child, ideally in Bettleheim's institute in Chicago. The disorder was thought to occur in middle-class Caucasian families where both parents were educated. During this period of history, not only did the mothers of children with autism have to care for a child with challenging and unusual behaviors, they also experienced the added burden of being blamed as the cause.

In 1964, Bernard Rimland published the book *Infantile Autism: The Syndrome and Its Implications for a Neural Theory of Behavior*, which attributed the cause of autism to biology rather than poor parenting. Rimland dedicated his career to addressing the biological issues that contribute to and result from autism spectrum disorders. He had long hypothesized that there are brain differences in individuals with ASD compared to the brains of typically developing children. Rimland founded the Autism Research Institute (ARI) that supports the project Defeat Autism Now (DAN). Annual conferences are held where physicians present information on possible metabolic (interrelated chemical interactions that provide the energy and nutrients) contributions to symptoms and suggest diets that can be used to avoid the side effects of toxins for individuals with ASD.

### Genetic Influences.

Autism is a behaviorally defined lifelong neurodevelopmental disorder, with strong evidence for a complex genetic predisposition. (Lamb, 2011, p. 669)

Autism is currently considered a **neurological disorder** that is influenced by both environmental (including the in-utero environment) and genetic factors (Sigman, Spence, & Wang, 2006). Initial evidence for a genetic contribution to ASD is found in a series of twin studies conducted across several countries (e.g., United Kingdom, Scandinavia, United States), with similar outcomes (Bailey et al., 1995; Ritvo, Freeman, Mason-Brothers, Mo, & Ritvo, 1985; Rutter, 2005; Steffenburg et al., 1989). When one twin in a monozygotic pair of twins (identical) was diagnosed with autism, there was a high likelihood that the second twin, with the same DNA, also was diagnosed with autism (Cook, 1998). However, in dizygotic twins (fraternal), the concordance for the diagnosis for autism was very low. In addition to the twin studies, it has been found that the risk of autism for siblings of those identified on the spectrum is 15 to 20%, considerably higher than the population risk (.05 to .1%) (Lamb, 2011). Results of surveys have revealed that relatives have an increased frequency of lesser variants of autism, including social, language, and repetitive behaviors (Dworzynski, Happe, Bolton, & Ronald, 2009; Rutter, 2005).

"Autism spans the genome" (Coleman & Betancur, 2005, p. 17), or is likely to be caused by multiple genes on several chromosomes. Our genes are found on 23 pairs of chromosomes numbered from 1 to 22 and an X or Y chromosome. The larger the number of the chromosome, the smaller the size of that chromosome. When using specialized equipment, each chromosome appears in an X shape with the top arms, or p part, shorter than the lower and longer q portion.

Research indicates that autism spectrum disorder is caused by 2 to 20 susceptible genes across various chromosomes acting in concert (Minshew, Sweeney, Bauman, & Webb, 2005) and that there is significant heterogeneity in both the genes involved and the mode of inheritance (Geschwind, 2011). Some of the genes on the following chromosomes are hypothesized to contribute to ASD: chromosome 1p21.3 and 1q25.1-1q25.2, chromosome 3p14 and 3q26.31 (Kaymakcalan & State, 2011), chromosome 7q31.2 (Lamb, 2011), chromosome 13q21.32 (Kaymakcalan & State, 2011; Rutter, 2005), chromosome 15q11-q13 (Abrahams & Geschwind, 2008) (or the same region that is missing in Prader-Willi and Angelmann syndrome), chromosome 16p13.2 (Kaymakcalan & State, 2011), chromosome 19p and 19q (Rutter, 2005), chromosome 22q13.3 (Kaymakcalan & State, 2011), and the X chromosome (Coleman &

**1.1** *IN THEIR WORDS*  Laura Wood

# Three Children on the Spectrum

My husband and I have three wonderful sons. They are all on the autism spectrum. Our oldest son Alex's diagnosis at age 2.5 came as a tremendous blow to us, as it does to every family grappling with this disorder. At that time our twins were 5 months old and we were thoroughly overwhelmed by our responsibilities. But we managed to launch a high-quality home intervention program for Alex and felt that we were doing everything we could do for him.

As the shock of Alex's diagnosis wore off a bit, I did start overanalyzing certain observations of the twins' behavior. Were they smiling? Paying attention to faces? During their first year of development, despite my hypervigilance, I believed it to be unlikely that they were autistic. I had not yet heard about the increased likelihood of autism in siblings of autistic children, so I told myself I was being unnecessarily paranoid.

But as the months went by and certain developmental milestones were missed or seemed ambiguous, the nagging feeling returned and slowly I realized that the nightmare scenario was coming to pass. The twins were both diagnosed with autism spectrum disorder shortly before their second birthday.

The most obvious impact of having kids "on the spectrum" is the financial commitment required for their home therapy. We are extremely lucky in Seattle to have a wonderful integrated preschool that all three kids attend for specialized instruction; but supplemental home programs are also recommended for two of our children, and the staggering cost of those programs is not covered by health insurance.

In addition, as many parents of children with special needs will tell you, guilt is ever-present. Sometimes the guilt has a specific source (Am I spending enough time encouraging communication and appropriate play? Have we set up *enough* hours of home therapy?). Other times the guilt is vague, intangible, and inexplicable.

I have times when I feel bitter and isolated. I look at other families with typically developing children with longing or even with anger. They can't know what it's like to take their children to countless therapy appointments and spend tens of thousands of dollars on essential therapy. How can I relate to these parents who take for granted their child's imaginative play skills or brag recklessly about their baby's first words? And how can they relate to me when I occasionally confess the reason why my kids don't always respond appropriately to a peer's invitation to play? Unless autism has touched their lives in some way, a blank look tinged with pity is all those parents can muster.

But in other ways I recognize the gifts sent our way by this unexpected path in life. There are several wonderful teachers and therapists who would never have been in our lives had it not been for the autism in our family. And my children have reminded me that there are different varieties of intelligence beyond what we think of as typical.

My kids are sweet, wonderful rays of sunshine in my life. They give me so much joy that all the worry and guilt and expense are absolutely worthwhile. I have already learned from them, and I'm sure they have more to teach me as we continue through our lives together.

Betancur, 2005; Rutter, 2005). Chromosome X is of particular interest due to the higher ratio of males to females with the disorder and because of fragile X syndrome (Hagerman, Narcisa, & Hagerman, 2011), which results in similar symptoms (Morrow & Walsh, 2011).

> As more and more autism genes are identified, putting them within a rubric of both molecular pathways and brain circuitry will be critical to understand how they lead to autism. (Geschwind, 2011, p. 819)

## Differences in Structure and Function of the Brain

In Kanner's original description of autism, he noted that 5 of the 11 children had large heads (Minshew et al., 2005). At birth the head circumference of infants who later were diagnosed with autism is near normal; however, by 6 to 14 months of age, the head circumference becomes enlarged, reflecting early brain and cerebrum overgrowth (Courchesne, Webb, & Schumann, 2011) that continues during the first two years of life (Courchesne, 2011). The most likely cause is excess neuron numbers due to dysregulation of neurogenesis, or the lack of the normal pruning and connecting of neurons. "Autism is undeniably due to abnormal brain development beginning in early life" (Courchesne et al., 2011, p. 611).

The implication of the early brain overgrowth is that it occurs at a time when language is typically expanding and consolidating, and this is not happening for young children with ASD. This continued growth of circuitry occurs when there should be pruning and stabilization that interferes with social communication (Courchesne, 2011).

When children with ASD reach age 5 to 6, brain growth becomes abnormally slow or arrested, reaching normal size, with possible decline in volume and size as individuals continue to age (Courchesne, 2011).

Autism does not result from a problem with one location in the brain but from abnormalities within one or multiple neural systems, and with underconnectivity of cortical systems (Minshew, Scherf, Behrmann, & Humphreys,

2011; Coleman, 2005). Magnetic resonance imaging (MRI) studies have revealed the overgrowth in the frontal and temporal lopes of the brain and the amygdala (Courchesne et al., 2011). The frontal lobes are considered to play a role in memory formation and emotional expression, and patients with frontal lobe damage demonstrate a decreased ability to respond to stimuli in the environment (Reichler & Lee, 1989). The frontal lobes are the part of the brain where planning, organizing, self-monitoring, inhibition, flexibility, and working memory, or the cognitive construct of executive functioning, is considered to occur (Ozonoff, South, & Provencal, 2005). The amygdala is responsive to stimuli that are highly rewarding, such as a mother's face, for typical infants (Courchesne et al., 2011).

Neuroimaging studies that access areas of the brain reacting during different tasks, or functional MRIs, have revealed that regions associated with object perception are more active during tests requiring the identification of embedded figures given to subjects with ASD compared with prefrontal regions more active in typical subjects (Ring, 1999). There is also a reported inability to shift attention accurately and rapidly between sensory modalities measured in reaction times to the random presentation of visual and auditory stimuli (Courchesne et al., 1994). Neuroimaging studies also provide evidence for abnormalities in the systems that underlie face and voice processing (Sigman et al., 2006). There is a pattern in high-functioning individuals with ASD having preservation or enhancement of simple feature processing of visual information with affected information processing that requires integration (Minshew et al., 2011). Hypoactivation has also been found in the amygdala during certain tasks that may reflect less interest or reduced emotional arousal during those tasks (Schultz & Robins, 2005).

## When Do the Impairments Occur?

When children have more than one syndrome, such as ASD with mental retardation, tuberous sclerosis complex, or a related disorder such as

Rett or Angelman syndrome, the disorder is likely to be manifested by the first trimester (Coleman & Betancur, 2005). For some disorders—such as tuberous sclerosis, where 43 to 86% of individuals have ASD—there may be an underlying disease process that results in autistic symptoms that occurs from the first trimester. However, a susceptible gene for autism may lie in close proximity to a tuberous sclerosis gene and is triggered along with tuberous sclerosis (Rutter, 2005). Certain environmental factors associated with autism, such as rubella infection, ethanol, thalidomide, and valprioc acid for seizures, affect the fetus in the first trimester (Rodier, 2011).

It is the second trimester, or the period of time most associated with brain development, that is associated with neuronal organization and the disordered development in ASD (Coleman & Betancur, 2005; Minshew et al., 2011). The cortex looks different during the second trimester compared with typical brain development (Courchesne, 2011).

## Environmental Toxins

The role of environmental toxins remains controversial, with various speculations for possible toxic influences without substantiating evidence. One of the most widely known possible toxins (because of several publications in the popular press) is the measles, mumps, and rubella (MMR) vaccine. The following sequence of events describes the rise and fall of the attribution of cause for the symptoms of autism related to the MMR vaccine.

## Evolution of the Attribution of Cause to the MMR Vaccine

- In 1996, a lawyer hired Andrew Wakefield, a British gastroenterologist reporting an increase in inflammatory bowel disease, to conduct research on behalf of families having children with autism to support litigation against the MMR vaccine.

- In 1998, a study published in *The Lancet* (a British medical journal) reported

there might be a connection between the MMR vaccine and autism. It reported that 12 children with autism spectrum disorder given this vaccine developed inflammation of the intestines.

- In 1998, the Medical Research Council of Britain set up a panel to study the link and found no association between vaccines and autism.

- In 1999, a study revealed that the preservative thimerosal, a mercury-containing compound present in many vaccines, caused several infants to have levels of mercury in their blood that exceeded the guidelines recommended by the Environmental Protection Agency (EPA). The CDC recommended that thimerosal be removed from the vaccine, even though "there is no data or evidence of any harm caused by the level of exposure," but it is perceived as safer by others. Consequently, the preservative was changed.

- In 2004, 10 of 13 scientists who produced the 1998 study retracted their conclusions. "In a statement to be published in the March 6 issue of *The Lancet*, a British medical journal, the researchers concede that they did not have enough evidence at the time to tie the measles, mumps, and rubella vaccine, known as MMR, to the autism cases. The study has been blamed for a sharp drop in the number of British children being vaccinated and the outbreaks of measles" (O'Connor, 2004).

- In July 2006, the *British Times* published that "Britain is now in the grip of what has every sign of becoming a measles epidemic. In March the first child in 14 years was killed by the virus. Clusters of infections, such as in Surrey and Yorkshire, have propelled the number of confirmed cases this year to 449, the largest number since the MMR jab was introduced in 1988."

- In May 2010, Andrew Wakefield had his license revoked by Britain's medical council.

- In January 2011, citing information obtained by journalist Brian Deer, the British Medical Journal states that Wakefield's data is fraudulent. Andrew Wakefield appears on several television stations in the United States and states that there was no fraud from him only from Brian Deer who he calls a "hit man."

Research on the MMR vaccine has not supported any major role in the manifestation of ASD (Hertz-Picciotto, 2011). "It may be concluded that it is quite implausible that MMR is generally associated with a substantially increased risk for autism" (Rutter, 2005, p. 435). Researchers who evaluated the effects of the MMR vaccine in Quebec, Canada, when there was a 93% uptake of the vaccine during the 11-year period studied, found no association between the MMR uptake and PDD rates when either one dose was administered at 12 months of age or when two doses were administered at 12 and 18 months of age (Fombonne, Zakarian, Bennett, Meng, & McLean-Heywood, 2006). There was no significant difference between the rate of dosing and the increase in PDD prevalence (Fombonne et al., 2006). The cells from a subset of the young children with PDD in Quebec who received the two-dose schedule of the MMR vaccine were compared with a control group and there was no significant difference in the anti-MV antibody titers (D'Souza, Fombonne, & Ward, 2006). The authors conclude, "Our data, together with the epidemiological evidence, demonstrate that arguments against vaccinating children with MMR because of fear of ASD are not defensible on scientific grounds" (D'Souza et al., 2006, p. 1674). Nonetheless, if parents want to take precautions regarding the MMR vaccine, they can ask for each of the vaccines separately, they can request that the titers for the antibodies in their child's system be obtained prior to receiving a booster shot in order to determine if a booster is necessary, and they can request preservative-free vaccines.

What environmental factors are associated with a greater risk of ASD? Although no definitive factors have been found, research has revealed a greater risk for the following: advanced parental age, children of recent immigrants, some infections during pregnancy, living close to a freeway, pesticide exposure, medically related exposures, and certain air pollutants (Hertz-Picciotto, 2011). "The environmental factors identified thus far account for a very small proportion of autism cases, but that does not diminish the importance of their contribution to our understanding of ASDs" (Rodier, 2011, p. 863).

## Physiological Interventions

### Medication Treatment

Treating the behaviors associated with autism spectrum disorders with drugs or medication has been occurring since individuals were placed in the care of the medical community in hospitals and institutions. Only those professionals who are trained with medical degrees, such as a medical doctor (MD) or a psychiatrist, can prescribe medication. An Internet survey of 552 parents of children with autism revealed that 52% reported that their child was currently using medication (Green et al., 2006). Survey respondents of 195 parents with 2- to 8-year-olds involved in early intervention in Indiana revealed that 27.7% indicated involvement in medical treatment (Hume, Bellini, & Pratt, 2005).

Drugs that have been developed to treat other psychological (schizophrenia, depression) and behavioral [Attention deficit hyperactivity disorder (ADHD)] symptoms have been used with individuals with ASD as a means of managing attention, arousal, aggression, irritability, and self-injury. Based on double-blind, placebo-controlled studies, the Food and Drug Administration (FDA) has approved the use of risperidone (Risperdal) in children, ages 5 to 16, diagnosed with autism with irritability (Blankenship, Erickson, Stigler, Posey, & McDougle, 2011). Common side effects of risperidone include increased appetite and weight gain, tremors, dizziness, drowsiness, and sedation (McCracken, 2011). Double-blind, placebo-controlled studies also have revealed benefits of serotonin reuptake inhibitors (e.g., Zoloft, Luvox) for addressing repetitive behavior (Blankenship et al., 2011). These drugs are better tolerated in adults than they are in children. Psychostimulants (e.g., Ritalin) are less efficacious in children with PDD than in typical children with ADHD and cause more adverse effects (Blankenship et al., 2011); however, they continue to be prescribed for children with ASD (McCracken, 2011) (see Table 1.2).

> To date, double-blind placebo-controlled studies have not identified a drug with consistent beneficial effects on the social or communication impairments of autism. (Blankenship et al. 2011, p. 1196)

Information on the drugs reported used with their children with ASD from 27,000 parents has been collected since 1967 by the Autism Research Institute (ARI), founded by Bernard Rimland. Parents volunteer the information about the prescriptions used and their opinions about the effectiveness (Pangborn & Baker, 2005). It is clear from the placebo studies described in this chapter that parents are more likely to report positive effects even if they are not demonstrated by research.

Table 1.2 was modified to include only drug interventions (Autism Research Institute, 2009). The variety of drugs used is notable. The highest number of cases reported used Ritalin, with only 29% of parents indicating that there was an improvement. It is notable that several of the drugs used where parents have reported that their child got better for greater than 50% of the time were those used to control seizures (see Table 1.2).

Sandler and Bodfish (2000) conducted a placebo-controlled study and found no difference between a placebo and a single dose of secretin. They reported an interesting finding that 75% of the parents continued to believe in the benefits of secretin even after being informed about the study results. In spite of this outcome, the researchers stated that we should strive to practice evidence-based medicine (Sandler & Bodfish, 2000). In their review of 17 quantitative studies, 13 of which were randomized, double-blind, and placebo controlled, Esch and Carr (2004) report that only one study found any evidence of a causal relationship between secretin and changes in the symptoms of the 600 participating individuals with autism spectrum disorders. These authors discuss that parents may elect secretin treatment perhaps because of stress due to the pervasiveness of their child' s symptoms, a high degree of motivation to try any promising treatment, and hope for a drug made from a substance naturally found in the human body that may seem safe (Esch & Carr, 2004).

## Diets

Special diets are classified with a group of treatments considered as complementary and alternative medical (CAM) treatments (Hyman & Levy, 2011). Parent surveys have revealed that 50% of the 121 parents who had children in applied behavior analysis treatment programs also tried elimination diets (Smith & Antolovich, 2000), and 27% of the 552 parents surveyed through the Internet indicated implementing a special diet (Green et al., 2006). It is advised that any special diet be supervised by a physician with knowledge about nutrition and the side effects of eliminating foods from the diet (Pangborn & Baker, 2005) and who follow the consensus guidelines developed by medical societies for the management of common gastrointestinal symptoms (Buie et al., 2010). There is an unsubstantiated theory that some individuals with autism spectrum disorders have a "leaky gut," in which opiate peptides typically digested are passed through the stomach and travel to parts of the body, including the brain, resulting in discomfort and the display of the behaviors associated with ASD (Hyman & Levy, 2011). Gluten, a common wheat product found in breads and cereals, is the main culprit for these events, and similar to celiac's disease,

**TABLE 1.2** Parent ratings of behavioral effects of biomedical interventions

The parents of autistic children represent a vast and important reservoir of information on the benefits—and adverse effects—of the large variety of drugs and other interventions that have been tried with their children. Since 1967, the Autism Research Institute has been collecting parent ratings of the usefulness of the many interventions tried on their autistic children.

The following data have been collected from the more than 27,500 parents who have completed our questionnaires designed to collect such information. For the purposes of the present table, the parents' responses on a six-point scale have been combined into three categories: "made worse" (ratings 1 and 2), "no effect" (ratings 3 and 4), and "made better" (ratings 5 and 6). The "Better: Worse" column gives the number of children who "Got Better" for each one who "Got Worse."

| Drugs | Got Worse[A] (%) | No Effect (%) | Got Better (%) | Number of Cases[B] |
|---|---|---|---|---|
| Actos | 19 | 60 | 21 | 140 |
| Adderall | 43 | 26 | 31 | 894 |
| Amphetamine | 47 | 28 | 25 | 1,355 |
| Amafranil | 32 | 39 | 29 | 440 |
| Antibiotics | 33 | 50 | 18 | 2,507 |
| *Antifungals*[C] | | | | |
| Diflucan | 5 | 34 | 62 | 1,214 |
| Nystatin | 5 | 43 | 52 | 1,969 |
| Atarax | 26 | 53 | 21 | 543 |
| Benadryl | 24 | 50 | 26 | 3,230 |
| Beta Blocker | 18 | 51 | 31 | 306 |
| Buspar | 29 | 42 | 28 | 431 |
| Chloral Hydrate | 42 | 39 | 19 | 498 |
| Clonidine | 22 | 32 | 46 | 1,658 |
| Clozapine | 38 | 43 | 19 | 170 |
| Cogentin | 20 | 53 | 27 | 198 |
| Cylert | 45 | 35 | 19 | 634 |
| *Depakene*[D] | | | | |
| Behavior | 25 | 44 | 31 | 1,146 |
| Desipramine | 34 | 35 | 32 | 95 |
| *Dilantin*[D] | | | | |
| Behavior | 28 | 49 | 23 | 1,127 |
| Seizures | 16 | 37 | 47 | 454 |
| Fenfluramine | 21 | 52 | 27 | 483 |
| Haldol | 38 | 28 | 34 | 1,222 |
| IVIG | 7 | 39 | 54 | 142 |
| *Klonapin*[D] | | | | |
| Behavior | 31 | 40 | 29 | 270 |
| Seizures | 29 | 55 | 16 | 86 |
| Lithium | 22 | 48 | 31 | 515 |
| Luvox | 31 | 37 | 32 | 251 |
| Mellaril | 29 | 38 | 33 | 2,108 |
| *Mysoline*[D] | | | | |
| Behavior | 41 | 46 | 13 | 156 |
| Seizures | 21 | 55 | 24 | 85 |
| Naltrexone | 18 | 49 | 33 | 350 |
| Low dose Naltrexone | 11 | 52 | 38 | 190 |
| Paxil | 34 | 32 | 35 | 471 |
| Behavior | 48 | 37 | 16 | 1,125 |
| Seizures | 18 | 44 | 38 | 543 |
| Prolixin | 30 | 41 | 28 | 109 |
| Prozac | 33 | 32 | 35 | 1,391 |
| Risperidal | 21 | 26 | 54 | 1,216 |
| Ritalin | 45 | 26 | 29 | 4,256 |
| *Secretin* | | | | |
| Intravenous | 7 | 50 | 43 | 597 |
| Transdermal | 9 | 56 | 35 | 257 |
| Stelazine | 29 | 45 | 26 | 437 |
| Steroids | 34 | 30 | 36 | 204 |
| *Tegretol*[D] | | | | |
| Behavior | 25 | 45 | 30 | 1,556 |
| Seizures | 14 | 33 | 53 | 872 |
| Thorazine | 36 | 40 | 24 | 945 |
| Tofranil | 30 | 38 | 32 | 785 |
| Valium | 35 | 42 | 24 | 895 |
| Valtrex | 8 | 42 | 50 | 238 |
| *Zarontin*[D] | | | | |
| Behavior | 34 | 48 | 18 | 164 |
| Seizures | 20 | 55 | 25 | 125 |
| Zoloft | 35 | 33 | 31 | 579 |

A. "Worse" refers only to worse behavior. Drugs, but not nutrients, typically also cause physical problems if used long term. B. The number of cases is cumulative over several decades, so the number does not reflect current usage levels (e.g., Haldol is now seldom used). C. Antifungal drugs and chelation are used selectively, where evidence indicates they are needed. D. Seizure drugs: behavior effects other than on seizures, effects on seizures.

*Source:* Adapted from *Summary of Biomedical Treatments for Autism.* Autism Research Institute Publication 34/March, 2009. Used with permission.

gluten is thought to be undigested. Casein from milk products also breaks down into a similar peptide (casomorphine) as gluten (gliadnomorphins) (Lewis, 2002). Some of the peptides obtained from gluten and casein are very similar to those endorphins found in the brain. These opioid peptides act as neuroregulators.

Shattock and Whiteley (2000), who work at the University of Sunderland in the United Kingdom, have designed a protocol for the removal of casein and gluten from the diet along with the promotion of enzyme activity from dietary supplements. In spite of the fact that it is unlikely that an early developmental disorder such as ASD can be caused by limited experience with gluten (Pavone & Ruggieri, 2005), many families of children with autism spectrum disorders have tried a gluten-free and casein-free (GFCF) diet. In some situations the reported changes in autism symptoms are great (Lewis, 2002; Seroussi, 2000). However, the children on the diets are typically also receiving educational interventions that may be the actual cause of change in behavior.

A randomized, double-blind, repeated-measures study was conducted on the gluten- and casein-free diet by professionals in the College of Nursing of the University of Florida (Elder et al., 2006). Fifteen children who were diagnosed using established assessment tools were given either the GFCF diet or a placebo for 12 weeks. Dependent measures included urinary peptide measures, language samples, and parent and child behaviors. The results indicated that there were no significant differences between the groups on any measures (Elder et al., 2006). However, parents of seven children reported improvements, and nine parents elected to maintain a GFCF diet, even though there was no empirical support for the diet (Elder et al., 2006). The authors call for additional well-controlled research on the use of diets.

A review of randomized, controlled trials involving GFCF diets revealed only one study that reported a reduction in the behaviors associated with ASD (Millward et al., 2004). Kern and colleagues (Kern, Miller, Evans, & Trivedi, 2002) used a double-blind, placebo-controlled study in children with ASD and found positive results only for those children with chronic, active diarrhea, and suggest that they may represent a subtype of autism/PDD.

> Well-designed trials are needed to develop an evidence base for optimal diagnostic and treatment strategies to manage gastrointestinal disorders in children with ASDs. (Buie et al., 2010, p. S19)

Some families report it is costly and time-consuming to organize an alternative diet for one child and that children often react badly to the initial withdrawal of their favorite foods (Elder et al., 2006). In addition, some children with ASD may be selective in their food preferences, further limiting their intake (Williams & Foxx, 2007). However, changing a child's diet is an intervention where parents may feel they can make a contribution. By controlling the food their child eats, parents may feel like they are taking action to address the characteristics of ASD.

## Sensory Activities

Difficulties with sensory input have long been associated with autism spectrum disorders. Early versions of the DSM listed sensory impairments as one of the diagnostic criteria (DSM-III), and this criteria is included again in the proposed DSM-5. Anecdotal reports of both hyper- and hyposensitivity to environmental stimuli are common (Anzalone & Williamson, 2000) with more evidence of hypo- than hyper-responsiveness reported (Rogers & Ozonoff, 2005). Descriptions of individuals with ASD who cover their ears when music is played or react to a generally considered light touch or mild odor as if it is painful are considered hypersensitive (Grandin, 1992; O'Neill & Jones, 1997). Individuals who act as though they are deaf or are nonreactive when a fire alarm goes off are considered hyposensitive (Anzalone & Williamson, 2000; Baranek, 2002). The repetitive or stereotypic behaviors exhibited by some individuals, such as waving fingers in front of the eyes, body rocking, or noncontextual vocalizations, are speculated to provide sensory input.

The percentage of individuals with ASD who display these atypical reactions to sensory stimuli remains unknown and is estimated to be between 42% and 88% (Baranek, 2002). Results from the implementation of The Sensory Profile (Dunn, 1999), with 86 individuals with Asperger syndrome and 86 diagnosed with autism, indicate that individuals with Asperger syndrome may have comparatively greater differences in the areas of emotional/social responses, emotional reactivity, and inattention/distractibility compared with individuals diagnosed with autism (Myles et al., 2004). Research with 104 individuals diagnosed with autism between 3 and 56 years of age found that results of The Sensory Profile correlated with the results of the severity score on the Childhood Autism Rating Scale (Schopler, Reichler, & Rochen Renner, 1998) for young children but not for adolescents and adults, indicating that there was an apparent lessening of abnormal sensory processing (Kern et al., 2007).

Theorizing about the interactions between the environment and the individual's nervous and sensory systems, and suggesting interventions based on these theories, has been considered the realm of occupational therapy (Miller-Kuhaneck, 2004; Wakeford & Baranek, 2011). Occupational therapists study physiology and neurology and have engaged in debates regarding theories that describe the characteristics of autism spectrum disorders (O'Neill & Jones, 1997; Rogers & Ozonoff, 2005). In general, occupational-therapy-based activities are child-directed and are designed to promote the development of skills in the context of work, play, and adaptive behavior (Dawson & Watling, 2000).

Sensory integration therapy is based on the theory developed in the 1970s by Jean Ayres (1972), who worked with individuals with learning disabilities (Dawson & Watling, 2000). Intervention strategies based on her theory consist of planned sensory experiences such as swinging, deep-pressure touch, and tactile

stimulation. The goal of the sensory integrative process is to address the following four *As*: (1) arousal level, (2) attention to the environment, (3) affect, and (4) action, or engagement in adaptive, goal-directed behavior (Anzalone & Williamson, 2000). In their review of the research literature for the American Occupational Therapy Association (AOTA), Case-Smith and Arbesman (2008) conclude that there is minimal research evidence for sensory integration approaches and suggest that this be a focus of future research.

> Sensory integration therapy is a frequently recommended intervention for children with autism, even though the empirical evidence of its efficacy in minimal. (Rogers & Ozonoff, 2005, p. 1265)

Deep-pressure touch has been reported by Temple Grandin, a high-profile adult with autism, as a helpful strategy for calming down (Grandin, 1992). She reports that she created a Hug Machine that she used to apply deep pressure when desired. Deep pressure from the Hug Machine was evaluated for five children with autism—on galvanic skin response (GSR) and parent ratings on created subscales from items off the Conners Parent Rating Scale—compared with seven children who received no deep pressure or a placebo control (Edelson, Edelson, Kerr, & Grandin, 1999). The authors indicate that the low numbers greatly reduced the power of the statistics, but they claim that there was a marginally significant finding on the GRS in support of the deep pressure and that parents rated their children who received deep pressure lower on the created Tension scale (Edelson et al., 1999).

Based on the reported benefits of deep pressure, occupational therapists have recommended that children with ASD wear vests with weights in them to assist with focus and attention to task. Two studies using alternative treatment designs evaluated the effect of weighted vests with children with ASD (Cox, Gast, Luscre, & Ayes, 2009; Reichow, Barton, Neely-Sewell, Good, & Wolery, 2010) and found that there was no difference between conditions and no functional relationship between wearing the weighted vests during classroom activities and attention to task or engagement. The effects of touch or massage by parents at bedtime was evaluated for the effects on sleep problems and social relatedness, stereotypic behavior, and on-task behavior during bimonthly observations of play at preschool (Escalona, Field, Singer-Strunck, Cullen, & Hartshorn, 2001). The 10 participants in the experimental group slept better and were comparatively more attentive with less stereotypic behavior when they received massages. The authors conclude that the increase in attentiveness could be due to getting better sleep or enhanced parasympathetic activity (Escalona et al., 2001). Eleven children who received touch therapy comprised of rubbing with moderate pressure and smooth strokes for 15 minutes per day, 2 days per week for 4 weeks, were observed less frequently as orienting to irrelevant sounds and exhibiting stereotypic behaviors compared to an attention control group. There were no differences in off-task behavior or touch aversion between the two groups (Field et al., 1997). More research, with larger numbers of students with ASD and in educational programs, is needed regarding the effects of weighted vests, massage, or deep pressure on behaviors, including attention to tasks presented for learning.

Occupational therapists have recommended the use of a ball or specially designed chair for sitting in order to assist in maintaining attention or arousal. Schilling and Schwartz (2004) evaluated the use of such therapy balls with young children with ASD and concluded that there was an improvement in in-seat behavior and engagement for the four participants in their study.

Sensory activities that modulate the four target areas can be considered a sensory diet (Anzalone & Williamson, 2000). The purpose of a sensory diet is to help the individual to attain and maintain optimal arousal states or to provide sensory input that is sufficiently consistent and intensive to change sensory processing capacities (Wilbarger, 1995). Similar to a nutritional diet, a sensory diet involves planning for someone's individual needs (Wilbarger, 1995).

It is recommended that activities be implemented throughout the day with sensory tune-ups scheduled at key times (Wilbarger, 1995). Educators typically schedule sensory activities at predetermined times of the day because it is not possible to determine someone else's sensory needs accurately.

Wilbarger and Wilbarger (1991) described a strategy called the sensory summation technique that involves a combination of brushing the arms, back, and legs rigorously with a surgical scrub brush, followed by 10 gentle joint compressions to the arm and leg joints and concluding with sensory input to the fingers and toes. This procedure, referred to as the Wilbarger Protocol, has been recommended by occupational therapists to be implemented by public school preschool teachers multiple times throughout the day. There is one weak study (Kimball et al., 2007) on the use of the Wilbarger Protocol with individuals with autism spectrum disorders (Schaaf, 2011), and only one case study (Stagnitti, Raison, & Ryan, 1999) reports outcomes of a sensory diet that included the Wilbarger Protocol (Baranek, 2002).

It is not uncommon for occupational therapists who work in schools to recommend sensory diets, or a series of sensory-related activities for individuals with ASD to be included as part of the student's educational program (Schaaf, 2011). Sensory diets or activities were compared to an attention control condition where one-to-one activities were presented in a public school preschool classroom (Bonggat & Hall, 2010). These interventions were evaluated using an alternative treatment design on the effects of on-task behavior during the scheduled activities that followed the intervention sessions. The results indicated no difference for the sensory diet or attention control condition on the on-task behaviors on the participants (Bonggat & Hall, 2010). Data was collected by the preschool teacher of the classroom demonstrating how educators can evaluate the effects of strategies recommended by occupational therapists.

Three studies obtaining information from parent surveys indicate a high percentage of the use of sensory integration therapy: 56% of those enrolled in intensive behavior analytic treatment (Smith & Antolovich, 2000), 40% from participation in early intervention programs (Hume et al., 2005), and 38.2% from the Internet survey (Green et al., 2006). It is important to note that even though many individuals with autism spectrum disorders who attend public schools receive services from occupational therapists to address sensory issues, there has been relatively little systematic, controlled research on the effectiveness of various interventions (Dawson & Watling, 2000; Rogers & Ozonoff, 2005).

Regardless of the form of sensory activity evaluated, it would be important to control for the typical one-on-one attention that students with ASD receive during the implementation of sensory activities. Recent policies that emphasize the use of evidence-based practices have resulted in a critique of current practices used by occupational therapists and a call for empirical research on sensory-based interventions by school psychologists (Shaw, 2002), special educators (Goldstein, 2000), and leaders in the field of occupational therapy (Wakeford & Baranek, 2011; Ottenbacker, Tickle-Degnen, & Hasselkus, 2002). Occupational therapists are required to complete assessments, design interventions, and complete intervention reviews as part of evidence-based practices (Wakeford & Baranek, 2011). Developing and testing intervention strategies or packages through systematic evaluation of child progress would be important for occupational therapists as a way to be accountable for their recommendations. In the conclusion of her chapter that reviews the research on strategies used by occupational therapists with individuals with ASD, Schaaf (2011) writes, "[T]he need for solid research has reached a critical level" (p. 269).

> We have tended to rely on other forms of evidence, such as the voice of an expert, uncritical acceptance of the findings of a single published study or published manual, and reliance on our own previous experiences and the experiences around us. . . . We believe that an urgent need exists for all of us in occupational therapy to develop and use the skills necessary to plan treatment strategies for individual clients based on what is supported by evidence. (Ottenbacker et al., 2002, p. 247)

## Working in Collaboration with Specialists

It is clear that our colleagues who work as geneticists and neurologists will be busy trying to find the pieces of the puzzle in the forms of genes and brain functions that result in the behaviors classified as autism spectrum disorders. The creation of a pharmacological intervention designed specifically for autism is a future prospect. In addition, research is needed from nutritionists and occupational therapists to determine the effects of individually designed diets on physiological changes that affect learning.

In the meantime, educators will be increasingly required to provide effective instruction to individuals classified with autism spectrum disorders. The remainder of this book will focus on strategies that can be used by educators, with comments regarding the research evidence, or lack thereof, in support of the strategies. When the term **autism spectrum disorders** is used, it will mean all individuals classified using the proposed DSM-5 criteria, which includes those previously described as pervasive developmental disorder and Asperger syndrome.

In addition to using effective and evidence-based strategies, educators can be most successful if they work in collaboration with parents and specialists. Parents are typically the interface between specialists such as physicians and nutritionists and the educator. Information regarding parents' choice to use medication or a special diet would be important for educators to be aware of, and good communication with families is an essential means of obtaining this information. It would also be important for families to learn about any noticeable changes in behavior that are observed by educators following implementation of a diet or medication regime. Certainly families would want to know if their children appear to be too sleepy to attend to an activity or lesson or if they are displaying an increase in challenging behaviors.

Because occupational therapists often work in public schools, it is likely that educators will communicate directly and work collaboratively with the assigned specialist. The occupational therapist can provide suggestions for curriculum modifications that take into account any preferences for, or sensitivities to, sensory stimuli. Efforts can be made to ensure that any suggested interventions are individualized for each student and that some form of data is obtained to determine the effectiveness of any specifically designed strategy. Janinne Karahalios is an occupational therapist who works with individuals with autism who attend public schools in Connecticut. She holds the perspective that it is important to work with educators in the context of the classroom to achieve maximum results (see In Their Words 1.2).

---

**1.2**  *IN THEIR WORDS*   Janinne Karahalios, *MS, OTR/L Occupational Therapist*

## Collaboration in a Public School Setting

As an occupational therapist in the school setting, my goal is to support the creation of an environment where children with autism spectrum disorders (ASD) can learn how to fulfill their roles as "student" with as much independence as possible. I encourage active participation in purposeful and meaningful tasks to promote the development of self-care, self-regulation, and motor skills. In order to achieve this goal I work directly with students and actively collaborate with team members in a consistent and effective manner.

I have found communication to be essential in achieving the consistency necessary for successful programming for children with ASD. It is important that parents, teachers, and other service providers share a vision of the student's future and develop a common path to achieve the desired results. The individualized education program (IEP) must represent this vision, and each team member should be familiar with all goals because goals are addressed across multiple settings throughout the day, not solely in individual settings. Students will not meet the goals that fall in the realm of occupational therapy (OT) if they are addressed only during an OT session. Occupational therapists rely on teachers, parents, and paraprofessionals to carry out their recommendations each time the opportunity presents itself within the context of the child's natural environment. It is similarly important for occupational therapists to address cross-disciplinary goals when given the opportunity.

Participation in all school settings—the classroom, recess, physical education, music, and art—is vital for the child with ASD to fulfill his or her role as "student." Occupational therapists believe that many children with ASD demonstrate differences in sensory processing patterns. Occupational therapists increase the awareness of the impact sensory input may have on a student's adaptive behavior and functional motor skills within each of these environments. A child's heightened responsiveness to sensory experiences can increase anxiety, especially in new situations. Provision of predictability, order, and routine can prevent "fight or flight" reactions that sometimes result in inappropriate behaviors. Visual schedules, first-then boards, use of visual and auditory timers, and creation of social stories are examples of strategies that can be used to ease anxiety during stressful situations. Modification of sensory experiences, such as allowing for use of tools when initially

*(continued)*

**1.2 *IN THEIR WORDS (continued)***

involved in messy play, and the use of sound-dampening headphones when attending a noisy assembly, can make the experiences tolerable for a student with ASD. These accommodations can be slowly and systematically altered to increase the child's tolerance to such activities. Occupational therapists also help create dressing and feeding routines to be practiced daily during toileting, snack, and lunch times, to increase independence in these skills.

Occupational therapists also provide suggestions for providing a sensory-friendly environment. Recommendations might include: offering a "quiet corner" for de-escalation; avoidance of seating in high-traffic areas; using rugs or carpets to absorb environmental noise; eliminating glare from fluorescent lighting; providing visual organization to clearly define space; and creating opportunities for movement activities, such as jumping, climbing, swinging, and running.

Each team member brings unique knowledge, skills, and experience to the educational program. Effective communication between team members and consistent implementation of agreed-upon strategies and programs will assist students with ASD to gain skills to navigate through learning and life, and to make strides toward independence.

## SUGGESTIONS FOR DISCUSSION

1. Discuss the evidence for a genetic influence on autism spectrum disorders. From your experience, do you notice characteristics or subtle traits from undiagnosed family members of an individual with ASD?

2. Identify the changes to the diagnostic criteria with the *Diagnostic and Statistical Manual*-5 (DSM-5) compared with the DSM-V. What do you think about not having a separate category for Asperger disorder?

3. Engage in a debate with one side arguing for an increase in the incidence of ASD due to the reported prevalence rates within the previous 10 years and the other side arguing for other factors contributing to the reported increase in prevalence.

4. What is the argument for a gluten- and casein-free diet, and why do you think some parents elect to place their child on this diet?

5. Describe the strength of the evidence from research using randomized, double-blind, placebo-control group designs.

6. Describe the aim of strategies and activities recommended by occupational therapists for children with autism spectrum disorders.

7. Discuss why there is so little research published on the effectiveness of sensory-based strategies and activities.

8. Identify the strengths and limitations of the physiological approach to addressing the (a) occurrence and (b) characteristics of autism spectrum disorders.

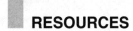

# RESOURCES

## Books

Amaral, D. G., Dawson, G., & Geschwind, D. H. (2011). *Autism spectrum disorders*. New York: Oxford University Press.

Coleman, M. (2005). *The neurology of autism*. New York: Oxford University Press.

Ozonoff, S., Rogers, S. J., & Hendren, R. L. (2003). *Autism spectrum disorders: A research review for practitioners*. London: American Psychiatric Publishing, Inc.

## Websites

*www.autism-society.org*
  Autism Society of America
*www.dsm5.org*
  The American Psychiatric Association proposed criteria for the DSM-5

# CHAPTER TWO

# Assessment

## CHAPTER OBJECTIVES

The reader should be able to:

- Explain why the ADOS and ADI-R are considered the gold standard for diagnosing individuals with autism spectrum disorders.

- Provide an example of a curriculum-based assessment and describe how assessment results are used for identifying goals and objectives for individuals with autism spectrum disorders.

- Illustrate how a teacher can arrange a classroom environment to facilitate the collection of ongoing assessment.

The form of assessment and the tools used depend on the purpose of the assessment. It is important to use the correct tool for the purpose for which it was intended. Using a screwdriver to put a nail in the wall to hang a picture may actually work, but it is far better to use a hammer for this purpose so that you get accurate results. Using a tool to obtain information for which it was not designed may give you inaccurate results. It is also important that the ethnic and linguistic background of the focal individual is considered when selecting assessment tools. Some tools devise their norms, or ages when behaviors are typically present, by testing the tool in one geographic location or with limited numbers of ethnic groups. Families

that have newly arrived in the United States may have very different expectations for the development of certain skills. Items on instruments may be unknown, irrelevant, or contrary to the values for families from specific culturally and linguistically diverse backgrounds. It is the responsibility of the assessor to try to eliminate cultural biases when selecting tools and administering assessments.

This chapter describes the assessment tools designed to obtain information about individuals with autism spectrum disorders (ASDs). Tools will be described by purpose and will include: screening instruments, diagnostic assessment tools, curriculum-based assessments, progress monitoring assessment, and program evaluation. The link between assessment outcomes and the planning of educational programs will be emphasized.

# Screening Instruments

A **screening** is a brief assessment aimed at identifying those infants and/or children who may be at risk for developmental delays due to differences compared with standard expectations for children of the same age range and cultural background (Losardo & Notari-Syverson, 2001). Screening tools are typically administered widely in order to identify individuals who require further testing. Screening tools are designed to be **sensitive** enough to identify those situations where the young child may be identified with autism spectrum disorders (Zwaigenbaum, 2011). It is also important that the instrument does not incorrectly identify those children not at risk, or that the **specificity** of the instrument is sufficiently accurate (Zwaigenbaum, 2011). The **positive predictive value** (PPV), or the proportion of children identified at risk who actually have the disability, is also a concern for screening developers.

More attention has been paid in recent years to the development and implementation of screening tools so young children can be identified early and so intervention can begin when the greatest outcomes are possible. Studies of infant siblings of children diagnosed with ASD who are at greater risk for ASD reveal that there are no differences observed at 6 months of age (Ozonoff et al., 2010; Rozga et al., 2011), but at 12 months of age, infants later diagnosed with autism have significant differences in their gaze to faces and directed vocalizations (Ozonoff et al., 2010) and lower rates of joint attention and requesting behaviors (Rozga et al., 2011). By 18 months there is a difference in the use of social smiles (Ozonoff et al., 2010). When symptoms appear early, by 12 months of age infants later diagnosed with ASD have "decreases in eye contact, social initiative, joint attention, and emotion sharing as well as a failure to respond to name" (Rogers & Wallace, 2011, p. 1085).

Overall, there is a convergent evidence from both retrospective and prospective studies that ASD symptoms emerge, in the vast majority of cases, in the first two years of life. (Zwaigenbaum, 2011, p. 76)

## Checklist for Autism in Toddlers (CHAT)

The CHAT (Baron-Cohen et al., 1996) is a nine-item screening tool for autism completed by parents with toddlers as young as 18 months of age. Five additional items for completion by a general medical practitioner or health visitor are also included (Brock, Jimerson, & Hansen, 2006). Research on the specificity and positive predictive value of the CHAT indicates that these are strengths of this measure (Coonrod & Stone, 2005). Three of the nine items appear to be the best predictors of autism spectrum disorders: lack of gaze monitoring, lack of proto declarative pointing, and lack of pretend play by age 18 months (Baird et al., 2000). A follow-up study of 16,253 18-month-old infants in England who were identified by the CHAT during an initial administration revealed that the initial administration and a repeated screening 1 month later resulted in a predictive value of 75% (Baird et al., 2000).

A *Modified Checklist for Autism in Toddlers* (M-CHAT)™ (Robins, Fein, & Barton, 1999), for use with toddlers between 16 and 30 months of age, was developed and implemented in the United States (Robins, Fein, Barton, & Green, 2001). This instrument contains the nine items from the CHAT and additional items that are more likely to be present in young children older than 16 months. Although more time is needed to evaluate the predictive validity of the instrument, the authors state that the M-CHAT can accurately detect children at risk for autism/pervasive developmental disorder (PDD). Table 2.1 lists the 23 items included in the M-CHAT.

## CSBS Infant-Toddler Checklist

The Infant-Toddler Checklist (ITC) is a 24-item tool designed to be completed by caregivers when children are ages 6 to 24 months (Wetherby

## TABLE 2.1 M-CHAT

Please fill out the following about how your child **usually** is. Please try to answer every question. If the behavior is rare (e.g., you've seen it once or twice), please answer as if the child does not do it.

| | | |
|---|---|---|
| 1. Does your child enjoy being swung, bounced on your knee, etc.? | Yes | No |
| 2. Does your child take an interest in other children? | Yes | No |
| 3. Does your child like climbing on things, such as up stairs? | Yes | No |
| 4. Does your child enjoy playing peek-a-boo/hide-and-seek? | Yes | No |
| 5. Does your child ever pretend, for example, to talk on the phone or take care of dolls, or pretend other things? | Yes | No |
| 6. Does your child ever use his/her index finger to point, to ask for something? | Yes | No |
| 7. Does your child ever use his/her index finger to point, to indicate interest in something? | Yes | No |
| 8. Can your child play properly with small toys (e.g., cars or bricks) without just mouthing, fiddling, or dropping them? | Yes | No |
| 9. Does your child ever bring objects over to you (parent) to show you something? | Yes | No |
| 10. Does your child look you in the eye for more than a second or two? | Yes | No |
| 11. Does your child ever seem oversensitive to noise? (e.g., plugging ears) | Yes | No |
| 12. Does your child smile in response to your face or your smile? | Yes | No |
| 13. Does your child imitate you? (e.g., you make a face—will your child imitate it?) | Yes | No |
| 14. Does your child respond to his/her name when you call? | Yes | No |
| 15. If you point at a toy across the room, does your child look at it? | Yes | No |
| 16. Does your child walk? | Yes | No |
| 17. Does your child look at things you are looking at? | Yes | No |
| 18. Does your child make unusual finger movements near his/her face? | Yes | No |
| 19. Does your child try to attract your attention to his/her own activity? | Yes | No |
| 20. Have you ever wondered if your child is deaf? | Yes | No |
| 21. Does your child understand what people say? | Yes | No |
| 22. Does your child sometimes stare at nothing or wander with no purpose? | Yes | No |
| 23. Does your child look at your face to check your reaction when faced with something unfamiliar? | Yes | No |

*Source: Modified Checklist for Autism in Toddlers.* D. L. Robins, D. Fein, & M. L. Barton. Used with permission. © 1999 Robins, Fein, & Barton.

& Prizant, 2002). This tool is part of an assessment package created by the same authors of the Communication and Social Behavior Scales (CSBS) Developmental Profile. Items are organized under seven categories that include emotion and eye gaze, communication, gestures, sounds, words, understanding, and object use. Most of the items are answered by identifying a frequency of *not yet*, *sometimes*, or *often*. Five items require the identification of a number. For example, the choices for "How many words does your child use meaningfully that you recognize (such as *baba* for *bottle*; *gaggie* for *doggie*)?" are: none, 1–3, 4–10, 11–30, and over 30.

Karen Pierce and colleagues at the University of California San Diego Autism Center for Excellence have been using the ITC as the screening tool recommended in their research with physicians in the greater San Diego area (Pierce et al., 2011). They worked with 170 pediatricians to recommend the screening of 10,479 infants at the 1-year well-baby checkup using the ITC. They found the positive predictive value of using this screening at age 1 to be .75, which is considered high, and conclude that this screening offers an alternative to focusing on screening baby siblings to study autism prospectively.

> Both the M-CHAT and ITC have shown considerable promise as ASD screens in community samples. (Zwaigenbaum, 2011, p. 84)

## Early Screening of Autistic Traits (ESAT)

The ESAT is a 14-item questionnaire that was developed in the Netherlands for identifying young children 16 to 48 months at risk for ASD (Swinkels et al., 2006). Parents are asked to report yes or no to items such as "Can your child play with toys in varied ways (not just fiddling, mouthing or dropping them)?" "When your child expresses his/her feelings, for instance, by crying or smiling, is that mostly on expected and appropriate moments?" and "Is it easy to make eye contact with your child?" The developers found that caregivers other than the parents were more likely to give negative answers (Swinkels et al., 2006).

The ESAT was implemented by a trained child psychologist in a random population of 31,724 children aged 14 to 15 months (Dietz, Swinkels, van Daalan, van Engeland, & Buitelaar, 2006). Eighteen young children with ASD were detected, which is lower than the reported prevalence rate in the Netherlands. The PPV was 25%, with false positives receiving diagnoses of mental retardation, language disorder, and attention deficit hyperactivity disorder (ADHD) (Dietz et al., 2006). None of the identified children were found to have typical development. The ESAT was used as part of a two-stage screening approach that led to earlier detection of ASD, particularly for children with low IQ, in the Netherlands (Osterling et al., 2010).

## Screening Tool for Autism in Toddlers and Young Children (STAT™)

The STAT is a screening tool developed in 1997 by researchers at Vanderbilt Kennedy Center to be used with young children between 24 and 36 months of age (Stone, Coonrod, Turner, & Pozdol, 2004). There are 12 items in the categories of imitation, play, and communication-requesting and communication-directing attention that are completed during observations of a play interaction. Items are scored as either pass or fail or by the number of requests of directing of attention. The utility of the STAT in community-based settings remains to be determined (Stone et al., 2000).

## Social Communication Questionnaire (SCQ)

The SCQ is a parent report measure that contains 40 items designed to screen for pervasive developmental disorders in children age 4 and older (Berument, Rutter, Lord, Pickles, & Bailey, 1999). There are two versions of the questionnaire: one for children under 6 years of age and another for children older than 6 years. Items are scored as either present or absent in the areas of reciprocal social interaction, language and communication, and repetitive and stereotyped behaviors. Examples include "How much language do you think [child's name] understands if you don't gesture?" "When [child's name] is approaching someone to get her/him to do something or to talk to her/him, does [child's name] smile in greeting?" and "Is [child's name] bothered by minor changes in her/his routine? Or in the way her/his personal things are arranged?" The sensitivity, specificity, and positive predictive values are all high when PDD is compared to other diagnoses (Coonrod & Stone, 2005). However, initial research has been completed on children referred to specialized centers for assessment and therefore are highly select samples (Zwaigenbaum, 2011).

## Childhood Asperger Syndrome Test (CAST)

This screening tool was developed to be used with children ages 4 though 11 years (Scott, Baron-Cohen, Bolton, & Bayne, 2002). The screening tool contains 37 items that are answered with yes or no and include questions such as "Does s/he tend to take things literally?" "Does s/he make normal eye-contact?" and "Does s/he try to impose routines on him/herself, or on others, in such a way that it causes problems?" (Brock, Jimerson & Hansen, 2006, p. 49).

In addition to the published screening measures designed to identify autism spectrum disorders, there are other screening tools that focus on the domains of social-emotional development and communication, or the domains that are delayed in children identified with ASD. Squires, Bricker, and Twombly (2002) have created a screening tool, the *Ages and Stages Questionnaires: Social Emotional,* and report acceptable rates of sensitivity and specificity.

Eight surveys completed by caregivers are designed for specific ages between 3 and 66 months. Items on the questionnaires are scored as occurring (a) most of the time, (b) sometimes, or (c) never or rarely. The categories included in each of the surveys are self-regulation, compliance, communication, adaptive behaviors, autonomy, affect, and interactions with others (Squires et al., 2002). It takes approximately 20 minutes to complete one of the surveys. The authors state that the tool can be used as a one-time screen, but it is most beneficial if it is used as a series of surveys to obtain an understanding of the child's social-emotional development over time. Data to determine cut-off scores were obtained by sampling 3,014 children with ethnic backgrounds taken from the proportions reported in the 2000 U.S. Census and include a group of young children identified with a social-emotional disability (Squires et al., 2002).

The future development of screening tools will focus on designing and validating tools that can be used with young children from diverse cultural and linguistic backgrounds internationally (Grinker, Yeargin-Allsopp, & Boyle, 2011). "Understanding how culture influences the recognition and definition of autism spectrum disorders will facilitate cross-cultural adaptations of screening and diagnostic tools" (Grinker et al., 2011, p. 125).

# Diagnostic Processes

Diagnostic assessments would be made following the identification from a screening assessment, a recommendation from a pediatrician, or from a suggestion from a parent who has concerns. Best practice in assessment includes obtaining information from multiple sources using multiple forms of measurement (Gotham, Bishop, & Lord, 2011; Sandall, Hemmeter, Smith, & McLean, 2005). The assessment process typically includes family input via an interview, and observation of child behavior during structured and unstructured activities. The tools described in this chapter are often used as part of the multiple measures included in making a diagnosis. In addition to the results from the diagnostic tools, another component in accurate diagnoses is the clinical judgment of the diagnostician, who is usually a psychologist or psychiatrist with experience working with individuals with autism spectrum disorders (Gotham et al., 2011).

## Childhood Autism Rating Scale (CARS)

One of the earliest developed and currently most widely used assessment tools is the *Childhood Autism Rating Scale (CARS)* (Schopler, Reichler, & Renner, 1988). The developers of this tool incorporated their 15 years of experience identifying children in the state of North Carolina as part of the Treatment and Education of Autistic and other Communication handicapped CHildren (Division TEACCH) program. The developers evaluated the tool with individuals representing the racial distribution in North Carolina of 67% Caucasian, 30% Black, and 3% other races (Schopler et al., 1988). Items are based on the DSM-IV and 1978 National Society for Autistic Children criteria.

A second edition of the rating scale (CARS2) comprises three instruments (Schopler, Van Bourgondien, Wellman, & Love, 2010). The original scale remains the same and is referred to as the standard version, or CARS2–ST. A second version, or CARS2–HF, also with fifteen items, was developed for high-functioning individuals. The standard scale is to be used for individuals under age 6, or over age 6 with an IQ estimated at 79 or lower with impaired communication; the high-functioning version is for individuals age 6 or older with estimated IQs of 80 or above with fluent communication (Schopler et al., 2010). There is also a questionnaire for parents and caregivers (CARS2-QPC). Each of the fifteen items are rated on a scale from 1 (within normal limits for the age) to 4 (severely abnormal use of the behavior for age); descriptions of the range of behaviors on the scale accompany each item to assist in the scoring (Schopler et al., 2010). Samples for Relating to People, item 1 from CARS2-ST and item 3 in CARS2-HF, are shown in Figures 2–1 and 2–2.

Considerations for each of the items are found in the CARS2 manual, which is to be used as a guide for the professional administering the scale. It is clear, however, that clinical judgment is required in rating CARS2 items. For example, distinctions between scoring a 3.5 and a 4 require previous knowledge and experience of individuals with autism spectrum disorders. The authors recommend that the CARS2 be conducted by professionals, including physicians, special educators, school psychologists, speech pathologists, and audiologists practicing with exposure to and training in autism (Schopler et al., 2010). Raw scores are used to categorize the results as nonautistic, autism spectrum—mild to moderate level of behaviors, and autism spectrum—severe level of behaviors.

## Gilliam Autism Rating Scale (GARS)

The GARS/GARS2 was designed as one tool to be used by a multidisciplinary team to differentiate those individuals likely to have autism from those who do not (Gilliam, 1995, 2005).

## I. RELATING TO PEOPLE

**1**

**1.5**

**No evidence of difficulty or abnormality in relating to people** • The child's behavior is appropriate for his or her age. Some shyness, fussiness, or annoyance at being told what to do may be observed, but not to an atypical degree.

**2**

**2.5**

**Mildly abnormal relationships** • The child may avoid looking the adult in the eye, avoid the adult or become fussy if interaction is forced, be excessively shy, not be as responsive to the adult as is typical, or cling to parents somewhat more than most children of the same age.

**3**

**3.5**

**Moderately abnormal relationships** • The child shows aloofness (seems unaware of adult) at times. Persistent and forceful attempts are necessary to get the child's attention at times. Minimal contact is initiated by the child.

**4**

**Severely abnormal relationships** • The child is consistently aloof or unaware of what the adult is doing. He or she almost never responds or initiates contact with the adult. Only the most persistent attempts to get the child's attention have any effect.

## Observations:

FIGURE 2–1    Item 1 from CARS2-ST: Relating to people

---

# 3. RELATING TO PEOPLE

This item is related to the first two items, which also rate aspects of social relationships. This item differs in that it is confined to dimensions related to direct interpersonal interactions and the person's expression and reaction to another person. The two dimensions that are rated in this item are the person's initiation of interactions and the reciprocal nature of the interactions.

**1**

**1.5**

**No evidence of difficulty or abnormality in relating to people** • Age-appropriate initiation of interactions to get help, to have needs met, and for purely social purposes. Interactions with others are fluid and show a reciprocal back-and-forth pattern.

**2**

**2.5**

**Mildly abnormal relationships** • Initiates interactions only to get obvious needs met or around special interests. Some give-and-take noted in interactions, but lacks consistency or fluidity or appropriateness. Aware of other people of same age and interested in interactions, but may have difficulty initiating or managing interactions. Minimal initiation for purely social purposes that does not involve special interests.

**3**

**3.5**

**Moderately abnormal relationships** • Initiates interactions almost totally around his or her special interests, with little attempt to engage others in these interests. Responds to overtures from others, but lacks social give-and-take or responds in ways that are unusual and not always related to original overtures. Unable to maintain an interaction beyond initial overtures.

**4**

**Severely abnormal relationships** • Does not initiate any directed interactions and shows minimal response to overtures from others. Only the most persistent attempts to get the person to engage have any effect.

---

**FIGURE 2–2**   Item 3: Relating to people from the CARS2-HF

*Source:* Schopler, E.,Van Vourgondien, M. E., Wellman, G. J., & Love, S. R. Material from the CARS copyright © 2010 by Western Psychological Services. Reprinted by permission of the publisher, Western Psychological Services, 12031 Wilshire Boulevard, Los Angeles, California, 90025, U.S.A. (www.wpspublish.com) not to be reprinted in whole or in part for any additional purpose without the expressed, written permission of the publisher. All rights reserved.

The scale is designed to be completed by a parent, teacher, or caregiver who responds about an individual age 3 through 22 years (Brock et al., 2006). The scale consists of 42 items scored from 0 (never observed) to 3 (frequently observed), and 13 yes or no questions regarding the child's development. The items are grouped into four subtests of stereotyped behaviors, communication, social interaction, and development. Normative data were collected on a sample of 1,092 individuals with autism in the United States and Canada (Gilliam, 1995). Sample items include the following:

Spins objects not designed for spinning

Repeats words or phrases over and over

Uses gestures instead of speech or signs to obtain objects

Non-imitative of other people when playing

Becomes upset when routines are changed (Gilliam, 1995)

Subtest scores above 12 indicate an above average to very high probability of autism, with a reported reliability of between .88 and .96. It is also important to note that the GARS was designed for use with children age 3 and older, and valid use with younger children is questionable (Coonrod & Stone, 2005). The authors state that the GARS can be used to target goals and objectives for students (Gilliam, 1995).

James Gilliam (2001) also has authored the *Gilliam Asperger's Disorder Scale (GADS)*, which is designed to be used with individuals ages 3 through 22 to determine the probability of Asperger disorder. The same rating scale of 0 to 3 as used in the GARS is used for the GADS for 32 items in the subscales of social interaction, restricted patterns of behavior, cognitive patterns, and pragmatic skills. A Parent Interview Form with six additional yes or no questions is also included as part of the GADS. Example items are: requires specific instruction to begin tasks, is unaware of or insensitive to the needs of others, attaches very concrete meanings to words, has difficulty identifying when someone is teasing (Gilliam, 2001).

Normative data for the GADS were taken from a sample of 371 individuals with Asperger disorder from the United States, Canada, Great Britian, Mexico, and Australia (Gilliam, 2001). Although the information for creating the GADS was obtained from the DSM-IV-TR and ICD-10 definitions of Asperger disorder and syndrome, the author states that the definition of Asperger as a separate disorder remains controversial (Gilliam, 2001).

## Diagnostic Interview for Social and Communication Disorders (DISCO)

The DISCO interview (Wing & Gould, 1978) is currently in its ninth edition. This semistructured interview was created by authors in the United Kingdom to assist clinicians with the diagnosis and management of individuals with autism spectrum and other developmental disorders (Wing, Leekam, Libby, Gould, & Larcombe, 2002). Information about a broad array of behaviors across domains is collected on the DISCO, including information regarding ratings of current levels of development, degree of delay in milestones, and the severity of atypical behavior. This data can be used to assist with the diagnosis of an individual, and a summary of DISCO ratings provides a detailed database of the percentage of different behaviors that are exhibited by individuals who are classified with autism spectrum disorders (Wing et al., 2002).

## Autism Diagnostic Interview–Revised and the Autism Diagnostic Observation Schedule (ADOS)

The combination of the *Autism Diagnostic Interview–Revised (ADI-R)* (LeCouteur, Lord,

& Rutter, 2003), a semistructured interview for caregivers, and the *Autism Diagnostic Observation Schedule (ADOS)*, a standardized protocol for observing the communicative and social behavior of toddlers to adults (Lord, Rutter, DiLavore, & Risi, 2001), is considered the gold standard of diagnostic processes (Lord & Corsello, 2005). The ADI-R is comprised of 93 items linked to DSM-IV and ICD-10 criteria and takes approximately 2 hours to complete by an experienced interviewer. Clinicians are encouraged to use videos as training materials and it is recommended that clinicians be experienced in working with individuals with autism (Gotham et al., 2011). The questions to be asked of the caregivers for each of the items are clearly marked in a colored box, with the scoring criteria to the right of the text. Interrater reliability is reported to be excellent for the domain scores of the three subscales: communication; social reciprocity; and restricted, repetitive behaviors (Chakrabarti & Fombonne, 2001).

The ADOS is comprised of four modules for use with individuals of varying developmental and language levels. Standardized activities that set the occasion for observation of behavior are recorded on a scale of 0 (regular use or typical behavior) to 3 (lack of skill or behavior). Module 1, Pre-Verbal/Single Words, is comprised of 10 activities, including free play, response to joint attention, and birthday party, where behaviors scored include: frequency of vocalization directed to others, pointing, responsive social smile, showing, and functional play with objects as examples (Lord et al., 2001). Module 2, Phrase Speech, is scored during some of the same activities as Module 1 (e.g., free play and birthday party) and requires additional activities such as construction task and description of a picture. Module 3, Fluent Speech—Child/Adolescent, overlaps activities with Module 2 with the addition of friends and marriage, loneliness, emotions, and creating a story as examples. Module 4 is designed for high-functioning adolescents and adults and includes the added activities of daily living and plans and hopes.

## 2.1 📖 IN THEIR WORDS
Natacha Akshoomoff, *Ph.D. Associate Professor, Department of Psychiatry University of California, San Diego*

## Information Obtained from the ADOS

The *Autism Diagnostic Observation Schedule (ADOS)* has been shown to be a reliable and valid component of the diagnostic process (Lord et al., 2001). The ADOS provides a standardized context in which to assess social interaction, communication, play and imagination, and repetitive behaviors and interests. The administration involves activities designed to press for social and communicative behaviors. The examiner chooses from one of four different modules, based upon the language level of the individual. The provision of separate modules was intended to minimize the potential bias introduced by differences in language ability upon making a diagnostic decision. The revised algorithms for scoring the ADOS now consist of two new domains, Social Affect and Restricted, Repetitive Behaviors, combined to one score resulting in improved predictive value (Gotham et al., 2007). These revised algorithms also take into account language level and age. Based on the overall sum, the ADOS results in a classification of autism, autism spectrum, or non-spectrum. The ADOS does not differentiate among autism spectrum diagnoses (such as Asperger disorder or PDD-NOS). The authors found that the distribution of ADOS items did not cluster but rather was continuous from autism to PDD-NOS, thus refuting the appropriateness of separate cut-offs for each diagnosis (Lord et al., 2001). It is expected that the ADOS will continue to be part of the gold standard for diagnosis using DSM-5 criteria for autism spectrum disorder.

Clinical information provided during ADOS administration can be very useful for program planning. For example, social overtures are broken down into requests, directing another person's attention to something of interest, giving objects to another person, comments, and giving information. This also provides information about the contexts under which the child currently exhibits social overtures. A young child with ASD may respond to bids for joint social attention but may not yet initiate such interactions with others. Basic aspects of social behavior are also closely observed, such as eye contact, facial expressions, use of gestures, vocalizations, and use of objects. Teachers have found it useful to observe the child during ADOS administration. In some cases, the child may exhibit certain behaviors more regularly in this semistructured interaction with an adult that may be less commonly observed in the classroom or when working with familiar adults who provide more support. These differences may provide helpful information regarding the emergence of new skills or a need to focus on generalizing more skills across settings.

A large number of research studies have demonstrated that the ADOS has good inter-rater reliability, test-retest reliability, and diagnostic validity. However, given the short time period provided by the ADOS administration, as well as the fact that it provides an observation only of current functioning, it is important that diagnosis be made not on the basis of the ADOS alone, but rather that the ADOS is used in tandem with parent interview. The test authors originally intended that experienced clinicians would use the ADOS as part of a comprehensive assessment.

The ADOS is overinclusive of very young children with mental retardation and underinclusive of verbal adolescents and adults with mild characteristics (Lord & Corsello, 2005). The ADOS has been widely used to determine diagnoses for research purposes and to assist in making clinical diagnoses (Akshoomoff, Corsello, & Schmidt, 2006). Researchers can attend a five-day workshop to ensure standard administration and reliability in scoring. A two-day workshop is recommended for training of those who administer the ADOS in clinical settings. Western Psychological Services also produces a guidebook and training videos. Dr. Akshoomoff (In Their Words 2.1) discusses the benefits of the ADOS.

The latest version of the DSM-5 (see Chapter 1) includes a rating of severity of symptoms. It is likely that diagnostic tools will need to be developed to reflect this shift from a categorical approach toward a more dimensional framework (Gotham et al., 2011). Along with more refined tools to measure and define severity of ASD, "quantitative approaches to measuring symptoms across domains could improve our ability to describe different developmental trajectories and responses to treatment" (Gotham et al., 2011, p. 39).

## Additional Measures Used to Assess Outcomes

### Vineland Adaptive Behavior Scales

The *Social-Emotional Early Childhood Scales (Vineland SEEC)* (Sparrow, Cicchetti, & Balla, 1998) containing a number of items that would be impaired in young children with ASD, was designed to be completed in a semistructured interview format with an adult familiar with the child's social-emotional behavior. Responses to items are compared to a standardized sample of young children from birth through 5 years 11 months taken from the national sample obtained for the *Vineland Adaptive Behavior Scales* (Sparrow, Balla, & Cicchetti, 1984). Items on the early childhood scales are grouped in the following clusters: interpersonal relationships, play and leisure time,

and coping skills, with an overall social-emotional composite score also obtained. Administration of the SEEC scales takes approximately 15 to 25 minutes (Sparrow et al., 1998).

### Mullen Scales

The *Mullen Scales of Early Learning* (Mullen, 1995) is a standardized tool frequently used by researchers to evaluate outcomes for young children from birth to 68 months to provide a measure of cognitive functioning. Test items are presented according to developmental stages, followed by tasks used to assess the expected developmental indicators (Overton, 2012). Results can be compared to normative data. It is not uncommon to measure pre- and post-intervention outcomes using the Mullen Scales.

## Assessments for Educational Planning and Intervention

Assessments for educational planning can be used by educators and related service personnel such as speech language pathologists. Obtaining relevant information from a psychoeducational assessment depends on making the necessary accommodations and selecting the specific assessments appropriate for use with learners with autism spectrum disorder (Brock et al., 2006). Suggested accommodations and considerations include preparing the student for the experience, placing the assessment session in the student's daily schedule, minimizing distraction, using preestablished physical structures and work systems, using powerful external rewards, carefully preselecting task difficulty, and allowing nonstandard responses (Brock et al., 2006).

### Autism Screening Instrument for Educational Planning (ASIEP-2)

The ASIEP-2 was initially designed to assist public school personnel with identifying individuals with autism (Krug, Arick, & Almond, 1993). The ASIEP-2 is comprised of five standardized subtests that can be used for diagnosis, placement, educational program planning, and progress monitoring. Included as part of this instrument is the *Autism Behavior Checklist (ABC)*, which provides 57 items, and teachers and parents circle the responses that describe the focal child. The ABC was intended to be the initial step in educational planning by teachers. Although the ABC has limitations as a screening instrument, it has value in documenting change, especially if the observed behaviors scored decrease in number following educational intervention (Lord & Corsello, 2005).

An Interaction Assessment Record Form is also included to guide observations of children during social interaction and constructive play. A Vocal Behavior Sample and a Prognosis of Learning Rate obtained by recording the child's responses during discrete-trial instruction are two additional subtests. The fifth subtest, typically administered by the teacher, is the Educational Assessment; it is comprised of four sections: receptive language, expressive language, body concept, and speech imitation. This subtest provides particularly relevant information that assists with the identification of educational needs (Krug et al., 1993).

## Psychoeducational Profile (PEP)

The *Psychoeducational Profile,* currently in the third edition (PEP-3) was designed by the TEACCH program to identify the strengths and weaknesses in skills of individuals with autism spectrum disorders age 6 months through 7 years for the purpose of educational planning (Schopler, Lansing, Reichler, & Marcus, 2005). The normative sample used for comparison of results was taken from 407 individuals with autism spectrum disorders collected from 21 states in the United States. The sample also reflected the U.S. Bureau of Census data with regard to ethnicity, race, income, and level of education (Schopler et al., 2005).

The assessment is to be conducted in two parts. The first, the Caregiver Report, is a new component in this third version of the PEP

(Schopler et al., 2005). Caregivers are asked to identify their child's developmental level in several categories and compare this with typical child development. They also report on developmental history, problem behaviors, personal self-care skills, and adaptive behavior skills that include responding to a hug and participation in new activities. Scores from the Caregiver Report can be compared to percentiles from the normative sample found in the examiner's manual (Schopler et al., 2005).

The second component, the Performance Profile, is comprised of 10 subtests—six that measure developmental abilities and four focused on maladaptive behaviors (Schopler et al., 2005). An educator can purchase a test kit with all of the materials needed to administer the performance measures. Through a series of test items and activities, the test administrator scores a possible 172 items as 0 (failing), 1 (emerging), or 2 (passing). Administration directions are provided for each item, but the order of administration can be flexible and does not need to be standardized. The six performance subtests scored are cognitive verbal/preverbal, expressive language, receptive language, fine motor, gross motor, and visual-motor imitation. The six performance and four maladaptive subtests—affective expression, social reciprocity, characteristic motor behaviors, and characteristic verbal behaviors—are recorded throughout the presentation of all activities and then summarized into composite scores for communication, motor, and maladaptive behaviors.

Multiple areas are scored during each activity of the PEP-3 on the Examiner Scoring and Summary Booklet. For example, during the activity with items hidden in a denim pouch, the subtests of cognitive verbal/preverbal (CVP), gross motor (GM), affective expression (AE), and characteristic motor behaviors (CMB) are scored. Each of the performance subtests is then summarized separately, and the examiner can identify areas of strength as well as areas of focus for educational planning. Educators can use individual strengths when designing curriculum. Information from the Caregiver Report can be used by educators to address those skills and behaviors reported to occur at home.

## Adolescent and Adult Psychoeducational Profile (AAPEP)

The AAPEP was designed for the purpose of developing individualized treatment goals for adolescents and adults over age 12 with autism spectrum disorders (Mesibov, Schopler, Schaffer, & Landrus, 1988). The tool is comprised of a direct observation scale and two interviews that include a home scale and school/work scale. Each scale is comprised of six functional areas: functional communication, leisure skills, vocational skills, vocational behavior, interpersonal behavior, and independent functioning (Mesibov et al., 1988). This instrument is one of the few available that can be used to target skills for intervention with adults with autism spectrum disorders (Lord & Corsello, 2005).

As part of their book, Quill, Bracken, and Fair (2000) have published the Assessment of Social and Communication Skills for Children with Autism. This assessment tool can be used as a caregiver or teacher interview measure and includes information about the child's play, communication, and social skills observed at home, at school, and in the community. It identifies motivators and describes challenging behavior. The person completing the interview is asked to identify whether any of the skills demonstrated generalize across environments. An assessment summary sheet is included to assist educators with the identification of target objectives. The book (Quill, 2000) contains suggested activities for teaching any of the skills targeted. The activities are designed for younger children.

## Functional Emotional Assessment Scale (FEAS)

The FEAS has been designed in two versions: a clinical version and one for research purposes (Greenspan, DeGangi, & Wieder, 2001). The authors of the FEAS are the same as those who developed the floor time approach described in Chapters 2–6. The research scales are comprised of a series of recording sheets organized by the child's age (7 months through 4 years), where the caregiver scores the child's behavior on a scale of 0 (not at all or very brief) to 2 (consistently present or observed many times) (Greenspan & DeGangi, 2001). The categories scored are based on the authors' use of six functional developmental levels: (1) self-regulation and interest in the world; (2) forming relationships, attachment, and engagement; (3) two-way, purposeful communication; (4) behavioral organization, problem solving, and internalization; (5) representational capacity (elaboration); and (6) representational differentiation (Greenspan et al., 2001). The assessments of younger children do not include all of the categories.

The FEAS was validated on a sample of infants and young children that included 197 normal children, 190 infants and children with regulatory disorders, 41 children with pervasive developmental disorders, and 40 children from multiproblem families, with the vast majority (94%) from White, middle-class communities (DeGangi & Greenspan, 2001). The authors state that the FEAS shows "better sensitivity for the majority of subscales" compared with specificity rates that "were quite low for most of the subscales" (DeGangi & Greenspan, 2001, p. 185).

The clinical version of the FEAS is comprised of a list of skills that typically occur at each of the six functional developmental levels from the research version (Greenspan & Wieder, 2001). The authors state that the scale can be used as a descriptive measure only to "systematize clinical thinking" (Greenspan & Wieder, 2001, p. 78) because the scale has not been used on a large number of normal, delayed, or dysfunctional children, or has not been validated.

## The McGill Action Planning System

The *McGill Action Planning System (MAPS)* (Vandercook, York, & Forest, 1989) is a process for transition planning that is person-centered and conducted with a team. The process is guided by a series of questions addressed to the entire team, including the individual with autism spectrum disorder (Myles & Simpson, 1998a). Some of these questions are: What is the individual's history? What is your dream and nightmare? What are the individual's strengths, gifts, abilities, and interests? What would the individual's ideal day in the community look like and what must be done to make it happen?

## Choosing Outcomes and Accommodations for Children (COACH)

The *Choosing Outcomes and Accommodations for Children* (COACH) is a guide for educational planning for students with disabilities ages 3 to 21 (Giangreco, Cloninger, & Iverson, 1998). The focus of the approach is designing an educational program with the aim of pursing valued life outcomes guided by a coordinated individualized education program (IEP) process. The assessment portion of the guide includes questions for a family interview and checklists by domain for establishing learning outcomes, with templates to aid in writing measurable annual goals and short-term objectives. The appendix in COACH has many user-friendly forms to assist teams with determining the supports needed, creating a schedule, and planning and adapting instruction.

## Curriculum-Based Assessment and Monitoring Progress

Curriculum-based assessment is defined as a methodology whereby (1) assessment is linked to the curriculum and instruction, (2) educational success is evaluated by students' progress across key indicators in the curriculum, and (3) the primary purpose is to determine students' instructional needs. (Shapiro & Elliott, 1999, p. 383)

Curriculum-based assessments are recommended for use with young children and students with disabilities as well as students from diverse backgrounds. A curriculum-based assessment involves selecting and measuring objectives

from the curriculum that will be taught to the learner with autism spectrum disorder. Initial skills are measured and recorded, and then probe, or periodic, measures are taken once intervention or teaching has begun in order to obtain information on progress with objectives. Ongoing data collection on specific goals and objectives to evaluate intervention strategies and monitor progress is integral to curriculum-based assessments (Wolery, 2004).

Curriculum-based measurement tools for basic skills such as reading and math were developed in the 1970s as a way for special educators to assess the effects of their instruction (Shinn & Bamonto, 1998). Curriculum-based measures are effective for monitoring students' progress because they (1) are tied to the curricula; (2) are of short duration to allow for frequent administration; (3) focus on direct, repeated measurement of performance; (4) are capable of having many forms; and (5) are sensitive to the improvements of students' achievement over time (Kratochwill, Sheridan, Carlson, & Lasecki, 1999).

Curriculum-based measures are considered best practice for use by educators of students with disabilities and students who are English language learners (Baker, Plasencia-Peinado, & Lezcano-Lytle, 1998). The Division of Early Childhood (DEC) has identified recommended practices that include recommendations for conducting authentic, collaborative, and useful assessments (Sandall, Hemmeter, Smith, & McLean, 2005). Recommended practices were devised from the synthesis of information from reviews of the research literature and from focus groups of parents, practitioners, administrators, and scientists (Smith, McLean, Sandall, Snyder, & Ramsey, 2005). It is recommended that professionals and families rely on curriculum-based assessment as the foundation or "mutual language" for team assessments and that professionals report assessment results in a manner that is immediately useful for planning program goals and objectives.

A four-step model describing an integrated curriculum-based approach has been outlined by Shapiro and Elliott (1999). Step 1 involves assessing the academic environment to determine the effect on successes or failure. The next step would be to assess the curriculum placement or determine if the curriculum materials are a good match for the learner with ASD or if they are too difficult or too easy. In step 3, modifications to the instructional information are made, such as including visual supports. The final step is progress monitoring of both short- and long-term outcomes (Shapiro & Elliott, 1999).

Published assessment and curriculum tools designed for use with young children provide a means for educators to obtain information about the learner's current performance and the hierarchy of skills typically obtained in standard domains such as communication or social development. These materials can be used as a guide for the selection of objectives for learners with autism spectrum disorders. It is important to note that learners with ASD do not always learn skills in the same order as their peers, and they may even present with skills that typically occur at an older age at the same time they have delays in some skills in the same domain.

Bagnato, Neisworth, and Munson (1997) have published a description, or "snapshot," of curriculum-based assessment instruments in their book *Linking Assessment and Early Intervention*. Each of the assessment instruments reviewed was rated on a scale of 1.0 (negligible) to 3.0 (exemplary) on six dimensions of quality. Several curriculum-based assessments received high ratings in all six dimensions.

## Curriculum-Based Assessment Tools

One of the tools that received high ratings by Bagnato and colleagues (1997) is the *Hawaii Early Learning Profile* (HELP) for children from birth to age 3 (Parks et al., 1994) and preschoolers (ages 3 to 6) (Vort Corporation, 1995). This is an assessment designed to be completed by observing the child's activity under ongoing or arranged circumstances (Bagnato et al., 1997). Another highly rated tool is the *Assessment, Evaluation, and Programming System (AEPS)*,

a set of assessment and curriculum materials for use with young children from birth through age 6 years. The administration guide, sample observational recording sheets, and sample Individualized Family Service Plan (used with families of young children birth through age 3) or IEP goals and objectives are found in Volume 1 (Bricker, Pretti-Frontczak, Johnson, & Straka, 2002). Volume 2 contains the assessment items listed by domain and separated in two sections for birth through 3 years and 3 to 6 years (Bricker, Capt, & Pretti-Frontczak, 2002). The curriculum for teaching skills found to be delayed is outlined in Volume 3 for birth through 3 years (Bricker & Waddell, 2002a) and Volume 4 for 3 to 6 years (Bricker & Waddell, 2002b). Assessment and curriculum items are organized into six key domains: social, social-communication, fine motor, gross motor, adaptive, and cognitive. There is a goal and objective written for each item and the objective contains a criterion for success.

Third and fourth highly rated (Bagnato et al., 1997) and widely used sets of curriculum-based assessments are, respectively, the *Carolina Curriculum for Infants and Toddlers with Special Needs* (Johnson-Martin, Attermeier, & Hacker, 2004) and the *Carolina Curriculum for Preschoolers with Special Needs* (Johnson-Martin et al., 2004). Organized into six domains of child development, child behaviors are listed following a suggestion for a situation for eliciting activities or a description of a position or activity where the skills are likely to be observed. The criterion skill or behavior is described for each item. A recording sheet, including a column for the date to record when the skill is mastered, is presented alongside each item. The curriculum includes daily routines and functional activities that would facilitate the development and learning of skills, including suggestions for group activities (Johnson-Martin et al., 2004).

The *Creative Curriculum* designed for infants and toddlers (Dombro, Colker, & Dodge, 2003) and for preschoolers (Dodge, Colker, & Heroman, 2006) is another assessment and curriculum set that provides suggestions for arranging the educational environment so that goals and objectives can be embedded into everyday routines and activities (Dombro et al., 2003) or within a daily schedule for preschool-age children (Dodge et al., 2006). The appendix of the curriculum guide for infants and toddlers includes a self-assessment to assist teachers and caregivers with identifying goals and objectives. There is also a form for individualizing goals and objectives for young children; the form is organized by skill areas and is presented in a family-friendly manner. Examples include "to learn about others" and "to learn about moving and doing" (Dombro et al., 2003).

Several curriculum guides have been designed to be used with discrete trial procedures that have been published for use specifically with learners with autism spectrum disorders (see Chapter 4 for a detailed description of discrete trial procedures). Each of these guides has information on select objectives, presented in order of difficulty for the areas found to be challenging by individuals with ASD (communication and social development) as well as other socially important skills (self-help, early academic skills) (Leaf & McEachin, 1999; Lovaas, 2003; Taylor & McDonough, 1996). Ongoing data collection for progress monitoring and suggestions for incorporating modifications to teaching strategies if needed are critical features of these materials.

## Assessment of Basic Language and Learning Skills (ABLLS)

The ABLLS was designed as an assessment and curriculum guide for children with autism and other developmental disabilities (Partington & Sundberg, 1998). The tool contains assessment and skills tracking grids, along with information that guides the development of individualized education program (IEP) goals for a child. The authors use behavior analysis, in particular Skinner's work on verbal behavior, as a guide for assessment items (see Chapter 4 for a description of verbal behavior). The tool has been revised and published as the ABLLS-R (Partington, 2006).

ABLLS-R items are scored 0 through 4 according to established criteria for 554 items distributed across the categories of basic learner skills (e.g., cooperation, imitation, receptive language, requests, play and leisure, following classroom routines), academic skills (reading, math, writing, and spelling), self-help skills (dressing, eating, grooming, and toileting), and motor skills (fine and gross) (Partington, 2006). The number of items under the 25 categories varies between 6 and 57.

The Skills Tracking pages provide a series of bar graphs where the number of items that meet criteria in each category can be depicted by filling in a box with color. Progress over time can be demonstrated by higher numbers of items colored, indicating meeting criteria following intervention (Partington, 2006; Partington & Sundberg, 1998). Data sheets and a curriculum guide are included as part of this assessment package.

The SCERTS Model for use with students with autism spectrum disorders, described in detail in Chapter 6, is presented in a two-volume set containing Volume 1, *Assessment*, and Volume 2, *Program Planning*. The assessment volume contains a description of the model and a list of child and partner skills under three competency stages of Social Partner, Language Partner, and Conversation Partner (Prizant, Wetherby, Rubin, Laurent, & Rydell, 2006a). The SCERTS assessment process (SAP) "is designed to meet the purpose of assessment for intervention or educational planning. The SAP would only be implemented with a child who is suspected of having ASD or another developmental disability affecting social communication and emotional regulation" (Prizant et al., 2006a, p. 131).

The authors describe the SAP as a curriculum-based assessment that is linked to items in their intervention model. Assessment information is gathered through interviewing of significant people, observation of daily activities, and behavior sampling and eliciting responses related to the social communication and emotional regulation of the child. Although different items are assessed depending on the stage of focus, the domains assessed remain the same across stages and include joint attention and symbol use under social communication, mutual regulation and self-regulation under emotional regulation, and interpersonal support and learning support under transactional supports. When transactional supports are assessed, the focus is on the partner and learning environment (Prizant et al., 2006a).

A criterion is established for each of the items that can be assessed across the three stages and the criterion is stated in the assessment volume (Prizant et al., 2006a). Observation forms are included in the volume; the observation forms have columns to the left of each item where scores of 0 (criterion not met) to 2 (criterion met consistently across two partners and in two contexts) can be placed. Data sheets for organizing and prioritizing objectives for the target child and the supporting partners, and Daily and Weekly Tracking Logs are also included in Volume 1 (Prizant et al., 2006a).

Aspy and Grossman (2011) have published a framework for creating comprehensive interventions for high functioning individuals with ASD entitled the Ziggurat Model. Multiple tools are included and are to be used by a multidisciplinary team including parents to identify the student's needs, establish goals, and develop interventions. Strategies suggested are drawn from those developed by the TEACCH model (see Chapter 7) and those based on applied behavior analysis (see Chapters 4 and 5). Another tool that can be used to guide planning is the Comprehensive Autism Planning System (CAPS) (Henry & Smith Myles, 2007), which comprises the following components: activities and times that the student requires support, target skills, structure/modifications, reinforcement, sensory strategies, communication skills, generalization plan, and data collection. The model includes forms located in the appendix that can be used for assessment, goal identification, and educational strategy planning.

In addition to skills and objectives related to the areas of communication, social-emotional development, and academic and self-help skills, adaptive skills may be an issue for a learner with ASD. Behavior in the form of tantrums when a less

preferred activity is scheduled, or refusal to transition or change attention to a preferred task, becomes a challenge for educators. Other behaviors such as self-injurious behaviors or hitting or pinching others may result in a restrictive placement. When behaviors that are considered problematic occur in a school setting, personnel are required to determine the function of the behavior through a functional behavior assessment. Although school psychologists often take the lead in conducting a functional behavior assessment, educators are often requested to collect ongoing data on these problem or challenging behaviors and to monitor progress with any program or intervention plan devised. Information about functional behavior assessment strategies to address the function of a problematic behavior, and ways to prevent problem behavior through positive behavior supports, is presented in Chapter 5.

An advantage of using curriculum-based assessments is that the assessment results are clearly linked to the selected goals and objectives that are the focus of educational planning. Some of the published curriculum guides provide suggestions for writing objectives for a particular skill, identifying the materials needed, and proposing an effective procedure and accommodations that can be used to modify the instruction for learners with specific disabilities (e.g., Bricker & Waddell, 2002a, 2002b). In addition to identifying delays in areas such as communication and social interaction skills, assessment results will also indicate strengths that can be incorporated into curriculum design. For example, a student for whom reading letters is a strength may be read books about sharing and friendship or use scripts to assist with the development of peer relationships.

## Ongoing Progress Monitoring

Following the identification of individual strengths and weaknesses through the assessment process, it is up to the educational team to prioritize goals and objectives. The interventionists then identify the activities and formats where the objectives will be embedded and begin to address skill-building activities. To determine if the strategies selected are working, ongoing progress monitoring is essential. Monitoring progress with all objectives is recommended on an ongoing basis so that engagement in activities is confirmed and changes to intervention or program activities can be made if progress is too slow (Wolery, 2004). Assessment should be planned as an integral component of an educational program rather than an event that occurs prior to or periodically during the year, such as for an annual review. However, incorporating progress monitoring systems requires personnel who value ongoing assessment; administrative support for program design that includes progress monitoring systems; and team members with skills in progress monitoring, modifying interventions, and communicating program changes (Wolery, 2004). Chapter 3 reviews the recommendations for best practice in working as a team and in implementation of evidence-based practices, and details on how to collect data effectively can be found in Chapter 4.

Guides are available to assist in the creation of curriculum activities that embed IEP objectives. In their book for preschool educators of children with special needs, Sandall and Schwartz (2002) provide many suggestions for curriculum modifications and activities that can be used to embed target skills. Relevant forms for assessing the quality of the classroom and child strengths and areas of concern, and creating a child activity matrix to ensure that IEP goals are embedded, and worksheets for evaluating any concerns are found in the appendix. In their *Quick Start Manual*, Webber and Scheuermann (2008) provide a comprehensive overview of how to implement strategies based on applied behavior analysis from classroom design, providing step-by-step descriptions of strategies (see Chapter 4) and providing instruction in how to collect data with various data collection forms (e.g., Naturalistic/Milieu Program Data Form and Trial-by-Trial Data Sheet) for ongoing progress monitoring embedded throughout the manual. They devote a chapter to collecting data for monitoring behaviors targeted for reduction.

Even when preservice training includes an emphasis on progress monitoring systems and educators agree about the value and importance of these systems, it is the rare public school classroom that incorporates a data collection and evaluation system. Educators are frequently not sufficiently fluent in data collection and interpretation, and they do not have the skills to design data collection forms and progress monitoring systems in order to implement ongoing curriculum-based programs. However, this can be done. Penelope Wong Bonggat successfully developed a data collection and monitoring system and trained the paraprofessionals in her classroom to monitor the IEP objectives for her preschool students, including learners with autism spectrum disorders (see In Their Words 2.2).

## Program Evaluation

Program evaluation occurs when the outcomes from a specific program are assessed to determine whether they are effectively addressing stated program objectives. For educational interventions to be effective, interventionists need to be able to implement evidence-based practices effectively (see Chapter 3 for description of best implementation practices) within a supportive environment. If the environment is a school, then the policies and practices at the federal, state, district, school, and classroom levels can affect whether programs are effective (Dunlap, Iovannone, & Kincaid, 2008). Recommendations for an effective program include: a school-wide positive behavior support plan in place (see Chapter 5 for a description), efficient management of instructional time is in place, a data-based accountability system is implemented, frequent feedback to the student is given, high expectations are evident, and interactions with students occur in a positive and

**2.2** ⬥ *IN THEIR WORDS*  Penelope Bonggat, *M.A. Preschool Teacher*

## Designing a Progress Monitoring System in a Preschool Classroom

As a teacher of preschool-age children with autism, data collection holds a special place in my heart and plays an even more vital role in the functioning of my classroom. It permeates every aspect of my teaching, from how I set up the physical environment to dictating students' individualized education programs (IEPs). There are many intricacies involved in creating a data collection system, and this involves dedication and constant fine-tuning. I have found that a successful data collection system relies on the following factors: desire, training, classroom staff, your students, and use of reinforcement. All teachers will find ways to individualize their system and make it work for them, but the key is to do it.

An important aspect of creating a data collection system within the classroom is the motivation of the teacher. Throughout my career in special education I have been fortunate to be exposed to some form of data collection system and always assumed this is how special education worked. I have also been fortunate to be mentored by professionals who dedicated themselves to data collection and impressed its importance onto me. However, exposure to and training in data collection do not always correlate with establishing and maintaining a detailed system in one's classroom. As I began establishing the data collection system I had envisioned in my head, I quickly became overwhelmed with the amount and the quality of the data I was gathering. So I asked myself two important questions, "Why take data?" or "What do you want to know?" and "How do I make this easy (therefore, more likely) to use?"

As an educator in special education, it is my job and my responsibility to know exactly where my students are functioning in relation to their previous performance, and in relation to their peers. A well-planned and executed data collection system can establish students' rate of learning, their learning style, what they are learning, what their strengths and weaknesses are, their ability to generalize skills. It allows me to individualize what I teach and document student progress in order to relay that information to parents and support providers. Accurately and consistently recorded data dictate the development of new goals and objectives for an IEP. Without documenting progress of existing IEP goals, there is no dependable way of knowing if mastery has occurred, and if not, data assist me in answering the question "why not?" Data allow a student to move ahead before his or her IEP is due or determine if modifications need to be made to the current IEP if goals and objectives are not being reached. In this way, I can collaborate with families and support providers and gauge what kind of goals to write (formal assessment data are also necessary) and what increments of measure will challenge but ensure success for each student.

In creating the physical environment of my classroom I modeled and modified the areas according to what research had suggested was best practice for both typical preschoolers and students with autism. But in order to gather data on every student and every goal, every day, this would demand the assistance of my two special education technicians (aides). My data collection system would need to be detailed yet practical, as data would need to be collected during daily activities. With my own ideas on what information needed to be gathered, I turned to my aides for input on how to create the data sheets. I found that it was only prudent to seek their input on how the data

(*continued*)

## 2.2  IN THEIR WORDS (continued)

sheets should be set up if I expected them to use the data sheets on a daily basis. Partnering with my aides on creating the data sheets made data collection training and data review the obvious next steps in our collaboration.

I wanted data collection to be a natural part of the daily operations of my classroom and in order to have the data collection system I wanted, my aides would have to be equally dedicated and well trained. Good relationships with my aides made communication easier and much more effective, and I encouraged them from the start to approach me with their ideas, questions, and concerns. Not only did my aides work with the students and thus would be able to provide vital information on their progress, but their participation made them equally vested in this process and accepting of the numerous changes I made. While I built time into our daily schedule to discuss student progress, I also made sure I spent adequate time with each aide, training and shadowing as I implemented a new data sheet or program to ensure consistency. Additional training I conducted with my aides during their nonworking hours only occurred because of the relationship I had established with my aides and in addition to their own desire to go above and beyond in order to support our students.

A well-established data collection system also became an effective time-management tool. While it was important for all classroom staff to take data in order to track progress and maintain consistency in how we taught specific skills, it also allowed my aides to introduce new skills to my students once they had met mastery criteria or to adapt how we were teaching a skill to facilitate progress. This natural flow of data collection and teaching eliminated the need for my aides to ask questions on a daily basis on what to teach next and gave me the opportunity to focus on teaching my students and not my aides.

Ultimately, the system I created involved data sheets strategically placed in every area of the room where these students worked on skills related to their IEP goals and objectives (keep in mind, confidentiality of students' identities, goals and objectives, and progress is crucial when determining how you will physically set up your system). As data sheets were completed, they were removed and placed in a data binder (one for each student), which organized old data for analysis or presentation at IEP meetings. Once the data collection system was functioning, a great deal of fine-tuning took place. To my surprise this process never ended! With each school year I was blessed with new students who challenged my existing system and required me to rethink and rework how to gather data effectively. While my experience produced a data collection system that was unique to my classroom, all teachers will find ways to individualize their system so it is informative and functional for them. It may seem like you're staring up at a mountain as you take your first steps to establishing or revising your data collection system. But like the journey our students make toward reaching their goals, small steps, the right attitude, and the support of those around you will make the journey easier.

caring way (Dunlap et al., 2008). When evaluating any program, it is important to determine that the program is effective for multiple individuals with autism spectrum disorders who have varying strengths and deficits.

## Autism Environmental Rating Scale (APERS)

To evaluate the context in which evidence-based practices are being implemented as a means for identifying strengths and improving weaker aspects, the National Professional Development Center on ASD (NPDC) (autismpdc.fpg.unc .edu) designed a tool to use with personnel across states in the United States, with a focus on overall program components. The evaluation tool, called the *Autism Environmental Rating Scale* (APERS), was created in two versions, preschool–elementary and middle–high school. To obtain a broad spectrum of information from multiple sources, the evaluation requires record reviews, interviews of parents and key personnel, and observation of interactions between individuals with ASD and peers and staff. The evaluators attend to how the environment is arranged, how much teamwork is evident, and whether evidence-based practices are implemented and monitored for effectiveness.

Parents and educators have the right to inquire about outcomes of any program for individuals with autism spectrum disorders. Suggestions for the criteria on which parents may evaluate educational programs for learners with autism spectrum disorders are found in Chapter 3. A definition and description of evidence-based practices are also found in Chapter 3. The published research on effectiveness is summarized for the programs described in Chapters 4 through 7. The strength of evidence in support of these programs is also indicated.

## SUGGESTIONS FOR DISCUSSION

1. Discuss why it is important to use assessment tools for the purpose for which they were designed.
2. State why is it important to monitor progress with each learning objective identified for an individual with ASD.
3. Conduct a debate, with one side arguing for the need for daily data collected during multiple educational activities and the other side arguing for probe data taken for one child at a time, at the end of the day, or weekly.
4. Describe how you would link assessment results to the curriculum developed for a learner with autism spectrum disorder.
5. Discuss the ways in which cultural and linguistic biases can affect the results of the assessment process.
6. Identify the program components that can support or hinder the effectiveness of the interventions for individuals with ASD.

## RESOURCES

### Screening and Diagnosis

Baird, G., Cox, A., Charman, T., Baron-Cohen, S., Swettenham, J., Wheelwright, S., & Drew, A. (2000). A screening instrument for autism at 18 months of age: A six year follow-up study. *Journal of the American Academy of Child and Adolescent Psychiatry, 39*, 694–702.

Gilliam, J. E. (2005). *Gilliam Autism Rating Scale (GARS2)*. Austin, TX: Pro-Ed.

Lord, C., Rutter, M. A., DiLavore, P. C., & Risi, S. (2001). *The Autism Diagnostic Observation Schedule*. Los Angeles, CA: Western Psychological Services.

Robbins, D., Fein, D., & Barton, M. (1999). *The Modified Checklist for Autism in Toddlers*. www2.gsu.edu (Diana L. Robins).

Schopler, E., Van Bourgondien, M. E., Wellman, G. J., Love, S. R. (2010). *The Childhood Autism Rating Scale-Second edition (CARS2)*. Los Angeles, CA: Western Psychological Services.

Swinkels, H. N., Dietz, C., van Daalen, E., Kerkhof, H. G. M., van Engeland, H., & Buitelaar, J. K. (2006). Screening for autistic spectrum in children aged 14 and 15 months. I. The development of the Early Screening of Autistic Traits questionnaire (ESAT). *Journal of Autism and Developmental Disorders, 36*, 723–732.

Wetherby, A., & Prizant, B. (2002). *Communication and Social Behavior Scales Developmental Profile—Infant-Toddler Checklist*. Baltimore: Brookes.

## Educational Planning and Program Design

Krug, D. A., Arick, J. R., & Almond, P. J. (1993). *Autism Screening Instrument for Educational Planning* (2nd ed.). Austin, TX: Pro-Ed.

Mesibov, G. B., Schopler, E., Schaffer, B., & Landrus, R. (1988). *Adolescent and Adult Psychoeducational Profile (AAPEP): Volume IV*. Austin, TX: Pro-Ed.

Partington, J. W. (2006). *The Assessment of Basic Language and Learning Skills (ABLLS-R Protocol): An assessment, curriculum guide, and skills tracking system for children with autism and other developmental disabilities*. Pleasant Hill, CA: Behavior Analysts.

Schopler, E., Lansing, M. D., Reichler, R., & Marcus, L. M. (2005). *Psychoeducational profile (Third edition) (PEP-3): TEACCH individualized psychoeducational assessment for children with autism spectrum disorders*. Austin, TX: Pro-Ed.

# CHAPTER THREE

# Collaborating for Effective Implementation of Evidence-Based Practices

## CHAPTER OBJECTIVES

The reader should be able to:

- Explain how research provides the evidence or empirical basis for the use of educational strategies and name the legislation that requires the implementation of scientifically based practices by educators.

- Indicate the identified factors that result in effective implementation of evidence-based practices according to Fixsen, Naoom, Blase, Friedman, and Wallace (2005).

- Identify the methods for developing partnerships with parents and paraprofessionals.

As described in Chapter 1, researchers are working to find the cause or causes of autism spectrum disorders (ASDs) on a neurobiological level and have found possible genes and proteins that may be influential in the development of the challenges that face individuals with ASD. However, there remains no intervention at the biological level to prevent autism spectrum disorders. At present and likely well into the future, educational interventions to build skills and replace problem behavior are necessary. Chapter 3 addresses the identification and implementation of evidence-based practices by educators as they design curriculum and instruction for individuals with autism spectrum disorders. Ideally the selection of strategies and educational objectives are considered in collaboration

with families to ensure a consistent approach and optimal outcomes.

Students with autism spectrum disorders can benefit from educational interventions and accommodations targeted to increase effective social interaction and address concerns with repetitive mannerisms (American Psychiatric Association DSM-5, 2013). Many also need educational strategies to develop and expand communication systems. Due to the uneven learning abilities and skill levels of students with ASD, individualizing any curriculum is essential (Webber & Scheuermann, 2008). Current policy requires that, when educators select strategies for teaching any curriculum, they use scientifically based practices, or those with research support that can be implemented with fidelity.

# Legislation Guiding Practice

Through the efforts of parent and professional collaboration, legislation has been passed in the United States that has influenced the quality of education for students with disabilities. The evolution of education legislation and some of the most influential legislation relevant for individuals with autism spectrum disorders and their families is described below.

## Evolution of Education Legislation

- 1954, *Brown v. Board of Education:* A decision by the U.S. Supreme Court ended "separate but equal" schools based on race because segregation based on unalterable characteristics resulted in inequitable educational opportunities.

- 1972, *Pennsylvania Association for Retarded Citizens v. the Commonwealth of Pennsylvania:* Decision mandated a free, public program of education appropriate to the child's capacity, with placement in the regular public school class preferred.

- 1973, The Rehabilitation Act (PL 93-112): This law included Section 504, which considered exclusion from any program or activity based on disability as discrimination.

- 1975, The Education of All Handicapped Children Act (PL- 94-142): This law ensures a free, appropriate public education (FAPE) that includes special education designed to meet the unique needs of all children with disabilities. This act was amended in 1986, and in 1991 and 1997 as the Individuals with Disabilities Education Act (IDEA).

- 1982, *Board of Education v. Rowley:* This court case addressed the appropriateness of the method for implementing an individualized education program for a child who was deaf. Consequently, it is often interpreted that a school must provide an appropriate, but not necessarily the best, educational program for each student.

- 1990, The Americans with Disabilities Act (PL 101-336): This legislation includes the Bill of Rights for Persons with Disabilities.

- 2001, No Child Left Behind Act: This legislation states that all children should have a fair, equal, and significant opportunity to obtain a high-quality education and reach minimum proficiency on challenging state academic standards and assessments.

- 2004, Individuals with Disabilities Improvement Act (PL 108-445): This act reauthorized the Individuals with Disabilities Education Act (IDEA). (Murdick, Gartin, & Crabtree, 2007)

- 2006, Combating Autism Act (P.L. 109-416): This act expanded coordination of federal activities in autism through the reestablishment of the Interagency Autism Coordinating Council.

- 2010, A Blueprint for Reform: The Reauthorization of the Elementary and Secondary Education Act: This act includes cross-cutting priorities, for example, technology, evidence, efficiency, supporting English learners and students with disabilities, and supporting rural and other high needs areas.

## The Individualized Education Program (IEP) and the Individualized Family Service Plan (IFSP)

The means by which a **free, appropriate education (FAPE)** has been implemented since 1975 is through an **individualized education program (IEP)**. The IEP is a document that results from the collaborative effort of parents, school personnel, and other service providers, called the IEP team (Murdick, Gartin, & Crabtree, 2007). IDEA 2004 requires that the IEP team must include at minimum, the student's parents, the special education teacher, a general education teacher, a representative of the local educational agency (school), someone that can explain the instructional implications of any assessment results, and others at the discretion of the student's parents or the school (Yell, 2012).

The IEP is created in collaboration between parents and the local educational agency (LEA). IDEA 2004 describes a parent as a natural, adoptive, or foster parent; a guardian; a person acting in the place of a natural or adoptive parent (including grandparent, stepparent, or other relative) with whom the child lives; or an individual who is legally responsible for the child's welfare (PL 108–446 602[23], 118 Stat. 2647 [2005]). Parents are required to consent to initial evaluation, reevaluation, and services (Murdick et al., 2007). "Parental involvement is essential both as a source of information and consent for programming and as an advocate for the student" (Murdick et al., 2007, p. 175).

The IEP describes both the abilities and needs of the child, and establishes the educational goals and objectives to be implemented in the least restrictive environment (Murick et al., 2007). Curriculum objectives are determined as an outcome of a dialogue among team members during preschool through the high school years. IDEA 2004 emphasizes the writing of measurable annual goals, evaluating progress toward each goal during the course of the year, and informing parents of progress at least every nine weeks (Yell, 2012). The implementation of ongoing measurement through curriculum-based assessment is recommended.

A requirement of the IEP is an explanation of the extent to which the child will not participate with nondisabled children in regular class and activities (Murdick et al., 2007), so that consideration of the least restrictive environment for education is considered. The least restrictive environment (LRE) is defined in IDEA 2004 as follows:

> To the maximum extent appropriate, children with disabilities, including children in public and/or private institutions or other care facilities, are educated with children who are not disabled, and special classes, separate schooling, or other removal of children with disabilities from the regular environment occurs only when the nature or severity of the disability of a child is such that education in regular classes with the use of supplementary aids and services cannot be achieved satisfactorily. (PL 108–446, 612 [a][5][A], 118 Stat. 2647 [2005])

In addition, education for children with disabilities should be provided as close to the child's home as possible, with children who are not disabled whenever possible, and both academic and extracurricular activities should be provided (Murdick et al., 2007). Each public agency is required to provide a continuum of alternative placements with increasing levels of educational supports (Murdick et al., 2007).

In 1986, the **individualized family service plan (IFSP)** was designed to address the individualized needs of infants and toddlers with disabilities and their families (Murdick et al., 2007). The IFSP is a process of addressing individualized outcomes based on the strengths, resources, priorities, and concerns of the family. Included as part of IDEA 2004 is the requirement of a statement of measurable results, or outcomes, expected to be achieved in preliteracy and language skills. Children ages 3 to 5 may have either an IFSP or an IEP depending on their individual needs (Murdick et al., 2007).

Another requirement of IDEA 2004 is that early intervention services are provided in natural environments and that a justification is provided in the IFSP of the extent, if any, to which services will not be provided in a natural environment. **Natural environments** are defined by federal definition as "settings that are natural or normal for the child's age peers who have no disabilities" (34 CFR Part 303.18). Natural environments comprise the everyday community activities that are opportunities for child learning of functional and adaptive skills (Dunst, Raab, Trivette, & Swanson, 2010).

## No Child Left Behind

The primary goals of the No Child Left Behind Act (NCLB) passed by the U.S. Congress are as follows: all students must achieve high academic standards by rewarding school districts that improve student achievement and reforming those that do not, all students will be taught by a highly qualified teacher using scientifically based methods, all students will be educated in safe and drug-free schools and classrooms, parents have the right to transfer their child from a "failing" or unsafe school, all limited-English-proficient students will become proficient, and all students will graduate from high school (Turnbull, Turnbull, Erwin, Soodak, & Shogren, 2011; Yell & Drasgow, 2005). This law contains 10 sections or titles. Accountability for results is emphasized, and research-based instruction, or the use of strategies based on scientifically based research, is a central principle (Yell & Drasgow, 2005).

The implications of NCLB for learners with autism spectrum disorders are that they are required to be taught by highly qualified teachers and paraprofessionals using **scientifically based instruction** (Yell, Drasgow, & Lowrey, 2005). Highly qualified special education teachers are those with a bachelor's degree and who are fully certified by the state in the area in which they teach and who have passed a test of subject matter knowledge and competency (Yell & Drasgow, 2005). A highly qualified paraprofessional is defined, as of January 8, 2006, as one with a secondary school diploma or equivalent, plus two years of study at an institute of higher education or competence in the subject matter taught, as demonstrated by passing a state test. According to NCLB, paraprofessionals can provide instructional support services only when directly supervised by a highly qualified teacher (Yell, 2012). NCLB requires states to provide high-quality professional development activities to all public school teachers (Yell & Drasgow, 2005).

The implications of NCLB for the instruction of learners with ASD are that teachers will need skills in constructing and administering relevant assessments, interpreting the findings of assessments, designing individualized curriculum that addresses assessment results, and implementing interventions grounded in scientifically based research (Yell & Drasgow, 2005; Yell et al., 2005). There is currently a large gap

between what is known to work from scientifically based research and what is implemented in many classrooms (Yell, 2012; Yell et al., 2005). To identify research-based instructional practices, educators need the skills of defining research evidence, evaluating research findings, and implementing effective practices.

## Identifying Evidence-Based Practices

No Child Left Behind states that only scientifically based practices should be used in education. **Scientifically based practices** are defined as those where there is a body of research demonstrating effectiveness with students with disabilities as opposed to strategies that have been created on convincing premises but have not been evaluated or assessed (Yell et al., 2005). Educators are expected to implement strategies that have been demonstrated as effective for individuals with ASD by research that has been reviewed by peers and published in discriminating outlets for research. In contrast, a self-published book describing an approach or strategy written by the strategy developer with testimonials by users would not be considered scientific evidence.

In their position statement on evidence-based practices in communication disorders, the American Speech-Language-Hearing Association (ASHA) recommends that speech-language pathologists and audiologists "incorporate the principles of evidence-based practice in clinical decision making to provide high quality clinical care. The term **evidence-based practice** refers to an approach in which current, high-quality research evidence is integrated with practitioner expertise and client preferences and values into the process of making clinical decisions" (American Speech-Language-Hearing Association, 2005).

It is important to consider that the research evidence is about the application of the educational strategy, ideally used with learners with autism spectrum disorders. Neurological research on brain functions may be interesting and provide evidence of atypical patterns of functioning; however, this research has not been used to inform the effects of educational practices. Similarly there may be a body of research on the effectiveness of a strategy or approach used effectively with typically developing children. However, this research does not inform about the effectiveness of the same approach used with a learner with ASD. For example, an educational strategy that incorporates modeling by adults or peers may be effective for typical children but ineffective for those children with ASD who have difficulties with the imitation of others (Rogers, 2006).

A hallmark of scientifically based evidence is whether or not it is replicable. A strategy or intervention should be defined well enough so that demonstrations of effectiveness can be repeated over time, with multiple students, and by multiple educators. A strategy that is shown to be effective only when used by the developer would have limited usefulness. Ideally, demonstrations of implementing the strategy or approach effectively for individuals with ASD could be repeated when used by experts, educators, parents, and paraprofessionals.

There have been several reviews of the published research literature in order to determine which strategies (National Autism Center, 2009b; Odom, Collet-Klingenberg, Rogers, & Hatton, 2010) or program models (Odom, Boyd, Hall, & Hume, 2010; Rogers & Vismara, 2008) have sufficient evidence to be determined as scientifically based. The term **evidence-based practices** began in medicine (Reichow, Volkmar, & Cicchetti, 2008), where the use of randomized group designs that compare a treatment with a placebo-control condition is commonly used to determine effectiveness. Randomized controlled treatment methods are considered the gold standard for addressing research questions (Odom et al., 2005). Educational practices evaluated using group experimental or quasi-experimental research designs would be considered evidence-based if two or more studies are of high quality or four or more studies are of acceptable quality with weighted effect sizes significantly greater

than zero (Gersten et al., 2005). Essential quality indicators regarding the selection of participants, implementation of intervention, outcome measures (including measures of generalized performance), and data analysis must be included in a quality study (Gersten et al., 2005).

School districts often do not allow random assignment of learners to a classroom or to maintain a control group with no intervention (Gersten et al., 2005). Therefore, single-subject, or single-case, experimental designs replicated across participants may be a better fit when evaluating some educational interventions (Horner et al., 2005; Odom et al., 2005). Evidence of effectiveness for single-subject designs is considered if five or more studies are published in peer-reviewed journals with: a clear description of the participants and settings; dependent variables that are operationally defined and measured repeatedly with inter-observer agreement; independent variables or practices that are operationally defined and implemented with fidelity, with a demonstrated functional relationship to the dependent variable; and a demonstration of social validity (Horner et al., 2005; Reichow et al., 2008). Fidelity is defined as the degree to which a strategy is implemented correctly or as it was designed to be used. Studies must have been conducted by three different researchers in three different geographic locations and include at least 20 participants, such as 20 participants diagnosed with autism spectrum disorders (Horner et al., 2005).

The National Autism Center (2009a, 2009b) coordinated a review of the research published between 1957 and 2007 involving participants with autism spectrum disorder, and using a Scientific Merit Rating Scale classified the evidence into four categories: established, emerging, unestablished, and ineffective/harmful. Their findings are presented in two reports entitled the *National Standards Project* (National Autism Center, 2009b) and *Evidence-based Practices and Autism in the Schools* (National Autism Center, 2009a). These reports list eleven treatments classified under those that are "established". The number of research studies with demonstrated outcomes in support of these treatments varies and ranges from 6 to 231. The list of established treatments and the number of research publications for each category is found in Table 3.1.

When summarizing these findings, the authors state that approximately two-thirds of these strategies are based purely on the behavioral literature and 75% of the other third are also based on behavioral principles. In other words, over 90% of the published studies reviewed by the National Standards Project focused on the implementation of behavioral strategies.

The National Professional Development Center (NPDC) on ASD also completed a review of the same research literature using the criteria established by Reichow, Volkmar, and Cicchetti (2008) and Odom and colleagues (2005). These reviewers categorize 24 strategies as evidence-based (Odom, Collet-Klingenberg, Rogers, & Hatton, 2010). Figure 3–1 is a matrix comparing the 11 evidence-based strategies determined by the NPDC on ASD with the 24 found by the National Standards Project, which can be found on the NPDC website at http://autismpdc.fpg.unc.edu.

In addition to this matrix, this website contains much more information. For each of the 24 evidence-based practices, there is a list of the references by age group that determined the classification. There is also a description of the practice in a brief form, and a checklist for measuring fidelity of intervention that can be used to guide skill acquisition for educators. Some of the practices are also connected to video modules (autism Internet modules) with examples of practices.

In addition to practices or strategies that are used to address the defining characteristics of autism spectrum disorders, program models also have been evaluated. Comprehensive treatments have been evaluated, with a focus on those used in early intervention (Rogers & Vismara, 2008) and those meeting six selected criteria with participants across the life span (Odom, Boyd, Hall, & Hume, 2010). Using the treatment classification criteria established by Chambless and colleagues (1998) that categorized models, Rogers and Vismara (2008) found only the Lovaas treatment approach in the category of "probably efficacious," having two or more strong group designs or three or more strong single-subject designs published prior to 2007.

Odom, Boyd, Hall, and Hume (2010) evaluated 30 comprehensive treatment models across six dimensions (operationalization, fidelity of implementation measures, replication, empirical evidence for the model, quality of the research evidence, and published focused intervention studies by model developers) using a 5-point rating scale. The Lovaas Institute was also rated highly, with scores of 4 or 5 for at least four dimensions. Others rated highly included the Denver Model, LEAP, May Institute, and the Princeton Child Development Institute (PCDI). The dimension that was scored highest overall for these models was operationalization, with many having clear manuals of procedures and curriculum. The dimension that was the weakest overall was in the measurement of fidelity of implementation. Many models incorporated staff training procedures where one supervisor evaluated a trainee until he or she met criteria, but few had inter-rater agreement between supervisors on staff performance, and only one program validated their staff training checklist.

**TABLE 3.1** National Standards Project

| Established Treatments | Journal Articles Comprising Category |
|---|---|
| Antecedent package | 99 |
| Behavioral package | 231 |
| Comprehensive behavioral treatment for young children | 22 |
| Joint attention intervention | 6 |
| Modeling | 50 |
| Naturalistic teaching strategies | 32 |
| Peer training package | 33 |
| Pivotal response treatment | 14 |
| Schedules | 12 |
| Self-management | 21 |
| Story-based intervention package | 21 |

**Overlap Between Evidence-Based Practices Identified by the National Professional Development Center (NPDC) on ASD and the National Standards Project (NSP)**

| Evidence-Based Practices Identified by the National Professional Development Center (NPDC) on ASD | Established Treatments Identified by the National Standards Project (NSP) | | | | | | | | | | |
|---|---|---|---|---|---|---|---|---|---|---|---|
| | Antecedent Package | Behavioral Package | Story-Based Intervention Package | Modeling | Naturalistic Teaching Strategies | Peer Training Package | Pivotal Response Treatment | Schedules | Self-Management | Comprehensive Behavioral Treatment for Young Children | Joint Attention Intervention |
| Promoting | X | | X | | | | | | | The NPDC on ASD did not review comprehensive treatment models. Components of The Comprehensive Behavioral Treatment of Young Children overlap with many NPDC-identified practices | The NPDC on ASD considers joint attention to be an outcome rather than an intervention. Components of joint attention interventions overlap with many NPDC-identified practices. |
| Antecedent-based intervention | X | | | | | | | | | | |
| Time Delay | X | | | | | | | | | | |
| Reinforcement | | X | | | | | | | | | |
| Task Analysis | | X | | | | | | | | | |
| Discrete Trial Training | | X | | | | | | | | | |
| Functional Behavior Analysis | | X | | | | | | | | | |
| Functional Communication Training | | X | | | | | | | | | |
| Response Interruption/Redirection | | X | | | | | | | | | |
| Differential Reinforcement | | X | | | | | | | | | |
| Social Narratives | | | X | | | | | | | | |
| Video Modeling | | | | X | | | | | | | |
| Naturalistic Interventions | | | | | X | | | | | | |
| Peer-mediated Intervention | | | | | | X | | | | | |
| Pivotal Response Training | | | | | | | X | X | | | |
| Visual Supports | | | | | | | | X | | | |
| Structured Work Systems | | | | | | | | | X | | |
| Self-Management | | | | | | | | | | | |
| Parent Implemented Intervention | The NSP did not consider parent-implemented intervention as a category of evidence and practice. However, 24 of the studies reviewed by the NSP under other intervention categories involve parents implementing the intervention. | | | | | | | | | | |
| Social Skills Training Groups | Social Skills Training Groups (Social Skills Package) was identified as emerging practice by the NSP | | | | | | | | | | |
| Speech Generating Devices | Speech Generating Devices (Augmentative and Alternative Communication Device) was identified as an emerging practice by the NSP. | | | | | | | | | | |
| Computer Aided Instruction | Computer Aided Instruction (Technology-based Treatment) was identified as an emerging practice by the NSP. | | | | | | | | | | |
| Picture Exchange Communication | Picture Exchange Communication System was identified as an emerging practice by the NSP. | | | | | | | | | | |
| Extinction | Extinction (Reductive Package) was identified as an emerging practice by the NSP. | | | | | | | | | | |

**FIGURE 3–1** Matrix of the overlap between the evidence-based practices identified by the National Professional Development Center on ASD and the National Standards Project

*Source:* Matrix of the overlap between the evidence-based practices identified by the National Professional Development Center on ASD and the National Standards Project. Website for the National Professional Development Center (NPDC) on ASD and the National Standards Project (NSP). http://autismpdc.fpg.unc.edu/content/national-standards-project. Used with permission.

Eikeseth (2009) evaluated the quality of the research for 25 outcomes studies of comprehensive treatment programs for young children with autism spectrum disorders. Only one study, by Smith, Groen, and Wynn (2000), met the highest criteria, or Level I, that included a randomized control design, and this research evaluated a model based on applied behavior analysis that was classified under the Lovaas approach in the study by Odom, Boyd, Hall, and Hume (2010). Four studies, all programs based on applied behavior analysis, were classified as a Level II scientific rating according to Eikeseth (2009). Studies of the TEACCH approach were rated among those that received a Level III rating in the system used by Eikeseth (2009). Edelvik and colleagues (2009) conducted a meta-analysis of the research outcomes for early intensive behavioral intervention only and concluded that the effect sizes indicate that there is established efficacy for this approach; the authors recommend it as the intervention of choice for children with autism.

The Interagency Autism Coordinating Committee (IACC), established by Congress to coordinate all efforts under the Department of Health and Human Services, published a list of the most notable publications representing advances in the field (Interagency Autism Coordinating Committee, 2011). Two of the four publications addressing the question, which treatments and interventions will help? are the two reviews by Odom and colleagues (Odom, Boyd et al., 2010; Odom, Collet-Klingenberg et al., 2010), underlying the importance of knowing which models and strategies are evidence-based so that practitioners can be most effective when working with individuals with ASD.

## Implementing Evidence-Based Practices Effectively

Knowing which strategies are evidence-based is important; however, implementing these strategies with fidelity is essential for effective outcomes. The method for putting research findings into practice is referred to as implementation science (McHugh & Barlow, 2010). Successful training in the use of evidence-based practices requires both providing didactic information and competency training "defined as the process of acquiring skills necessary to administer a treatment skillfully and with fidelity" (McHugh & Barlow, 2010, p. 74). A review of the literature evaluating the research regarding the implementation of evidence-based practices across fields, including education, by the National Implementation Research Network (NIRN) contains clear recommendations for research to practice (Fixsen et al., 2005). The authors state that good outcomes for consumers (individuals with autism spectrum disorders and their families) occur when evidence-based practices are implemented effectively. In other words, educators need to have the skills to implement evidence-based practices, and they need the support to use these skills in their work environment.

Information alone, or workshop training, is *not* an effective implementation method (Fixsen et al., 2005). The research completed by Smith, Parker, Taubman, and Lovaas (1992) illustrates the point that workshops alone are insufficient. These authors investigated training and generalization in a two-part study. The focus of the first study was the skill acquisition of behavioral techniques after providing a one-week intensive workshop for 31 staff members working in various group homes throughout the United States. The workshop provided didactic information, role-plays with instructors, analysis of videotapes of teaching, and the opportunity to practice newly introduced strategies one-on-one with individuals with autism spectrum disorders (Smith et al., 1992). The result of the training was an increased demonstration of skills by those who participated in the study during the training week compared to a comparison group not attending the workshop. During the second study, however, it was revealed that the use of learned skills did not generalize to the group home. The second part of the study included observations of the developmentally disabled clients residing in the group home before and after the intensive staff workshop. Again, no evidence of generalization or client benefit was observed.

Lerman, Vorndran, Addison, and Kuhn (2004) found a similar lack of generalization of direct teaching strategies following a week-long workshop in strategies based on applied behavior analysis for public school teachers. Skills obtained at the workshop for the implementation of preference assessments did generalize to their work in the public school classrooms. However, teachers performed less than 80% of the direct teaching steps correctly in the absence of feedback in the main classroom, and the authors recommend ongoing consultation and support in the generalization setting (Lerman et al., 2004).

The additional components needed for generalization of training to practice include: *coaching on-site, performance evaluation, program evaluation, facilitative administrative practices,* and *methods for systems interventions* (Fixsen et al., 2005). Vismara, Young, Stahmer, Griffith, and Rogers (2009) found that, although there was no difference in whether or not training was conducted live or through distance learning, both forms needed to include didactic information with video examples and supervisor feedback from a trained and skilled therapist for increases in the skills of professionals and the learners with ASD to occur.

## Coaching, Mentoring, and Supervisory Support

On-the-job coaching is one of the core components necessary for the implementation of evidence-based practices (Anderson et al., 1993; Fixsen et al., 2005). The opportunity to apply knowledge about teaching in the complexity of the classroom under supervised guidance is critical in preparing educators effectively (Boreen, Johnson, Niday, & Potts, 2009; Lerman et al., 2004; McGee & Morrier, 2005). The coach, or supervisor, provides feedback and support for the educator as he or she attempts to implement a new or different evidence-based practice. The coach, or purveyor of the evidence-based practice, must

be clear about the key components of the strategy and skilled in the intervention use with individuals with autism spectrum disorders. If the strategy is indeed evidence-based, clearly defined interventions will be identified that have been replicated by researchers and practitioners.

Knowing the core components of intervention programs and practices and their underlying principles may be important for successful implementation (Fixsen et al., 2005). This knowledge is necessary in order for the coach to be able to determine whether the educator is implementing the strategy with **fidelity**. In other words, the coach has to know how to do the strategy well and has to know the parameters for determining whether the educator is doing it right. If the coach does not understand the critical aspects of the intervention or does not have the implementation skills, then it would be difficult to ensure that new practices are done well by the educator. Dean Fixsen describes why effective coaching is needed to assure fidelity of implementation by educators (In Their Words 3.1).

Effective coaching consists of providing a demonstration of the strategy, providing an opportunity for practice of the skill, followed by immediate feedback of the implementation of the strategy (Joyce & Showers, 2002). This requires the coach to be available to work alongside the educator who is trying new strategies. The coach, or mentor, also provides emotional support and encouragement to the educator, who may be trying to teach in a different style of practice (Boreen et al., 2009; Gibson, 2005). Good mentors are supportive, committed, sensitive, flexible, enthusiastic, diplomatic, and willing to give credit and recognition (Harvard Business Essentials, 2004; McCormick & Brennan, 2001).

The coach also assists the educator in the craft of implementation. It takes an understanding of the context of the educational environment, the individual characteristics of the learner with autism spectrum disorder, and a good understanding of the critical features of the strategy in order to implement the strategy in a flexible way that takes these factors into account without jeopardizing the integrity of the strategy,

**3.1**

# The Importance of Coaching in Conjunction with Training for Educators

Innovations represent new ways of providing education. The implementation of an innovation requires teachers (and others) at a school to learn when, where, how, and with whom to use new approaches and new skills. *Preservice* and *in-service training* are efficient ways to provide knowledge of background information, theory, philosophy, and values; introduce the components and rationales of key practices; and provide opportunities to practice new skills and receive feedback in a safe training environment. Most skills needed by successful teachers, staff, and administrators can be introduced in training but really are learned on the job with the help of a *consultant/coach* (e.g., craft information, engagement, teaching to concepts, good judgment). Implementation of evidence-based innovations requires behavior change at the teacher, staff, and administrative support levels. Training and coaching are the principal ways in which behavior change is brought about in the beginning stages of implementation and throughout the life of evidence-based practices and programs (Fixsen et al., 2005).

During training, information about history, theory, philosophy, and rationales for program components and practices can be conveyed in lecture and discussion formats geared to knowledge acquisition and understanding. Skills and abilities related to carrying out the program components and practices can be demonstrated (live or recorded) then followed by behavior rehearsal to practice the skills and receive feedback on the practice (Joyce & Showers, 2002). While they are not effective by themselves for producing sustainable changes in school settings, training workshops are an efficient way to impart important information to teachers and staff and, when coupled with coaching, can contribute to important outcomes (e.g., Joyce & Showers, 2002). As found by Sparks (2004) in his review of staff development for teachers, training for new innovations and programs, especially large-scale programs, requires more than a day or two of training. Preparation to conduct several innovative programs needed 10 to 15 days. Sparks (2004) also noted that coaching is an important component when teachers implement a new program and "face the day-to-day challenges of their work" (p. 249).

With newly learned behavior there are several simultaneous problems that must be faced:

1. *Newly learned behavior is crude compared to performance by a master teacher or administrator.* Training usually is designed to introduce the learner to the essential elements of a new set of skills. However, there are uncounted nuances of when and how to use the components in various combinations in proactive teaching, reactive teaching, conceptual teaching, effective praise, proactive prompting, and so on, given the immediate behavior of students and others. With experience and effective coaching, teachers, staff, and administrators develop a personal style that is comfortable for them while still incorporating the core intervention components of the evidence-based practice.

2. *Newly learned behavior is fragile and needs to be supported in the face of reactions from consumers and others in the service setting.* Behavior change directly impacts others in the environment.

For example, when a teacher makes a significant change in his or her behavior in the classroom, 20 to 30 children and their families react to that change. When teachers and staff change their behavior, the reactions from consumers and stakeholders initially may not be positive; effectively punishing the teacher for making a change. For fragile, new behavior, the negative reaction may be enough to discourage the teacher from persisting. One role of a coach is to prepare the teacher for potential reactions and support the teacher through the early stages of implementation until the new behavior is more skillfully embedded in the school environment.

3. *Newly learned behavior is incomplete and will need to be shaped to be most functional in a service setting.* When designing workshop training experiences, there is only so much that can be accomplished effectively within the time available. Preservice workshop training can be used to develop entry-level knowledge and skills. Then coaching can help teachers and others put the segmented basic knowledge and skills into the whole education context. Coaches can help teachers see how their personal beliefs and attitudes can be integrated with the skills, knowledge, philosophy, values, and principles of the program as well as other aspects of the education context.

or without implementing the strategy without fidelity. Assisting the educator to adapt skills and craft knowledge to fit the personal style of the educator is one of the core components of effective coaching (Chance, 2008; Kise, 2006).

Selecting the supervisor or coach may be important in whether or not the evidence-based practice is implemented effectively; however, more research is needed on the selection of staff to act as change agents or purveyors of new practices (Harvard Business Essentials, 2004; Fixsen et al., 2005). It would be logical that selecting someone who has a good knowledge and understanding of the system in which the evidence-based practice will be implemented may have advantages over an outsider, no matter how competent the outsider may be.

Effective instruction can make a significant difference in the quality of life for an individual at any age. Although there are multiple definitions of **quality of life**, it is primarily measured by determining the individual's level of satisfaction along the dimensions of emotional well-being, interpersonal relationships, physical well-being, self-determination, social inclusion, and rights (Schalock, 2000). The value placed on each of the quality-of-life dimensions is likely to vary over the individual's life span, but meeting a person's basic needs and providing the same opportunities as others have to pursue goals will always remain important (Schalock, 2000).

It is critical that educators understand the importance of selecting and implementing educational strategies in an ethical manner. The Council for Exceptional Children (CEC) and the Behavior Analysis Certification Board (BACB) have established codes of ethics to be followed. The following Code of Ethics for CEC was first adopted in 1983 (Murdick et al., 2007).

## CEC Code of Ethics for Educators of Persons with Exceptionalities

The Council for Exceptional Children Board of Directors approved the following statement and ethical principles for special education professionals. Professional special educators are guided by the CEC ethical principles and practice standards in ways that respect the diverse characteristics and needs of individuals with exceptionalities and their families. They are committed to upholding and advancing the following principles:

A. Maintaining challenging expectations for individuals with exceptionalities to develop the highest possible learning outcomes and quality of life potential in ways that respect their dignity, culture, language and background.

B. Maintaining a high level of professional competence and integrity and exercising professional judgment to benefit individuals with exceptionalities and their families.

C. Promoting meaningful and inclusive participation of individuals with exceptionalities in their schools and communities.

D. Practicing collegially with others who are providing services to individuals with exceptionalities.

E. Developing relationships with families based on mutual respect and actively involving families and individuals with exceptionalities in educational decision making.

F. Using evidence, instructional data, research and professional knowledge to inform practice.

G. Protecting and supporting the physical and psychological safety of individuals with exceptionalities.

H. Neither engaging in nor tolerating any practice that harms individuals with exceptionalities.

I. Practicing within the professional ethics, standards, and policies of CEC; upholding laws, regulations, and policies that influence professional practices; and advocating improvements in laws, regulations, and policies.

J. Advocating for conditions and resources that will improve learning outcomes of individuals with exceptionalities.

K. Engagement in improvement in the profession through active participation in professional organizations

L. Participation in the growth and dissemination of professional knowledge and skills. (The Council for Exceptional Children, 2010. Reprinted with permission.)

Ethical dilemmas, or situations in which it is difficult to determine the right action, frequently arise for educators working with individuals with autism spectrum disorders. Educators may have a conflict between the action they would take as an individual and the action suggested by their role as an employee of an agency or public school (Murdick et al., 2007). For example, the educator may have a different opinion about inclusion than that of the parents or the school district.

## Implementing a Systems Approach

Implementation of evidence-based practices is a process involving multiple decisions, actions, and corrections (Fixsen et al., 2005). To be effective, an educator needs the support of the system or the key personnel such as administrators, peers, and supervisors. Anderson and colleagues (1993) implemented a comprehensive training model for behavioral support using a trainer-of-trainers model with case-study teams comprised of key personnel in the service delivery setting. A key component of the SCERTS model is transactional support that is required for the learner with ASD, the family, and the educator or service provider (Prizant, Wetherby, Rubin, Laurent, & Rydell, 2006a). In this model, support is addressed in four ways: interpersonal support from adults and peers toward the individual with ASD, learning supports embedded in curriculum and methods, support to families, and support among professionals (Prizant et al., 2006a).

Whenever possible, educators must be provided with a working context that recognizes and allows for discussion about the emotional challenges and rewards inherent in working with children with autism spectrum disorders (Prizant et al., 2006b). The goal for the organization should be fostering a sense of personal growth and competence among members of a network of people who direct their energies toward supporting children and families (Prizant et al., 2006b) or creating a community of practice with this common aim (Fixsen et al., 2005).

## System Accountability for Effective Practice

Evidence-based programs consist of a set of practices with accountability to the consumers and funders of those practices (Fixsen et al., 2005). Involvement of stakeholders in planning and selection of programs to implement encourages ownership of the implementation process (Fixsen et al., 2005; McClannahan & Krantz, 2004). Developing **communities of practice** (Fixsen et al., 2005) that support, inform, and are accountable to each other (Duchnowski & Kutash, 1997) for quality service delivery is a noble goal.

The Princeton Child Development Institute (PCDI) is an example of a program that implements evidence-based practices using a system of on-site staff training with an accountability system that documents student progress and revises program components based on feedback from staff, family, and community stakeholders (McClannahan, 2005). Most staff training is hands-on, with supervisors who model the effective practice, create practice opportunities, and provide immediate, positive, and corrective feedback (McClannahan & Krantz, 2001). Good relationship-building skills are a focus of staff development, in which public recognition and acknowledgment of accomplishments is modeled and fostered, and a subculture of cooperation is supported (McClannahan & Krantz, 2004).

The content of the training is specified by a protocol that includes evidence-based practices such as the use of behavior-specific and contingent praise, providing opportunities to respond, incorporating incidental teaching episodes, and maintaining learner engagement (McClannahan & Krantz, 2004). Data are collected by the supervising staff member on these skills as well as on the engagement of the students with autism (McClannahan & Krantz, 2004). After 6 to 8 months of hands-on training, the staff members' skills are evaluated by a supervising staff member different from the one who was providing the hands-on training. "Training and evaluation procedures are designed to maximize staff member successes" (McClannahan & Krantz, 2004, p. 195). All staff members are evaluated at least annually, and passing the evaluation is necessary for reappointment.

An important aspect of the accountability system at PCDI is that the outcomes for the learners, trainees, trainers, and administrators are all yoked (McClannahan & Krantz, 1993). In other words, trainees, or newer staff members succeed when their students make progress. Staff members know when their students are making progress because they are trained to collect and graph data. Trainers' skills are recognized and appreciated when their trainees and their students succeed. Administrators succeed when children, trainees, and trainers are all successful (McClannahan & Krantz, 1993). In this system, everyone has a common goal—the success of the learner with autism spectrum disorder—and everyone must work together to accomplish this goal.

PCDI does not operate in isolation. It is important that satisfaction with the program is obtained from stakeholders such as family members, employers, neighbors, and the governing board (McClannahan, MacDuff, & Krantz, 2002). Families play a key role in the selection of intervention goals, participation in instruction, and hands-on training so they can be effective partners in intervention and provide encouragement for participation (McClannahan & Krantz, 2004). If issues of satisfaction arise, the administrators make changes to the program to address this consumer feedback.

In addition, it is important for the data to be reviewed by an external evaluator who can act as an inter-rater regarding learner successes and offer suggestions for program changes in those skill areas with slower progress. Each year, an impartial professional with expertise in applied behavior analysis reviews a randomly selected sample of learner programs. A protocol developed and validated at PCDI is used to rate each of the intervention programs on components such as the response definition of the objective, the written description of the data collection procedure, a written description of the intervention procedure, and a graph (McClannahan & Krantz, 2006). The evaluator scores whether the behavior has changed in the desired direction and the appropriateness of the intervention strategy, and records whether there is a signature from a parent indicating consent for the program (McClannahan & Krantz, 2006).

The model of intervention and accountability used by the Princeton Child Development Institute has been disseminated to programs in the United States (three in New Jersey and one in New York), and internationally in Poland, Russia, Greece, Australia, and Turkey. The administrators of all programs were trained at the Princeton Child Development Institute for at least a year and until they had acquired the skills in the intervention strategies and supervision necessary to replicate the staff-training component so critical for success. Each of the replication sites is assigned an administrator from PCDI who works as a consultant to the program director and assists with the support, problem solving, and community collaboration necessary for program success (McClannahan, 2005). PCDI is an example of a program that incorporates the recommended components of successful implementation outlined by the National Implementation Research Network (Fixsen et al., 2005). Unfortunately, not many models of exemplary practice have been disseminated across programs (McGee & Morrier, 2005).

# The Who, When, Where, What, and Why of Effective Systems

It is clear that educators are most effective when they use scientifically determined or evidence-based strategies that they learn to implement by (1) obtaining an understanding of the theoretical principles behind the strategies through didactic means, (2) along with practice in individualizing the strategies for learners with autism spectrum disorders, with guidance from a coach in the educational setting. Details about who comprises the team, when is the optimal time to begin educational interventions, where interventions should take place, what the curriculum should entail, and why collaboration is important for effective systems will now be addressed.

## Who Is Part of the IEP/IFSP Team?

The IEP/IFSP team includes professionals with various training and expertise, including the special education teacher or early interventionist who often serves a key role in coordinating the team. Some school districts hire autism specialists to help teachers design curriculum for students with ASD. This specialist can also help with the physical arrangement of the classroom environment to help facilitate social interaction, maximize student participation in activities, and decrease the likelihood of problem behavior. Autism specialists may provide ongoing support to educators in the design, implementation, and evaluation of educational strategies. Important to the work of an autism specialist are knowledge of and skills in implementing evidence-based practices and experience in working with individuals with ASD.

General education teachers will be working with the team to ensure that the student with ASD has access to the general education curriculum used with same-age peers. The general education teacher will arrange for any modifications and supports needed for successful inclusion in activities with peers, including those with an academic focus. The attitude toward and skills displayed in working with students with autism spectrum disorders will be important for effective instruction by the general education teacher.

Specialists who complete discipline-specific assessments and work with teachers to implement individually designed instruction are frequently included on the IEP team. Due to the fact that many students with ASD have some form of communication impairment, it is common that the services of speech-language pathologists (SLPs) are frequently requested. Speech-language pathologists may provide educators with strategies to assist with the articulation of words or the formation of complete sentences. These specialists also are likely to know about activities that can strengthen the oral-motor muscles that support spoken language and when and for whom these activities are prescribed.

Students who are delayed or who fail to develop oral language may benefit from an augmentative or alternative communication (AAC) system (Beukelman & Miranda, 1998). Speech-language pathologists, along with assistive technology specialists, can design augmentative or alternative communication systems if needed, and provide training for staff in the use of such systems. An assistive technology service is defined under IDEA as any service that directly assists a child with a disability in the selection, acquisition, or use of an assistive technology device (Murdick et al., 2007). Collaboration with the assistive technology specialist or the speech-language pathologist is vital because any communication system works only if it is used consistently throughout the day.

As described previously, the sensory systems are considered the domain of the occupational therapist. The occupational therapist can assist with the design of fine and gross motor activities or in using preferred sensory modalities in the design of curriculum and instruction. Occupational therapists often consult in situations when the learner is hyper- or hyposensitive to environmental stimuli, such as avoiding any activity with music or being highly motivated by the sound of music.

The school psychologist also has a role in working with individuals with autism spectrum disorders and their families. The psychologist has the skills to work with the family as a counselor to offer advice and reassurance. All too frequently, however, school psychologists are asked to consult only when there is a behavior problem to address. It is often the school psychologist who is responsible for conducting a functional assessment of a problem behavior prior to suggesting an intervention strategy (see Chapter 5 for detailed descriptions of functional assessment). The psychologist must work with the teacher and develop a strategy that the teacher is willing and able to implement if there is any chance that the intervention will be effective.

## Working Effectively with Paraprofessionals

Although curriculum adaptation is the responsibility of the teacher, paraprofessionals often implement educational interventions and aim to foster the development of social and academic skills (Giangreco, 2010). In some cases, the paraprofessional is working with students with autism spectrum disorders on a one-to-one basis (Young & Simpson, 1997). To work effectively, the paraprofessional needs skills in communication and collaboration as well as the effective delivery of instruction.

One of the many skill sets needed by educators in order to work effectively is the supervising of paraprofessionals. Management strategies must be explicitly taught so that educators can be effective with students with autism spectrum disorders (Mehring & Dow, 2001). Although No Child Left Behind requires paraprofessional training, a review of the literature illustrates that preservice training is generally unavailable or deficient, and in-service training is limited in scope and inconsistently available (Giangreco, Suter, & Doyle, 2010). In general, when surveyed, paraprofessionals have indicated an interest in more training (Griffen-Shirley & Matlock, 2004). Similar to the training provided to educators, the format for much of the training of paraeducators is in workshop or didactic format only (Jahr, 1998).

Research outcomes have demonstrated that training of paraprofessionals does make a difference (Hall, Grundon, Pope, & Romero, 2010). A workshop followed by feedback in the classroom and home setting from the teacher of record resulted in effective use of prompting for various evidence-based strategies by six paraprofessionals across three settings (Hall et al., 2010). With training, four paraprofessionals were more likely to facilitate interactions with students with disabilities, and consequently these students were better able to interact with typically developing peers (Causton-Theoharis & Malmgren, 2005). Feedback to reduce overprompting by paraprofessionals and the addition of activity schedules increased the independent completion of tasks by a student with autism included in a general education classroom (Hall, McClannahan, & Krantz, 1995). The scant research focused on paraprofessional skill development is clearly insufficient considering the prolific use of paraeducators hired to work directly with students with ASD under supervision.

French and Picket (1997) list some concerns about paraprofessional training gathered from their research: (1) Opportunities for ongoing training and supervision are often limited, (2) professionals have limited to no training on how to supervise paraprofessionals, and (3) the roles of professionals and paraprofessionals have begun to overlap and become unclear. Giangreco, Broer, and Suter (2011) question the model of using paraprofessionals to assist students in inclusive environments and identify some of the detrimental effects of excessive proximity with paraprofessionals to include: unnecessary dependence, interference with peer and teacher interaction, limited access to competent instruction, and feelings of stigmatization (Giangreco, 2010). Leblanc, Ricciardi, and Luiselli (2005) echo these concerns for paraprofessionals who use discrete trial teaching formats and describe three elements that were found to be important: (1) training needs to be practical; (2) staff should find the training favorable; and (3) long-term, ongoing support for trained skills is necessary for maintenance. In addition, the paraprofessional's skills in working collaboratively with parents in autism intervention are critical (Marcus, Kunce, & Schopler, 2005).

# Working Collaboratively with Families

Family members are key partners with educators because they can do so much more together than either partner can do alone. "One of the most important components of any treatment including an evidence-based practice is family involvement" (Association for Children's Mental Health, 2004, p. 2). The DEC recommended practices for policies, procedures, and systems change begin by listing actions that families and professionals can do to shape policy at the federal, state, and local levels. This partnership between families and professionals is essential.

To be effective advocates and partners, it is important for parents and educators to try to prevent problems, form alliances, be alert for opportunities to advocate, pinpoint and document problems when they arise, and seek win-win solutions (Turnbull et al., 2011). Turnbull and colleagues have identified seven principles of an effective partnership, with trust as the cornerstone to the relationship (see Figure 3–2). Trust is built when partners communicate in open and honest ways, there is mutual respect, there is a commitment, power and advocacy is shared, and professionals are competent in providing a quality education (Turnbull et al., 2011). Turnbull and colleagues (2011) describe partnerships between families and professionals as relationships in which there is mutual agreement to defer to each other's judgments and expertise as appropriate for securing outcomes for students, other family members, and professionals.

## Challenges to the Family/Professional Partnership

Weaknesses in any aspect of the arch (see Figure 3–2) can challenge the family/professional partnership, but lack of trust is reported as most related to conflicts between parents and school personnel (Turnbull, Zuna, Turnbull, Poston, &

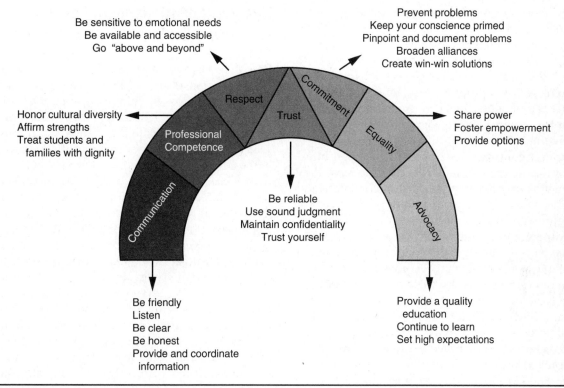

Be sensitive to emotional needs
Be available and accessible
Go "above and beyond"

Prevent problems
Keep your conscience primed
Pinpoint and document problems
Broaden alliances
Create win-win solutions

Respect

Commitment

Trust

Professional
Competence

Equality

Honor cultural diversity
Affirm strengths
Treat students and
    families with dignity

Share power
Foster empowerment
Provide options

Communication

Advocacy

Be reliable
Use sound judgment
Maintain confidentiality
Trust yourself

Be friendly
Listen
Be clear
Be honest
Provide and coordinate
    information

Provide a quality
    education
Continue to learn
Set high expectations

**FIGURE 3–2**   The seven principles of partnership
*Source:* Turnbull, Ann; Turnbull, H. Rutherford; Erwin, Elizabeth J.; Soodak, Leslie C.; Shogren, Karrie A.; *Families, Professionals and Exceptionality: Positive Outcomes Through Partnerships and Trust,* 6th edition,© 2011. Reprinted by permission of Pearson Education, Inc., Upper Saddle River, New Jersey.

Summers, 2007). Turnbull and colleagues (2011) discuss the importance of educators trusting themselves and their own empowerment. However, it is not unusual for educators to feel disempowered when working with students with ASD and their families. Many parents have taken on a professional role themselves as the teacher, case coordinator, and advocate for their child (Marcus et al., 2005). These parents develop a greater expertise in autism than many professionals who may be new to the disability and the field (Marcus et al., 2005). Educators may feel insecure when interacting with knowledgeable families. In addition, some parents enter new situations with educators prepared to argue or fight for services for their child with autism spectrum disorder because of

previous experiences. It is helpful if both parents and educators begin any new relationship with the aim of working together as collaborative partners who have the best interest of the learner with autism as the priority.

Educators may feel caught in the middle between families who want the most quality, resources, and skilled professionals to teach their child in a way that is likely to result in the best outcomes, such as the implementation of evidence-based practices, and a district that needs to distribute resources fairly, has limited funds, and is obligated to provide a beneficial education but not the best possible education (Yell & Drasgow, 2005). A review of the litigation by parents to receive discrete trial teaching (referred to by them as the Lovaas approach) for their children with autism revealed that parents won their cases in the majority of (34 of 45) court cases (Yell & Drasgow, 2005). The courts found that the districts had not complied with the IEP process and that the school's programming was inappropriate (e.g., it was not individualized or showed lack of progress monitoring) in the majority of the winning cases (Nelson & Huefner, 2003; Yell, 2012).

If educators have recently received information about evidence-based practices, they may be eager to implement those practices and find a lack of support or other preferences for intervention from families or administrators. Although educators know they are required to develop the individualized education program as part of a team that includes families, they may be challenged by their role as a mediator between the family and the district, and they may find it difficult to know how to interject their own perspectives regarding the educational content and practices. To work effectively, respectfully, and diplomatically in such situations takes a lot of interpersonal skills that come with time and experience.

Educators need to acquire the skills to work through any cultural and linguistic differences between the educator and the family so that misunderstandings can be avoided and a system for effective communication can be used between home and school. Interviews with African American families of children with severe emotional or cognitive disabilities, including autism, revealed that over half of the parents (64%) did not feel respected by teachers and other school staff members (Zionts, Zionts, Harrison, & Bellinger, 2003). Some parents felt that the school unfairly blamed them for their child's disability or behaviors, and one-third did not feel that the school treated them as a partner. "The relationship between cultural differences and satisfaction with the special education system seemed to these parents to be inextricably tied to issues of respect and levels of comfort [among] parents, teachers and children/youth with moderate to severe disabilities" (Zionts et al., 2003).

# Recommendations to and by Parents Regarding Evidence-Based Practices

Research has demonstrated that students with ASD experience difficulties if there is limited consistency across learning environments, and therefore it is essential that service be consistent and carefully coordinated (Prizant et al., 2006b). This need for consistency includes the practices in the educational and home environments.

"ABA is a science of behaviour, which, when applied to autism, empowers parents with the skills to harness principles of behaviour for bringing out the best in their children" (Keenan, 2006, p. 48). Keenan describes how a parent of a child with autism instigated the application of his work in applied behavior analysis to the community issue of designing effective programs for individuals with ASD in Ireland (Keenan, 2006). The parents of children with ASD in Ireland and New Zealand describe the process of designing and obtaining educational services for their children with ASD, including starting new programs and their successes, failures, and recommendations (Keenan, Henderson, Kerr, & Dillenburger, 2006). It is clear from each of the stories the great amount of time and effort that parents put into obtaining an evidence-based education for their children.

When guiding parents through the special education process, Chantal Sicile-Kira (2004), a parent herself, provides some suggestions, including: getting to know how your child learns and the educational strategies that work for learners with ASD, learning about the local school district and visiting different schools and classrooms, learning about intensive behavior therapy, keeping good records and notes, developing good relationships, and not being afraid to ask questions.

In their book, parent and professional coauthors Koegel and LaZebnik (2004) provide guidelines for choosing the right teacher. Some of the questions they suggest that parents consider are: Does the teacher have good behavioral control of her students? Is the teacher able to individualize instruction for the variety of different student abilities in her classroom? Are the teacher's classroom activities and curriculum meaningful? Does the teacher incorporate motivational strategies into the teaching?

In an article describing a list of guidelines for evaluating intervention programs for children with autism spectrum disorders, the first and last guidelines are: "Approach any new treatment with hopeful skepticism. Remember the goal of any treatment should be to help the person with autism become a fully functioning member of society," and "be aware that often new treatments have not been validated scientifically" (Freeman, 1997, p. 647).

## When to Begin Intervention

It is important to begin intervention at an early age because children's brains are still developing and major changes to development can occur that will have an impact on the future in many ways (Dawson & Osterling, 1997; Smith, Groen, & Wynne, 2000). Interventions that provide the most intensive, direct, and appropriate individualized services to children will alter early experiences and have the greatest benefits (Ramey & Ramey, 1999). It is important to note that the timing and intensity of services may vary depending on ethnic and socioeconomic factors. The most intensive services are often received by children with parents that have the time and resources to negotiate intervention, and children from ethnic minority backgrounds are more likely to be diagnosed and receive intervention at a later age than those from Caucasion families (Akshoomoff & Stahmer, 2006).

Outcomes from research indicate that **early, intensive behavioral treatment (EIBT)** has resulted in approximately half of participating young children with ASD entering the school system in classrooms with typical peers (Birnbrauer & Leach, 1993; Lovaas, 1987). Howard, Sparkman, Cohen, Green, and Stanislaw (2005) found that early intensive behavioral intervention resulted in children diagnosed with autism gaining skills at a rate

of approximately one year of development per year of age, or with demonstrated learning rates similar to their peers without autism. The meta-analysis of 34 studies of EIBT with participants beginning treatment between the ages of 2 and 7 years revealed a large effect size for changes in full scale IQ and a moderate effect size for changes in adaptive behavior as a result of intervention (Eldevik et al., 2009).

Fenske, Zalenski, Krantz, and McClannahan (1985) found that age at entry was related to treatment outcome for students with autism. Children who received intensive behavioral intervention prior to 60 months of age were more likely to live with their parents and attend public school classes compared with students who began attending the school after age 5 (Fenske et al., 1985). McGee , Morrier, and Daly (1999) reported that approximately 80% of the children who enter the Emory Autism Resource Center in Atlanta go on to kindergarten with typical peers.

Two-thirds to three-quarters of individuals with autistic disorder also have some degree of cognitive delay or intellectual disability (Towbin, Mauk, & Batshaw, 2002). Even the most skilled practitioners find it difficult to predict which children with ASD will make the most gains with effective intervention. However, all children are able to learn new skills. The number of skills acquired and the learning rate may vary depending on the degree of delay and the skill of the instructor.

## Where Intervention Should Take Place

Due to the importance of starting educational programs at a young age, many programs begin in the home. The home is the "natural environment" for early intervention services, as most children are at home before age 3. Research has demonstrated that home programs implemented by parents have resulted in increased gains by their children with autism spectrum disorders (Meadan, Ostrosky, Zaghlawan, & Yu, 2009; Ozonoff & Cathcart, 1998; Weiss, 1999), and parent-implemented strategies is one of the identified evidence-based practices by the

National Professional Development Center on ASD. In their review of the literature, Meadan and colleagues (2009) identified 12 studies of parent-implemented interventions that were conducted, at least in part, in the home setting.

The home is the setting for many educational programs for children with autism spectrum disorders, as either the exclusive setting or as a supplement to center-based programs and public schools. Currently there are many private, nonprofit agencies that provide home educational programs for children with autism spectrum disorders. Some of these programs are international, such as the Center for Autism and Related Disorders (CARD), Autism Partnerships, and TEACCH. Others are national or local (e.g., Autism Spectrum Therapies [AST]).

Working collaboratively with families is a critical aspect of all early intervention services (Turnbull et al., 2011). Home programming with parents is also the hallmark of effective educational programs (Ozonoff & Cathcart, 1998). Collaboration with families is particularly important for individuals with autism spectrum disorders who often have difficulty with change and may respond to different expectations, environmental cues, and behavioral consequences here by exhibiting challenging behavior (Scheuermann & Webber, 2002). Consistency across settings can act as prevention of such problems (Alberto & Troutman, 2009). The Center for Evidence-Based Practice also supports working with young children in the natural environment— described as the optimal location for intervention.

## Inclusion

Where the educational program takes place when children reach school age is one of the controversial issues in the area of autism spectrum disorders. Included in discussions of where education takes place are factors such as the staff–child ratio, the educational approach implemented, the presence of typical peers, the number of hours of intervention, how related services are utilized, and proximity to the home. Many parents and professionals have strong opinions about where educational strategies should take place. Some educators feel that education with typical peers located in the home community, or inclusion, is a priority (Renzaglia, Karvonen, Drasgow, & Stoxen, 2003; Ryndak & Billingsley, 2004). For some parents and educators, inclusion is the only option. These parents and educators believe that not to educate students with disabilities with their peers is to segregate them because of their disability and that such separation is unjust or immoral.

The Division of Early Childhood (DEC) of the Council for Exceptional Children and the National Association for the Education of Young Children (NAEYC) published a joint position statement in April 2009 supporting early childhood inclusion. According to the statement, the desired results of an inclusive experience for young children with and without disabilities are a sense of belonging and membership, positive social relationships and friendships, and development and learning to reach children's full potential. One of the recommendations for using the position statement is to "establish a system of service and supports that reflect the needs of children with varying types of disabilities and learning characteristics, with inclusion as the driving principle and foundation for all of these services and supports" (DEC/NAEYC. 2009, p. 2).

When evaluating where a student with autism spectrum disorders receives educational services, it may be helpful to address three possible priorities for an inclusive placement: the opportunity to be with typical peers for social development, increasing academic skills that are adapted from general education standards, and the ability to be increasingly independent in the community. Some parents and IEP teams place one of these priorities above the others. Also, priorities may change as students age.

## Opportunity to Be with Typical Peers for Social Development

It is very difficult to interact with typical peers during the day if they are not part of your educational program. Research outcomes have demonstrated, however, that placement alone is not sufficient to promote social interaction between peers with and without autism spectrum disorders, and some form of intervention is necessary in order to facilitate social interaction with peers (Strain, Schwartz, & Bovey, 2008).

Students with autism spectrum disorder often need to be taught to imitate others, including how to imitate the play behaviors of peers (Buffington, Krantz, McClannahan, & Poulson, 1998; Rogers, 2006; Stahmer, 1995). Social skills such as greetings, conversation skills, and initiating and responding to social bids have been taught to children with autism spectrum disorders (Strain et al., 2008). Even if students have social skills, the teacher needs to arrange the environment to support social interaction (Harrower & Dunlap, 2001; Myles & Simpson, 1998b). Also, it may be important to discuss issues of disability with typical peers so they are prepared for atypical social interaction styles. If supports are in place, typical peers may perceive students with autism spectrum disorders as desirable playmates and members of social groups in inclusive settings (Boutot & Bryant, 2005).

If interacting with peers is a priority for an inclusive placement, then it is important to ensure that the student with autism spectrum disorders is getting this opportunity during educational activities and during recess times. In addition, it is important to ensure that the student has the necessary skills to take advantage of the opportunities when they arise and that peers are accepting of the occasional atypical initiations or social responses.

## Increased Academic Skills Adapted from General Education Standards

If academic skill gain is a priority, it is important to ensure that there is a method in place to monitor student progress and that any teacher or paraprofessional has a good understanding of what the individual goals and objectives are, and how to address these through evidence-based educational strategies. To adapt curriculum to meet the individual needs of the student with autism

spectrum disorders, educators must be willing and adequately trained (Simpson, de Boer-Ott, & Smith-Myles, 2003). If a student with autism is in a classroom with typical peers but is working one-to-one in the back of the classroom with a paraprofessional on unrelated activities, then the student is not really included with access to the general education curriculum or to peers.

It is likely that some form of classroom adaptations would be needed in order to make the educational experience for the student with ASD successful. Almost all students with autism spectrum disorder benefit from a schedule of daily activities (Schopler, Mesibov, & Hearsey, 1995). In her chapter entitled, "Tools to Give Information," Linda Hodgdon (1998) has several suggestions for using visual materials to create schedules.

Modifications can be made to facilitate instruction. Adaptations to materials may include adding a list of instructions, presenting a graphic organizer, or incorporating manipulatives (Hubbard, 2005). Modifications to the presentation of instruction may include supplementary cues embedded in worksheets or read to the student, changes to the pacing of delivery, including breaks in activities, and increasing the rate of feedback (Hubbard, 2005).

## Increase Independence

A priority for a student with autism spectrum disorders may be increasing self-determination by making independent choices and by obtaining skills related to future employment areas (Wehmeyer & Schalock, 2001). Attending school in the home community may be perceived as a step closer to this goal compared with attending a school at a distance or with students with disabilities only. Again, attending school alone will not result in the student with autism spectrum disorders gaining the skills to be a content and contributing member of the community.

Perhaps because paraprofessionals are hired to work specifically with students with disabilities, they may spend too much time assisting the student with autism spectrum disorders.

In fact this happens so often that it is referred to as *hovering* (Giangreco, Edelman, Luiselli, & MacFarland, 1997). Even with those skills identified as those where the student can complete the task independently, paraprofessionals have a tendency to provide too many prompts or too much assistance (Hall, McClannahan, & Krantz, 1995). Strategies to develop and maintain independent task completion of work activities need to be taught to paraprofessionals who serve as instructors. If fostering independence is a priority for inclusion, it is important that this is communicated to all staff.

Goals and objectives that relate to long-term planning of vocational interests should be included. Information about how much independence is achieved by the student with autism spectrum disorders needs to be shared with the team, including interested family members. Self-management of tasks completed can be taught to young children and is a foundational skill for working with decreased supervision in the future. Self-management is considered an evidence-based practice by both the National Standards Project (National Autism Center, 2009b) and the National Professional Development Center on ASD.

Sheila Wagner (see In Their Words 3.2) has written two books to assist educators who work in inclusive settings, one focused on elementary-age students (Wagner, 1999) and one for students in middle and high school (Wagner, 2002). Included in these books are strategies that can be used by the general education teacher to work with students with autism spectrum disorders as individuals or as part of class-wide interventions.

One suggestion for elementary-age students is the creation of the Lunch Bunch as a means of promoting social interaction during lunch periods (Wagner, 1999). The Lunch Bunch is a teacher-facilitated activity for which the student with autism spectrum disorders selects peers and the teacher facilitates by identifying a topic for conversation or suggesting an organized game. Wagner (2002) also provides suggestions for middle school students regarding

ways to build friendships between the student with autism spectrum disorders and peers. Topics relevant for this age group, such as issues around the formal and informal dress code and transition to employment, are included. Sample data sheets for monitoring behavior and progress are found at the end of these books.

Placing students in a general education environment without the supports to access the curriculum or without educators who are skilled in working with students with autism spectrum disorders is unlikely to result in learning. Myles and Simpson (1998b) have devised the *Autism Inclusion Collaboration Model*, for use by parents and public school personnel in which a set of interwoven components are considered as essential for effective learning. These program modifications and supports include: availability of trained support personnel, reduced class size, adequate teacher planning time, availability of paraprofessionals, collaborative problem-solving relationships, and in-service training. Even with these components in place, these authors state that including students with autism spectrum disorders effectively will continue to be a challenge for school systems.

## Specialized and Separate Educational Programs

In contrast to those who hold the opinion that inclusion in general education environments is the optimal place for the education of students with ASD, other parents and educators believe just the opposite—that placing a student with autism spectrum disorders in a general education classroom will deny them the quality education that can make the most meaningful difference in their lives. These parents and educators agree with the necessary components for successful inclusion outlined by Myles and Simpson (1998b) but believe that it is the rare public school program that can effectively address each of these components and thus have a school-wide effective program for their students with autism spectrum disorders. In contrast, educational programs that specialize

## 3.2 IN THEIR WORDS

Sheila Wagner, *M.Ed. Assistant Director Emory Autism Resource Center Atlanta, Georgia*

Inclusive programming for students with autism spectrum disorders has opened a world of opportunities for generalizing skills out of the isolated setting of the past and into the local community and everyday living experiences. This style of education poses intense challenges, and it is difficult to achieve success when processes are not conducted in a systematic manner. Too often, inclusive programs are initiated without proper analysis of the many necessary components that can ensure success over the long term for students with ASD. Frequently, "dumping" a student with a non-autism-related disorder into a general education classroom can succeed with very little effort. However, that is rarely true when students with ASD are concerned. This is a disability that demands strict attention to detail, consistency over time, and research-based methods for implementation. When considering inclusive programming for children with ASD, the components must be carefully considered, or the attempt will very likely haunt the school system and family when the programming disintegrates into bedlam.

Let us briefly examine only a few components of inclusive programs that must be analyzed in order to achieve positive outcomes for students with ASD:

- **Training**—for all staff and administration involved with this student. Training in the disability, teaching strategies, positive behavioral methods, peer programs, social skills, academic modifications, imbedding language, and so on, must be thorough and ongoing as needs change.

- **Collaboration**—daily, weekly, and monthly between special and general education teachers, between home and school, and between school therapists and community therapists (including physicians). This effectively promotes the generalization of skills from school to life.

- **IEP driven**—no two students with ASD are alike, so why should inclusion programs be? What works for one student with ASD may not work for another student with this disability. Individual needs still drive inclusion programs.

- **Administrative support**—teachers need to know that their efforts at conducting inclusive programs are appreciated and supported by their supervisors and that they are there to take part in problem analysis. Without it, teachers can become frustrated and discouraged. Families need their support even more.

- **Philosophically aligned**—all involved with this student need to believe in the program and have a positive attitude toward the student and his or her potential for learning within this environment. It is a myth to think that students with ASD cannot detect negative opinions that teachers project; such opinions seriously damage efforts for true inclusion.

- **Adequate support levels**—it is unfair to ask a student to participate in the general education setting without providing the student the needed supports to ensure success—that is, paraprofessional support *when needed* (full or partial), necessary modifications/accommodations for academics, organized natural supports (peer programming, hierarchy of cues, etc.), behavior programs, and so on.

*(continued)*

## 3.2 ☐ IN THEIR WORDS (continued)

■ **Flexibility and creativity**—students with ASD will challenge teachers' widely held and often firmly entrenched beliefs about how to teach students. Therefore, teachers will need to think "outside the box" and embrace new ideas and strategies, ultimately improving their own teaching skills.

Too often, students with ASD have been underserved and underestimated by traditional conventions of isolation and exclusion; but they can and do learn and progress when programs are well developed and systematically implemented. Inclusive programs can be a gateway to the wider social community in the lives of our students with ASD.

in the implementation of evidence-based strategies for students with ASD are more likely to be successful.

Jane Howard and her colleagues (2005) conducted a study in northern California where they compared outcomes for young children with autism spectrum disorders across three types of programs. One of the three groups received intensive behavioral treatment from Therapeutic Pathways staff in the home, school, and community for 25 to 40 hours per week of one-on-one intervention. Instructional assistants who were college students were trained and supervised by staff with master of arts (MA) degrees in psychology or special education and training in evidence-based practices.

The second group was comprised of children who attended public school classrooms designed for children with autism with a one-to-one or one-to-two staff-to-child ratio for 25 to 30 hours per week. Typically one teacher supervised between four and eight paraprofessionals. The credentialed special education teachers received consultation from MA degree candidates who had not yet completed their MA degrees. They used a variety of behavioral, structured teaching, and developmental approaches to practice. The third group was comprised of children enrolled in special education classrooms along with peers labeled with

various disabilities. They had 15 hours of service per week with a one-to-six adult-to-child ratio that included a certified special education teacher and paraprofessionals. Developmentally appropriate educational activities were used in these classrooms according to staff.

The results were that the group receiving intensive behavioral intervention showed significantly higher mean standard scores in all domains except motor skills, and better learning rates compared with the other two groups. The authors argue for the importance of the educational approach (intensive behavior therapy), the number of hours of intervention, and the training of staff (Howard et al., 2005) and suggest that these factors would be difficult to obtain in most public school systems.

## What Curriculum or Skills to Select

A good curriculum should have a conceptual structure, offer details of the implementation, and be used in a child-specific manner (Anderson & Romanczyk, 1999). States have developed standard general education curriculum for students by grade level. IDEA requires that special educators use these same standards for students with IEPs as their peers in general education whenever possible (Yell, 2012). Students with autism without intellectual disabilities frequently use the same curriculum standards, in both number and content, as their typical peers. Students with autism spectrum disorders with moderate to severe intellectual disabilities usually have IEPs guided by general education standards but adapted in both number based on team priorities and in content. For example, math goals may include more functional use of mathematic skills. Webber and Scheuermann (2008) recommend that the curriculum goals and objectives be developed by a team, including the family, that will facilitate the student's ability to live a productive and fulfilling life. According to these authors, the chosen curriculum should be longitudinal, horizontally integrated, age appropriate, and community referenced, and should include communication and social skills. Ben-Arieh and Miller (2009) add that goals should focus on the student's interest, serve as prerequisites for other important skills, have the potential to reduce or eliminate problem behavior, and promote independence.

Several published curriculum guides were developed particularly for individuals with autism spectrum disorders. Some of these guides are domain-specific, or focus on one or two areas of possible delay or difficulty. For example, one guide focuses on self-help or self-care skills (Wrobel, 2003). Others focus on developing social skills as the primary area. McAfee's (2002) social-emotional curriculum was designed for individuals with high-functioning autism and Asperger syndrome. Curriculum items found in the text by McAfee include recognizing emotional expressions, using an anger meter, and using preferred activities to calm down. Gutstein and Sheely (2002a) have published a social-emotional curriculum guide with items that facilitate development in very small steps. Taubman, Leaf, and McEachin (2011) have created a social skills curriculum that focuses on teaching social awareness, social communication, social interaction, social learning, and social relatedness. Fiore (2000) has also addressed social objectives as well as communication skills in the

curriculum activities found in Quill's publication. Beginning items of this curriculum include social attention (looks at person/object/novel activity), uses eye gaze (uses eyes to maintain social interaction), gestures (points), motor imitation, and verbal imitation. Communication skills have also been a focus of curriculum materials. Freeman and Dake (1997) developed a language curriculum guide for students who already have more advanced skills, such as the ability to communicate in some way and knowledge of basic colors, shapes, 5 to 10 animals, numbers 1 through 10, and the alphabet. Items from their text include pretend play, topical conversation, and analogies.

Multiple domain curriculum guides include those written for instructors who use applied behavior analysis as the approach (Lovaas, 2003; McEachin & Leaf, 1999; Taylor & McDonough, 1996). All program guides suggested that compliance with instruction, cooperation, or attending is the initial focus of instruction so that teaching can be effective. All of these curricula have initial, or foundational, skills comprised of imitation (of motor skills), expressive language (either pointing or verbal imitation), receptive language (e.g., one-step direction), and matching (identical objects).

Each of these texts includes suggestions for teaching these skills, such as the materials you would use, the prompts you could embed, and ways to generalize the skill. Which items you would target and in what order would need to be individualized. There is a paucity of research on the order of presentation of skills in order to determine which are most important for later skill development or which items are truly foundational for more complex skills.

The curriculum content of the multidomain publications is consistent with what Dawson and Osterling (1997) found in their review of eight clinically judged as effective early intervention programs for children with autism. They stated that these programs all focused on the child's ability to attend to the environment, imitate others, comprehend and use language, play appropriately with toys, and socially interact with others. It remains unclear, however, when educators should begin to work on pretend play or social interaction. Some practitioners believe it is important to work on social targets from the beginning (Gustein & Sheely, 2002a), whereas others state that imitation and receptive language skills are prerequisites for teaching play and social skills (Lovaas, 2003). "There is no agreed-upon curriculum in the field at this time" (Frea & McNerney, 2008, p. 93).

Teaching skills that enable access to a less restrictive environment is a priority for the individual with ASD. For example, if a child learns to use the toilet, then lots of opportunities become available, such as participation in community activities that may exclude children in diapers. This skill alone can make a major difference in how LRE is defined for that person. Learning functional skills such as dressing, sight-word reading, computer use, cooking, and public transportation use can have an effect on future lifestyle and interaction with the community.

It is recommended that curriculum objectives or what the teacher will target be individualized, and that person-centered planning be used to obtain family priorities for skills to be addressed (Browder, 2001; Test, Mason, Hughes, & Konrad, 2004). In person-centered planning, described as an ongoing process used to gather information about the hopes and dreams of an individual to be used in the development of long- and short-term goals (Held, Thoma, & Thomas, 2004), family expectations are taken into account when determining objectives. Strengths may be shaped at a young age for future vocational options (Grandin, 1999). Educators can use the individual's strengths when designing curriculum in order to increase skills in areas of weakness. For example, if a student is good at drawing, he could illustrate a story after he has correctly read the words of the text. Regardless of the type of goals and objectives for each student, it is important for educators to keep their expectations high, yet realistic, for every student and to celebrate progress and successes.

Regardless of what skills are selected as part of the IEP, it is required by IDEA 2004 that annual goals be measurable so that progress toward the goal can be monitored (Ben-Arieh & Miller, 2009; Yell, 2012). It is a legal requirement that there is information in the IEP regarding how the goal will be measured and when and how student progress will be reported to parents (Murdick et al., 2007; Yell, 2012). If a student takes an alternative assessment to the statewide test, then short-term objectives, or benchmarks, are also required (Murdick et al., 2007). These, too, must be written in measurable terms (Yell, 2012).

Mager (1997) describes the aspects of an instructional objective so that educators can measure student performance: "An objective is related to the intended outcome of instruction, rather than the process of instruction" (p. 5). According to Mager, three characteristics must be included in an objective: performance, conditions, and criterion. The performance is an observable description of what the learner is expected to do or produce. The objective must also include the conditions under which the behavior is expected. It is also important to include the criterion or the level of competence that must be reached or surpassed (Mager, 1997). When a behavior reaches criterion level, it may be considered as demonstrated or mastered. Once mastered, skills are reviewed to ensure maintenance of newly acquired skills.

All special educators write goals for identified target skills. However, goals and objectives may be unclear or not measurable. Some educators are simply following a formula without understanding how they can write a goal that is observable and replicable for data collection purposes. A goal stating:

> **By April and in the presence of teachers and peers, Maria will greet others with 80% accuracy on 9 out of 10 trials as measured by teacher records.**

has little meaning if the teacher does not know why teaching greetings is important, does not keep records, if the greeting behavior is not operationally defined (Is waving okay? Is a "Hi" without eye contact correct?), and if accuracy is not a relevant dimension of the behavior.

How does someone greet another person with 80% accuracy? (See Alberto & Troutman [2009], for descriptions of dimensions of behavior.)

A clearer objective would be written as follows:

> **Maria will greet adults or peers with a clearly audible "Hi" followed by the person's name a minimum of twice a day for three consecutive school weeks.**

## Maintaining and Sustaining Effective Practice

Supportive and hospitable leadership and organizational structures are core implementation components (Fixsen, et al., 2005). Positive administrative attitudes and support are critical for improving schools (National Research Council, 2001). When educators perceive that the instructional practice is valued by the school leader, it is more likely that they will implement the strategy or practice. The National Implementation Research Network provides a framework for developing evidence-based intervention practices within organizations (see Figure 3–3).

A key point made in the report by the National Implementation Research Network is that effective implementation takes time. Organizational change is always required for successful and sustainable implementation of evidence-based practices, and *systems change takes time* (Fixsen et al., 2005). Implementation occurs in six stages, with the first four (exploration, installation, initial implementation, and full implementation) taking approximately 2 to 4 years to complete. Innovation, or the adaptation to the organization, and sustainability, in the form of expanding the support base and maintaining effectiveness demonstrated with an accountability system in a changing context, are the final two stages of implementation (Fixsen et al., 2005). For something as complex as meaningful systems change, it will probably take from 3 to 5 years of sustained effort (Duchnowski & Kutash, 1997).

Making these changes requires communication and trust between the administrators of educational programs and facilities and university personnel. "We have a situation in which the state of practice is problematic and the field does not readily turn to the research community for help. This is in spite of the fact that the special

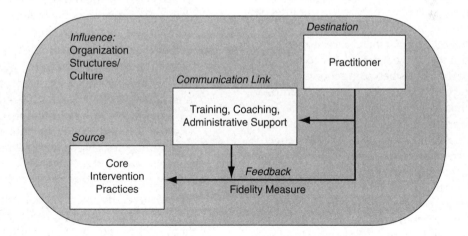

**FIGURE 3–3**  Implementation framework applied to developing evidence-based intervention practices within organizations
*Source:* From D. L. Fixsen et al. (2005). *Implementation research: A synthesis of the literature.* Tampa, FL: University of South Florida, Louis de la Parte Florida Mental Health Institute, The National Implementation Research Network (FMHI Publication #231) p. 28. Used with permission.

education research community has accumulated an impressive knowledge base that has been empirically derived" (Duchnowski & Kutash, 1997, p. 237). It is important for university personnel to initiate dialogues with school administrators, to share information, and to begin the exchange of ideas so that there is mutual problem solving. It is important that the people in the research community and the field work together to establish evidence-based practices that result in a quality education for learners with ASD.

"It seems that organizations exist in a shifting ecology of community, state, and federal social, economic, cultural, political, and policy environments that variously and simultaneously enable and impede implementation and program operation efforts" (Fixsen et al., 2005, p. 58). If programs or organizations are not aligned to integrate staff selection, training, performance evaluation, and ongoing training, and do not provide the resources in the forms of financial allocations, materials, manuals, and expertise so that current organizational practices can change, it is difficult to implement evidence-based practices. Organizations that are not committed to the needed resources and support are likely to be more vulnerable to the external influences of government policy and politics. Figure 3–3 depicts the system of support for the effective implementation of evidence-based practices.

School reform that includes changes to policy and administrative practices is accomplished through partnerships between schools and businesses, industry, and government (Simpson, 1994). In the recommended practices for systems change from the Division of Early Childhood of CEC, it is noted that "[t]he work of effective leaders is grounded in their ability to develop effective partnerships; to align policies, structures, and practices to promote change; and to cultivate a culture within the organization that not only supports, but encourages, data-informed decision making and change" (Sandall, Hemmeter, Smith, & McLean, 2005, p. 168). Cooperative partnerships have a direct bearing on the lives of individuals with autism spectrum disorders and their families (Simpson, 1994).

Many of the approaches and strategies used in education are adopted prior to determining whether scientifically based evidence exists for the practice. Educators may believe that a strategy is effective and hold the opinion that there is no harm in using strategies that have not been supported by research. However, if parents and educators are spending time and resources implementing strategies that are not effective or do not work, then valuable time is wasted when a different, more effective strategy may have resulted in better outcomes for the individual with autism spectrum disorder. Some interventions, such as facilitated communication, have been demonstrated through research as not effective and may even have harmful effects for some families. The evolution of the use of facilitated communication—a strategy without research-demonstrated effectiveness—illustrates this point.

## Evolution of Facilitated Communication: A Strategy without Evidence of Support

- 1970s—Rosemary Crossley, a teacher at St. Nicholas Hospital in Melbourne, Australia, introduces facilitated communication to a group of 12 children.

- 1979—One of the individuals with cerebral palsy, Anne McDonald, sues for the right to leave St. Nicholas Hospital and move in with Crossley. Rosemary Crossley states that holding the hand of Anne while she types (facilitated communication) helps her to control her spasms.

- 1985—Professor Biklen from Syracuse State University visits Australia to give a talk and has dinner at the Crossley home, where he observes facilitated communication.

- 1990—Biklen publishes an article on facilitated communication in the *Harvard Education Review* and reports a moral obligation to get it in place in the United States for individuals with autism (Makarushka, 1991).

- 1993—Research evaluations of facilitated communication are published with consistent findings of no support and the conclusion that it is the facilitator that is communicating (Hudson, Melita, & Arnold, 1993; Smith & Belcher, 1993; Szempruch & Jacobson, 1993; Wheeler, Jacobson, Paglieri, & Schwartz, 1993).

- 1993 —*Frontline* airs "Prisoners of Silence," a report on facilitated communication, and describes how individuals with disabilities in various countries were removed from their family homes due to claims of abuse by family members revealed through facilitated communication (Schreibman, 2005).

- 1999–2005—Evaluation of research evidence causes reviewers *not* to recommend facilitated communication as a practice (New York State Department of Health, 1999; Schreibman, 2005; Simpson, 2005).

- 2004—*Autism Is a World,* a documentary short-subject film coproduced by Biklen about an adult who uses facilitated communication, is nominated for an Academy Award (State of the Art Productions, Inc., 2004).

- 2008—Professionals, including Biklen, continue to recommend facilitated communication under various names for the approach.

Facilitated communication occurs when a facilitator provides physical assistance by sitting on the right side of an individual with disability and using her hand to support the individual's index finger, hand, or arm to push the keys on a keyboard (Hudson et al., 1993). For some, a specially designed keyboard with letters in alphabetical order is used. After each stroke, the facilitator pulls the hand back to help the learner avoid errors of hitting multiple strikes of the same key (Smith & Belcher, 1993). Biklen has stated that the support of the facilitator's hand goes well beyond the physical support and that the relationship of trust between the facilitator and the learner is paramount and cannot be measured (Makarushka, 1991).

Several studies were conducted to evaluate the communicated messages of the individual with disabilities. The format for these studies included a condition when the individual with disabilities sees a card with one object or question and the facilitator sees a different object/question. For example, Wheeler and colleagues (1993) placed the individual with ASD with the facilitator seated to the right with both parties across from the researcher. A partition divided the line of sight between the facilitator and individual with ASD. During one condition the facilitator and the individual with ASD were shown the same object on a card to be identified through typing using facilitated communication 50% of the time and different objects the other 50% of the time.

In all studies that controlled for the content viewed by the individual with disabilities compared with the content viewed by the facilitator, the responses were consistent with what the facilitator viewed (object or question) and not with what the individual with disabilities viewed (Hudson et al., 1993; Szempruch & Jacobson, 1993; Wheeler et al., 1993). Facilitators were surprised to learn how much they were influencing the typing of the person they were facilitating. In addition, Smith and Belcher (1993) found that the communication output during facilitated typing was consistent with individuals' verbal communication without any of the unexpected literacy skills reported by promoters of facilitated communication.

Several professional teams have reviewed the literature in order to determine whether or not to recommend that this approach be used with individuals with autism spectrum disorders. Consistently, the outcome of these reviews has been *not* to recommend facilitated communication (New York State Department of Health, 1999; Simpson, 2005). Facilitated communication is not recommended because the intervention has undergone a substantial amount of rigorous research and the evidence demonstrates that the intervention does not increase skill acquisition (Green & Shane, 1994). It is considered an unestablished treatment according to the National Standards Project (National Autism Center, 2009a). In addition, there have been serious detrimental effects for some children with autism spectrum disorder, such as removal from their families (Simpson, 2005). Schreibman (2005) writes that facilitated communication is a prime example of what can go terribly wrong with unproven treatments.

## Selecting Evidence-Based and "New" Strategies

"New" strategies for individuals with autism spectrum disorders are being marketed continuously. Educators, including teachers and school district personnel, are often the target of this marketing. Without knowledge about the research evidence, or lack thereof, educators can be susceptible to intervention fads and trends (Green, 1996). Teachers are often encouraged to attend workshops or to recommend strategies to parents. Workshop attendance or purchase of these strategies can be costly in terms of both time and money (Green, 1996). It would helpful to have some prepared questions that can be asked about any new approaches. Several authors have suggested that educators approach any new treatment with hopeful skepticism (Freeman, 1997) and consider the following questions and cautions:

- What is the intervention supposed to do? (Green, 1996)

- What is the impact of the method on the individual's general quality of life? (Simpson & Myles, 1998)

- Will the intervention detract from the overall educational and treatment program? (Simpson & Myles, 1998)

- Have its effects been tested in controlled experiments using direct observation? Has the research included children with autism spectrum disorders? Have those results been published in peer-reviewed journals? (Freeman, 1997; Green, 1996)

- Can these methods be maintained in the long term with appropriately trained personnel and other resources? (Simpson & Myles, 1998).

Some strategies that have been established as evidence-based can be selected to increase skills and replace challenging behavior of individuals with ASD. When making a choice, it is essential that educators know why they are targeting a skill and using a specific strategy. Without knowing why a strategy is used, it is difficult to implement the strategy effectively. An understanding of why a strategy is used necessitates an understanding of the theory underlying the approach and the key concepts of the theory. Many instructors are not sufficiently trained in multiple theories and the strategies based on key concepts of the theory, yet they implement strategies from diverse approaches. The outcome of selecting strategies with limited understanding and skills is likely to be mediocre (Howard et al., 2005).

In addition, using multiple strategies to address the same goal based on different theoretical approaches could be wasting valuable time with at least one ineffective intervention. If, for example, a student had an annual goal to use a phone independently to call home, this could be taught using several methods. A specialist may be teaching the learner to sing a song with the phone number embedded as part of a game entitled "Who do you call?" that includes turn-taking with a peer. The paraprofessional who has learned about visual supports may create worksheets that have seven boxes separated by a dash and ask the student to write the correct numbers in the boxes from a written model. Neither strategy incorporates a real phone or number pad. The teacher could be incorporating a strategy to teach number discrimination using a touch-tone phone pad during math rotations using errorless learning.

Without taking ongoing data and monitoring student progress as required by IDEA 2004, the educator would not be aware of what strategies were effective. And if the learner did increase her skills in using the phone to call home, the teacher would not know which strategy accounted for the change. Perhaps the teacher believes it is the music and game activity or the use of the squares as a guide that accounts for the change. It is also possible that neither of these strategies was effective but would be used again because of the teacher's belief in what caused the change.

Each time the method of instruction is selected, an important choice is made. If the educator is using evidence-based practice, then research studies will demonstrate that the strategy selected has been effective for others with disabilities, including individuals with autism spectrum disorders. Even though there are demonstrations of the effectiveness of the strategy, however, it is important that educators evaluate if the strategy is effective for the individual learners with ASD with whom they work by using ongoing progress monitoring.

Because it is important to know the theory behind the strategies and the key concepts of strategies used by educators working with individuals with autism spectrum disorders, the following four chapters will describe three different theoretical approaches and the key concepts of each approach. The three approaches are: applied behavior analysis (Chapters 4 and 5), social-relational and developmental (Chapter 6), and cultural (Chapter 7). Strategies that are used by educators based on these theoretical approaches will be described. Each chapter will begin with a description of the theoretical basis for the approach followed by the history of application for individuals with autism spectrum disorders. Key concepts that define the approach will be explained, with examples of strategies used for students with ASD that incorporate these key concepts. Strategies that are used by educators or key concepts put into practice will be defined and illustrated for each theory. What a classroom would look like if these key concepts were put into practice will be described. In addition, the research evidence for each approach will be reviewed throughout the chapters and summarized near the end of each respective chapter. Each chapter will conclude with suggestions for discussion and a list of resources for further information.

## SUGGESTIONS FOR DISCUSSION

1. Discuss the statement "Intervention and education make a difference in the quality of life for individuals with ASD."

2. Why do you think intervening early can have such an impact?

3. Conduct a debate with one side arguing for inclusive education with typical peers and the other side arguing for education in specialized programs using evidence-based practices designed for children with autism.

4. Define *evidence* for a practice and state how evidence-based practices are determined.

5. Explain why training conducted in a workshop format alone does not result in the effective implementation of practices.

6. (a) State how feedback can be given in a manner that facilitates the effective use of evidence-based strategies and (b) describe how you like to receive feedback from a supervisor.

7. What are the factors that contribute to the wide appeal of some strategies, such as facilitated communication, that do not have support from research?

8. Indicate how you would respond to a parent who requests the use of an invalidated intervention in his child's program.

# RESOURCES

## Books, Monographs, and Reports

Fixsen, D. L., Naoom, S. F., Blase, K. A., Friedman, R. M., & Wallace, F. (2005). *Implementation research: A synthesis of the literature*. Tampa: University of South Florida, Louis de la Parte Florida Mental Health Institute, the National Implementation Research Network (FMHI Publication #231).

Handleman, J. S., & Harris, S. L. (2006). *School-age education programs for children* with autism. Austin, TX: Pro-Ed.

Myles, B. S., & Simpson, R. L. (1998). Inclusion of students with autism in general education classrooms: The autism inclusion collaboration model. In R. L. Simpson & B. S. Myles (Eds.), *Educating children and youth with autism* (pp. 241–256). Austin, TX: Pro-Ed.

Schreibman, L. (2005). *The science and fiction of autism*. Cambridge, MA: Harvard University Press.

Turnbull, A., Turnbull, R., Erwin, E., Soodak, L., & Shogren (2011). *Families, professionals, and exceptionality: Positive outcomes through partnership and trust* (6th Edition). Upper Saddle River, NJ: Pearson.

Wagner, S. (1999). *Inclusive programming for elementary students with autism*. Arlington, TX: Future Horizons.

Wagner, S. (2002). *Inclusive programming for middle school students with autism/Asperger's syndrome*. Arlington, TX: Future Horizons.

Yell, M. L., & Drasgow, E. (2005). *No Child Left Behind: A guide for professionals*. Upper Saddle River, NJ: Merrill/Prentice Hall.

## Websites

*autismpdc.fpg.unc.edu*
   National Professional Development Center on ASD

*http://www.fpg.unc.edu/~nirn/*
   National Implementation Research Network

*www.autism-society.org*
   Autism Society of America

*www.autismspeaks.org*
   Autism Speaks

*www.cec.sped.org*
   Council for Exceptional Children (contains information about the Code of Ethics and evidence-based practices)

*www.nationalautismcenter.org*
   The National Standards Project (evaluations of the quality of the empirical literature of educational interventions for individuals with ASD is organized by this center)

## CHAPTER FOUR

# Applied Behavior Analysis: Increasing Skills

## CHAPTER OBJECTIVES

The reader should be able to:

- Describe the theoretical basis on which the principles of behavior analysis have been formulated and explain what it means to be an "applied" science.

- Define the key concepts of the principle of reinforcement, stimulus control, selecting socially important behaviors, operational definitions of behavior, prompt dependency, generalization, and collecting and graphing data.

- Identify what is meant by a motivational system for a student with autism spectrum disorders.

Chapters 4 and 5 describe the behavioral approach. The emphasis in Chapter 4 is on strategies for increasing skills; in Chapter 5, strategies based on the same approach are described with the aim of decreasing and replacing problem behavior. In this chapter the theoretical basis for the behavioral approach is identified, the history of applied behavior analysis used with learners with autism spectrum disorders (ASDs) is listed, key concepts are described, strategies based on these key concepts are explained, and an illustration of a model classroom based on this approach is provided. The research evidence for the strategies based on the behavioral approach is summarized at the conclusion of the chapter.

applied—Principles used with people in all types of environments such as schools, homes, offices, and factories that have social significance to the individual or to society.

behavior—An observable and measurable act or movement that is the focus of intervention.

analysis—Measurement of behavior to determine functional and replicable relationships between interventions and outcomes.

Analytic behavioral application is the process of applying sometimes tentative principles of behavior to the improvement of specific behaviors, and simultaneously evaluating whether or not any changes noted are indeed attributable to the process of application—and if so, to what parts of the process. In short, analytic behavioral application is a self-examining, self-evaluating, discovery-oriented research procedure for studying behavior. (Baer, Wolf, & Risley, 1968, p. 91—quotation from the first issue of the *Journal of Applied Behavior Analysis*)

## Theoretical Basis for Applied Behavior Analysis

Similar to other fields of science, behavior analysis consists of the measurement of observable phenomena. The science of behavior can be organized by three foci, philosophical or theoretical analysis of behavior, the experimental analysis of behavior, and applied behavior analysis (Cooper, Heron, & Heward, 2007). Practice is guided by the theory and research from all three domains. The theoretical foundations can be found in the positivism movement in the 19th century that held that only knowledge that was objectively observable was valid (Alberto & Troutman, 2009). Charles Darwin's work that linked animal and human behavior, thus indicating that we can learn about human behavior from experimental studies with animals, also contributed to the developing science. The scientific study of behavior revealed well-established general laws, or principles, that hold true for a wide range of species, including human behavior (Mayer, Sulzer-Azaroff, & Wallace, 2012).

John Watson used the term **behaviorism** to describe the focus in the area of psychology on observable phenomena in contrast to a focus on the mind or emotions from the psychodynamic approach (Alberto & Troutman, 2009). Watson's focus was on the direct observation of the relationships between environmental stimuli (S) and the responses (R) that are evoked by such stimuli, known as stimulus-response psychology (Cooper et al., 2007). B. F. Skinner, often considered the founder of the principles of applied behavior analysis, built on Watson's work on stimulus-response psychology by describing respondent behavior, or behavior elicited by stimuli that precede the behavior, also known as antecedents. In addition, he described operant behaviors, or those influenced by stimuli that follow a behavior, also known as consequences (Skinner, 1938).

Skinner focused on the philosophy of behavior throughout his career (see Skinner, 1974, *About Behaviorism*). He also conducted many experimental studies, mostly with rats and pigeons, to support these basic principles of behavior. Through the experimental analysis of behavior, a great deal was learned about the effects of different aspects of antecedents (e.g., clarity and familiarity) and consequences (rate or schedule of delivery, interest to the subject) on the behavior of focus. It was also determined that factors related to the individual subject also influenced their own behavior (such as their history with consequences, deprivation and satiation with consequences, etc.). A central concept underlying how learning occurs is found in the **three-term contingency** of antecedents-behavior-consequences (Mayer et al., 2012).

## History of Applied Behavior Analysis and Autism

Montrose Wolf, Todd Risley, and Hayden Mees (1964) were among the first to apply the principles of behavior analysis to work with children identified with autism. These researchers were working under the supervision of Sidney Bijou, a colleague of Skinner's, at the University of Washington. One of the first applications occurred when a request was made to work with a little boy named Dicky (not his real name) who was placed in an institution. Because Dicky was not making progress, and in fact was injuring himself with his own behavior, the institutional staff decided to try this "new" approach to treatment. Wolf, Risley, and Mees (1964) used principles of behavior, such as reinforcement, to get Dicky to wear his glasses and to stop self-injuring. By placing any injurious behaviors on **extinction** (withholding reinforcement of the behaviors they wanted to decrease) while they simultaneously gave him lots of praise and attention for the behaviors they wanted to increase **(reinforcement)** for periods of time without self-injurious behavior, Dicky began to wear his glasses for longer and longer periods of time. His engagement in learning activities increased and his self-injurious behaviors decreased (Wolf, 2003). Extinction and reinforcement are two principles of behavior that were demonstrated repeatedly in experimental studies with animals (Skinner & Epstein, 1982).

Other colleagues and graduate students who worked with Baer, Wolf, and Risley developed their own programs or schools for children with autism, including Ivar Lovaas (UCLA Psychiatric Unit) and Patricia Krantz and Lynn McClannahan (Princeton Child Development Institute [PCDI]). Lovaas began his work at the UCLA Young Autism Project in 1970 (Lovaas, 1987), and Krantz and McClannahan became executive directors of the PCDI in 1975. Also in the early 1970s, Dr. Sandra Harris started the Douglas Developmental Center on the Rutgers University campus. These behavior analysts and those working with them (such as Schreibman, Carr, Koegel, Handleman, and Romancyck) began by using discrete trials made up of a stimulus or cue that provides an opportunity to emit a behavior and that is followed by a consequence. For example, the teacher says, "Find the red ball" (cue), the student correctly selects the red ball from a group of toys (behavior), and the teacher responds, "Well done! You can play with the red ball you chose" (consequence). This instructional sequence of **antecedent-behavior-consequence (ABC)** is a common example of how the principles of behavior analysis can be used in teaching.

In 1985, PCDI staff members published their first outcome study indicating that children identified with autism who began their program before age 5 had comparatively better treatment gains (Fenske, Zalenski, Krantz, & McClannahan, 1985). They had already published research demonstrating skill acquisition of students in their program including gains in using descriptors, answering *wh-* questions, and speaking in paragraphs in a home–school project (Krantz, Zalenski, Hall, Fenske, & McClannahan, 1981). In addition they published a series of studies on using incidental teaching to increase language and conversational skills conducted with McGee (McGee, Krantz, Mason, & McClannahan, 1983; McGee, Krantz, & McClannahan, 1984, 1985). Prior to 1985, they published a description of their model program for working with parents (McClannahan, Krantz, & McGee, 1982).

In their review of behavioral treatment for individuals with autism, Matson and colleagues stated that over 200 studies were published between 1970 and 1980 (Matson, Benavidez, Compton, Paclawskyj, & Baglio, 1996). These studies demonstrated that by the 1980s, behavioral strategies could be used to teach children with autism to answer questions (Freeman, Ritvo, & Miller, 1975), to respond to multiple cues (Koegel & Schreibman, 1977), to increase language (Hart & Risley, 1975) and conversational skills (McGee et al., 1984), to initiate (Strain, Kerr, & Ragland, 1979) and respond to the social initiations of peers (Shafer, Egel, & Neef, 1984), and to increase prevocational work rates (Sugai & White, 1986), as some examples.

Ivar Lovaas (1987) conducted a study where he evaluated the effects of the number of hours of one-to-one applied behavior analysis treatment on the outcomes for children with autism. The group ($n = 19$) that received a minimum of 40 hours per week had better outcomes compared with the group ($n = 19$) that received 10 hours a week, with 47% of the 40-hour group attending public school and scoring within the normal range of intelligence on standardized assessments. Only 2% of the control group receiving 10 hours a week achieved this outcome (Lovaas, 1987).

When participants were retested four and one-half years later, eight of the nine students from the 40-hours-a-week group maintained their gains, demonstrating that this approach may result in significant and long-lasting effects (McEachin, Smith, & Lovaas, 1993). Birnbrauer and Leach (1993) replicated that Lovaas study in Australia and also found that 47% of the children with autism who received 40 hours a week of behavioral intervention were approaching normal levels of functioning. Due to the impact of this research some people refer to the approach used as the Lovaas method, instead of correctly identifying the approach as applied behavior analysis.

Also in 1993, Catherine Maurice published a book about her struggle as a parent to obtain a diagnosis and find effective treatment for her two children with autism. Her book, *Let Me Hear Your Voice* (Maurice, 1993), was influential in encouraging parents to search for educators with knowledge and skills in applied behavior analysis. This book was disseminated at a time when additional programs implementing applied behavior analysis procedures were publishing the gains made by young children with autism (Harris, Handleman, Gordon, Kristoff, & Fuentes, 1991).

The reviews of the literature on comprehensive models (Odom, Boyd, Hall, & Hume, 2010) and strategies used with individuals with ASD (National Autism Center, 2009a; Odom, Collet-Klingenberg, Rogers, & Hatton, 2010) reveal that the majority of comparatively highly rated comprehensive treatment models and identified evidence-based practices are those based on behavior analysis (see Chapter 3 for details of these studies). In their report describing strategies with sufficient research evidence to be identified as one of the 11 "established" strategies, the authors of the National Standards Project (NSP) conclude that "two-thirds of these strategies are based on behavior analysis" (National Autism Center, 2009b, p. 50).

Odom and colleagues found a great deal of overlap with the National Standards Project in their identification of evidence-based practices (Odom, Collet-Klingenberg, et al., 2010)

and not only agreed that there was sufficient evidence for all of the practices identified by the NSP that were based on behavior analysis (prompting, antecedent-based interventions, time delay, reinforcement, differential reinforcement, response interruption/redirection, task analysis, discrete trial teaching, naturalistic interventions, pivotal response training, functional communication training, functional behavior analysis, video modeling, self-management, and peer mediated intervention), they added to the list (e.g., extinction, Picture Exchange Communication, parent implemented intervention). These strategies will be defined and discussed in this chapter as well as in Chapters 5 and 8 of this book. The results of these reviews indicate that educators who are required to use strategies that are scientifically based (see Chapter 1 for legislation) are therefore required to have a good understanding of applied behavior analysis because the majority of the evidence-based strategies are based on this theoretical approach.

An understanding of some key concepts of applied behavior analysis by practitioners is essential so that any intervention can be truly individualized. Limited skills by an interventionist may result in an inability to tailor strategies to the individual's history, preferences, current skills, and program objectives. Using one strategy or tool, even well, is limiting in any profession. It is no different for an educator. A complete introduction to applied behavior analysis is beyond the scope of this text. However, practitioners who work with learners with autism spectrum disorders should be familiar with some basic elements of applied behavior analysis because strategies based on this approach are considered evidence-based.

## Key Concepts

It is important to identify some key concepts so that strategies based on applied behavior analysis can be recognized. Examples of how educators can incorporate these concepts in educational strategies will be described.

## Principle of Reinforcement

*Positive reinforcement.* **Positive reinforcement** has occurred when there is a presentation of a stimulus (consequence) immediately following a response (behavior) that results in an increased probability of the response (behavior) in the future (Cooper et al., 2007). When we refer to reinforcers, we are focusing on the consequences following behavior. Reinforcement only results in an increase in behavior or targeted skills. **Negative reinforcement** also results in an increase of targeted skills; however, the negative reinforcement procedure occurs when a behavior produces the contingent removal, reduction, or postponement of a stimulus, resulting in an increase in the future probability of the occurrence of that behavior (Cooper et al., 2007). An example of negative reinforcement is provided in Chapter 5. The focus in this chapter is on positive reinforcement.

Educators often select rewards for students and give them contingent on "good" behavior, including correct responses. However, if the teacher-selected reward does not result in an increase in the behavior, then it is not, by definition, a positive reinforcer. Sometimes we select rewards based on what we think students like or are motivated by, but our selection is incorrect or has lost its appeal. For example, a student may have a favorite toy at the beginning of the school year, but after several months he or she may grow tired of the same toy. Sometimes the delivery is too delayed, such as at the end of the class period or end of the day. Sometimes the student does not know why the reward was given because **descriptive praise** was not used or contingencies for receiving the reward are unclear. If the reinforcement contingencies are not clear, then the student does not know why praise or rewards are given and will be less likely to repeat the behavior in the future. Only if data are collected to assess whether the reward results in an increase in the target behavior will

it be known if a positive reinforcer was used and whether the positive reinforcement procedure was used effectively.

This point is illustrated by a teacher who uses fish crackers as a reward for children sharing toys during a preschool play period. Because most of the children in her classroom like fish crackers, the teacher carries a big bowl of them and gives them to the children when she notices them sharing toys. She has asked one of the classroom assistants to collect data on Chris's sharing behaviors during play. When Chris receives a fish cracker, he either licks it or puts it down because he does not like the texture of the cracker. Chris often leaves the play area after receiving a cracker. His teacher changes the reward to a hand stamp of a dinosaur. Then, according to the data, Chris stays at play longer and shares more with his peers. The dinosaur stamps are a reinforcer because they increase the probability of sharing when given contingently for sharing behavior. The fish crackers did not result in an increase of the target behavior (sharing) and therefore were not a reinforcer.

Research has demonstrated that the schedule of reinforcement also affects behavior. If a teacher wants to increase a new or weak skill, then a consistent or continuous schedule of reinforcement may be selected. A continuous schedule is when the established reinforcer is given each and every time the behavior is emitted (Mayer et al., 2012). The use of continuous reinforcement increases the probability that the behavior or skill will occur and that the student will practice the behavior to the point where it is presented with some degree of fluency.

Once the target behavior is established, the teacher can begin to work on maintaining the skill over a period of time. To support maintenance of the skill, the teacher may want to thin the schedule of reinforcement or use a more intermittent schedule of reinforcement, when the reinforcer is presented on some but not every occurrence of the behavior (Cooper et al., 2007). Research has demonstrated that intermittent schedules maintain a behavior longer (Cooper et al., 2007). In addition, the schedule is more likely to approximate the schedule found in the "natural" environment (Cooper et al., 2007).

Incorporating student preferences and developing a system that supports student motivation are essential to creating a successful educational experience for a student with autism spectrum disorder (Dyer, 1989; Mayer et al., 2012). Establishment of student preferences for activities, topics, academic subjects, and form and intensity of sensory stimulation may be obtained by asking them, their parents, caregivers, and previous teachers. For some students, a more formal preference assessment may need to be conducted.

## Preference Assessments

Mason, McGee, Farmer-Dougan, and Risley (1989) adapted a **paired-stimulus preference assessment** for use with nonverbal students with autism. They presented an array of objects (edibles, vibrating toys, music boxes) and activities (hugs, spinning in the air, clapping hands) in pairs and defined a preference as the one reached for within 5 seconds after presentation. Following the identification of a group of preferred items, students chose several items from this group each day to use as rewards for completing educational activities. Incorporating these preferred items increased attention to task and decreased problem behaviors.

Lavie and Sturmey (2002) demonstrated that staff members can be taught to use the paired-stimulus preference assessment when the skills are taught with brief instruction, video modeling, and rehearsal with feedback. They clearly outlined the steps for staff training that included (1) putting two stimuli in front of the child and if the child touches a stimulus, removing the unchosen one immediately, and (2) if the child does not approach either, prompt him or her to sample each item for 5 seconds and present both again.

DeLeon and Iwata (1996) used a method called **multiple stimuli without replacement** and found that presenting an array of seven items and having the student choose one item at a time to be an effective method of determining preferences. In this method, the item chosen by the student is not replaced and the remaining items of the array are rearranged prior to the student making another choice. This method provides educators with information about an array of potential reinforcers to use with the student. Researchers have confirmed that this method is effective for determining the preferences of students with autism (Carr, Nicholson, & Higbee, 2000).

After student preferences are identified, they can be incorporated into motivational systems. Examples of such systems include arranging the student's schedule so that preferred activities and/or items follow less preferred activities (Cooper et al., 2007) or incorporating the student's choice of activities following a teacher-identified task. Embedding preferred topics, items, and materials into educational activities can increase engagement. The selection of teaching strategies that include preferred modalities, such as visual cues (McClannahan & Krantz, 1999), and preferred consequences, such as the use of identified reinforcers (Dyer, 1989; Mason et al., 1989), can maximize teaching effectiveness and prevent problem behaviors.

## Motivational Systems

The aim of any motivational system is to maintain or increase behavior with a system that approximates the "natural" rate of reward. Typical motivational systems for students with autism spectrum disorders include both contrived rewards arranged by educators and natural rewards scheduled into the daily routine (snack or computer time). Examples of behaviors maintained by natural reinforcers might include elementary-age students who remain on-task until it is time for recess, or employees who are productive until they receive their paycheck at the end of the week. However, typical rates of reward are often too low or too thin to increase or maintain the behaviors of individuals with autism spectrum disorders, and it is often too difficult for students who receive a consistent high rate of reinforcement for demonstrating new skills to jump to a typically lean schedule of reinforcement. A common strategy to address delays of reinforcement is the creation of a token system.

> From the supermarket to the stock market, any economic system of exchange involves some form of token reinforcement. (Hackenberg, 2009, p. 257)

A formal **token economy system** is comprised of a set of tokens (such as pennies or photos of favorite characters) that are collected contingent on specific target behavior(s) and then traded for preferred activities or for backup reinforcer items after the select number of tokens has been obtained by the student (Cooper et al., 2007). We all use money and therefore live in a token economy. By creating an individualized token system for our students with autism, we can teach them the value and use of money at the same time we teach them to delay obtaining a reward. "The impact that token systems have as a tool for teaching behavior improvement in a positive way remains one of the major contributions to behavioral psychology" (Ayllon, 1999, p. 2). A sample token board that includes pennies as tokens to be exchanged for a choice activity (photo or symbol to be attached to Velcro) is found in Figure 4–1.

Ganz and Sigafoos (2005) demonstrated that an adult who was blind and diagnosed with autism and cognitive disabilities was able to use a token system and self-administer his own rewards in a vocational public school setting. Self-management of tokens was found effective

for increasing sharing in children with autism during play activities (Reinecke, Newman, & Meinberg, 1999). Some very young children with autism spectrum disorders can be taught to self-deliver tokens and self-deliver their own rewards (P. J. Krantz, personal communication, June 1, 2005). In Their Words 4.1 is a discussion of the importance of motivational systems for children with autism by McClannahan and Krantz.

## Stimulus Control

Antecedent stimuli, or stimuli that precede a behavior, also may acquire some control or set the occasion for a behavior to occur (Cooper et al., 2007). **Stimulus control** is demonstrated when the rate or frequency of a response is altered concurrently with the presence of a **discriminative stimulus**. For example, you are more likely to go to the door and open it following the ringing of the doorbell. The bell becomes a discriminative stimulus for your door-opening behavior. Similarly, we want to teach children with autism to say hi in the presence of an adult or peer and not just randomly throughout the day.

Our environment has a multitude of stimuli that may be related to our behavior. Visual stimuli such as clocks, written schedules, sunlight, food on the table, facial expressions, and so on, are related to many forms of our behavior. We also use auditory stimuli to occasion behavior: the words from our teachers, school bells, car horns, and crying from babies all may be related to specific behaviors. Children with autism spectrum disorders frequently have difficulty with stimulus control, and the stimulus that typically elicits behavior for many individuals may have little effect (no apparent reaction to facial expressions) or may elicit unusual behavior (tantrums when the school bell rings). Some individuals with autism spectrum disorders react with **stimulus overselectivity**, or by attending to an irrelevant dimension of the stimulus (Lovaas, Koegel, & Schreibman, 1979; Rosenblatt, Bloom, & Koegel, 1995). For example, a student shown

**FIGURE 4–1** Sample token board

## 4.1 IN THEIR WORDS

**Lynn E. McClannahan and Patricia J. Krantz,** *Executive Directors, Princeton Child Development Institute*

### Motivational Systems for Children with Autism

All children have motivational systems—systems of rewards that strengthen and maintain behavior. For example, typical children's motivational systems may include parents' attention and praise, allowance money, and special trips to toy stores or fast-food restaurants. These systems are usually effective, although they are often informal and casual. But children with autism spectrum disorders need motivational systems that are programmed. The responses to be rewarded must be defined, rewards must be selected on the basis of each individual's preferences, rewards must be varied and contingently delivered, reinforcement schedules must be selected thoughtfully and executed carefully, and performance data must be reviewed to determine the effectiveness of each youngster's motivational system. Perhaps the biggest challenge is to decrease prompts and program for independent performances while maintaining an appropriate rate of reinforcement.

a photograph of a boy who is laughing may attend to the color of his hair or an emblem on the shirt pocket. It would be important for educators to identify the critical features of any items included in a discrimination task—for example, to attend to the boy's mouth and eyes for facial expression.

Students with autism can be taught to attend to relevant stimuli and to discriminate stimuli in the environment through the reinforcement of the desired behavior by an educator in the presence of the discriminative stimuli and not in the presence of other stimuli. This process is referred to as **discrimination training** (Green, 2001). For example, we teach children to pick up the spoon, and not the fork, in the presence of the cereal. Children are taught to label photographs correctly by saying Mom only when a photo of mother is shown and not when there is a photo of a sibling.

One common method used to teach discrimination is through **matching-to-sample procedures** (Green, 2001). Using matching-to-sample, conditional discriminations are taught, or the student is taught that the correct answer

or the correct response is conditional on the context, antecedent, or sample. For example, a spoon is the correct match in an array of spoon, fork, and knife *only* under the condition when a spoon is the sample to match (see Figure 4–2). With matching-to-sample, one object or photo is the sample and two or more (preferably three) objects or photos serve as the comparison stimuli. The student is asked to choose, from the comparisons, the correct match to the sample. The correct choice depends, or is conditional upon, the sample. When presenting the trials, randomly vary the positions of the comparison stimuli (sample of three) and avoid presenting the same items more than twice in a row (Mayer et al, 2012). Change the position of the correct item so that it is clear if the student has a position bias, or always chooses the item on the left. Discrimination between items or categories of items is a basic skill that educators can teach using the match-to-sample procedure.

**Stimulus generalization,** or responding in the same way to similar antecedent stimuli with a history of reinforcement, is also taught. It is important that a spoon is identified as the

**FIGURE 4–2** Matching-to-sample of spoon

correct utensil to use with cereal, regardless of whether it is a teaspoon or tablespoon, plastic or metal, white or silver, with a fancy or plain handle. Once a student uses a spoon correctly in the presence of the cereal with a utensil not previously reinforced, stimulus generalization has occurred (Ghezzi & Bishop, 2008).

Frequently, stimulus generalization must be taught systematically to individuals with autism spectrum disorders. It is often necessary to add cues or prompts to the environment in order to facilitate stimulus control. **Prompts** can take the form of verbal instruction ("This is the spoon"; "Write your name here"), gestures (pointing), modeling (demonstrating the behavior), or physical guidance (placing the student's hand on the correct choice). Prompts are used to increase the likelihood that the discriminative stimulus will occasion the desired response (Alberto & Troutman, 2009) or that the student will see the bowl of cereal and select and use a spoon.

**Errorless learning** techniques utilize cues or prompts that result in correct responses each time the stimulus is presented as a way to prevent, or substantially minimize, errors (Mayer et al., 2012). For example, the spoon ladle (the

critical feature) can be made much larger than the fork prongs, and hand-over-hand prompts can be used to assist the student to pick up the spoon following the delivery of the cereal. The student is then reinforced for correctly selecting the spoon. In this example, the reinforcer is embedded in the activity because the student really likes cereal and is allowed to eat some.

Certain factors, referred to as **motivating operations** (Michael, 2007) can influence the effectiveness of this training. If the child has not eaten cereal earlier in the day, this may increase his motivation to choose a utensil and eat more. If another child is crying at the table, the child with autism spectrum disorders may become distracted, or if breakfast is served at an unusual time of day, the child with autism may refuse to change his routine and eat the cereal. These factors need to be considered when evaluating the effectiveness of strategies used.

*Fading extra or artificial cues.* Regardless of how additional cues are used for teaching, they need to be **faded** so that the relevant stimuli can serve as discriminative for the desired behavior. Planned fading of the hand-over-hand prompts and the gradual reduction of the size of the spoon ladle may be necessary before it can be said that the child can discriminate a spoon from a fork. The **time-delay procedure** is a strategy that can be used to fade prompts. Progressive time delay involves initially providing a prompt to the student with autism immediately when the cue is presented and then gradually increasing the interval of time before the prompt is given until the student responds to the cue without a prompt (Charlop & Walsh, 1986). In constant time-delay, a fixed time interval is always used prior to a prompt (Alberto & Troutman, 2009; Mayer et al., 2012).

A challenge facing educators who teach students with autism spectrum disorders is that the children can become dependent on the use of added cues or prompts (MacDuff, Krantz, & McClannahan, 2001). Some students develop a dependency on prompts from adults. It can be a common occurrence for students to look for a head nod or pointing gesture in order to make a correct choice, or to wait for adult instruction in order to complete any task. Students may learn that they do not have to attend to and comprehend what the teacher is saying because someone else will repeat the instruction for them or provide some other cue. These students are not demonstrating mastery of a skill because they are not completing the skill independently, and they are not using the cues typically found in the environment but rather depend on artificial prompts.

An effective strategy used to avoid such **prompt dependency** (MacDuff et al., 2001) is the incorporation of **photographic activity schedules** (McClannahan & Krantz, 2010). The researcher-practitioners who developed this strategy have found that even young children can be taught to follow independently picture cues placed in a book format. Schedules can be made for older students to facilitate completion of vocational activities. Banda and Grimmett (2008) reviewed the literature on the use of activity schedules with individuals with autism and found 13 articles that demonstrated increases in social interaction and on-task and transition behaviors, and decreases in tantrums and other problem behaviors. These reviewers conclude, "[T]he reviewed studies support the use of activity schedules as an effective intervention strategy for modifying various social, daily living, on-task, and transition behaviors in persons with autism" (Banda & Gimmett, 2008, p. 331).

In their book, *Activity Schedules for Children with Autism*, McClannahan and Krantz (2010) describe how they teach students with autism spectrum disorders first to obtain picture/object correspondence and then to follow photographic cues. They teach the students to turn the pages of a book, point to the photograph, and then complete the activity represented in the photograph. Students are able to complete all the activities depicted before they are included in the schedule. Students are taught to use schedules they can follow and independently complete tasks and activities.

*Prompting.* An important aspect of using photographic activity schedules (McClannahan & Krantz, 2010) is the method used to teach the students. **Most-to-least prompts** (hand-over-hand to gesture) are administered from behind the student so that the student does not learn to wait for an adult cue but rather follows what is in the photographic schedule independently. If the learner is a reader and text is included in the activity schedules, eventually the photographs will be faded, resulting in the student following a written schedule just as a typical student does. In summary, the use of activity schedules incorporates visual cues and graduated guidance (physical touch) as prompts for instruction that are then faded to a text schedule that approximates what is used by typical peers.

Activity schedules and instruction to paraprofessionals to avoid using verbal prompts increased the independent on-task behavior of three students in an inclusive school (Hall, McClannahan, & Krantz, 1995). Baseline observations revealed that these paraprofessionals used multiple forms of prompting even for activities that they had identified as activities the students could accomplish independently. **Overprompting** from classroom assistants, including paraprofessionals assigned to assist individuals with autism spectrum disorder, is a common problem.

Another commonly used sequence of prompting is the **least-to-most sequence** that starts with a verbal prompt and ends with physical guidance. Although this sequence begins with the least intrusive method of prompting, it may not be the best sequence for some students with ASD who learn to wait until an adult provides graduated guidance or completes the task for them. In other words, some students with autism spectrum disorders may become prompt-dependent when using this sequence of prompting.

### Operationalize Target Behaviors

Describing behavior in observable and measurable terms is a critical aspect of applied behavior analysis, just as it is for writing complete and clear objectives for individualized educational programs (IEPs). A target behavior should be described clearly enough that it can be understood and replicated by others (Baer et al., 1968). A teacher, paraprofessional, and substitute should be able to read a description of the target behavior for a student and understand clearly what behavior earns a reward, or which behavior is ignored. If definitions are left up to interpretation, then any data collection system will be meaningless because everyone will be recording different behavior. Skills such as communicating wants and needs, initiating social bids, turn-taking, sharing, following a schedule—in fact, all behaviors—need operational definitions. A recording sheet in the classroom can be used to record the date and any occurrences of the target behavior, and the teacher and others can clearly identify when the objective has been met.

Some target goals include a set or sequence of skills that each need to be acquired and mastered in order to complete a more complex chain of behaviors. Educators often write these steps following a **task analysis** of how to complete skills such as teeth brushing, making a sandwich, or going to the library and choosing a book. Either by doing the set of behaviors by yourself or by watching one or more people, a task analysis can be written in small enough steps to be understood clearly and accomplished by the learner. The steps can be described in photos, drawings, or written instructions or presented orally. Educators can also conduct a **discrepancy analysis** to evaluate the skills of a typical peer completing the same task compared with the student with autism spectrum disorders. The instructional strategies would be aimed at narrowing or eliminating the discrepancy between the skills of the students.

Once the set of steps has been identified, and information is obtained about which steps the student is currently able to complete and which steps need instruction or guidance, a time and a place to work on the task is identified. With any skills, it is important, if possible, to work in the environment where the task will be accomplished independently in the future. In other words, teeth brushing should be taught

in a bathroom; making a sandwich should be taught in a kitchen or lunchroom.

Because task analyses are used frequently, many sources are available from which educators can obtain task analyses for a variety of skills. The educator needs to tailor the sequence to the individual student and the environment where the task will take place. Step size, materials used, and form of presentation can all be modified. Once a task analysis is completed, the instructor can decide how to teach the individual component skills.

The sample task analysis for stapling shown in Figure 4–3 was obtained from the website for the Murdoch Center Program Library (www.murdochfoundation.org) where curriculum materials with over 1,000 task analyses can be purchased (Wheeler et al., 1997). See also Resources at the end of this chapter.

As you can see from the figure, there are many steps to this task. For some students, you will need to add some steps; for others, you can simplify a task analysis. The recommended strategy used to teach stapling in this example was the **backward chaining procedure**. The task analysis can be considered a chain of behaviors, with each link acting as the discriminative stimuli for the next link in the chain (Cooper et al., 2007). When using backward chaining, the educator completes all but the last link of the task or the one closest to the reward. When that step is completed, the student gets a reward. When that step is mastered, the student is then required to complete the last two steps before the reward is given, and so on.

## Selecting Socially Important Behaviors

A key concept in applied behavior analysis is that socially important behaviors are targeted for change. Is greeting an important behavior for Maria and for her family? The answer is likely to be yes because many students with autism spectrum disorders have difficulty learning basic social rules and interacting with others effectively. Greeting others is often used to begin a social interaction and focus the student with autism's attention toward others, and it is a skill

**Specific Target Behavior:** When given the instruction, "_____, put these together," student staples two pages together.

**General Instructions:** Method I—Backward Chaining Procedure. This program teaches stapling two pages together. Once mastered, use Collating & Stapling (VO-OP-25) to teach multiple sets with varying numbers of pages. Arrange pages on table so that first page is immediately to left of second page and bottom edges of pages are lined up near edge of table. Have stapler to right of pages and about 12 inches back from front edge of table. Have several pairs of pages already stapled and placed in stack to right of stapler near forward edge of table. If student has difficulty aligning pages in stapler correctly, jig may be helpful. Step 4 may also be difficult for some students who might otherwise master remaining steps. If so, adjust program to allow help on that step or consider using a jig to align pages.

**Prerequisites:** Turning Page (VO-OP-01).

**Materials:** Two pieces of 8½ × 11-inch paper, stapler, table.

| STEP | METHOD |
|---|---|
| 9. Picks up first page with left hand. | 9. Give instruction, "_____ put these together." Have student pick up first page in left hand by placing fingers on top of bottom edge of page and sliding and lifting off table, grasping with thumb behind page as page lifts up. |
| 8. Transfers page to right hand. | 8. As page is lifted, have student use right hand to grasp right edge of page about halfway up with thumb on top, fingers under, and release left hand. |
| 7. Picks up second page. | 7. Have student pick up second page in left hand as in Step 9. |
| 6. Places second page under first page. | 6. Have student slide second page under first into right-hand grasp. |
| 5. Holds pages with both hands. | 5. Have student grasp left edge of stacked pages with left hand so that pages are held in both hands. |
| 4. Jogs pages. | 4. Have student hold pages loosely and tap bottom edge lightly on table to align. |
| 3. Inserts upper-left corner of pages in stapler. | 3. Have student slide pages forward so that upper-left corner is in stapler. |
| 2. Staples pages. | 2. Have student press down firmly on stapler with left hand until pages are securely stapled. |
| 1. Places pages in stack. | 1. Have student place stapled pages in stack to right of stapler. |

**FIGURE 4–3** Task analysis for stapling

*Source*: Murdoch Center Program Library. A. J. Wheeler, R. A. Miller, B. M. Springer, N. C. Pittard, J. F. Phillips, & A. M. Myers, 1997. North Carolina: Murdoch Center Foundation, Inc. Used with permission.

that has been demonstrated to improve with behavioral strategies (Halle, 1987).

It is often important that the skills targeted are functional and age-appropriate for the student. It is easy to argue for the time and effort needed to teach communication skills, reading, and basic math. It is less clear how many colors students need to know, if learning all the words to a song correctly is necessary, or if learning to write a phone number is important to a student who can be taught to use a telephone directly.

Decisions about which behaviors to target are usually made by the IEP team, which includes family members. Educators who follow a behavioral perspective focus on those skills most important for the student at present and in the future. Assessment focuses on current levels of performance or current skills that are then shaped to the desired target performances. Whenever possible, foundational skills that can be used throughout the student's life and across environments are targeted.

The interview with Eric (see In Their Words 4.2), a graduate from the Princeton Child Development Institute, clearly shows that he has learned foundational life skills. His quality of life is very good. He has paid employment, enjoys leisure activities such as reading and watching movies and plays, attends church, and has friends and hosts parties. When asked if he remembered learning these foundation skills he replied, "No." However, when asked if he would recommend his school to others he replied, "Oh, yes."

## Planning for Generalization and Maintenance

Once a student has obtained a skill, it is important to facilitate the generalization of that skill. **Generalization** is a key concept in applied behavior analysis (Anderson & Romanczyk, 1999). Generalization is considered to have occurred if the student's behavior occurs under different, untrained conditions such as with a different teacher, at home, or on the playground. Generalization can be claimed if no extra manipulations were made in the different condition or if some manipulations occur but they are clearly less than those required in the intervention condition (Stokes & Baer, 1977).

Students with autism spectrum disorders have difficulty generalizing new skills to new contexts (Alberto & Troutman, 2009). It is not unusual for a student with ASD to learn to respond to a question or to follow the oral instructions of one adult very well, but when asked the exact question by a peer or a stranger, the student does not answer. Consequently, it is important to *plan for generalization at the beginning* of the development of any curriculum objectives (Mayer et al., 2012).

Stokes and Baer (1977) offer some suggestions for facilitating the transfer of skills or generalization. They suggest that the naturally maintaining contingencies be identified and introduced early. For example, if you are teaching a student to respond to a bell or to a teacher's instruction, then using the actual bell or saying what the teacher is likely to say would facilitate generalization. Using common stimuli is helpful. For example, teaching ball-playing skills with the same ball that will be found in the playground will make it more likely that the student with ASD will use the ball-playing skills in the different environment.

Providing sufficient examples is also important. If you teach discrimination of a fork and spoon, then using larger and smaller, both plastic and wooden, salad and serving utensils would assist the student to understand that *spoon* is used for a class of items with similar characteristics. Training loosely or using the contingencies that will be found in the new environment facilitates transfer. In other words, students are more likely to respond to adult questions if they eventually do not get praised or rewarded after every question because they are not likely to receive a continuous reinforcement schedule in most settings.

Finally, Stokes and Baer (1977) suggest that we teach generalization—that we arrange for opportunities to practice skills in many environments, using different materials, and in the presence of various peers and adults. For social situations, facilitating generalization

## 4.2  *IN THEIR WORDS*

## Interview with Eric, PCDI Graduate

**E:** My name is Eric, I work at [company] for over 14 years. I'm now 36. I live in a condo for over 7 years. I live alone.

**I:** Do you prefer to live alone?

**E:** I prefer to live alone.

**I:** OK. Well, what are some of the things that you do in your own apartment?

**E:** I like to clean it up a little. And I like to exercise on my treadmill and do my exercise program. And go to Blockbuster video and rent some videos or DVDs. Or go to movie theaters, like to Cinema Plaza, or sometimes [name of adult life coach] comes and, and we go to the library, or we do some shopping.

**I:** What kind of movies do you like best?

**E:** I like comedies and horrors.

**I:** Give me a good example. What's one of your favorite movies?

**E:** *Ruthless People.*

**E:** I like to read. I read magazines.

**I:** What kind?

**E:** *National Geographic.*

**I:** Oh, well that's a good magazine to read. Do you cook for yourself?

**E:** Yes, I.do.

**I:** What are some things that you make?

**E:** Capellini with fresh tomato sauce.

**I:** Mmm, that sounds great.

**I:** What do you do at work?

**E:** I work there in different departments of that company. And now I work in the library, and I work there for over 5 years now.

**I:** And what do you do in the library?

**E:** I shelve books alphabetically. I copy articles from medical books and journals.

**I:** Mmm, oh, so people ask and request a certain article?

**E:** And yes, and deliver priority mail and microfilming.

**I:** Oh, I see. So basically you respond to the requests that other people have for articles and things?

**E:** Yes, I do.

**I:** How do you get to work?

**E:** I go to, I take a van pool there.

**I:** Oh, well that's really good. You're a member of the Unitarian Church, aren't you?

**E:** Yes, I am.

**I:** And what kind of activities do you do at that church?

**E:** I like to help the kids.

**I:** In what way? What do you do with kids?

**E:** I read to them.

**I:** You also do some other things with the Unitarian Church, don't you? Sometimes make signs for them?

**E:** Yes, I do.

**I:** Oh, I see. OK. Well, why do you enjoy going there so much?

**E:** 'Cause I want to make special friends.

**I:** I see. That's good. So there you find them to be friendly and helpful to you?

**E:** Yes.

**I:** OK, do you try to go every Sunday?

**E:** Yes, I do.

**I:** Did you have a party at your house and invite some friends to come?

**E:** Well, I remember one time I, I had my millennium party. Some of my friends from church came.

**I:** Well, that was nice. Right. One of the things you've learned how to do is to entertain people, haven't you?

**E:** Y—Yes.

**I:** What's important when you're hosting a party? Or hosting guests?

**E:** I, I serve them drinks and keep them entertained.

**I:** Oh, alright. That's good. I wonder if you can talk to me a little bit about when you were a student at PCDI. Can you tell, can you remember some things you learned as a student at PCDI?

**E:** I learned how to be friendly and to be a good friend.

**I:** Anything else you can remember about your time at, at PCDI?

**E:** No.

**I:** Well, what about your life coaches that work for PDCI now? Is there anything that you particularly appreciate or enjoy about your life coaches?

**E:** Yes, they're fun. [Name of coach] used to be my life coach and [another name] used to work here but not anymore.

**I:** OK. Well, do you think that other students might be happy if they went to PCDI?

**E:** Oh, yes.

**I:** OK, why?

**E:** Because, I, and [another student] was my friend, uh, was my best friend for about 22 years, or over 25, years I think.

(*continued*)

## 4.2 IN THEIR WORDS (continued)

**I:** Of course, of course. Well, are you still friendly at work and friendly at other places?

**E:** Oh, yes, yes. I, I have been.

**I:** I'm glad to hear that. Why is it important to be friendly?

**E:** Because I want to show them that I care.

**I:** Excellent, a great answer. Well, I'm proud of you.

**E:** Thanks.

means including multiple social partners while the student is learning a new skill. It is especially important that a student with autism spectrum disorders does not interact exclusively with an assigned classroom aide because it is likely that any skills will be demonstrated for that person alone.

The reauthorization of IDEA (2004) emphasizes the importance of inclusive educational experiences with children without disabilities and requires an explanation of the extent to which the child will not participate with typical children (Murdick, Gartin, & Crabtree, 2007). Planning for generalization from the initiation of educational programs means addressing where you teach, how you teach, and what you teach. Wagner (1999) describes strategies based on behavior analysis that she has used successfully with students with autism who are fully included in elementary schools (see Chapter 3).

### Collecting and Graphing Data Linked to Objectives

Applied behavior analysts use the technology of measurement to evaluate both the behavior of the participant and the interventionist (Baer, Wolf, & Risley, 1987). Evaluating the effectiveness of any strategy is a critical aspect of this approach. Behavior analysts collect data and evaluate the effectiveness of strategies through the use of reliable and valid measures of performance and through single-subject research designs that

demonstrate replicable functional relationships between changes in the target behavior and the intervention strategy implemented. One of the hallmarks of ABA is the collection, analysis, and utilization of objective data (Taubman, 2008).

**Multiple-baseline designs** are often used to measure functional relationships. The design provides evidence of a **functional relationship** between behavior and intervention that is replicated at least two times. Baseline data on a target behavior is collected prior to intervention in at least three conditions (with different settings, people, or behaviors of one individual). The intervention is introduced at different times across the three conditions in order to control for any event occurring at the same time as the intervention. Demonstration of the functional relationship between variables (target behavior and intervention) occurs when the target behavior systematically changes when—and only when—the intervention is introduced.

Multiple-baseline designs are one of the single-case research designs that are considered an effective method of evaluation for interventions. Suggested criteria for determining if there is sufficient evidence of effectiveness of a strategy when using single-subject designs (Horner et al., 2005) has been described previously. Many single-subject studies demonstrate that the strategies described in this chapter have been effective for individuals with autism spectrum disorders. These studies are published in peer-reviewed journals, including the *Journal of Applied Behavior Analysis,* which is devoted to this approach.

Even if you are not interested in or sufficiently skilled to produce publishable research on your practice, it would be critical as an implementer of behavioral strategies to collect data on their effectiveness with your students. Effective data collection is a hallmark of the applied behavior analysis approach (Mayer et al., 2012). It does take skill, however, to plan a valid measurement system and to interpret the data. Recording pluses and minuses that are not reviewed or have little meaning for educators and their supervisors is not beneficial to anyone. In contrast, meaningful data that are interpreted in a timely manner could make the difference in how much progress is made by a student. Changes can be made if progress is too slow or an effective strategy can be used more often to facilitate skill acquisition.

The **data collection** form and frequency should be tied to the behavioral objective. If we are measuring greeting twice a day, then it is important to know the date and how many times per day the defined behavior occurred. If we are measuring vocabulary words used, we would want to be clear about which words are targeted. Too often, educators attempt to collect data on too many words, too infrequently, resulting in a pattern of correct and incorrect responses that is difficult to interpret.

Another way in which data collection becomes unclear is when educators record the level of prompting used even when the target behavior is to be accomplished independently or without prompts. Educators may think they need to document that the student went from a verbal prompt of instruction to the use of a gesture only for a particular skill. Considering the frequent issue with prompt dependence, this change in level of prompt may not indicate real progress, only the substitution for the form of assistance as the individual is working toward independence. It would be more impressive to demonstrate fewer skills performed independently and generalized rather than lots of skills where students are continuing to depend on some form of prompt.

The design of the data sheet can serve as a helpful reminder of the goal or target objective. A good data sheet makes it very easy for anyone to keep an eye on the goal. Compare the two accompanying data forms for the noted objective.

The right-hand column is easier to read and you can easily see the frequency when

| When given a touch-tone phone and asked to "Call home," Jose will independently and accurately dial his home phone number and identify himself to a family member on 9 out of 10 consecutive opportunities. | | | | | | |
|---|---|---|---|---|---|---|
| Date | FP PH V G C | Comments | Date | + = correct <br> − = error | | Comments |
| 1  3/7 | FP PH (V) G C | | 3/7 | − | | |
| 2  3/9 | (FP) PH V G C | Bad day | 3/9 | − | | Verbal |
| 3  3/10 | FP (PH) V G C | | 3/10 | − | | gestures |
| 4  3/12 | FP PH (V) G C | | 3/12 | − | | |
| 5  3/15 | FP PH V G (C) | | 3/15 | + | | Yeah! |
| 6  3/18 | FP (PH) V G C | | 3/18 | − | | |
| 7  3/19 | FP PH V G (C) | chatted | 3/19 | + | | |
| 8  3/22 | FP PH V G (C) | | 3/22 | + | | |
| 9  3/23 | FP PH V G (C) | | 3/23 | + | | |
| 10  3/26 | FP PH V G (C) | | 3/26 | + | | After weekend |
| FP = full physical, PH = partial physical, <br> V = verbal, G = gestural, C = correct | | | | 50% | | |

the objective of independent telephone skills has been met. If Jose continues the trend of correctly calling home for the next five sessions, then he will have met his goal. The scoring sheet on the left has information that is less relevant for the objective and requires the reader to review the objective to see what level of performance is required.

The following table is another example of two data forms for a vocabulary objective. The

| When asked questions following oral reading, Lee will correctly identify vocabulary words from a field of three text words on 9 out of 10 trials for 5 consecutive trial days. | | | | | | |
|---|---|---|---|---|---|---|
| Words | FP PH V G C | Comments | | Date | + = correct<br>− = error | Words:<br>Car<br>Camp<br>Map |
| car | FP (PH) V G C<br>FP PH V (G) C<br>FP PH V G C | | 1 | 3/7 | − − − − −<br>− − − − − | |
| fast | (FP) PH V G C<br>(FP) PH V G C<br>FP (PH) V G C | | 2 | 3/9 | − − − − −<br>− − − − − | |
| slow | FP PH (V) G C<br>FP PH V G (C)<br>FP (PH) V G C | | 3 | 3/10 | − − − − −<br>− + + − − | |
| motor | FP PH V (G) C<br>FP PH V G C<br>FP PH V G C | | 4 | 3/12 | − − + − −<br>− + − + − | |
| drive | FP (PH) V G C<br>FP PH (V) G C<br>FP PH V G C | | 5 | 3/15 | − + − + −<br>− − + + + | |
| camp | FP PH (V) G C<br>FP PH V G C<br>FP PH V G C | | 6 | 3/18 | − − + + +<br>− + + + + | − = camp |
| map | FP PH V G (C)<br>FP PH (V) G C<br>FP PH V G (C) | | 7 | 3/19 | + − + − +<br>+ + + − + | − = camp |
| push | FP (PH) V G C<br>FP PH V G C<br>FP PH V G C | | 8 | 3/22 | + + − + +<br>− + − − + | |
| pull | FP PH V (G) C<br>FP PH V G (C)<br>FP PH (V) G C | | 9 | 3/23 | + − + + +<br>+ + + + + | Yeah! |
| truck | FP PH (V) G C<br>FP PH V G C<br>FP PH V G C | | 10 | 3/26 | + + + + +<br>+ + + + + | Again |
| FP = full physical, PH = partial physical,<br>V = verbal, G = gestural, C = correct | | | | | | |

right-hand column is, once again, the clearer of the two forms.

In this table, the data recorded on the right-hand side clearly depict when the objective has been met. We also know the date when the skill was addressed and assessed. The data are presented in chronological order. The data sheet on the left indicates that different words are worked on at different dates and there is insufficient practice with any word. In addition, the words focused on by the student are left to the discretion of the instructor, who may choose those that are easier rather than words that are similar and often confused.

## Strategies Based on Key Concepts

In the behavior analytic view, autism is a syndrome of behavioral deficits and excesses that have a biological basis but are nonetheless amenable to change through carefully orchestrated, constructive interactions with the physical and social environment. Behavior analytic intervention seeks to redress those deficits and excesses by providing multiple planned opportunities for the learner to develop and practice skills that are useful in a variety of situations. (Green, 2001, p. 73)

Once socially important target behaviors or skills are identified, then the strategy for increasing these skills is selected. Webber and Scheuermann (2008) describe how to select target behaviors and other curricular considerations in their manual. They suggest that the curriculum is developed as a team (e.g., the IEP team) that includes family members and that practitioners choose a curriculum that facilitates a student's ability to live a fulfilling and productive life. They suggest that the chosen curriculum should result in functional skills; be longitudinal, horizontally integrated, age appropriate, and community referenced; and include communication and social skills.

### Discrete Trial Teaching

**Discrete trial teaching** is one strategy based on the principles of applied behavior analysis (Anderson, Taras, & Cannon, 1996; Tarbox &

Najdowski, 2008; Lovaas, 1981). Each trial is comprised of a three-term contingency with a clear antecedent or discriminative stimulus—a target behavior—followed by a consequence. This teaching unit, called a trial, has a clear beginning and end, or is discrete (Fovel, 2002; Leaf, 2008). Trials are frequently initiated by adults and often with a verbal prompt. If the student's response is correct, or the desired response is emitted, then that behavior is rewarded. If the behavior is not the desired response, an error correction procedure is used.

Trials can be initiated while seated at a table in a quiet corner of the classroom, or in any environment where the target behavior and consequences have been identified. "Please put your socks away" is an antecedent for discriminating socks from shirt and opening the correct dresser drawer. If done correctly, the skill can be rewarded with praise or a preferred activity.

Discrete trials are relatively easy to record because it is clear when the trial begins and what behavior follows. It is likely that data on discrete trials is taken more frequently than with other strategies based on the principles of behavior. A contributing factor is that individuals are often taught to collect data as part of any training on the use of discrete trials.

Discrete trials are often used to teach beginning skills and when the student is acquiring new skills because the adult can control the frequency of practice and because the contingencies for reinforcement are very clear (Webber & Scheuermann, 2008). If a new professional is learning to use strategies based on behavior analysis, it is likely that the professional will be taught discrete trial teaching. However, knowing how to deliver a discriminative stimulus and a consequence is just one tool that an educator can use. If the educator using this tool does not have a good understanding of the principle of reinforcement or of stimulus control, the educator will be very limited in the use of this strategy. It is also less likely that the educator can tailor the strategy to be effective with each individual student.

Implementing the ABC strategy is not simple. Awareness of motivating operations, an understanding of the pacing of delivery of antecedents, maintenance of clear expectations for performance, and knowledge of schedules of reinforcement and preference assessments are necessary. Knowledge of how to interpret data so that instructional decisions can be made in a timely manner is also important.

Discrete trials have been used to teach many skills to children with autism spectrum disorders, including verbal and motor imitation (Lovaas, 2003), preacademic and academic skills (Matson et al., 1996), communication and language (Quill, 2000), social interaction skills (Taylor & Jasper, 2001), and affection comments (Gena, Krantz, McClannahan, & Poulson, 1996) and responding to emotional statements. In other words, this strategy has been used to address many of the typical skills needed by individuals with autism spectrum disorders.

Use of only discrete trial teaching can result in prompt dependency because the student becomes overly accustomed to waiting for adults to initiate the teaching sequence. In addition, skills learned with one instructor or with one set of environmental conditions may not generalize to other situations. Consequently, behavior analysts use a variety of strategies based on behavioral principles when working with individuals with autism spectrum disorders, including incidental teaching, which has been shown to facilitate generalization of skills.

## Incidental Teaching

**Incidental teaching** was first used to increase language skills during naturally occurring adult–child interactions (Hart & Risley, 1974, 1975). The focus in incidental teaching is on child-initiated interactions. Incidental teaching can be used to increase the skills of individuals with autism spectrum disorders (McGee, Morrier, & Daly, 1999). Contrary to its name, incidental teaching requires a good deal of planning for instruction. Arranging the environment to elicit student initiation is essential to using this approach effectively. Placing items out of reach, providing access to preferred items contingent on expanded language, and requiring sharing to continue with motivational activities are all examples of how incidental teaching opportunities can be organized by the educator.

Even when there are preferred items or activities nearby, educators may need to "talk up" an item by describing the item near the individual with autism until he or she initiates a request for that item (McGee et al., 1999). Once the initiation occurs, the educator can request a behavior or skill that is part of an IEP objective and then reinforce that skill with access to, or continued interaction with, that item.

McGee and her colleagues use the Wait-Ask-Say-Show-Do sequence of prompting, or a least-to-most sequence, in their approach:

*Wait*—Take the child to the area where environmental cues will be evident. If there is no response within 5 seconds . . .

*Ask*—Ask the child a generic question, such as "What do you need to do?" Following 5 seconds of no response . . .

*Say*—Say what is expected in the form of a simple direction. A gesture may then be used to . . .

*Show*—Direct the child's attention to the object or materials. If the direction is not followed . . .

*Do*—Use gentle physical guidance to help the child complete the task.

Whenever the child completes the task, provide praise and access to the materials or preferred activity (McGee et al., 1999, p. 142). Incidental teaching has been used to teach individuals with autism spectrum disorders to increase sign language (Schepis et al., 1982), label objects (McGee et al., 1983), use prepositions, and read (McGee, Krantz, & McClannahan, 1985, 1986).

## Pivotal Response Training

Behavioral researchers who have focused on embedding choice-making and turn-taking as part of the child-initiated teaching interaction have called their approach **pivotal response training (PRT)** (Koegel, Koegel, & Carter, 1999; Schreibman, Kaneko, & Koegel, 1991). PRT was developed by Lynn Koegel, Robert Koegel, and Laura Schreibman, who have extensive experience as researchers and practitioners using applied behavior analysis. In their training manual published in 1989, Koegel, Schreibman, and colleagues identify **motivation** and **responsivity to multiple cues** as pivotal behaviors for acquisition of new skills. Using the natural environment to foster response generalization (Ghezzi & Bishop, 2008) is a key feature of PRT. Other pivotal behaviors that, when used, produce improvements in nontargeted behaviors (Baker-Ericzen, Stahmer & Burns, 2007) include self-initiation and self-management. Important components for the implementation of PRT include following the child's lead, providing child choice, interspersing maintenance tasks, reinforcing attempts, and using natural consequences (Koegel, Schreibman, Good, Cerniglia, Murphy, & Koegel, 1989; Stahmer, Suhrheinrich, Reed, Bolduc, & Schreibman, 2011).

PRT was initially designed to increase language skills, and was used primarily in clinic settings and with parents. Research has also demonstrated that peers can be taught to use PRT strategies effectively (Pierce & Schreibman, 1995). Publications in the early 1990s focused on teaching self-management as a pivotal behavior (Koegel & Koegel, 1990; Pierce & Schreibman, 1995) and using strategies to teach self-initiation (Koegel, Camarata, Valdez-Menchaca, & Koegel, 1998; Koegel, Carter, & Koegel, 2003). The PRT package of strategies has been demonstrated as effective for teaching children with ASD symbolic play skills (Schreibman, Stahmer, & Pierce, 1996; Stahmer, 1995), sociodramatic play (Thorp, Stahmer, & Schreibman, 1995,

and increasing social interaction skills with peers (Pierce & Schreibman, 1995; Schreibman et al., 1996). An evaluation of 158 families with young children with ASD who participated in PRT revealed that children showed significant improvements in adaptive functioning regardless of race or ethnicity, with children age 3 or younger showing the least impairment and making the most improvement (Baker-Ericzen et al., 2007). In another study it was determined that the most favorable results for the clinic-based PRT intervention was found for children who exhibited a moderate to high interest in toys and rates of verbal stimulatory behavior, exhibited low to moderate rates of nonverbal self-stimulatory behavior, and were tolerant of another person in close proximity (Sherer & Schreibman, 2005).

To expand the use of PRT to the classroom (CPRT), researchers have designed a model and a manual to assist educators working with students with autism spectrum disorders who attend preschool through grade 3 to implement CPRT effectively (Stahmer et al., 2011). The authors of the manual begin by explaining the principles of applied behavior analysis on which CPRT is based, followed by descriptions and illustrations of the key strategies of CPRT: gaining student attention, using clear and appropriate cues, providing a mix of easy and difficult tasks (maintenance and acquisition), sharing control, using multiple cues, using direct reinforcement strategies, using contingent reinforcement, and reinforcement of attempts (Stahmer et al., 2011). Sections on troubleshooting address issues that can occur when educators first attempt to implement strategies such as CPRT. Key components of a program based on applied behavior analysis (identifying target goals; targeting educational goals in educational activities; and collecting data for ongoing progress monitoring, including suggested data sheets) are addressed in the manual. Cindy Bolduc, an author of the CPRT manual and a special education teacher in a public preschool classroom, discusses how she implements CPRT in her work (see In Their Words 4.3).

When using any of the teaching strategies just described, educators implementing the behavioral approach are likely to incorporate a **shaping procedure**. **Shaping** is defined as the systematic reinforcement of successive approximations of a target behavior (Alberto & Troutman, 2006). To use the shaping procedure, the educator needs to have a powerful motivator, a clear definition of the target or goal behavior, and knowledge (data-based, of course) of the current skill level of the student. All educators working with the student should know and require the next step or approximation of the skill before delivering reinforcement. Shaping is used for language skills, motor skills, and any other behavior that can have an approximation to the goal.

## Video Modeling

Peter Dowrick (Dowrick & Dove, 1980; Dowrick & Hood, 1981) was one of the first to promote the use of video modeling, particularly video self-modeling, as a strategy for use with individuals with disabilities. Ayres and Langone (2005) published a review of articles on the use of

**4.3 IN THEIR WORDS** Cindy Bolduc, *M.A., Special education preschool teacher*

Classroom pivotal response training (CPRT) is designed to utilize a more natural approach for teaching young children in combination with structured goals and within a classroom setting—both individually and with peers. As a teacher of preschool-age children on the autism spectrum, I have tried a variety of empirically based strategies for working with this population. The thing I have noticed with CPRT is that it is so adaptable to almost any activity within my daily curriculum: circle, art, snack, one-to-one interactions. The students respond well to the incidental presentation of the lessons and show less disruptive behaviors because CPRT allows them to take the lead in their choice of materials and activities they enjoy.

While I choose the goals and objectives for each lesson, my students maintain interest longer because I allow them the choice of what they want to work with or for. For example, when using CPRT during circle, I would have prepared in advance a data collection sheet for a staff member to record the behaviors/skills I am looking to see. If I wanted a child to response verbally to a question, I might ask him or her about the name of a peer and wait for a response. My aide would record what response the student made, freeing me to continue my lessons. At art, I would require students to request the items needed to do a project, such as the glue, a pen, paper, crayons, etc. Where one child's goal might be to point to, or choose a picture of what he needs, another would be required to request the item with a single word, or a phrase. Still another child, depending on her or his goal, might need to request the item from a peer. Again, the data record sheet would be prepared ahead of time for ease of use. It is also important to make the activity something the child enjoys, or to have available a reinforcing item to give the child after he or she responds.

CPRT has become my favorite practice in helping my students gain or increase their verbal response repertoire. Incorporating these strategies allows me the flexibility to present objectives at any time, in any area.

video with students with autism in 2005 that comprised a description of 15 studies. Two years later, in 2007, McCoy and Hermansen (2007) published a review of video modeling and by that time, the number of publications had doubled: Their review evaluated 34 articles.

> Video modeling is a behavioral technique that uses videotapes rather than live scenarios for a child to observe, thus allowing the focus of attention to be concentrated on the stimulus tape. (McCoy & Hermansen, 2007, p. 183)

Modeling is an evidence-based practice where a learner observes and then imitates a demonstrated or modeled behavior (Buggey, 2009; Nikopoulos & Keenan, 2006). There are a number of hypotheses about why individuals with ASD may prefer to imitate behaviors they observe from a video model rather than from live models; these hypotheses may account for the success that video modeling has had with this population. In fact, some practitioners and individuals with ASD describe many individuals with this disorder as visual learners (Grandin, 1999). Research has revealed successful acquisition of skills by learners with ASD when models were adults (e.g., Charlop-Christy & Daneshvar, 2003; MacDonald, Clark, Garrigan, & Vangala, 2005), peers (e.g., MacDonald, Sacramone, Mansfield, Wiltz, & Ahearn, 2009; Nikopoulos & Keenan, 2004), siblings (e.g., Reagon, Higbee, & Endicott, 2006; Taylor, Levin, & Jasper, 1999), and the self (e.g., Buggey, 1995; Wert & Neisworth, 2003). Researchers have also evaluated comparisons of the type of model on the behaviors and skills of individuals with ASD (e.g., Cihak & Schrader, 2008; Sherer et al., 2001).

Published studies have included individuals with ASD across ages and target skills. Studies with preschoolers have addressed play skills (Hine & Wolery, 2006; MacDonald et al., 2009; Reagon et al., 2006; Wert & Neisworth, 2003) and social skills (Gena, Couloura, & Kymissis, 2005). Elementary age students have been taught purchasing skills (Alcantara, 1994) and social skills (Buggey, 2005; Charlop-Christy & Daneshvar,

2003; Nikopoulos & Keenan, 2004) via video modeling. Video modeling with adolescents and young adults was used to evaluate increases in vocational skills (Cihak & Schrader, 2008). Adults ages 34 to 36 were taught to use a microwave oven for making popcorn (Sigafoos, O'Reilly, & Cannella, 2005) using video modeling.

Point-of-view modeling is considered when the video is made from the perspective of the individual watching and is focused on what the learner may see (McCoy & Hermansen, 2007). For example, Hine and Wolery (2006) created a video of adult hands using toys appropriately during play. Video has also been used to prepare an individual for a potentially stressful or unknown event such as going to the local shopping mall, taking a flight on an airplane, or going to the dentist. This strategy, referred to as video priming (Schreibman, Whalen, & Stahmer, 2000), uses a video taken at the actual mall, dentist's office, or other place that may be visited from the perspective of the individual with ASD; the video is shown to the individual as close to the event as possible to prepare him or her for what will happen in the near future.

## Incorporating Peers and Parents

You may want peers or parents to manage contingencies for some skills. Social skills in particular may benefit from involvement of peers or family members. Strategies that have resulted in increased peer interactions have included the use of **peer tutors**, or enlisting the assistance of a peer to facilitate the practice of skills such as greetings, play initiation, and knowledge of math facts and vocabulary words (Odom & Strain, 1986). Time delay is a demonstrated effective practice used to teach a variety of skills, including increasing social and communication abilities in children with autism spectrum disorders (Hwang & Hughes, 2000).

Parents have been, and continue to be, actively involved in programs for their children with autism. Dr. Ivar Lovaas and Drs. Krantz and McClannahan, developers of some of the earliest models, taught parents how to implement behavioral strategies and worked in the home to ensure consistency across educators. Family involvement is an essential component of programs that use strategies based on applied behavior analysis (Handleman & Harris, 2001), including those developed for school-age children with autism (Handleman & Harris, 2006). Parents can be taught to use strategies based on behavior analysis effectively (Moreland, Schwebel, Beck, & Wells, 1982; Sheinkopf & Siegel, 1998), and parents and professionals working collaboratively can increase the skills of students with autism spectrum disorders (Devlin & Harber, 2004). Parent or family education is an essential component of effective models (Rogers & Vismara, 2008; Strain & Bovey, 2011) and it is necessary to foster skill generalization and maintenance (Schreibman & Ingersoll, 2011). In their guide for parents, Harris and Weiss (2007) describe behavioral interventions used with young children with autism, provide examples of some model programs, and provide guidelines for choosing a program.

Parents have been instrumental to the progress of their children and to the dissemination of the science of behavior analysis. Parents are often on the board of directors of educational programs, and they have been an important force behind the dissemination of the ABA Consumer Guidelines (2004) from the Autism Special Interest Group of the Association for Behavior Analysis, International. Parent-organized groups, such as the Empowering Long Island's Journey through Autism (ELIJA) Foundation, Inc., offer support and advocacy for families of children with autism spectrum disorders who prefer applied behavior analysis interventions.

## Key Concepts Put into Practice

A model educational program based on the principles of applied behavior analysis would have motivational systems in place for each student. A variety of reinforcement procedures would be used, all aimed at increasing new skills and increasing time without challenging behavior. Data on student behavior would be recorded accurately by all staff members so that information about effective strategies and the rate of child progress would be shared. IEP objectives would be incorporated into educational activities and individualized for each student.

The environment would be arranged to facilitate stimulus control for relevant and natural cues. Multiple forms of prompts would be in place (visual schedules, auditory instructions, written scripts, palm pilot schedules), as would plans for fading these prompts so that the stimulus control is transferred to the cues used in the natural environment. Parents would be informed and involved, and they would implement strategies at home so that expectations and contingencies for behavior are consistent across settings.

Communication skills would be targeted, and many opportunities to practice would be provided. Oral communication would be the long-range targeted form of communication for all students. Augmentative systems such as sign language or pictures would be used in some programs. Play skills would be taught in a naturalistic manner by enthusiastic educators who incorporate preferred items and use lots of praise statements. Social interaction skills such as initiations and responses to peers would be taught using modeling, scripts, and reinforcement for targeted behaviors. Activities throughout the day would be scheduled, and periods when new skills are targeted would be interspersed with opportunities for students to practice and become fluent with newly acquired behaviors.

Staff training, including feedback to all staff members on performance with implementing behavioral strategies, would be common. Consistency across all staff members would be emphasized in order to maximize student progress. Plans for generalization would be incorporated from the beginning of teaching any new skills. Students would be engaged in activities, making choices, and working independently whenever possible. Both staff members and students would appear to be enjoying their time in the program.

## Ethical Applications

Individuals with autism spectrum disorders can be considered part of a vulnerable population, and it is important that ethical practices are adhered to whenever working with learners with ASD. Families are also vulnerable. Many parents will do just about anything within their means to assist their child and will put their trust into the hands of professionals who claim to have knowledge and skills that can improve the quality of life for their child and family. The increased diagnosis of ASD has resulted in an increased demand for practitioners who can work effectively in the implementation of evidence-based practices such as those based on applied behavior analysis. It is the responsibility of each professional to be aware of, and act in accordance with, ethical guidelines.

> Unlike scientific discovery, which is based on solid data derived from research, ethical guidelines are fluid, value-based, and changing from one time, place and society to another. They are shaped by cultural contingencies. Your responsibility as an investigator and/or practitioner is to stay abreast of your field's current local, regional, and national ethical guidelines. (Mayer et al., 2012, p. 667)

Shook and Favell (1996) identified effective implementation of applied behavior analysis, with a focus on the acquisition of new skills and the ethical application of behavioral principles as the minimum qualification for personnel working with children with autism and their families. Understanding ethics and making choices for practice based on codes of conduct is important for educators in general, including those who use a behavioral approach. Ethical guidelines are created to ensure that the technology based on the principles of behavior analysis is applied in a manner that does not cause harm.

Certification as a behavior analyst that includes a review of the *Guidelines for Responsible Conduct* (2010) is available through the Behavior Analysis Certification Board® (www.bacb.com). Certification as a Board Certified Behavior Analyst (BCBA®) or a Board Certified Associate Behavior Analyst (BCABA®) requires the completion of a board-approved sequence of courses offered at a university, documented field experience guided by a qualified supervisor, and passing an exam. The focus in the courses and practicum experience includes 10 content areas: ethical considerations; definition and characteristics; principles, processes, and concepts; behavioral assessment; experimental evaluation of interventions; measurement of behavior; displaying and interpreting behavioral data; selecting intervention outcomes and strategies; behavior change procedures; and systems support (Cooper et al., 2007; Mayer, et al., 2012). The ethical guidelines reviewed include information on interacting in a professional and ethical manner with reliance on scientifically and professionally derived knowledge. The rights of and responsibilities to clients are also emphasized.

One of the guidelines under treatment efficacy is: "The behavior analyst always has the responsibility to recommend scientifically supported most effective treatment procedures" (Bailey & Burch, 2011, p. 301). However, Bailey and Burch (2011) identify two of the most frequent ethical problems for behavior analysts as (1) the right to effective treatment and (2) the responsibility to recommend scientifically supported and most effective treatments. Working with colleagues and in systems that support the implementation of strategies based on ABA, including data collection, will be one of the likely challenges faced by behavior analysts. Another challenge is that parents and colleagues may choose to implement strategies that are not scientifically based, or they may not value the outcomes from research. This is illustrated in Chapter 1 when parents elected to continue with the GFCF diet in spite of lack of reported effectiveness from a controlled study.

# Research Support for Practice

Evaluations of comprehensive treatment models for individuals with autism spectrum disorders have consistently reported that models based on the principles of behavior analysis have sufficient well-designed research publication to conclude that there is evidence for the effectiveness of this approach. In their review of early intervention programs, Rogers and Vismara (2008) concluded that program models implementing the Lovaas treatment, or discrete trial teaching, was the only model that was in their topic category of "well established." Other reviewers (Howlin Magiati, & Charman, 2009; Reichow & Wolery, 2009) came to the same conclusion; in their reviews of early intensive behavioral intervention (EIBI), "EIBI is an effective treatment, on average, for children with autism" (Reichow & Wolery, 2009, p. 23). The studies included in these reviews were completed in home-based programs (Remington et al., 2007; Sallows & Graupner, 2005; Smith, Groen, & Wynne, 2000) and in preschool classrooms in community settings (Cohen, Amerine-Dickens, & Smith, 2006; Eldevik, Eikeseth, Jahr, & Smith, 2006; Howard, Sparkman, Cohen, Green, & Stanislaw, 2005). Researchers also have compared outcomes from programs using intensive behavioral intervention with other approaches, including special education classes in public schools, and reported positive outcomes for the behavioral approach (e.g., Howard et al., 2005).

Strain and Bovey (2011) published the outcomes of a randomized controlled trial of their model in 28 inclusive preschool classes compared with classrooms receiving their manual alone. The Learning Experiences and Alternative Programs for Preschoolers (LEAP) model is based on the principles of applied behavior analysis, uses incidental teaching, and employs a variety of evidence-based strategies. The inclusion of typical peers, embedding IEP objectives within classroom routines typically found in preschool programs, and providing skill training to family members are essential model components. The intervention consisted of a two-year program with in-vivo demonstrations, training, coaching, and relationship building with staff members who were knowledgeable and skilled in the LEAP model compared with a group of classroom teachers receiving the manuals only. Outcome data were obtained from children with ASD by teachers using a fidelity checklist and teacher ratings on a social validity scale. Results revealed significantly better gains for children in the intervention group on measures of cognitive, social, language, and problem behavior and on autism symptoms (Strain & Bovey, 2011). Not only does the study by Strain and Bovey (2011) provide additional support for the effectiveness of models based on applied behavior analysis, but the result from their study that teachers' scores on the fidelity of intervention checklist predicted child outcomes indicates the importance of implementing the strategies as designed and effectively (review Chapter 3 for discussion of implementation science).

Outcomes from a program from a model similar to LEAP were collected from the Children's Toddler School. Compared with LEAP, this model has more of an emphasis on PRT and includes some one-to-one sessions using discrete trial teaching in a separate room from the inclusive classroom. The Children's Toddler School is located in a clinical setting; the LEAP classrooms were located in public schools. An evaluation of this program revealed that there were significant increases in scores on standardized assessments and in performance on functional measures, with 37% of the young children with ASD functioning in the typical range at exit compared with 11% at program entry (Stahmer & Ingersoll, 2004).

There is now a large corpus of data supporting the effectiveness of behavioral interventions for the treatment of children with autism spectrum disorders (ASDs). In fact, treatments based upon a behavioral (learning theory) model are the only treatments with a strong empirical basis. (Schreibman & Ingersoll, 2011, p. 1056)

In conclusion, a large body of research has demonstrated the meritorious effects of using strategies based on the principles of applied behavior analysis (ABA) with individuals on the autism spectrum (National Autism Center, 2009b; Odom, Boyd, Hall, & Hume, 2010; Odom, Collet-Klingenberg, Rogers, & Hatton, 2010). The vast majority of the identified evidence-based strategies (National Autism Center, 2009a; Odom, Collet-klingenberg et al., 2010) and the models with the highest ratings across categories (Odom, Boyd et al., 2010) are those based on applied behavior analysis.

## SUGGESTIONS FOR DISCUSSION

1. State what the letters ABA stand for and define each of the terms.

2. What are some of the key concepts that are used in any strategies or programs based on the ABA approach?

3. Conduct a debate with one side arguing in support of using discrete trials in any ABA-based program and the other side arguing against the use of discrete trials as the primary or only intervention strategy in a program.

4. Discuss the importance of arranging individualized motivational systems and illustrate the concept with examples.

5. List the technology, or the strategies, based on ABA used to address communication and social skills.

6. Describe the possible outcomes from programs based on ABA using research studies and the interview with Eric (see In Their Words 4.2) as your sources.

7. Explain why ABA is considered a scientifically based or evidence-based approach.

8. One of the defining aspects of ABA is that it is used to address "socially important behaviors." Discuss what these behaviors are for individuals with autism spectrum disorders.

## RESOURCES

### Textbooks on Applied Behavior Analysis

Alberto, P. A., & Troutman A. C. (2009). *Applied behavior analysis for teachers* (7th ed.). Upper Saddle River, NJ: Pearson Education.

Cooper, J., Heron, T., & Heward, W. (2007). *Applied behavior analysis* (2nd ed.). Upper Saddle River, NJ: Pearson Education.

Mayer, G. R., Sulzer-Azaroff, B., & Wallace, M. (2012). *Behavior analysis for lasting change.* Cornwall-on-Hudson, NY: Sloan.

### Curriculum Guides

Leaf, R., & McEachin, J. (1999). *A work in progress: Behavior management strategies and a curriculum for intensive behavioral treatment of autism.* New York: DRL.

Lovaas, O. I. (2003). *Teaching individuals with developmental delays: Basic intervention techniques.* Austin, TX: Pro-Ed.

LEAP Outreach Project (2003a). *Classroom management in the inclusive classroom.* Teacher's Toolbox.

LEAP Outreach Project (2003b). *Nurturing social skills in the inclusive classroom.*

Taylor, B. A., & Jasper, S. (2001). Teaching programs to increase peer interaction. In C. Maurice, G. Green, & R. Foxx (Eds.), *Making a difference: Behavioral intervention for autism* (pp. 97–162). Austin, TX: Pro-Ed.

Taylor, B. A., & McDonough, K. A. (1996). Selecting teaching programs. In C. Maurice, G. Green, & S. Luce (Eds.), *Behavioral intervention for young children with autism: A manual for parents and professionals* (pp. 63–177). Austin, TX: Pro-Ed.

## Websites

*www.bacb.com*

The Behavior Analysis Certification Board.

*www.behavior.org*

Autism section of the Cambridge Center for Behavioral Studies.

*www.murdochfoundation.org*

Program library has task analyses available for purchase.

# CHAPTER FIVE

# Applied Behavior Analysis: Replacing Behavior

## CHAPTER OBJECTIVES

The reader should be able to:

- List the most common functions of problem behavior.
- Identify the skills needed to design, implement, and monitor a behaviorally based assessment and intervention plan.
- Identify strategies to prevent problem or challenging behaviors from occurring.
- Describe how to include self-management as a program component of a reductive intervention.

The same theoretical basis of behavior analysis is used to guide practices to increase behavior or skills, or decrease behavior. The key concepts of selecting socially important behaviors, reinforcement, and observation and measurement will be addressed again, but in relation to replacing problem behavior with meaningful and functional skills. The concept of punishment will be introduced. Strategies used to address problem or challenging behavior for individuals with autism spectrum disorders, beginning with a functional assessment, will be identified. How strategies can be put into practice will be explained. The chapter will conclude with a review of the research support for the strategies discussed.

In their review article on behavioral treatment of autism, Matson, Benavidez, Compton, Paclawskyj, and Baglio (1996) identify the most frequently addressed challenging behaviors as stereotypy, aggression, and self-injurious behavior. These targets remained consistent as determined in a review of published articles from 1968 to 2003, focusing on participants with autism spectrum disorder (ASD), in the *Journal of Applied Behavior Analysis* (Wolery, Barton, & Hine, 2005). The highest percentage of targeted behaviors for deceleration in the 605 articles analyzed were found for unspecified or multiple behaviors, and stereotypic, self-injurious, aggressive, and disruptive behaviors.

The most effective way an educator can address the behaviors of individuals with autism spectrum disorders that are problematic for learning or challenging to participation in an environment with others is to gain a good understanding of the information and procedures described in Chapter 4. In other words, the ability to teach new skills to individuals with ASD is of critical importance. For example, individuals with many communication and social skills are less likely to use inappropriate behavior to communicate their wants and needs.

> The practice of reducing or eliminating problem behavior must be reconceptualized as the practice of teaching replacement behaviors that are at once adaptive, prosocial, functionally equivalent and socially valid. (Powers, Palmieri, D'Eramo, & Powers, 2011, p. 86)

The best way to prevent problem behaviors from occurring is to create a motivating environment with built-in reinforcers for students with ASD so that they maintain high levels of engagement. Environmental arrangements and the inclusion of motivational systems are important aspects of positive behavioral supports that function as preventive strategies (McGee & Daly, 1999). If challenging behaviors are targeted for decreasing, then it will be important for educators to know how to teach replacement behaviors and skills. If an educator designs and implements an intervention to reduce problem behavior but does not design a plan to teach replacement behaviors, it is unlikely that the intervention will be effective over time. It is worth repeating that knowledge of the principles of applied behavior analysis and competence in teaching new skills through the evidence-based strategies of shaping, modeling, prompting, and positive reinforcement (Odom, Collet-Klingenberg, Rogers, & Hatton, 2010) are fundamental to creating a positive, functional, and enjoyable educational environment (see Chapter 4).

The effectiveness of applied behavior analysis to reduce problem behavior has been demonstrated through research spanning the previous 30 years. Examples include decreasing echolalia (Schreibman & Carr, 1978), stereotypic behavior (Dyer, 1987; Haring, Breen, Pitts-Conway, & Gaylord-Ross, 1986; Harris & Wolchik, 1979), and forms of aggressive behavior toward others (Matson et al., 1996). The history of the use of principles to address behavior that has interfered with learning or is a problem for individuals, including those with autism spectrum disorders, is described in the next section.

## Evolution of Applied Behavior Analysis to Decrease Behavior

- In the late 1960s, Todd Risley and colleagues demonstrated how applied behavior analysis can be used effectively to reduce self-injurious behavior with Dicky (not his real name), a young child with autism (Risley, 1996).

- In the early 1970s, research was published demonstrating the effectiveness of punishment to reduce challenging behavior (e.g., Harris & Wolchik, 1979; Koegel, Firestone, Kramme, & Dunlap, 1974).

- In 1977, Edward Carr (1977) published "The Motivation of Self-Injurious Behavior: A Review of Some Hypotheses" in the *Psychological Bulletin*, where he stated that different motivational factors are likely to influence treatment selection.

- In the 1970s and early 1980s, concerns arose regarding the misuse of aversive strategies. Some professionals called for laws prohibiting the use of aversive strategies. Some behavior analysts debated the issue, stating that not using known effective strategies to address severe injury would also be unethical and harmful.

- In the 1980s, many states created policies to govern the use of any aversive strategies with individuals with disabilities. Educators are required to try to use positive approaches whenever possible and to document the lack of effect of these strategies prior to using any, more restrictive procedures.

■ In 1982, Brian Iwata and colleagues, who worked with individuals with severe self-injurious behavior, began to hypothesize that these behaviors served multiple functions. They developed an experimental technology for identifying the functions of problem behavior (Iwata, Dorsey, Slifer, Bauman, & Richman, 1982).

■ Durand and Crimmins (1987) published a 16-item survey, the Motivation Assessment Scale, that can be completed by service professionals working with individuals exhibiting self-injurious behavior as a first step for identifying the possible function of this behavior. The four possible categories of function include sensory reinforcement, escape, attention, and wanting tangibles.

■ In 1989, the Association for Behavior Analysis completed a position statement on the Right to Effective Behavioral Treatment.

■ In 1994, the research by Iwata and colleagues was republished in the *Journal of Applied Behavior Analysis*, with their results from single-subject research of 152 individuals with self-injurious behavior. Through functional analyses conducted in clinical settings, they determined that escape from demand or positive social reinforcement was the function for 64% of the sample.

■ In 1997, the revision of the Individuals with Disabilities Education Act (IDEA) stated that a functional behavioral assessment must be conducted (IDEA, 20 USC P 1414 [d][3][B][i]) if the individualized education program (IEP) team is aware of a pattern of behavior that impedes the learning of the student or of another student, or the behavior subjects the student to disciplinary action such as suspension, expulsion, or removal of an interim alternative educational setting. In the second situation, if a behavior intervention plan (BIP) does not exist, the team must develop one, or if one exists, it must be reviewed for necessary modifications.

■ In 2004, with the reauthorization of the Individual with Disabilities Education Improvement Act, the use of positive behavioral interventions and supports was emphasized. The conduct of functional behavior assessment by districts is now mandated, and the implementation of a behavior intervention plan (BIP) is required when a behavior is determined to be a manifestation of a student's disability (Ryan, Katsiyannis, Peterson, & Chmelar, 2007).

## Selecting Socially Important Behaviors

When determining which behaviors to target, it is important to address those behaviors that are dangerous to the individual or others (Glasberg, 2005) or those that pose a safety risk (running into the street). Those that interfere with the adaptive functioning of the individual or those that result in the individual remaining in a more restrictive environment (hitting others, engaging in high rates of stereotypy, lack of attending skills) are also important behaviors to target. If the challenging behaviors are not dangerous and do not interfere with adaptive functioning, then it is suggested that the interventionist start working with the challenging behavior where the intervention is the most likely to be successful (Glasberg, 2005). Kratochwill, Sheridan, Carlson, and Lasecki (1999) suggest guidelines for selecting target behaviors, beginning with those that are physically dangerous to the individual or others, are aversive by virtue of the deviance, maximize the individual's opportunities in the long-term, and are constructive rather than reductive. They suggest that targets are selected in collaboration with significant others; targets that are most irritating to interventionists and significant others should also be considered a high priority. These authors agree with Glasberg that the team may want to start with the behavior with the greatest potential for success.

# Reinforcement

Reinforcement, both positive and negative, is a focus when addressing challenging behaviors. Positive reinforcement has occurred when a behavior is followed immediately by the presentation of a stimulus and, as a result, similar responses occur more frequently in the future (Cooper, Heron, & Heward, 2007). **Negative reinforcement** occurs when a behavior produces the contingent removal, termination, reduction, or postponement of a stimulus, which leads to an increase in the future probability of the occurrence of that behavior (Cooper et al., 2007). If the consequence for kicking a chair or tantrums is the removal of the demand for an educational activity or removal of the presence of an adult, then negative reinforcement could be what is maintaining the challenging behavior.

Challenging behavior used by individuals with ASD that serves the function of escaping from demands made by others is a commonly determined function (Alberto & Troutman, 2009; Iwata et al., 1994). In these situations, it is typically negative reinforcement that is maintaining the behavior. In other words, if a teacher stops making demands every time the student yells or pinches or contingently removes the demanding task, then the teacher has been using negative reinforcement, resulting in an increased probability that the challenging behavior will maintain or increase. Of course, this is not what the teacher intends to do.

## Extinction

Extinguishing or withholding reinforcement for a previously reinforced behavior, or using an **extinction procedure** (Cooper et al., 2007; Mayer,

Sulzer-Azaroff, & Wallace, 2012), is a procedure that has been demonstrated in experimental and applied situations by behavior analysts. Sensory extinction can be used for behaviors that are maintained by automatic reinforcement, such as physical sensation from scratching or pinching of the hand or arm (Cooper et al., 2007). If the child is required to wear gloves, the reinforcing effect of the scratching is removed (Cooper et al., 2007). Both the desired outcome of behavioral reduction when using extinction and the likely pattern or reactions to the use of extinction have been well researched (Mayer et al., 2012).

An example of extinction used for a behavior maintained by attention would be a child who receives a drink of water, or several drinks from a caregiver, if he or she begins to cry or call out that he or she is thirsty. The child would be receiving positive reinforcement for the crying or calling out. If extinction is recommended so that the drinks of water are terminated or withheld, several outcomes are likely. Initially the child is likely to increase his or her rate of the behavior, referred to as **extinction bursts** (Mayer et al., 2012). Demands will get louder and the crying will get more intense. There also may be **extinction-induced aggression**. If the louder cries continue to be ignored or put on extinction, then a shoe may be thrown across the room as a way to obtain attention and the withheld reinforcer (Mayer et al., 2012).

It is important to note that the extinction process takes time. If the behavior is one that needs to be reduced immediately, then extinction may not be the procedure of choice. There also must be consistency across all people implementing the procedure in all environments to prevent the occurrence of intermittent reinforcement. For example, if the child's grandmother comes to visit and answers the cry for water with drinks and attention, then it will take that much longer for the strategy to work. In a classroom, this means that all educators and paraeducators need to act consistently if an extinction procedure is recommended for behavioral reduction so that the procedure will be effective.

If extinction is put into place in one setting and not another (e.g., at school but not at home) then **behavioral contrast** can occur. Learners, including those with autism spectrum disorders, are quick to learn the contingencies in place within a specific environment. Behavioral contrast occurs when there is an increase in a behavior in one setting due to the implementation of a reductive procedure such as extinction in another setting (Mayer et al., 2012). It is important to note that research has revealed that if a behavior is targeted for a procedure to decrease the occurrence in one setting and not in another setting where the behavior occurs, it is likely that there will be an increase in the setting without the procedure (Cooper et al., 2007). In other words, if you target a behavior at school, it will be important to inform the family because they may see an increase in the behavior at home.

Even if there is consistency across people and across settings and the behavior is reduced for a period of time, it can recur. This reoccurrence is referred to as **spontaneous recovery**. If the same response occurs or it is ignored consistently, then it is likely to go away again.

Although extinction may appear to educators as a relatively easy procedure to implement, it is important to the success of the procedure that the educator knows about extinction bursts, behavioral contrast, extinction-induced aggression, and spontaneous recovery. In addition, it may seem easier to withhold reinforcement than it is in practice. It may be difficult to control facial expressions or the reactions of peers. It is often necessary to include a plan for what behaviors the others, including those implementing the procedure, will do when a problem behavior targeted for extinction does occur.

## Differential Reinforcement

Behavioral reduction is not recommended without the implementation of strategies to increase replacement or alternative behaviors. Differential reinforcement is an evidence-based procedure (Odom, Boyd et al., 2010) that can be used to build replacement skills. The definition of **differential reinforcement** is the process of reinforcing one response class and withholding reinforcement for another (Cooper et al., 2007). Differential reinforcement can be used to provide positive reinforcement at the same time that extinction of targeted problem behaviors is used. For example, if the behavior is maintained by attention, then extinction for that behavior while providing lots of attention for an alternative and appropriate behavior (**differential reinforcement of alternative behavior [DRA]**) is likely to reduce the challenging behavior. If a learner's calling out in class is ignored but hand raising is immediately responded to with attention and praise, it is probable that hand raising will increase and calling out will decrease.

This procedure works best if the alternative behavior selected is incompatible with the challenging behavior. When an incompatible behavior is selected, the procedure is referred to as **differential reinforcement of incompatible behavior (DRI)** (Alberto & Troutman, 2009; Mayer et al., 2012). An example that has been used successfully is reinforcing the behavior of holding books or a toy during transitions between activities for a student who either touches others or uses his or her hands for stimulatory behavior. If the behaviors targeted for reduction (in this case inappropriate touching) are not possible while the student is holding books, then the new behaviors are considered incompatible.

**Differential reinforcement of other behavior (DRO)** is a procedure in which a reinforcer is delivered for the absence or omission of problem behavior (Mayer et al., 2012) during a set time interval. A preschooler may receive a reinforcer for participating in circle for a brief period of time without touching his peers. Educators would ensure through data collection that the targeted problem behavior (in this case, inappropriately touching peers) had not occurred before any delivery of the reinforcer.

Tolerating delayed reinforcement is important for all students. Some individuals with autism spectrum disorders need to be taught to wait for a reinforcer or reinforcing consequence. One procedure to teach delay of reinforcement involves the following four steps: (1) the individual makes a request; (2) the educator then asks the individual to carry out some constructive activity in exchange for reinforcement afterward; (3) when the activity is completed, the individual requests again; and (4) the educator acknowledges that the activity has been completed satisfactorily and then honors the request (Carr et al., 1994).

## Noncontingent Reinforcement

Noncontingent reinforcement is another procedure that can be used with decreasing challenging behavior as a goal (Alberto & Troutman, 2009). To create a reinforcing environment for the individual, rewards are provided regularly on fixed or variable schedules of administration rather than presented contingent on identified behavior (Mayer et al., 2012). The rationale for using this procedure is that the educator is providing the reinforcers that are valued and thereby reducing the likelihood that the learner will engage in problem behavior in order to access these rewards. The disadvantage of selecting this approach is that replacement behaviors are not targeted and increased. In addition, a behavior that happens to occur just prior to the delivery of the reward, including the behavior targeted to be decreased, may be inadvertently reinforced and increased (Alberto & Troutman, 2009).

# Punishment

Punishment is another principle of behavior analysis that has been identified through experimental research with animals and people in laboratories and in applied settings. **Punishment** is defined by its function of decreasing or reducing behavior (Alberto & Troutman, 2009). Similar to reinforcement, punishment can also be **positive** (the contingent presentation of a stimulus) or **negative** (the termination or removal of an already present stimulus) (Cooper et al., 2007; Mayer et al., 2012). This term is challenging to many because of the common understanding of

the concept of punishment in the general public as a negative consequence that is harsh.

The following is an illustration of punishment that is consistent with the technical definition but differs from how most people would think of a punishing event. If a child with autism spectrum disorder who usually talks to adults is required to participate in a group activity with peers, and group activities consistently result in a decrease in vocalizations by this learner, then technically the decreased vocal behavior is a consequence of punishment in the presence of peers. However, the term *punishment* is considered by most to mean something aversive that is presented rather than the actual consequence of behavior. It is important for educators who are designing intervention strategies based on applied behavior analysis to understand this different interpretation of punishment.

Similarly, some individuals with autism spectrum disorders may seek behaviors (physical restraint, raised voices by adults) that most people would consider punishing. If these responses were delivered contingently following a problem behavior, the behavior might increase or actually be reinforced. The only way to know what the real consequences are is to collect data and review the pattern of behavior of the learner. The use of punishment can have negative side effects that have been determined through research; consequently, the use of punishment is not recommended unless other approaches have been tried first. Punishment should not be implemented without informed consent.

Physical restraint as a reductive procedure, especially when the learner is doing harm to self or others, has been used for brief periods or to remove the learner to a safe environment. Typically, specialized training in use of such procedures is required before they are implemented so that the safety and comfort of all students are addressed. It is also important to understand that the use of aversive procedures has demonstrated negative consequences. The demonstrated negative side effects of the use of punishment include aggressive or withdrawing behavior in the presence of the punisher, and the student may try to escape or avoid the situation where there has been a history of punishment (Alberto & Troutman, 2009). It is also particularly important to avoid using behavior reduction procedures that can lead to increased social avoidance by learners with autism spectrum disorders (McGee & Daly, 1999).

When selecting intervention procedures, it is the ethical responsibility of the educator to follow the doctrine of the **least restrictive alternative** and try the less intrusive procedures first; only if they have been found to be ineffective are more intrusive procedures to be implemented (Cooper et al., 2007). If any aversive procedures are considered for an individual with autism spectrum disorder, it is required by law that the procedures follow the guidelines set out by the local school system and courts. Only a team of professionals directly involved with the student and the student's parent or guardian can design and approve such a program. Data indicating that the behavior is severe enough to warrant such intrusive strategies and that previous procedures have been implemented effectively without success must be presented. Ongoing staff training, including an understanding of the negative side effects of such procedures, is a requirement.

## Motivating Operations

**Motivating operations (MOs)** are variables that have a value-altering effect on reinforcement or punishment (Glasberg, 2005; Michael, 2007). The motivating operation (MO) can be an establishing operation that increases the reinforcing effectiveness of a stimulus. The MO can also be an abolishing operation that decreases the reinforcing effectiveness (Michael, 2007). For example, if a student with autism has been given raisins as a reward all day, the raisins may lose their reinforcing power because the student is satiated. The amount of food would have an abolishing effect on the potency of the raisins used as a reinforcer. Another example is that a

student may be likely to exhibit a specific behavior, such as playing with a musical toy in a quiet room with one adult, but not in a crowded room with lots of noise and many adults. A quiet room would be an establishing operation that increases the effectiveness of play with the musical toy.

Individuals can be establishing operations for social interaction; in other words, conversation with a particular person may increase the reinforcing value of that dialogue for a child with ASD. The medication Risperidone may act as an establishing operation for food because it has a side effect of increased appetite, or it may act as an abolishing operation by making certain events less reinforcing (Crosland et al., 2003). It is important to evaluate the effects of any medication on the behavior of the individual with autism spectrum disorder.

## Observation and Measurement

Although challenging behavior is not a defining characteristic of autism spectrum disorders (www.dsm5.org), lack of communication skills and the strong adherence to ritual and routine can lead to problem behaviors if proactive and educational strategies are not put into place (Horner, Albin, Sprague, & Todd, 2000). Skills in observation and measurement in order to collect valid and reliable data are critical for the educator who is planning any intervention plan. Without knowledge of how to define, observe, record, and analyze data, educators are unable to determine if any intervention plan is working. The issues related to observation and measurement that were addressed in Chapter 4 are relevant for the observation and measurement of behaviors targeted for reduction or replacement.

### Stimulus-Response-Consequence or Antecedent-Behavior-Consequence (ABC)

Knowledge about antecedents and consequences related to a problem behavior is equally important when planning strategies to decrease challenging behavior as it is when planning to increase skills. An **ABC analysis** can be used when observing the problem behavior to determine possible triggers or antecedent events associated with the behavior and possible controlling consequences. In her follow-up book on functional behavior assessment, Glasberg (2008) provides a checklist for collecting ABC data, with columns labeled with questions such as, What happened *just* before the problem behavior? What was the behavior? What happened *just* after the problem behavior? Did the behavior immediately stop?

The behavioral concepts previously reviewed are described in a workbook for preschool staff as part of the manual *Classroom Management in Inclusive Classrooms* developed by the LEAP Outreach Project directed by Philip Strain (LEAP Outreach Project, 2003a). The manual is easy to read and clearly describes behavioral principles so the preschool educator can respond to undesirable behaviors and build alternative skills such as communication. Strategies for ongoing progress monitoring or keeping track of behavior are also included.

## Functional Analysis and Assessment

A functional analysis of behavior is an experimental method used to determine the function of a behavior considered challenging or problematic (Mayer et al., 2012). Functional analyses are typically conducted in well-controlled settings such as clinics and research facilities. Funcational assessments use multiple measures to determine the possible function of a problem or challenging behavior and are more likely to be conducted in less controlled settings such as in public schools. Functions can be grouped into two categories: those used to obtain or maintain access or those used to escape or avoid stimuli. For example, escaping from a less preferred activity or from social interaction may be the function of challenging behavior such as crying or yelling, especially if the behavior has been previously negatively reinforced.

The outcomes from the experimental analyses of behavior conducted by Iwata and colleagues (1982) with individuals with self-injurious behavior yielded four functions: to gain attention, to access sensory stimulation, to request items or activities, and to escape from demand. In their research, environmental conditions were systematically manipulated by presenting and removing attention, demanding tasks, time alone, and preferred objects or items under controlled conditions in a clinic to determine the **functional relationships**. If the behavior increases under any of these conditions, it can be concluded that there is most likely a functional relationship. In other words, by systematically altering the conditions, such as the amount of attention given following the display of the problem behavior and altering the various conditions over time, the team could determine the functional relationship between rates of behavior and the condition based on response differentiation. Once a function has been **hypothesized**, a strategy is selected based on **functional equivalence**. In other words, you want to teach a skill that serves the same or equivalent function as the problem behavior (Scheuermann & Hall, 2012). Only after you implement a strategy for a replacement skill that occurs reliably with a demonstrated decrease in the problem behavior can the assumed function be confirmed.

## Brief Functional Analysis

A brief functional analysis is an adapted version of the experimental analysis intended for use due to staffing constraints or urgency in addressing the problem behavior (Glasberg, 2005). In this analysis, all possible functions are tested once and then the conditions with the highest and lowest rates of behavior are analyzed further to determine a pattern, or functional, relationship.

Brief functional analyses were conducted by teachers in a classroom setting followed by the implementation of strategies that resulted in decreases in challenging behaviors (self-injury, hand-mouthing, aggression) of five students (Northup et al., 1994). The teachers were trained in a two-day workshop with opportunity for practice in a similar situation. They also received weekly half-day consultation visits by the researcher (Northup et al., 1994). This study provides a demonstration of the effective use of brief functional analyses by teachers who had support from a consulting researcher.

## Functional Behavior Assessment

> Functional assessment is a process for gathering information that can be used to maximize the effectiveness and efficiency of behavioral support. (O'Neill et al., 1997, p. 3)

This assessment process, used in applied settings such as schools, typically includes (1) interviewing multiple sources regarding the target behavior, including interviewing the individual with ASD if possible; (2) direct observation of the problem or challenging behavior over time and in multiple contexts; and (3) systematic manipulation of variables to determine the function of the behavior or the completion of a functional analysis (O'Neill et al., 1997).

Sample interview forms can be found in a number of published texts, including *Functional Assessment and Program Development for Problem Behavior* (O'Neill et al., 1997), *Functional Behavior Assessment for People with Autism* (Glasberg, 2005), and *Functional Assessment* (Chandler & Dahlquist, 2006). These tools are used to gather information about the form of the target behavior in order to better operationalize it, and to determine perceived times and situations when the behavior is most likely to occur. In addition, information about preferences, communication skills, and physiological factors that may influence the behavior is also collected.

The Motivation Assessment Scale (MAS) was developed (Durand, 1988; Durand, 1990) as a questionnaire to be completed by staff members who work directly with individuals who display challenging behavior. This 16-item tool provides input that is a start for determining the function of a behavior as either sensory, escape, attention getting, or obtaining tangibles. Researchers caution that the MAS may not show

good agreement with observational measures and should not be used as the only assessment tool (Johnston & O'Neill, 2001).

Direct observation of behavior confirms the impressions reported in the interview (Carr et al., 1994). Behavioral observation and measurement begin with a clear description of the target behavior or by operationalizing the behavior (Cooper et al., 2007). For example, the broad term *aggression* can be defined as hitting or pushing a peer with an open or closed hand for a single stroke or in an episode of multiple strokes to any part of the body. It is important that all observers have a clear definition of the behavior to be recorded for reliability purposes.

In addition to collecting data on the occurrence of the identified behavior, it is important to collect information on the antecedents and consequences. Antecedent information includes the general activities, times of day, interactive partners, comments directed to the student, and so on, in order to identify possible triggers or consistent antecedents that occur prior to, or along with, the target behavior. It is also important to collect data throughout the day in order to collect information about the possible effects of motivating operations.

Collecting data on the pattern of consequences provides valuable information about the possible function of the behavior. At this point in the process, a hypothesis regarding the functional relationship may be created (Glasberg, 2005). Perhaps it appears from the interview that attention is maintaining the behavior. The next step would be to verify your hypothesis or to observe the student under the condition that is thought to result in high rates of the behavior and compare it to another condition that is thought to result in low rates (Glasberg, 2005).

For example, if the student is consistently removed from the activity or consistently receives attention following the behavior, a reinforcing consequence may be identified. Research has demonstrated that challenging behavior is often maintained by attention. Even if the teacher approaches a student who just kicked a chair and says, "Please stop kicking chairs. You are not following the class rules," the student is receiving attention as a consequence of his behavior. It is important that a team member with knowledge of the principles of behavior analysis is monitoring the verification of the hypothesis. It is important to know about extinction and the likely escalation of a behavior under these conditions if the plan is to remove attention. These skills are especially important when addressing behaviors that are severe (Glasberg, 2005).

Once data are collected, the hypothesis about the function can be tested (Glasberg, 2005, 2008). Antecedents can be manipulated, such as by arranging for one-to-one and group instruction or changing the demand of tasks presented. The sample data sheet in Figure 5–1 includes information about multiple conditions and the frequency of the target behavior.

Eliminating the setting events (conditions related to the problem behavior in that setting) successfully reduced the associated problem behavior of two adolescents attending a public high school (Kennedy & Itkonen, 1993). The addition of a visual cue card (red circle with a line through it) helped reduce stereotypic behavior of a kindergarten student with autism spectrum disorder by providing a discriminative cue associated with environments where stereotypic behavior was not appropriate (Conroy, Asmus, Sellers, & Ladwig, 2005). Enriching the environment with preferred toys reduced the automatically reinforced scratching behavior of two children with autism (Sidener, Carr, & Firth, 2005). Changing the antecedent in the form of instruction from directive to nondirective prompts effectively reduced the noncompliant vocal behavior of a 10-year-old with autism (Peyton, Lindauer, & Richman, 2005). Each of these antecedent interventions was made following a functional analysis or assessment.

Suggested strategies when the behavior is maintained by automatic reinforcement include making sure the individual with autism always has direction about how to stay on task, ensuring that the activity is stimulating enough to compete with the automatic reinforcement behaviors, ruling out illness or injuries, providing free access to similar but appropriate activities, and

considering free access to automatic reinforcement in a certain place (Glasberg, 2008).

Note that behaviors can serve multiple functions or different functions at different times. Also, more than one behavior can be used to serve the same function (Glasberg, 2005). The same behavior may serve different functions at school and at home. Parents have been instrumental in completing functional assessments and identifying replacement behaviors to target at home (Lucyshyn, Kayser, Irvin, & Blumberg, 2002). Conducting an assessment of family routines and ecology is included in a functional assessment completed in the home to ensure a contextual fit for any plan. Frequently, the inclusion of supports for the family members as they implement and evaluate any intervention plan over the long term is needed (Lucyshyn, Kayser, et al., 2002.).

## Implementation of Functional Assessments in Collaboration with Families

Fox, Dunlap, and Buschbacher (2000) describe comprehensive **positive behavioral support** (PBS) as being comprised of a functional assessment, person-centered planning, the development of behavioral hypotheses, and support plan development. Families are partners in the functional assessment process. Because families report that problem behavior negatively affects many aspects of their lifestyle, interventions that are acceptable to the family, and effectively implemented across environments, will improve the quality of life for all family members (Fox, Dunlap, & Buschbacher, 2000).

Lucyshyn and colleagues have outlined 12 key features of positive behavior support with families (Lucyshyn, Horner, Dunlap, Albin, & Ben, 2002). Included in these features are building collaborative relationships with families, adhering to family-centered principles, and helping families identify and achieve meaningful lifestyle outcomes for their child with a disability. They also identify conducting a functional assessment, developing individualized, multicomponent support plans, and ensuring that positive behavior support plans are a good contextual fit with family life as key

**Antecedent Manipulations Data Sheet**

**Behavior:** _____

**Definition of Behavior:**

_____

_____

_____

_____

**Date:** _____

**Length of sessions:** _____

**Observer:** _____

**Observed with:** _____

**Define each condition here:** _____

1)

2)

3)

4)

5)

6)

| Condition | Session 1 Total | Session 2 Total | Session 3 Total | Overall Total |
|---|---|---|---|---|
| 1) | | | | |
| 2) | | | | |
| 3) | | | | |
| 4) | | | | |
| 5) | | | | |
| 6) | | | | |
| Which condition elicited the most target behaviors for each session? | | | | |

**FIGURE 5–1** Sample antecedent manipulation data sheet
*Source:* From Glasberg, B. A. 2005, p. 146. *Functional behavior assessment for people with autism: Making sense of seemingly senseless behavior.* Bethesda, MD: Woodbine House. Used with permission.

features. Other key features include providing implementation support, and continuous evaluation of child and family outcomes.

Working in partnership with families is a fundamental aspect of early intervention services. Moes and Frea (2000) found that behavior change was more likely to occur when behavioral supports were contextualized within the family setting, with parents and siblings of a young child with autism as partners, compared with when an intervention was prescribed to the family. As part of their early intervention model in Florida, the **Individualized Support Project (ISP)**, Dunlap and Fox (1999) report reduced problem behavior (tantrums and stereotypy) and increased skill acquisition for six young children with autism spectrum disorders. Essential to the ISP framework is comprehensive family support in the form of teaching the family effective strategies for prevention of problem behavior and the development of replacement skills (Dunlap & Fox, 1999). A detailed and individualized support plan is developed in collaboration with each family, written in simple language, and distributed to all of the child's caregivers (Fox, Benito, & Dunlap, 2002). If desired by the family, the ISP interventionist assists with the generalization of skills to community activities, including those with typical peers.

## Implementation of Functional Assessments by Educators

Although the implementation of functional behavior assessment (FBA) is mandated by IDEA, a research-to-practice gap exists in the effective use of FBA in public schools (Stichter, Shellady, Sealander, & Eigenberger, 2000). It is difficult to control the conditions sufficiently to conduct an experiment in a classroom, and educators rarely have the skills needed to implement and interpret the experimental data. The clinical model therefore must be adapted for use by educators and other school personnel (Stichter et al., 2000). It is also important to consider cultural factors when implementing functional behavior assessments as described by Dr. Angela McIntosh, In Their Words 5.1.

Authors caution that, although predesigned assessment tools and indirect measures such as interviews and surveys are relatively easy to administer, they may not provide valid information (Johnston & O'Neill, 2001; Stichter, 2001). In addition, if the educator does not have the competencies needed to implement a behavior change program and evaluate outcome, the information from the assessment process will be irrelevant. Core knowledge in the principles of applied behavior analysis, discussed in Chapters 4 and 5, is a requisite skill (Stichter et al., 2000).

"Teachers need to be given sufficient time and training to conduct the functional assessment, including analyses" (Stichter, 2001, p. 238). Practitioners need to be able to apply critical thinking along with keen observation skills and be able to interpret data in order to create an effective intervention plan (Stichter et al., 2000). Without these key skills, practitioners are likely to develop ineffective behavior support plans that do not take into account the information obtained from the functional assessment (Johnston & O'Neill, 2001).

The foundational knowledge and skills needed to implement a functional assessment design and behavior management plan can be obtained by completing the requirements for a Board Certified Behavior Analyst® as described in Chapter 4. The competencies obtained in behavioral assessment, observation and measurement of behavior, behavior change procedures, and ethical considerations would be especially relevant to replacing problem behavior. Continued education is one of the requirements of maintaining certification with this board so that behavior analysts remain up to date with research outcomes.

Teachers' opinions about the acceptability of intervention procedures are likely to influence implementation and outcome (Erbas, Tekin-Iftar, & Yucesoy, 2006). Researchers have demonstrated that training in the form of instructional material on functional analysis, a lecture by a scholar, demonstrations of the functional assessment process, and three individual consultations that included feedback resulted in increased

## 5.1 IN THEIR WORDS
**Angela McIntosh,** *Ph.D. Associate Professor,*
*Department of Special Education, San Diego State University*

### Considering Culture with a Functional Behavioral Assessment (FBA)

A functional behavioral assessment approach to addressing problem behavior can be very valuable, particularly in cases where inappropriate or undesirable behavior is rooted in an individual's cultural or ecological basis. Problem behaviors may be occasioned or maintained by variables that would be unidentified through traditional intervention methods, and the influence of these variables might prevent remediation of the problem behavior. For example, it might be difficult to remediate loud vocalizations by a student with autism if those vocalizations are valued and reinforced as indicators of engagement in family and community social settings where high levels of movement, sound, and verbal communication are typically present. Functions of problem behavior are related to student needs and desires; are valid for each individual based on what he or she has experienced; and cannot typically be classified as good or bad, right or wrong. It is the behavior through which these functions are manifested that we identify as appropriate or inappropriate, acceptable or unacceptable.

Functional behavioral assessment helps teachers understand more about their students' home and family lives, communities, customs, and cultures. These understandings are essential to planning and implementing behavioral interventions that will not only promote positive behavior changes in current school settings, but that can also be maintained in other environments. Because culture and environment influence behaviors, we must plan and implement behavioral interventions to decrease problem behaviors within a framework that reflects the dynamic interactions among individuals, their cultural context, and the behaviors we seek to influence.

teacher skills and positive changes in their opinions about functional assessment (Erbas, Tekin-Iftar, & Yucesoy, 2006). Teachers' performances were rated lower during the escape condition. Surveying acceptability was one of the outcomes measures used in a study of functional behavioral assessment in 10 elementary and middle school settings (Crone, Hawken, & Bergstrom, 2007). One year following a team-based training in FBA, 49 team members gave the highest rating to the fact that the team model was effective and that the model is sustainable; they gave the lowest ratings to statements about the training improving BSP implementation skills and having a positive impact on the staff.

Training in how to conduct a functional assessment requires more than a workshop alone and requires an adequate system to support FBA team practices, including coaching within the system where educators work (Scott, Liaupsin, Nelson, & McIntyre, 2005). A training of trainers model that includes the provision of technical feedback, analysis of the application to the individual, and personal facilitation by the trainer or coach is important for the implementation of practice. Several websites provide information and tools for educators that can be used to supplement training or coaching in the use of strategies for replacing problem behaviors, as described next.

The Technical Assistance Center on Social Emotional Intervention for Young Children is a multisite collaborative center that conducts research and disseminates information on best practices for parents and educators on its website, www.challengingbehavior.org. Information at the center is aimed at young children ages 18 to 48 months and their families. The collaborators of the center have reviewed the literature on developing skills in these areas and have recommended practices. *Teaching Tools* (which can be found at the website) is intended to assist teachers in developing plans, including preventive strategies, to support young children who are displaying challenging behavior during routine activities. An important aspect of the center's approach is to connect with the public and disseminate information through strategic partners of grassroots organizations so that the information does not remain with university personnel alone.

The Center for the Social Emotional Foundations for Early Learning (csefel.vanderbilt .edu) is focused on providing support and training to states, and aims to disseminate research and evidence-based practices for work with young children from birth to age 5. Using a pyramid model, personnel begin to develop the foundation for effective practices identified as an effective workforce, nurturing and responsive relationships, and high-quality supportive environments. Targeted social emotional supports and intensive intervention strategies are identified through research reviews with young children and described in What Works Briefs, which is available on the website.

Blair, Lee, Cho, and Dunlap (2011) demonstrated how positive behavior support can be implemented for young children with autism in Korea through a family–school collaboration. Through a partnership among the teachers and mothers for three children, a functional assessment was completed, the function of problem behavior (noncompliance, disruption, aggression, self-injury) was determined, adult behavior (positive and negative interactions) was recorded, and a behavior support plan was created. The result of these collaborations was a decrease in problem behavior both at school and at home. All participants rated the family–school collaboration as acceptable and effective.

## Behavior Intervention Plan (BIP)

The reauthorization of IDEA in 1997 and 2004 requires a functional assessment and behavior intervention plan (BIP), and has resulted in a focus on the development of forms and training protocols to facilitate the process of the creation of a behavioral support plan. School psychologists, special educators, and autism specialists have been the primary targets for education and training in this area. In addition, a focus on positive behavioral supports as preventive strategies is a current emphasis for both approaches aimed at individuals and those intended for larger communities, such as school-wide systems (Lewis & Sugai, 1999).

IDEA requires a behavior intervention plan (BIP) at the following times: (1) at the time of development, review, or revision of an IEP when the team is aware of a pattern of behavior that impedes learning of the student or a peer; and (2) at the time that the occurrence of a behavior subjects a student to disciplinary action (suspension up to 10 days, change of placement, or removal to an interim alternative educational setting). In these situations, a team must create a BIP if it does not exist or review it for necessary modifications if one is in place (Alberto & Troutman, 2009). Any behavior intervention plan must have clearly defined operational definitions of behavior, address generalizations, and require the collecting and graphing of data.

Note that, even with the best information from any form of behavioral assessment, the intervention strategy will be effective only if it is selected and implemented by educators skilled in applied behavior analysis. If a practitioner conducts an extensive functional behavioral assessment but can suggest only a few strategies—such as using a "take a break" card for those individuals who try to escape from demands, or a prearranged social time for individuals seeking attention—the outcomes of such limited intervention options will often be ineffective. An understanding of how to individualize interventions based on the principles of behavior analysis is needed in order for the practitioner to be effective at identifying and implementing strategies to increase and maintain replacement skills.

## Strategies Based on Key Concepts

At present, the emphasis is on prevention of problem behaviors, and if any challenging behaviors occur, the use of positive behavior supports (Carr et al., 2002). Campbell (2003) reviewed behavioral interventions to reduce problem behaviors used with individuals with autism. He found 117 articles published between 1966 and 1998 that included 181 individuals with autism spectrum disorders. Almost half of the studies (53) were published between 1990 and 1998, reflecting the increased use of functional analysis, or assessment and strategies based on function, as required by IDEA. Most of the publications evaluated the use of positive procedures alone ($N = 58$). Extinction alone was used and assessed in 10 articles, aversive procedures in 21, and a combination of strategies in 28 (Campbell, 2003).

Carr (2011) suggests a tripartite model for considering intervention that includes either (1) avoiding, (2) mitigating, or (3) coping. The avoid strategy includes eliminating the trigger stimuli and setting events that evoke the challenging or problem behavior. The focus when mitigating is on altering the problem context, or environmental redesign. Coping includes teaching the learner strategies that address the problem behavior such as functional communication training, self-management, and relaxation. Self-management is discussed later in this chapter.

### Preventing Problem Behaviors

Behavioral educators try to prevent challenging behaviors as the first approach. One of the most important preventive strategies for challenging

behavior in students with autism spectrum disorders is to teach them new skills to communicate (Carr & Durand, 1985), to interact socially with the environment, to remain engaged with tasks, and to access the positive consequences of using acquired skills (Scheuermann & Hall, 2012). When designing positive behavior supports, it is important to consider student preferences and cultural expectations (Koegel, Koegel, & Dunlap, 1996). Parents can also provide invaluable information from their own assessments of their child's behavior in the natural environment (Mullen & Frea, 1996).

> A key principle of positive behavioral supports "is that problem contexts produce problem behaviors; therefore, by modifying problem contexts and the behavioral consequences that help to create these contexts, we should be able to reduce or eliminate problem behaviors." (Carr, 2011, p. 1149)

Creating a learning environment that learners find interesting and fun can result in a high degree of engagement in activities that result in the acquisition of skills (McGee & Daly, 1999). Using a high-probability (high-p) request sequence to prevent problem behavior that functions to escape from tasks or situations has been effective for individuals with ASD (Powers et al., 2011). The requested behaviors that comprise these sequences should be in the learner's repertoire so that he or she earns the opportunity for reinforcement at high levels. Eliminating or reducing periods of time when learners with ASD are required to wait for the next activity or to transition to another environment will reduce the opportunity for the display of problem behaviors (McGee & Daly, 1999). Providing opportunities for making choices has been demonstrated to be related to reductions in problem behavior (Repp, 1994). Trained staff, including teachers and other educators who are good observers of student behavior, can intervene or redirect a learner prior to the display of problem behavior (McGee & Daly. 1999).

Repp (1994) demonstrated that variables related to instruction can be related to the occurrence of problem behavior, and consideration of these variables as they relate to individuals with ASD can serve to prevent challenging behaviors. These variables include presenting a choice of tasks or activities, varying the tasks presented, reducing the task difficulty, embedding low-probability or less preferred tasks in a series of high-probability or preferred tasks, and increasing the pace of instruction. Knowledge about a learner's interests and strengths is important for determining which tasks are considered high-probability for engagement.

McGee and Daly (1999) state that the preventive approach takes a lot of effort from educators—however, so does any problem or challenging behavior. If a behavior of a learner with ASD is considered a problem for the individual or others, an assessment is completed in order to determine the function of the behavior. A collaborative, assessment-based approach to developing individualized interventions for students with challenging or problem behavior is another definition of positive behavior support **(PBS)** (Lucyshyn, Kayser, Irvin, & Blumberg, 2002).

## School-Wide Positive Behavior Supports (SWPBS)

School-wide positive behavior supports (SWPBS) is a systems-level intervention aimed at improving student academic and behavior outcomes. SWPBS has four integrated elements: (1) data for decision making, (2) measurable outcomes supported and evaluated by data, (3) use of practices based on evidence that they are achievable, and (4) systems that support the implementation of these practices. The description of SWPBS, presentations on the topic made by the model developers, and resources such as books and journal publications can be found at the Positive Behavior Interventions and Supports website hosted by a national center offering technical support to states (www.pbis.org). The model used to provide intervention is depicted in a pyramid with primary prevention by the creation of school- and classroom-wide systems as the foundation. Secondary prevention is aimed at

students with at-risk behavior, and tertiary prevention is for a small percentage of the school community and is an individualized and specialized system for students with high risk.

Research using randomized, controlled trials has demonstrated the effectiveness of SWPBS in fewer office detention referrals and suspension rates, greater academic achievement scores (Bradshaw, Mitchell, & Leaf, 2010), and greater perceived safety (Horner et al., 2009) compared with wait-list schools, or those waiting to receive PBS programs. Although program-wide positive behavior supports (PWPBS) has been determined as a socially valid practice for stakeholders working in pre school programs (Frey, Park, Browne-Ferrigno, & Korfhage, 2010), focus groups conducted by other researchers found consistency in the perceived barriers to sustaining school-wide efforts that include a school culture with stakeholders holding various points of view about discipline, lack of administrative leadership and support, lack of a support structure and time, need for ongoing professional development, and need for increased participation from families and students (Bambara, Nonnemacher, & Kern, 2009).

# Functional Communication Training

Functional assessments reveal that problem behaviors may serve as a means to obtain wants and needs or to protest in as many as 75% to 80% of individuals displaying challenging behavior (Koegel, Koegel, Boettcher, Harrower, & Openden, 2006). In some circumstances, teaching the learner an appropriate form of communication to express the same function, such as a means to request wants and needs, to ask for help, or to take a break, instead of using the problem behavior will result in a reduction of problem behavior (Carr & Durand, 1985; Durand, 1990). **Functional communication training** involves using differential reinforcement to teach individuals to request in a socially acceptable way for the same reinforce that has been serving to maintain the problem behavior (Mayer et al., 2012). Functional communication training is identified as one of the evidence-based practices by the National Professional Development Center on ASD (Odom, Collet-Klingenberg, Rogers, & Hatton, 2010).

By teaching an appropriate escape response from difficult tasks, such as using the phrase *help me*, Durand effectively reduced psychotic speech in a child with autism (Durand & Crimmins, 1987) and self-stimulatory behavior in four children with developmental disabilities (Durand & Carr, 1987). Yi and colleagues taught three students with autism to *mand*, or request, the removal of nonpreferred items as a replacement for exhibiting challenging behavior (Yi, Christian, Vittimberga, & Lowenkron, 2006). When taught requests for assistance, students with autism spectrum disorders are less likely to want to escape interactions with educators, and therefore challenging behaviors often decrease when an alternative and appropriate means of getting what is wanted is used. (See Chapter 8 for a description of and research outcomes for functional communication training.)

In another study (Durand & Carr, 1991), a student was taught to get attention from teachers by asking, "Am I doing good work?" which resulted in decreased challenging behavior that was maintained across three school years. Halle, Brady, and Drasgow (2004) suggest that multiple forms of the same function be taught so that individuals with problems in communication can have sufficient strategies for communicative repairs. They provide the example of teaching a child to request wants and needs by using the word for *want* in addition to teaching how to point, so that the child has a choice of effective strategies.

Developing a communication system has the added benefit of preventing problem behaviors that develop because the student does not have another means of expression. Establishing rapport with the student and establishing yourself as a conditioned reinforcer is important when working with students who have communication challenges (Carr et al., 1994). See Chapter 8 for more information regarding the development of communication skills.

## Self-Management

Behavioral strategies have been used to assist students with autism spectrum disorders in monitoring their own behaviors and administering their own rewards. **Self-management of contingencies** is defined as the personal application of behavior change tactics that produces a desired change in behavior (Cooper et al., 2007). It is important for students with autism spectrum disorders to learn to monitor their own progress with acquiring new skills and decreasing the frequency of inappropriate behavior. Self-management skills are an important component of independence. Self-management is an identified evidence-based strategy (National Autism Center, 2009a; Odom, Collet-Klingenberg, et al., 2010).

Self-management consists of **goal setting**, self-recording or **self-monitoring**, **self-instruction**, and **self-reinforcement** (Alberto & Troutman, 2009). Goals selected in collaboration with the student are more likely to be met. In addition, the student who is about to engage in a self-management procedure must be aware of the goal he or she is working toward. Goals should be clearly defined and agreed upon. Clearly defined or operationalized behaviors are important so the learner knows exactly what to record.

As part of self-monitoring, students typically learn to identify the behavior to be recorded (replacement behavior) and learn how to monitor and record their own behavior. For example, a high-functioning second-grade student with autism increased his on-task behavior with self-management and reduced out-of-seat and off-task behaviors (Callahan & Rademacher, 1999).

Teaching self-recording can be done in multiple ways. Video samples of the students can be used to help the students record themselves. Students can learn to use wrist counters to record the frequency of a discrete behavior or skill. Even children as young as age 5 or 6 with autism spectrum disorders can use wrist counters to monitor their own behavior, such as when monitoring the number of compliments (e.g., "Neat!" "I like . . .") given to others (Apple, Billingsley, & Schwartz, 2005). A digital watch with a repeat alarm set for 10-second intervals and a recording sheet were part of a strategy used by a 12-year-old girl with autism to monitor quiet and noisy behavior (Mancina, Tankersley, Kamps, Kravits, & Parrett, 2000). This self-recording and self-reinforcement program effectively reduced her inappropriate vocalizations across environments (Mancina et al., 2000). Correspondence training can also be used to teach students to plan and accurately report their own behavior (Mayer et al., 2012).

Initially, the accuracy of the student recording is monitored and rewarded by a second observer, such as the teacher, to ensure that the student is collecting valid data. The accuracy of data collection is rewarded. When the student records accurate data reliably, the student learns to administer his or her own reward. Kratochwill and colleagues (1999) have identified seven factors that affect the accuracy and reliability of self-monitoring: (1) training in self-management for better accuracy; (2) the use of systematic methods, such as the use of a recording form, will result in more reliable and accurate data than informal and unsystematic methods; (3) the use of a self-monitoring device such as a wrist counter allows for simple and accurate data collection and reduces reliance on memory; (4) generally, a short time interval between the self-monitoring act and the occurrence of the target behavior results in more accurate data; (5) monitoring one response at a time avoids the interference and inaccuracies of response competition; (6) the more time and energy spent on the self-monitoring activity, the less accurate the data may be; and (7) contingent positive reinforcement for accurate recording tends to increase accuracy.

Some self-management strategies include a self-instruction component (Alberto & Troutman, 2009). Typically, an adult models the completion of an activity while providing oral instructions such as "Turn the computer on and open Excel." Then the student performs the task just modeled, including the use of self-instruction in a low voice. The task is then practiced without self-instruction. Self-administered rewards can be delivered following successful completion of the task during self-instruction or for any successful task completion identified during the goal-setting process.

One of the advantages of selecting self-management procedures is that self-monitoring is cost effective and less intrusive or stigmatizing than monitoring by a clinician, therapist, or other adult (Koegel, Frea, & Surratt, 1994; Kratochwill et al., 1999). The strategy can be used across a wide range of environments and throughout the day, increasing the opportunity for implementation and practice. Self-management skills, once taught, can be used for multiple behaviors, giving the individual increased self-control and independence (Koegel et al., 1994). Self-management is an important component of the skills needed for self-determination.

## Token Economies

The use of **token or point systems** can be an important component of an intervention aimed at decreasing problem behavior as well as increasing skills. Tokens or points can be delivered following the occurrence of replacement behaviors, providing positive reinforcement. Tokens and points can be delivered by the student him- or herself or others on the absence of challenging behavior during a set period of time, thus incorporating differential reinforcement of other (DRO) behavior. Self-delivery of tokens can be managed by young children, as demonstrated by two 6-year-olds who delivered tokens contingent on varied responses of a target behavior (Newman, Reinecke, & Meinberg, 2000).

Included in some token systems is response cost. **Response cost**, a form of negative reinforcement, occurs when tokens either are not delivered or are taken away following the occurrence of a behavior target to be decreased (Cooper et al., 2007). Intervention procedures that incorporate response cost need to be considered by relevant ethics committees. It is also important to start with a set of points or tokens so that if tokens are lost, the student is not at zero and thus will not lose motivation to use the system. Some systems also incorporate opportunities to earn bonus points for some identified behaviors, enabling students to make up for any points lost due to response cost procedures (Alberto & Troutman, 2009). Charlop-Christy and Haymes (1998) found that tokens created from objects of obsession (letters, trains) resulted in faster acquisition compared to typical tokens (stars, happy faces) implemented on the same reinforcement schedule. The authors discuss the added motivational effect of using specialized tokens at some point in the lesson.

### Behavioral Contracts

Like any other contract between two parties, a **behavioral contract** is a written agreement between parties, one of which is a learner with autism spectrum disorder, that clearly delineates the terms for obtaining rewards and the consequences of not completing the contract, if any. Points or tokens for completing parts of the contract may be embedded. Myles and Simpson (1998a) outline the steps for developing a contract with an individual with Asperger syndrome as follows: meet with the concerned parties and determine the conditions of the contract; determine who will use the contract, where it will be used, the reinforcement menu, and if any negative consequences will be used; take baseline data; determine the reinforcement schedule and

goals; write, discuss, and sign the contract to ensure understanding; and, finally, monitor the contract.

## Combinations of Strategies

A combination of self-management, a token system using points, and reinforcement of replacement behaviors was used with three learners with autism spectrum disorders (Koegel, Frea, & Surratt, 1994). A wrist counter was used to assist the three students with autism to self-monitor replacement skills for problematic social behavior that included appropriate responses to questions; describing observations in the community by stating, "I see a . . ."; initiating conversation; and responding to peers (Koegel et al., 1994).

The self-management of a token system that included differential reinforcement of other behavior (DRO) was used to reduce the stereotypic behavior of three adolescents with autism in a special education classroom (Haring, Breen, Pitts-Conway, & Gaylord-Ross, 1986). Students received five tokens for correct responses and five tokens for omitting stereotypic behavior. A token system had been established in their classroom (Haring et al., 1986). The same combination of self-management and DRO strategies was used successfully by three students with autism to reduce out-of-seat behavior and inappropriate nail flicking (Newman, Tuntigian, Ryan, & Reinecke, 1997).

An individualized self-management and DRO procedure was designed for a student with autism spectrum disorder as part of the educational program at Alpine Learning Group in New Jersey. The student had a game board created with his face as the token and a pathway toward a preferred reward. At the designated interval, the student moved his game piece one step closer to his reward (see Figure 5–2). Students can self-manage their own DRO reward systems by checking boxes, moving a token toward a goal, crossing out boxes, or any other form of self-administered data collection system.

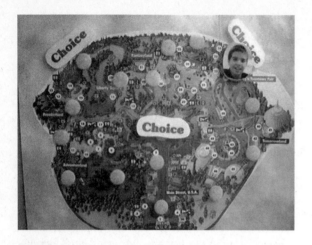

**FIGURE 5–2**  DRO game board
*Source:* The DRO game board created for a student attending Alpine Learning Group, Paramus, New Jersey. Used with permission.

Koegel, Koegel, and colleagues describe the use of an intervention package consisting of self-management, prompts, and reinforcement for replacement behavior that successfully reduced the challenging behavior of two young children with autism (Koegel, Koegel, Boettcher, Harrower, & Openden, 2006). The challenging behaviors included inappropriate contact and aggressive behavior toward peers for one child and yelling and inappropriate statements for the second child. Replacement behaviors were selected following a functional assessment and included appropriate statements for demanding tasks, such as "I need help" and "Let's take a break" for the child for whom problem behavior was used to escape demand, and teaching the child to ask "What are you doing?" or say "Let's go play!" for the child for whom the function was seeking attention (Koegel, Koegel, et al., 2006).

Parents have also implemented combination strategies to reduce the challenging behavior of their child with autism spectrum disorder toward younger siblings (Koegel, Stiebel, & Koegel, 1998). In collaboration with skilled clinicians, replacement behaviors for aggression in the forms of hitting, punching, yelling, pinching, and so on, effectively reduced these problem behaviors in three sibling pairs. The intervention package included environmental arrangement to reduce the variables associated with problem behaviors, enriching the environment with preferred toys, and parental prompts for use of alternative behaviors (Koegel, Stiebel, & Koegel, 1998).

In another example, a combination of strategies was used to decrease the aggressive behavior of a 10-year-old with autism toward his infant sibling, and was implemented in collaboration between the family and two university professors (Barry & Singer, 2001). It is clear from this effective program that the clinicians had a comprehensive understanding of behavior measurement and analysis, and sophisticated skills in implementing interventions. This elaborate program is a reminder of the skills needed to address complex challenging behavior. The authors worked with a family to address a crisis in which a boy (age 10 years and 8 months) with autism was acting in an aggressive manner toward his infant sibling by smothering the infant with his own face, overturning the stroller, shaking the infant when the infant was in a baby seat, choking by grabbing the infant's neck, and jumping on a chair while gesturing to the infant to climb on the chair (Barry & Singer, 2001).

A functional analysis revealed that the behavior occurred when the boy had access to the infant and was maintained by verbal attention and physical contact from parents and other siblings. Replacement behaviors included speaking in motherese, singing songs to the infant, and playing appropriate games such as hide-and-seek. Parents were taught to speak to the child when he was behaving appropriately (that is, differential reinforcement of alternative behavior [DRA]), to redirect the child by calming, and to ask the child with autism to notice the infant's emotional reaction to the problem behavior. He was also asked to notice that the infant was smiling and happy when the boy was interacting with the replacement behavior (Barry & Singer, 2001).

The boy was taught the replacement behaviors through the development of a task analysis, verbal prompting, verbal reinforcement, error correction, and modeling of replacement behaviors. The boy with autism spectrum disorder was taught to self-monitor his own behavior. The clinician-implemented training program was faded through the introduction of self-management and was successful (Barry & Singer, 2001). Clearly, these clinicians not only understood how to conduct a functional analysis to determine that attention was maintaining the behavior, they also used many behavior analytic skills in the development of alternative behaviors and analysis of outcomes.

## Key Concepts Put into Practice

By creating an environment that is motivating for individuals with autism spectrum disorders and implementing strategies to maintain engagement and the acquisition of new skills, educators are actively preventing problem or challenging behaviors. A token system for working toward or gaining rewards may assist the students to learn to tolerate delays in reinforcement. Opportunities for making choices and self-management should be introduced early in the educational program. If problem behaviors arise, it is required by IDEA that a functional assessment be conducted to determine the relationship of the behavior to either antecedent or consequential variables, or both.

Changes to setting events associated with the behavior targeted for reduction or the implementation of positive strategies such as differential reinforcement of alternative behavior and functional communication training are implemented. It is required that data are collected on the outcomes of these strategies.

If positive approaches are not effective and strategies—including response cost or time-out—are introduced, then the team must meet to approve such a plan.

## Research Using Applied Behavior Analysis to Decrease and Replace Behaviors

Campbell concludes his review of 117 articles published in 15 journals between the years of 1966 and 1998 that focused on behavioral interventions for persons with autism with the following comment, "First and foremost, behavioral treatments were found to be significantly effective in reducing problem behavior in individuals with autism" (Campbell, 2003, p. 133). The author also concludes that the type of target behavior and the type of treatment did not influence the average effect. He did find that there were greater effects when an experimental functional analysis was used. Although a clear understanding of the function of a behavior is helpful with designing intervention plans, the outcomes of the Campbell review could be related to the correlation between those studies that used an experimental analysis of behavior and the clinicians' skills in behavior analysis. Experimental analyses are more likely to be completed by doctoral-level clinicians than by educators who work in environments that make manipulations of antecedent and consequent events more challenging.

Effective interventions to reduce problem and challenging behavior designed after a functional assessment continue to be published since Campbell completed his review in 1998. Some of these interventions are described in this chapter. There is currently an increased emphasis by behavior analysts on the design of strategies that can be maintained by systems such as those found in public schools. The importance of working within a system is emphasized in Chapter 3 of this book.

## SUGGESTIONS FOR DISCUSSION

1. Discuss why it is important to replace any problem behavior that is reduced or eliminated.

2. Provide examples of how the key strategies based on applied behavior analysis used to increase skills can be used to decrease problem behavior.

3. Conduct a debate with one side in support of the statement "Punishment should never be used!" and the other side arguing that punishment may be difficult to avoid if one is using the technical definition of the term.

4. List some common functions of a problem or challenging behavior that you have noticed from your own experience.

5. Explain the rationale for using self-management programs for individuals with autism spectrum disorders from a young age.

6. Discuss at what point you would intervene with stereotypic behavior.

7. Identify situations where the use of a token economy system would be beneficial.

8. Explain why it is so important to work collaboratively with families when addressing problem behavior.

## RESOURCES

### Books

Cooper, J., Heron, T., & Heward, W. (2007). *Applied behavior analysis* (2nd ed.). Upper Saddle River, NJ:Pearson Education.

Glasberg, B. A. (2005). *Functional behavior assessment for people with autism: Making sense of seemingly senseless behavior*. Bethesda, MD: Woodbine House.

Glasberg, B. A. (2008). Stop that seemingly senseless behavior! *FBA-based intervention for people with autism*. Bethesda, MD: Woodbine House.

O'Neill, R. E., Horner, R. H., Albin, R. W., Sprague, J. R., Storey, K., & Newton, J. S. (1997). *Functional assessment and program development for problem behavior: A practical handbook*. Pacific Grove, CA: Brookes/Cole.

Scheuermann, B., & Hall, J. A. (2012). *Positive behavioral supports for the classroom*. Upper Saddle River, N.J: Pearson.

### Websites

*csefel.vanderbilt.edu*
   Center for the Social Emotional Foundations for Early Learning
*www.challengingbehavior.org*
   Technical Assistance Center on Social Emotional Intervention
*www.pbis.org*
   Positive Behavior Interventions and Supports
*www.pent.ca.gov*
   Positive Environment Network of Trainers—California Department of Education

## CHAPTER SIX

# Developmental and Social-Relational Approaches

The reader should be able to:

- Explain the role of cognition in development according to Piaget and Bandura and sociocultural influences according to Vygotsky.
- Describe the strategies that are typically used by those who follow a developmental, social-pragmatic approach to working with children with autism spectrum disorders according to Ingersoll (2010).
- Discuss why it is important to facilitate play with peers when working with young children with autism spectrum disorders.

## Theoretical Basis for the Developmental and Social-Relational Approaches

The models and strategies described in this chapter include those based on the developmental or social-relational approach. Model and program developers have referred to one or more of the theorists described in the beginning of this chapter when providing a rationale for the focus of suggested strategies. Similar to behavior analysis, developmental theorists attribute skill development to the interface between the individual's biological and behavioral history and environmental or sociocultural factors

(Bandura, 1977; Piaget, 1950; Vygotsky, 1978). In contrast, developmental theorists refer to a mediating factor such as cognition (Piaget) or the individual's social-emotional response (Vygotsky) to account for changes in behavior. Bandura, a social-learning theorist, writes that interaction is determined by the interlocking factors of behavior, other personal factors, and environmental factors, with varying degrees of influence depending on the situation or context.

Psychiatrist Daniel Stern (1985) draws on both traditional psychoanalytic and attachment theories in his approach, which emphasizes a subjective sense of self as the organizing principle. According to Stern, several senses of the self may exist in preverbal forms and are revealed later through language and self-reflection. Stern describes the development of the sense of self in four stages. The first stage, the **emergent self**, is described as the coming-into-being of organization, which is the heart of creating and learning. The infant has unrelated experiences of changing passions and confusions that are yet to be integrated and connected.

In the next stage, the **sense of core self**, the typical infant of 2 to 3 months of age appears more integrated during social interaction (Stern, 1985). Infants in this stage are beginning to connect affective experiences with other experiences of self and note regularities in the flow of events. During this stage, the infant regulates the level of excitation, such as by use of gaze aversion to cut out stimulation above the optimal range, as well as gaze and facial expression to seek out stimulation. Caregiver behavior can overstimulate the infant, and the infant can become disregulated by occurrences in the environment.

The third stage, the **subjective self**, occurs "when the infant discovers that he or she has a mind and that other people have minds as well" (Stern, 1985, p. 124). Pointing gestures and following another's line of vision, or the establishment of joint attention, occurs during this stage. Intentional communication (reaching for a cookie held by mother) also occurs during this stage. Parents often begin to imitate the child with affect attunement, in which the parent responds in kind to the affect of the child.

Typically during the second year, language emerges, and with language emergence comes the final stage, the **verbal self**. Children begin to imagine and represent things in their minds, and symbolic play and language become possible. Young children now have the mechanisms to share their interpersonal world knowledge and can work on imagination, which differs from reality. Interpersonal interaction can now involve past memories, current experiences, and expectations of the future.

Educators who are influenced by Stern would provide opportunities to increase the development of the sense of self across stages. Creating opportunities for joint attention and encouraging imaginative play would be a focus. Building communication by responding to intentional gestures would be recommended.

Piaget (1950) writes that cognition and affect are both aspects of intelligence. As the individual continues to assimilate information about the environment, with some cognitive construct such as memory or schema, he or she increases in cognitive development and intelligence. Piaget writes that assimilation occurs by grouping factors about reality. This assimilation, or development, occurs in stages with four principal periods. The first stage, symbolic and preconceptual thought (from 1½ to 4 years of age), is focused on the acquisition of language.

Memory is also an important component of the Piagetian framework. Piaget argues that there are multiple forms of memory, and thus the young child's ability to recall and act on events changes with development. What is most important, according to Piaget, is that the young child is actively engaged with materials and the environment rather than practicing rote memory tasks (Piaget, 1973). He also believed that positive affect during interactions and learning activities facilitated memory. Piaget (1950) writes that speech and language are fundamental for learning. Examples of ways educators support young children using a Piagetian framework include creating opportunities for them to be actively engaged in activities, helping them with concepts of categorization or groupings, focusing on sensorimotor activities as a precursor for verbal language, and assisting with practice in shapes and sizes to foster perceptions of spatial relationships.

L. Alan Sroufe (1995) writes that development is an integrated process and that understanding emotional development sheds light on cognitive and social development. He defines emotion as "a subjective reaction to a salient event, characterized by physiological, experiential, and overt behavioral change" (Sroufe, 1995, p. 15). According to Sroufe, when emotional reactions are observed, there is commonly a notable arrest in behavior, even if this is followed by some motoric reaction. During the first months and years of life, new emotions become available and the emotional process undergoes fundamental changes.

In Table 6.1, the emergence of emotions over the first 54 months, as outlined by Sroufe, are presented. Sroufe (1995) writes that emotional and social development during early childhood is so closely tied that the term **socioemotional development** is widely used in the field. The main socioemotional task for preschoolers is the movement from dyadic regulation towards self-regulation of emotion. Young children have the twin tasks of learning how to express affect directly and yet to control and modulate it when necessary. Through fantasy play, children can express vital feelings in a controlled context. Educators influenced by Sroufe's work would arrange for many opportunities for social interaction with adults and peers, including arranging fantasy or imaginative play activities.

**TABLE 6.1** The emergence of emotions in early life

| Age, in Months | Developmental Issue | Anger/Frustration | Wariness/Fear | Pleasure/Joy |
|---|---|---|---|---|
| 0 | Absolute stimulus barrier | Distress due to physical restraint, extreme discomfort | Startle/pain, obligatory attention | Endogenous smile |
| 1 | | | | |
| 2 | | | | Turning toward, pleasure |
| 3 | Regulation of tension (positive affect) | Frustration reaction | | |
| 4 | | | Wariness | Delight, active laughter |
| 5 | | | | |
| 6 | Development of reciprocity (active participation) | | | |
| 7 | | Anger | | Joy |
| 8 | | | | |
| 9 | Formation of an effective attachment relationship | | Fear (stranger aversion) | |
| 11 | | | | |
| 12 | Practicing (exploration and mastery) | Angry mood, petulance | Anxiety, immediate fear | Elation |
| 18 | Emergence of self | Defiance, rage | Shame | Positive valuation of self, affection |
| 24 | | Intentional hurting | | |
| 36 | Mastery through play and fantasy | | Guilt | Pride, love |
| 54 | Identification, sex-role development, and peer competence | | | |

*Source:* From *Emotional Development: The Organization of Emotional Life in the Early Years*, by L. A. Sroufe, 1995, New York: Cambridge Press, p. 68. Reprinted with the permission of Cambridge University Press.

Bandura's (1977) **social learning theory** differs from the learning theory previously described by the acknowledgment of cognition as a factor that can influence behavior. Psychological functioning is explained as a result of continuous reciprocal interaction of personal and environmental determinants. An example given by Bandura (1977) explains the difference in social learning theory. He writes that even with a history of consistent reinforcement of a behavior, an individual will not emit the behavior if he or she *believes* that the behavior will not be rewarded on future occasions. For example, if a parking space is available each day when the person arrives at 11:00 a.m., the person could start believing that his or her luck has run out one morning at 11:00 and so not arrive until noon. In other words, the individual's cognitive thought or belief has a strong influence over behavior. Self-arousal, including fear responses, to neutral events can be developed by cognitive responses to the event. Some individuals who are highly aroused by events or stimuli direct their attention to extraneous or irrelevant features of the event. This social learning theory approach emphasizes self-regulatory capacities; the use of symbols for interaction with the environment; and observational learning, particularly through modeling.

Bandura (1977) also states that emotional responses can be learned through vicarious expectancy learning. Displays of emotion conveyed by facial, vocal, and gestural cues of a model can become emotionally arousing to the observer if they have a history of being paired with a positive experience. There is variability in the degree to which an individual is influenced by the modeling of others, or by following the crowd. Individuals with autism spectrum disorders (ASD) may have difficulty learning by imitating or modeling others, and the imitation of nonverbal behaviors is often a skill taught early (McEachin & Leaf, 1999; Taylor & McDonough, 1996). Strategies that include the modeling of the behaviors of peers via in-vivo or recorded situations have been influenced by Bandura. Strategies that address behavior due to anxiety,

fear, or overarousal with self-management and self-regulation of skills also have their theoretical bases in Bandura's work.

Lev Vygotsky, who began his career as an educator of individuals with physical and cognitive disabilities (Vygotsky, 1978), describes a developmental approach with a focus on supporting learning through a sociocultural context. He proposes that most learning takes place in a social context, so working with peers and in groups is essential. An important contribution of Vygotsky's (1978) work is a description of the **zone of proximal development**. Vygotsky states that it is important for educators to determine what auxiliary assistance or information (**scaffolding**) might be used to assist a student to reach success or mastery. He writes that many assessment instruments focus on the skills that someone can perform at mastery. The assessments then describe that the person assessed is functioning at a particular age level. He writes that if you take the zone of proximal development into account, you may find that one child who scores at a 5-year-old level on a task but can reach a 7-year-old level with some assistance is different from another child who also scores at the same 5-year-old level but, with assistance, can perform at a 10-year-old level. In other words, children have different zones of proximal development and are in reality operating at very different levels.

Educators who follow Vygotsky's work would aim to find the zone of proximal development for each skill and would challenge each student to increase skills by arranging for tasks to be targeted at each individual's potential development. Potential development would be determined through the guidance of adults (scaffolding) or in collaboration with peers. This method allows educators to assess the process of "accomplishing a task by the aid of specific auxiliary means" (Vygotsky, 1978, p. 74).

The Vygotskian approach to social interaction is fundamentally cultural (Adamson & Chance, 1998; Wolfberg, 2003). Caregivers are the agents of culture who interpret their infant's expressions as meaningful within the context of their own culture. When an infant displays a new behavior, such as a smile, the adult reaction transforms the behavior into a social act. After many repeated experiences of supported expression, the infant masters the action that has cultural meaning. "The act has passed through the zone of proximal development during which the adult has educated the child in its use" (Adamson & Chance, 1998, p. 21). Vygotskians maintain that the development of joint attention occurs as a process of acts of the child and reactions of the caregivers who support and enculturate the child. As the child consolidates the skill of attending simultaneously to people and to shared objects, a foundation is laid for the use of symbols.

Vygotsky writes that social interaction is fundamental for intellectual development. He writes that play is also a fundamental developmental activity. Through play, a child learns to relate to the environment in a new way. During play, the child learns that an object represents, or is a sign for, another object, such as a piece of wood is a baby if the gesture of cradling is used with the wood. "Children's symbolic play can be understood as a very complex system of 'speech' through gestures that communicate and indicate the meaning of playthings" (Vygotsky, 1978, p. 108).

Vygotsky writes that play is a primary social activity through which young children acquire interpersonal skills, social knowledge, and symbolic capacities (Schuler & Wolfberg, 2000). It is also through interaction with peers during play activities that children learn about the peer culture or the unique social worlds that children construct out of their everyday experiences that is separate from the world of adults.

The process of writing symbols is very important, according to Vygotsky. He believes that writing is often too focused on the formation of letters in contrast to the meaning of the symbols on the paper. He also states that a focus on writing is important in the preschool years. According to Vygotsky, instead of teaching writing as a motor skill, it should be taught as a complex cultural activity.

## Transactional Model

This model focuses on the influence of interaction on development. Both the individual child and the environment change over time and affect each other in a reciprocal fashion (Sameroff & Chandler, 1975). Developmental outcomes are viewed as a result of a continuous dynamic interplay among child behavior, caregiver responses to the child's behavior, and environmental variables that may influence both the child and the caregiver (Sameroff & Chandler, 1975; Wetherby & Prizant, 2000). Early achievements serve as a foundation for subsequent development (Warren, Yoder, & Leew, 2002). Ideally, over time, the young child's social behavior is interpreted accurately by a caregiver, and the caregiver is then able to respond in a way that supports the social exchange and both child and caregiver develop a sense of efficacy (Wetherby & Prizant, 2000).

Several programs designed for individuals with autism spectrum disorders are based on developmental or social-relational theories or use transactional models. Each of the following programs will be discussed as examples based on these theoretical bases: Developmental Individual-Difference Relationship-Based (DIR)/floortime, responsive teaching, Hanen, and relationship development intervention (RDI). Each of these models is to be used by parents and caregivers as the key intervention agents. Other models also focus their approach with parents, blend theoretical approaches in their design, and incorporate strategies based on applied behavior analysis with those based on developmental and social-relational theories—Enhanced Milieu Teaching, the Early Start Denver model, and Project ImPact. Two additional models that focus on individuals with ASD across ages—Pivotal Response Treatments, and the SCERTS model—are also included in this chapter. An ideal example of a program that puts the developmental and social-relational strategies into practice will be described. The research or evidence for each of these programs and models will be discussed at the end of each program description.

# The DIR®/Floortime Approach™

The floortime philosophy, developed by Stanley Greenspan, M.D., is an approach for parents and educators that fosters the development of the whole child by engaging and creating partnerships (Hanna & Wilford, 1990). Influenced by Piaget, there is a focus on logical thinking and sensorimotor activities in this approach. Consistent with Sroufe, the authors state that emotion is critical to the growth of the mind and brain (Greenspan & Wieder, 2006, 2011).

## Evolution of the DIR®/Floortime Approach™

- In 1990, Greenspan published a video and guide for use of floor time (then two words) with young children, including those with disabilities.

- In 1998, Stanley Greenspan, along with Serena Wieder, published a book that described the use of the "individual-difference, relationship-based, developmental approach to intervention" for children with special needs, including children with autism spectrum disorders (Greenspan & Wieder, 1998, p. 14).

- In 2002, in collaboration with colleagues from speech-language and occupational therapy, Greenspan and Lewis (2002) published an affect-based language curriculum that includes activities for applied floor time for those children who need systematic instruction conducted in semistructured activities.

- In 2005, the Developmental, Individual-Difference, Relationship-Based (DIR)® Floortime approach for working with autism spectrum disorders was published by Greenspan and Wieder (2005b) in a three-piece set, providing examples with video footage of floortime intervention with families.

- In 2006, Greenspan and Wieder (2006) published *Engaging Autism*, a book describing the DIR® Floortime approach in detail.

## Key Concepts of the DIR®/Floortime™ Approach

The DIR model uses the child's natural emotions and interests to enhance the functional emotional capacities of joint attention, engagement, two-way communication, problem solving, and symbolic thought (Greenspan & Wieder, 2011). The model emphasizes the development of functional emotional capacities, with a focus on individual differences in sensory modulation, processing, and motor planning and sequencing through relationships and interactions. Stern's (1985) concepts are evident in this model with its focus on regulation of behaviors, sensations, and use of gestures.

Floortime is a specific intervention technique derived from the DIR model. It is a **developmental approach**, with a primary goal of enabling the child to form a sense of him- or herself as an intentional, interactive individual by helping the child to progress through the six functional emotional developmental levels (Greenspan & Wieder, 2005a; 2011). These levels are (1) shared attention and regulation; (2) engagement and relating; (3) purposeful emotional interactions; (4) shared, social problem-solving (joint attention); (5) creating ideas; and (6) building bridges between ideas (logical thinking) (Greenspan & Wieder, 2011). Each child's unique way of taking in and responding to the world represents this child's **individual difference**. It is assumed that each child will have some qualitative differences regardless of diagnostic category or cultural background. These differences can be considered in three categories: difficulty with sensory reactivity, processing difficulty, and difficulty in motor planning and sequencing (Greenspan & Wieder, 2005a). These individual differences serve as the basis for the focus of floortime (Greenspan & Wieder, 1998, 2005b). In the floortime model, the parent or educator determines where in the normal sequence of development that individual child went off track, and a strategy is created for getting development back on track. "Floortime emphasizes the child's initiation, reciprocity, continuous flow of interactions, reasoning, and empathy" (Greenspan & Wieder, 2011, p. 1068).

**Relationship-based interaction** with primary caregivers is a critical element in helping children to return to a healthy developmental path (Greenspan & Wieder, 2005b). "Healthy relationships throughout childhood are critical to emotional development, which, in turn, creates a basis for learning in several important areas" (Greenspan, 1990, p. 1). According to Greenpan and Wieder (2005b), "emotions make learning possible" (p. 7), so by interacting with children in ways that capitalize on emotions, by following interests and motivations, adults can help children climb the developmental ladder.

It is recommended that DIR®/Floortime™ be conducted in an intensive manner, or in at least six to ten 20- or 30-minute sessions a day for those children (Greenspan & Wieder, 1998, 2011). Children with autism and related disorders require extra practice. First steps for involvement include sharing in activities that provide mutual pleasure and holding the child's attention through the senses (Greenspan & Wieder, 1998, 2006). Floortime for children with autism spectrum disorders has two goals: (1) to follow the child's lead, and (2) to bring the child into a shared world (Greenspan & Wieder, 2006). Greenspan and colleagues recommend that, in addition to floortime with parents and educators, children with autism spectrum disorders be given an opportunity to play with peers and to receive intervention from a team of professionals such as speech, occupational, and physical therapists (Greenspan & Lewis, 2002; Greenspan & Wieder, 2005b, 2006, 2011).

## Strategies Based on Key Floortime Concepts

According to Greenspan and Wieder (2006), the floortime technique is effective when the adult tunes into the child's emotions and engages with the child on the child's level by opening and closing many circles of communication together. This can be accomplished by using a five-step approach (Hanna & Wilford, 1990): (1) observation (listening and watching the child); (2) approach, or opening the circle of communication (responding with words and gestures appropriate to the situation); (3) following the child's

lead; (4) extending and expanding (language or play); and (5) allowing the child to initiate closure of the circle. When attempting to engage a child, getting down to the child's level and using a soft voice in a respectful manner is recommended (Hanna & Wilford, 1990).

Greenspan and Lewis (2002) write that adults can implement systematic instruction to teach new skills. Systematic instruction is described as teaching a new skill while maintaining pleasurable back-and-forth engagement. Skills are considered mastered when a child can perform them independently during applied floortime with four to five back-and-forth "circles of communication" across unrehearsed novel contexts. Applied floortime is when adults take a systematic instruction goal and elicit and teach it in a less structured activity, such as during a game or when making objects out of play dough. Applied floortime and systematic instruction is not mentioned in later descriptions of the model, and DIR-based interventions are distinguished from models based on other theoretical perspectives by clarifying that the primary goal is "to enable children to form a sense of themselves as intentional, interactive individuals; to develop cognitive, language and social capacities from this basic sense of intentionality; and to progress through the six Functional Emotional Developmental capacities" (Greenspan & Wieder, 2011, p. 1072).

## Evidence for Key Concepts of DIR®/Floortime™ Approach

The model developers published a retrospective review of clinical records for 200 clients and their families who participated for a minimum of 2 years (Greenspan & Wieder, 1997, 1999). All records were from the children who had been diagnosed as having autism spectrum disorders between 22 months and 4 years of age (Greenspan & Wieder, 1997). It was reported that parents were highly motivated and often traveled great distances to receive clinic services (Greenspan & Wieder, 1999). Outcomes were determined based on record review from an interdisciplinary team and scores on the Childhood Autism Rating Scale (CARS) (Schopler, Reichler, & Renner, 1998).

The authors report that approximately 58% (118) of the 200 cases reviewed showed "good to outstanding" outcomes (Greenspan & Wieder, 1997). These positive outcomes were attributed to the child's ability to sequence actions (motor planning) and use this to form complex, reciprocal, problem-solving interactions; the ability to imitate; as well as a great number of interactive opportunities geared at the child's developmental level (Greenspan & Wieder, 1999). What is unclear is which interventions were used to obtain these outcomes—such as whether or not applied floortime or systematic instruction was included.

In their book that describes the basic assessment model used in the DIR® approach and research applications, Greenspan, DeGangi, and Wieder (2001) reported that they compared 20 of the children with the best outcomes to 14 typically developing children using the Functional Emotional Assessment Scale. This scale provides criteria to be used with recorded samples of parent–child interactions. They determined that there was no difference between the best outcome group and their typical peers (Greenspan & Wieder, 1999). A follow-up study, which was published 10 to 15 years post-treatment for 16 of the children diagnosed with ASD from the 200 cases with the best outcomes, revealed that these gains were maintained and that, according to the model developers, these adolescents were empathetic, reflective, and creative, with solid academic skills and healthy peer relationships (Greenspan & Wieder, 2005a).

A study, implemented by researchers other than the model developers, included an intervention by two speech-language pathology graduate students (Hilton & Seal, 2007). One student implemented strategies based on DIR®; one implemented strategies based on ABA with each of two monozygotic twins. According to the results from the Communication and Symbolic Behavior Scales (CSBS), the twin who received ABA made more gains that the one who received DIR® treatment; however, the twin under

that ABA condition exhibited more negative behavior (crying, tantrums etc.). As the researchers conclude, these outcomes may be due to the skills of the interventionists (Hilton & Seal, 2007). These outcomes may indicate the relative challenges of implementing the DIR approach effectively for novice interventionists.

Outcomes of a study of a model, entitled The PLAY Project (Solomon, Necheles, Ferch, & Bruckman, 2007) based on the DIR®/Floortime model, revealed that 45.5% of 68 children ages 2 to 6 years with ASD receiving this 8- to 12-month program made good to very good functional developmental progress according to the results of the Functional Emotional Assessment Scale (FEAS) (Greenspan et al., 2001). There was no change in the parents' FEAS scores from pre- to post-intervention with the PLAY Project (Solomon et al., 2007). The authors of the FEAS (DeGangi & Greenspan, 2001), and the researchers of this study, state that additional measures of development with additional tools are needed to obtain valid information of outcomes (Solomon et al., 2007).

Researchers recommend that future studies include multiple measures of outcomes of interventions based on the DIR® floortime approach (Solomon et al., 2007). It is also important for the creators of this approach to identify the critical strategies (e.g., circles of communication), define these strategies, describe how to implement the strategies clearly enough so that they are replicable by parents and educators, and then measure outcomes for children with autism spectrum disorders. Until such outcomes are published, evidence for floortime remains limited (Odom, Boyd, Hall, & Hume, 2010).

## Responsive Teaching

**Responsive teaching** is an intervention approach that is the result of collaboration between Gerald Mahoney, Ph.D., a clinical psychologist, and James MacDonald, CCC-SLP, Ph.D. According to the model developers, responsive teaching is a parent-mediated approach that is derived from contemporary child development research and theory (Mahoney & MacDonald, 2005). The program is designed for children under age 6 with developmental disabilities, including autism and pervasive developmental disorder (Mahoney & Perales, 2005).

The curriculum is designed for implementation by parents and other caregivers who spend significant amounts of time interacting with young children. Responsive teaching was developed to assist caregivers in maximizing the potential of each of the routine interactions with children (Mahoney & MacDonald, 2007). The three domains of cognition, communication, and social-emotional development are the focus of this intervention. The authors state that this approach has been influenced by the work of Piaget and Vygotsky, the communication theory of Bruner, and the attachment theory of Bowlby (Mahoney & MacDonald, 2005).

## Key Concepts of Responsive Teaching

The responsive teaching curriculum promotes development by encouraging children to use pivotal behaviors, such as initiation, social play, exploration, problem solving, joint attention, vocalization, intentional communication, conversation, trust, empathy, cooperation, self-regulation, and feelings of confidence and control (Mahoney & MacDonald, 2005, 2007). The term *pivotal behaviors* was taken from the research of Robert Koegel and colleagues, who describe pivotal response training (PRT), an approach based on applied behavior analysis described later in this chapter (Koegel & Frea, 1993; Koegel, Koegel, & Carter, 1999). The premise underlying responsive teaching is that the developmental and social-emotional outcomes that young children obtain are strongly related to the use of pivotal developmental behaviors during daily interactions.

It is recommended by the model developers that caregivers and parents use daily routines to encourage pivotal behaviors. Parents and caregivers have the most opportunity for interactions and are essential to the development of the child. "No matter what professionals do with children, the stimulation parents provide while interacting with their children ultimately accounts for how effectively intervention promotes children's developmental well-being" (Mahoney & MacDonald, 2007, p. 12).

The teaching or interaction style used by caregivers is very important. The authors recommend five dimensions that result in a style that is highly responsive: (1) *match*, in which actions are adjusted to the child's developmental level, interests, and behavioral style; (2) *reciprocity*, or interactive episodes that have a balanced, give-and-take relationship that supports engagement during joint activity routines; (3) *shared control*, or encouragement of the child's control of the topic or focus that facilitates and moderates the direction of the interaction; (4) *contingency*, or interactions that have an immediate and direct relationship to a child's previous behavior and that encourage the child's intentions and communication and include the factors of awareness, timing, frequency, and intent; and (5) *affect* that is animated, accepting, and warm and fosters enjoyment (Mahoney & MacDonald, 2007).

## Strategies Based on Key Responsive Teaching Concepts

Approximately 70 responsive teaching strategies are included in the curriculum guide (Mahoney & MacDonald, 2007). The strategies are tied to the five key aspects of a highly responsive teaching style. For example, the strategies listed under the dimension of joint activity routines for developing reciprocity include play face-to-face games without toys, sustain repetitive play or action sequences, join perseverative play and make it interactive, play with the child with toys, and make a habit of communicating during joint activity routines (Mahoney & MacDonald, 2005, 2007). **Joint activity routines** are situations in which children and parents are both actively involved in doing the same thing together (Mahoney & MacDonald, 2007). These activities become predictable exchanges that can be enhanced in order to promote learning.

Under "animation to promote affect," the following strategies are listed: be animated, wait with anticipation, respond to the child in playful ways, be more interesting than the child's distractions, and accompany communication with intonation and nonverbal gestures (Mahoney & MacDonald, 2007). By providing opportunities for young children to make choices, doing what they prefer, and influencing their personal outcomes, they are more likely to have feelings of being in control (Mahoney & MacDonald, 2007). These feelings of control are strong predictors of children's performance on and persistence with tasks (Findley & Cooper, 1983).

## Evidence for Responsive Teaching

Research by Mahoney and Perales (2003, 2005) has been cited by others as evidence for positive outcomes of interventions based on a developmental and social-relational theoretical framework (e.g., Greenspan & Wieder, 2011; Wakeford & Baranek, 2011). Mahoney and Perales (2005) evaluated the effects of responsive teaching strategies used in weekly individual parent–child sessions for 20 preschool-age children with pervasive developmental disorder (PDD) compared with 30 preschoolers with developmental disabilities. Parents reported using strategies taught for approximately 15 hours per week. Pre- and post-treatment assessments included ratings of temperament, social-emotional characteristics, and play and social behaviors from a Temperament and Atypical Behavior Scale (TABS) (Neisworth, Bagnato, Salvia, & Hunt, 1999) and from the Transdisciplinary Play Based Assessment (Linder, 2008). Results indicated that changes in parents' responsiveness were moderately associated with changes in children's pivotal behaviors (attention, interest, persistence, initiation, cooperation, joint attention, and affect). Increases in children's pivotal behaviors were significantly related to improvements in children's developmental functioning, particularly in the areas of cognitive and language development, but not socioemotional functioning. The authors state that additional research is needed to gain greater confidence in these results (Mahoney & Perales, 2005).

Mahoney, Kim, and Lin (2007) evaluated a program focused on teaching parents to be responsive to their child and consequently increasing the child's use of pivotal behaviors during interactions of 45 mother–child dyads (eight children with ASD). The pivotal behaviors of focus were persistence, initiation, reciprocity, and self-regulation. They concluded that there is a relationship between children's use of pivotal behaviors and their level of developmental functioning, and between their use of these behaviors and the degree to which parents were engaged with them. When the authors divided the children into high and low pivotal behavior users, they found that high users had higher developmental age scores from the Vineland Adaptive Behavior Scales (Sparrow, Balla, & Cicchetti, 1984) and the Transdisciplinary Play Based Assessment (Linder, 2008). The authors conclude that pivotal behaviors mediate the relationship between maternal responsiveness and children's development (Mahoney et al., 2007).

Additional research on the use of the five key responsive teaching strategies, such as on parents' ability to implement strategies with fidelity and the effect on child outcomes, would be of interest. For example, there is little data on the outcomes of use of affect or matching a child's developmental and behavioral style on engagement. The identification and evaluation of specific strategies that facilitate the use of the pivotal behaviors described by Mahoney and colleagues by young children with ASD would be a major contribution.

## The Hanen Program

The Hanen program was developed in 1975 by Ayala Hanen Manolson, a speech-language pathologist living in Montreal, Canada. The initial focus was on assisting parents in facilitating improvement of communication skills in their children with significant language delays. This work resulted in the publication of the manual entitled *It Takes Two to Talk: The Hanen Program* (Manolson, 1992) and the establishment of the Hanen Centre, now offering workshops in eight countries. In 1999, a guide was created for parents of preschoolers with autism spectrum disorders entitled *More Than Words* (Sussman, 1999). This manual is a guide to help parents facilitate the development of communication, play, and social skills. Professionals such as speech-language pathologists can attend workshops where they are trained to use the manual and accompanying CD examples in their work with groups of parents. There are typically eight sessions held for groups of parents, and facilitators (e.g., speech-language pathologists) guide parents in implementing the key strategies with their child.

## Strategies Based on Key Hanen Centre Principles

The *More Than Words* manual (Sussman, 1999) is a well-illustrated guide for parents that includes suggested strategies in a curriculum beginning with learning about the child's likes, dislikes, and sensory preferences. Different learning styles (rote, gestalt, visual, auditory, hands on) are reviewed so that parents can identify how best to provide opportunities for communication. Communication acts (requests, protests) and stages (own agenda, requester, early communication, and partner) are reviewed in an easy-to-understand format. Parents' roles as communication partners are also addressed. Setting goals and using visuals, including the Picture Exchange Communication System (Bondy & Frost, 2001), are addressed.

Following the child's lead (using the four *I*s of include your child's interest, interpret, imitate, and intrude) is illustrated with examples of each of the four *I*s. Turn-taking during interactions using natural cues is discussed and how to embed these interactions in "people games" is described. The initials ROCK remind parents to do the following when engaged in people games: "*R*epeat what you say and do; *O*ffer opportunities for your child to take his turn; *C*ue your child to take his turn; and *K*eep it fun! Keep it going!" (Sussman, 1999, p. 141). When communicating with their child, parents are encouraged to "[s]ay less and stress, and to [g]o slow and show" (Sussman, 1999, p. 193). Embedding activities in everyday routines is emphasized and incorporating music, songs, and books is suggested. Finally the manual describes the stages of play, suggests games with toys, and provides six guidelines for helping children make friends through play dates.

### Evidence for the More Than Words Program

Three studies evaluating the Hanen More Than Words (HMTW) were published. A delayed control design was used to evaluate a three-month program for parents of 51 preschool-age children suspected of having autism spectrum disorder (McConachie, Randle, Hammal, & LeCouteur, 2005). Two effects of the intervention were compared to the control condition: (1) parents' use of facilitative strategies and (2) children's increased vocabulary. Another study used a case study method to evaluate the effects of the HMTW for three mothers and their preschool children with autism spectrum disorders (Girolametto, Sussman, & Weitzman, 2007). The researchers report child outcomes of increased vocabulary, engagement in social interaction, and social initiation. They also report that mothers increased their use of responsive comments during play interactions (Girolametto et al., 2007). The authors of both articles recommend further research with stronger research designs (McConachie et al., 2005; Girolametto et al., 2007).

A randomized, controlled trial design was completed with 62 toddlers with autism spectrum disorder in the HMTW program ($n = 32$) compared to a "business as usual" ($n = 30$) control group (Carter, Messinger, Stone, Celimli, Nahmias, & Yoder, 2011). The research was completed across three sites in different states in the United States. The results of the study were that there were no main effects for the HMTW program on parent responsivity or child communication; however, there were changes yielding noteworthy effect sizes for parent responsivity when pre-intervention was compared to both post-intervention and follow-up. In addition, child interest in objects was a moderating factor, with children with interest in fewer toys (three or less) prior to the program making gains in communication. The authors conclude that parents of children with higher object interest (four to six objects) may require strategies other than those focused on in the HMTW curriculum (Carter et al., 2011). This study begins to address the issue of selecting intervention strategies based on the skills of the individual child.

# Relationship Development Intervention (RDI)

Relationship development intervention (RDI) is a trademark of Gutstein, Sheely, and associates (Gutstein & Sheely, 2004). In his review article (2009), Steven Gutstein describes RDI as an approach that uses methods that are continually evolving to address the information-processing disability of individuals with autism spectrum disorders by carefully building dynamic intelligence. The work of Sroufe (1995) was influential on this approach, particularly the described notable arrest in behavior when a child is engaged in a highly motivating activity.

The focus of RDI has been on assisting parents in developing a relationship with their child with ASD in the area of social-emotional development by focusing on guided participation (Gutstein, 2009). The initial work was conducted in a clinic setting, but now it is focused on everyday environments for family activities. Parents have adapted the approach for use in the living room, backyard, neighborhood, and shopping mall (Gutstein, 2004). In his 2009 publication, Gutstein reported that there were over 200 trained RDI consultants caring for a minimum of 5,000 families in 16 countries.

## Key Concepts of RDI

The goal of RDI is competence or obtaining generalized motivation to enter situations perceived as having greater uncertainty with anticipation of success and mastery (Gutstein, 2004). Unlike other approaches that start with what the child with autism does well, this approach facilitates the aspect of the brain not working well (Gutstein, 2005). Remediation is about correcting deficits.

According to Gutstein (2005), the mind develops as part of a dynamic system that processes continual variation. RDI aims to develop mindfulness by focusing on emotions, roles, ideas, perspectives, and levels of complexity, areas frequently difficult for individuals with ASD. The ability to generalize is also an important aspect of **mindfulness**.

RDI begins at this initial aspect of the development of social-emotional relationships with the child's natural caregivers as the recipients of services from consultants. Once the parent readiness curriculum, which aims to "rebuild parent's faith in their own competence" (Gutstein, 2009, p. 178), is completed, parents attend the guided participation program. Social communication interactions between parents and their children with ASD are set up to provide experience sharing. Rather than asking instrumental questions such as "What is your favorite food?" or "How many cars do you have?" parents comment more often, "My favorite food is pizza" or "I am going to draw one now" as an effort to engage the child in sharing the experience.

According to Gutstein (2005), RDI is a cognitive-developmental model that helps children with ASD learn to maintain productive uncertainty by providing opportunities for the child to master deviations from initial regulatory patterns. "Through observation and active participation, the apprentice gradually learns to view [his or her] environment through the eyes of the master" (Gutstein, 2005, p. 19). The motivation for being an apprentice is the participation in a safe position that leads to the gradual competence of the master. It is important to begin with activities where the child is successful and can learn to feel competent. Competence—not joy, fun, or laughter—is the focus of RDI.

Once the child learns declarative communication and the nonverbal aspects that accompany it, the focus of remediation shifts to communication repair, or the monitoring of social interaction and self-regulation of communication in the form of self-talk, reflection, controlling stress, and managing impulses (Gutstein, 2005). By addressing this area of social-emotional development, which is challenging for individuals with autism spectrum disorders, RDI is aiming at the "heart of autism" (Gutstein, 2005).

## Strategies Based on Key RDI Concepts

The aim of **spotlighting** communication is to create a clear boundary around a critical event so that the child with ASD is clear about the importance of that event and remembers it (Gutstein & Whitney, 2002). Examples of spotlighting include pausing prior to the gesture, expression, or words; changing the pace of oral communication; exaggerating facial expression; leaning over or toward the individual with ASD; head nods; and silence (Gutstein, 2005).

When activities are modified to amplify desired objectives, the objectives are considered to be **framed**. This can be accomplished by minimizing the peripheral aspects of the activity, modifying the environment by adding structures such as written schedules, or adding additional structure to the activity. Certain activities can be framed to include a climax or moment of uncertainty about what will happen next. Gutstein states that this can be a powerful learning opportunity for the child.

Scaffolding, used by Vygotsky, is included as part of RDI in the same manner. Supports are provided so that the individual with ASD can experience or preview competence. This support is gradually withdrawn as the child gains mastery. Elaboration is the process of gradually adding complexity to activities so they become more like real-world conditions (Gutstein, 2005). Examples of elaboration include using materials in different ways; using a variety of modalities such as auditory, kinesthetic, and visual; reducing the amplification of spotlighting; increasing the necessity for more rapid shifts in attention; and adding more background noise or distractions.

A curriculum is used to build dynamic intelligence and guide the development of relationship competence from a novice focused on external, relationship-bound abilities such as social referencing (Gutstein, 2009; Gutstein & Sheely, 2002a) through internal, self-referencing abilities necessary for intimate relations (Gutstein, 2009; Gutstein & Sheely, 2002b).

## Evidence for RDI

"A controlled, blinded study of RDI has yet to be done" (Gutstein, 2009, p. 174). Sixteen children diagnosed with autism, Asperger syndrome, and PDDNOS with IQ scores of at least 70 participated in a clinic where RDI was developed. These 16 children were evaluated using chart reviews and follow-up assessments (Gutstein, Burgess, & Montfort, 2007). Five of the 16 children had participated in biomedical treatment and 12 in behavioral treatment prior to RDI; however, there was no reported correlation of pretreatment or concurrent treatment with outcome. Of the 12 children who initially received a diagnosis of autism (10) or autism spectrum (2) rating on the Autism Diagnostic Observation Schedule (Lord, Rutter, DiLavore, & Risi, 2001) at pretreatment, no child received a rating in the autism category post-treatment of at least 30 months of RDI. Parents reported improvement in experience-sharing items on the ADI-R (Lord, Rutter, & Le Couteur, 1994) and age-appropriate flexibility ratings on a survey. Following treatment, 10 of the 16 participants attended mainstream classrooms without an aide compared with two prior to treatment. The authors identify the limitations of their study as a lack of a control or comparison group, the lack of participants with more severe cognitive delays, and the implementation in the primary setting where RDI was developed alone (Gutstein et al., 2007).

RDI was one of the comprehensive programs evaluated by Odom, Boyd, Hall, and Hume (2010) and received a low rating on the criterion of additional studies due to the lack of research on the effects of the strategies recommended. Outcome research on programs implemented by interventionists other than the model developers as well as on the effects of the key strategies on the social skills and dynamic intelligence of individuals with ASD would be welcome.

# Enhanced Milieu Teaching

**Milieu teaching** was initially developed to increase communication with mother–child dyads in which children were developmentally delayed (Yoder & Warren, 1993). Milieu teaching is based on a developmental perspective and uses behavioral principles; its focus is to increase the number of opportunities for teaching new skills by "eliciting child communication through environmental arrangement, the mand model, and time delay procedures" (Yoder and Warren, 1993, p. 46). Milieu teaching combines strategies of environmental arrangement, prompting communication in functional contexts, and responsive interactions (Kaiser, Nietfeld, & Roberts, 2010). Teaching is embedded in typical activities, and adults are taught to implement incidental teaching procedures and to encourage spontaneous and prompted imitations. If the child does not initiate interaction, however, then the adult can use a mand-model sequence of interaction earlier than suggested with incidental teaching procedures (Allen & Cowan, 2008). **Enhanced milieu teaching** is described as a hybrid approach to early language intervention that incorporates the behavioral and social interactionist approaches (Hancock & Kaiser, 2002; Kaiser & Hester, 1994). Enhanced milieu teaching includes the additional strategies from responsive teaching such as turn-taking and a responsive conversation style (Kaiser & Hester, 1994). The three main

components of enhanced milieu teaching are (1) arranging the environment, (2) responsive interaction strategies, and (3) milieu teaching strategies (Kaiser & Hester, 1994).

## Strategies Based on Enhanced Milieu Teaching

Milieu teaching procedures (1) begin with the child's verbal or nonverbal requests; (2) are followed by the use of specific prompts; (3) incorporate corrective prompts if needed; and (4) end with an expansion of the child's utterance, positive feedback, and access to the requested object (Hancock & Kaiser, 2002). Like other natural language strategies, milieu teaching uses naturally occurring activities and arranges the environment in a similar manner to incidental teaching. (See the description of incidental teaching in Chapter 4.)

When using enhanced milieu teaching, practitioners are taught to use a mand model. **Mand** is a term used by Skinner to describe verbal communication that functions as a request. (See Chapter 8 for a description of verbal behavior and terms.) In enhanced milieu teaching, the practitioner gains the attention of the child with ASD (e.g., holding a toy of interest) and then instructs, or mands, for the use of language or other functional behavior (Webber & Scheuermann, 2008). If the child produces the behavior, praise and access follows. If the child does not produce the behavior, it is modeled for the child ("Truck, please"). If the child imitates the model, the behavior is praised and the truck is given to the child (Allen & Cowan, 2008).

**Time delay** is another strategy emphasized in enhanced milieu teaching. Time delay is used when the learner has the behavior or skill but does not readily exhibit the skill. In milieu teaching, the identified steps of time delay include (1) identify a situation when the student might need assistance or want something; (2) establish joint attention; (3) wait 5 to 15 seconds for a correct behavior while maintaining attention with an expectant look; and (4) if the response is correct, praise and allow the desired effect (or if the response is incorrect, implement mand-model or modeling procedures) (Webber & Scheuermann, 2008).

In this approach, parents are taught to interact in a responsive interaction style, with a focus on positive affective relationships, while implementing strategies that are individualized for each child (Kaiser & Hester, 1994). The responsive interaction strategies in this model include following the child's lead and balancing turns, maintaining the child's topic or interest, using linguistically and topically appropriate language with the child, matching the child's level with the language and the complexity of actions introduced, expanding and repeating the child's utterances, and responding to the child's verbal and nonverbal communication to build social interaction.

## Evidence for Enhanced Milieu Teaching

The initial research on enhanced milieu teaching demonstrated that parents could implement the strategies effectively with their preschool-age children with moderate to severe disabilities (Hemmeter & Kaiser, 1994) and that language skills increased when used by parents and teachers of children participating in early intervention programs in metropolitan Nashville (Kaiser & Hester, 1994). Enhanced milieu teaching was shown to increase the complexity and diversity of expressive language of four preschool children with autism (Hancock & Kaiser, 2002). Using a randomized group design, Yoder and Stone (2006) demonstrated that, compared with the group receiving the Picture Exchange Communication System (PECS) intervention (Bondy & Frost, 2001), the 17 preschool age children with autism spectrum disorders assigned to the enhanced milieu teaching group increased their frequency of generalized turn-taking and increased their generalized initiation of joint attention. Pretreatment initiating of joint attention predicted treatment effects. Those in the PECS intervention made more requests (Yoder & Stone, 2006).

# The Denver Model and Early Start Denver Model

The Denver model is a multidisciplinary model developed to serve young children (toddlers and preschoolers) with autism. It began as a federally funded treatment program for young children in 1981 (Rogers & Lewis, 1989). This five-day-a-week, 4.5 hours per day, program called The Playschool was part of the JFK Center for Developmental Disabilities affiliated with the University of Colorado Health Sciences Center (Rogers, Hall, Osaki, Reaven, & Herbison, 2001). The program was initially directed by Sally Rogers, Ph.D., developmental psychologist, and coauthored with Diane Osaki, OTR.

The theoretical perspective guiding program practices was strongly influenced by Daniel Stern (Rogers et al., 2001). Initially, nearly all therapies and activities were presented through play (Rogers & Lewis, 1989). Adults expanded activities to introduce social games so that interactions became a source of pleasure. Positive affect was stressed, and all adults who worked with children were trained in reactive language strategies (Rogers, Herbison, Lewis, Pantone, & Reis, 1986). Discrete-trial-teaching methods based on the principles of applied behavior analysis were introduced to teach imitation in 1989 (Rogers, 2000). Diane Osaki, the director of the Aspen Center for Autism in Denver, Colorado, describes her current program as a "fusion of applied behavior analysis and developmental and social-relational approaches" (D. Osaki, personal communication, January 12, 2006).

The Early Start Denver Model (ESDM) extends the model to toddlers ages 12 to 36 months with autism (Rogers & Dawson, 2010b). Key features of the Denver Model are maintained along with teaching strategies based on applied behavior analysis and PRT in particular (Vismara, Colombi, & Rogers, 2009). The model is designed to be implemented by parents and professionals across settings, and includes a developmental curriculum and accompanying child skills checklist (Rogers & Dawson, 2010a). The curriculum is divided into the domains of receptive communication, expressive communication, social skills, imitation, cognition, play, fine motor, gross motor, behavior, and personal independence (eating, dressing, grooming, chores) for four skill levels (Rogers & Dawson, 2010a, 2010b). Parents and professionals are encouraged to identify short-term learning objectives using the Early Start Denver Model Curriculum Checklist for Young Children with Autism (Rogers & Dawson, 2010a). Figure 6–1 provides an example of an item from the checklist under level 1 for expressive communication.

## Key Concepts of the Denver Model

"Families should be at the helm of their children's treatment" (Rogers et al., 2001, p. 100). Partnerships with families are emphasized, and parents are integral parts of an interdisciplinary team, which is comprised of an early childhood special education teacher, speech-language therapist, psychologist, occupational therapist, and paraprofessionals (Rogers et al., 2001; Rogers & Dawson, 2010b). According to Rogers and colleagues (2001), the emphasis of treatment must be on the social disability because autism is a social disorder, and relationships are therefore at the core of treatment.

Play is one of the most powerful cognitive and social learning tools (Rogers et al., 2001; Rogers & Lewis, 1989), and the cognitive aspects of play implemented within dyadic play routines are emphasized in the Denver model (Rogers & Dawson, 2010b). Other core features of the model are a focus on interpersonal engagement and implementing a developmental curriculum to foster fluent, reciprocal, and spontaneous imitation of gestures, facial expressions, and use of objects (Rogers & Dawson, 2010b). Various intervention approaches have demonstrated effectiveness, but effective programs require that

| Skill | Level 1 | Observed | Parent Report | Other/ Teacher Report | CODE |
|---|---|---|---|---|---|
| 1 | Uses a goal-directed reach to request. | | | | |
| 2 | Vocalizes with intent. | | | | |
| 3 | "Asks" for help by handing object to adult. | | | | |
| 4 | Takes turns vocalizing with communication partner. | | | | |
| 5 | Expresses refusal by pushing away object or giving the object back to another person. | | | | |
| 6 | Points proximally to request desired object. | | | | |
| 7 | Makes eye contact to obtain a desired object when adult blocks access/ withholds desired object. | | | | |
| 8 | Points to indicate a choice between two objects. | | | | |
| 9 | Combines vocalization and gaze for intentional request. | | | | |
| 10 | Points distally to request desired object. | | | | |
| 11 | Points distally to indicate a choice between two objects. | | | | |
| 12 | Vocalizes with CVCV reduplicative babbling (not necessarily word approximations). | | | | |
| 13 | Produces five or more consonants in spontaneous vocalizations. | | | | |
| 14 | Produces CVCV with differing CV sequences (variegated babbling). | | | | |

CV stands for consonant vowel.

**FIGURE 6–1** Expressive Communication items from Checklist 1-14

*Source:* Rogers, S. J., & Dawson, G. (2010). *Early Start Denver Model Curriculum Checklist for Young Children with Autism* (p. 3). New York: The Guilford Press. Used with permission.

most of the waking hours be spent in socially orienting activities, with more than 20 hours per week of structure for optimum progress (Rogers et al., 2001).

## Strategies Based on Key Denver Model Concepts

Following comprehensive assessment that includes standardized measures, identified goals and objectives for children are embedded in activities and are individualized (Rogers et al., 2001; Rogers & Dawson, 2010a). Joint activity routines are used as the context for interaction; they include an opening or set-up phase that establishes the theme of the play, the theme or when the child and adult are engaged in a definable play activity, elaboration of the theme to keep it interesting or to highlight different aspects of the play, and then the final phase of closing when attention is waning or the teaching value of the activity is over (Rogers & Dawson, 2010b).

**Sensory social routines** that include turn-taking are an integral part of each activity. These routines are "dyadic interactions involving simple, repeated social routines that engage the child at both sensory and affective levels" (Rogers et al., 2001, p. 112). Shared control and positive emotions are emphasized. The focus of communication is on intent rather than product during self-directed activities in natural environments (Rogers & DiLalla, 1991). During these routines, each partner is focused on the other person instead of on objects, and there is mutual pleasure and engagement in the play (Rogers & Dawson, 2010b). Positive approaches to address unwanted behaviors are used whenever possible. Visual-spatial cues (Mesibov, Schopler, & Hearsey, 1994) and visual supports, including the Picture Exchange Communication System (Bondy & Frost, 2001) are used (Rogers & Dawson, 2010b).

A fidelity coding sheet for the ESDM can be used for training and to guide the therapist or adult in the use of the identified strategies for the model, including those from the Denver Model

and from PRT (Rogers & Dawson 2010b). The strategies are listed on the fidelity checklist and are scored on a scale from 1 (weak) to 5 (strong) on the following items: management of child attention, use of the ABC format, use of instructional techniques, modulation of child affect/arousal, management of unwanted behaviors, quality of dyadic engagement, adult optimization of child motivation, adult use of positive affect, adult sensitivity and responsivity, multiple varied communication opportunities, adult's language for child's level, joint activity and elaboration, and transition between activities. The ESDM also includes a decision tree for choosing teaching procedures and guides the adult in consideration of changing variables in the categories of reinforcement, structure, and visual supports if there is no measurable progress after a determined period of time (Rogers & Dawson, 2010b).

## Evidence for the Denver Model and the Early Start Denver Model

Several outcome studies for children with autism spectrum disorders who participated in the Denver model have been published in peer-reviewed journals. One study reported outcomes obtained for 26 children ages 2 to 6 with autism, PDD, or severe emotional disturbance, through the use of teacher ratings and observations of play and social skills as well as from videotapes of parent–child interaction (Rogers et al., 1986). The primary vehicle for intervention was play. All adults received 40 hours of training in reactive language strategies. All children demonstrated statistically significant progress in cognitive, communication, and social-emotional domains. Of the 26 participating children, 7 were functioning within the normal range and attended a nonspecialized school after leaving the playschool program (Rogers et al., 1986).

In 1989, Rogers and Lewis published outcomes for 31 children diagnosed with autism or PDD following a six-month intervention period. The Denver model used is described as one that incorporated use of play, pragmatic language development strategies, interpersonal relationships, and activities to foster symbolic thought. Of the children who entered treatment without any useful speech, 47% acquired it by the end of treatment, and 73% in total had useful speech. Results of statistical analyses revealed that children had better-than-projected scores in cognition, language, social-emotional, perceptual/fine motor, and gross motor areas. The authors conclude that these data demonstrate the effectiveness of a developmentally based, affectively oriented treatment approach.

Rogers and DiLalla (1991) reviewed the charts of 49 children with autism and compared outcomes with 27 children with other behavior/emotional and developmental disorders (attention deficit disorder with hyperactivity, oppositional disorder) who attended the developmentally based program since 1981. Although children in the autism group were more delayed at entry, both groups made equal progress, with greater developmental gains than predicted as determined by post-treatment measures (Rogers & DiLalla, 1991). Gains were particularly impressive for language acquisition. The Denver model was replicated in four independent agencies and outcomes were assessed for 11 children with autism and mental retardation (Rogers, Lewis, & Reis, 1987). There were no increases in staff ratios, treatment hours, or other services when the Denver model was introduced. Measures were obtained for fidelity of implementation of the play-based strategies and child progress. Children made statistically significant treatment gains (Rogers, Lewis, & Reis, 1987).

A case study implementing the Early Start Denver Model with the father of a 9-month-old infant demonstrated child gains in social communicative behavior and provided support for the model (Vismara & Rogers, 2008). The father received weekly 1.5 hour sessions for 12 weeks that were focused on the strategies of the ESDM. By the fifth session, the father was able to establish shared attention and child engagement during meaningful play activities and was implementing intervention techniques such as modeling, prompting, reinforcing, shaping, and fading.

A brief intervention using the ESDM was implemented with eight parents for twelve weekly one-hour sessions (Vismara et al., 2009). The ESDM Fidelity Checklist was used to measure parents' use of key strategies taught. Outcomes for the young children (less than 36 months old) with autism were scored from video sessions of parent–child and therapist–child interactions in a clinic. The results revealed that parents were implementing the key components of the ESDM (scoring 85% or better) by the fifth or sixth session. Compared with baseline levels, children's use of functional verbal utterances and imitative behaviors increased and maintained at follow-up for the six children remaining in the study (Vismara et al., 2009). The authors conclude that parents can be taught to implement the ESDM effectively in a short-term education program with positive outcomes for their young children with ASD. An additional study demonstrated that the ESDM can be implemented by parents effectively when training by therapists was conducted via distance learning using the videotaped sessions and teleconferencing (Vismara et al., 2009). Comparisons of distance versus live methods of instruction showed that both methods of intervention were found to be equally effective.

Reported as possibly the first randomized, controlled trial of an intervention for toddlers with autism, the Early Start Denver Model was compared with the typical community intervention in greater Seattle (Dawson et al., 2010). Forty-eight toddlers ages 18 to 30 months were randomly assigned as follows: either the experimental condition comprising a mean of 15.2 hours per week of the ESDM plus an average of 16.3 hours a week in additional interventions, or the comparison condition that averaged 9.1 hours of individual therapy and 9.3 hours of group intervention for two years. Composite scores from the Mullen Scales of Early Learning (MSEL) and the Vineland Adaptive Behavior Scales (VABS) were used to measure outcomes at baseline and at years one and two post-intervention. Scores on both assessments were better for the group receiving the ESDM, with scores on the MSEL increasing

17.6 points compared with 7.0 points for those receiving the typical community intervention and scores on the VABS remaining steady for the ESDM group and declining by 11.2 points for the community intervention group (Dawson et al., 2010). In addition, seven of the children receiving the ESDM had a change in diagnosis from autism to PDD-NOS compared with only one in the community group.

The Denver Model was one of the highest rated comprehensive treatment models of the 30 reviewed by Odom, Boyd, and colleagues (2010). If the randomized, controlled trial study (Dawson et al, 2010) had been included (it was published following the review), the model would have received high ratings in additional criteria. The authors of the ESDM are to be commended for their development and use of a fidelity checklist (Rogers & Dawson, 2010a). It would be of interest to know which of the strategies that comprise the ESDM are easier for parents to implement with fidelity (Vismara et al., 2009) and which are more challenging for parents, and if these are also a challenge for professionals.

## Project ImPACT

Project ImPACT is a parent training program that incorporates intervention techniques from the developmental, social-pragmatic, and behavioral literature (Ingersoll & Dvortcsak, 2010b). One of the model developers, Brooke Ingersoll, describes the theories and strategies of this model (see In Their Words 6.1). The program was originally designed for clinicians in a one-to-one setting in a hearing and speech center in Portland, Oregon, in 2005, and has been implemented with over 200 families in Oregon and Michigan since then. The developers of the model brought their backgrounds as a psychologist and Board Certified Behavior Analyst (Ingersoll) and a speech-language pathologist trained in the DIR floortime approach (Dvortcsak) to the creation of the model. Project ImPACT is described in two manuals, one for practitioners (Ingersoll &

Dvortcsak, 2010b) and one for parents (Ingersoll & Dvortcsak, 2010a).

The recommended format of the parent training program includes 12 weeks of six 2-hour group sessions with 6 to 10 parents without children and six 45-minute individual coaching sessions with the trainer (Ingersoll & Dvortcsak, 2010b). The program is designed to be used with children diagnosed with autism spectrum disorders from time of diagnosis to age 6. Forms to be used to guide parents in gathering information about their child in order to select treatment goals such as the Child History Form, Social-Communication Checklist, and Goal Development Form are provided in the practitioner's manual (Ingersoll & Dvortcsak, 2010b). Intervention techniques are introduced in the group sessions, practiced for assigned homework, and observed during the individual coaching sessions. There is an accompanying CD with illustrations of each of the teaching strategies to be used for demonstration purposes.

## Strategies Based on the Project ImPACT Model

The intervention techniques used in the Project ImPACT model are illustrated using a pyramid and presented to the parents starting with those at the base of the pyramid (those considered foundational or almost always used) (see Figure 6–2 for the pyramid illustration). The initial strategies of focus include following the child's lead, imitating the child, using animation and modeling, and expanding language. Other interactive techniques taught include using playful obstruction to elicit communication, balancing turns, and communication temptations. Once parents are using these techniques, they are taught the direct teaching techniques such as prompting, and reinforcement (Ingersoll & Dvortcsak, 2010b).

Parents are taught to put all the strategies together and use those strategies that work best with their child. They are also told that they will be moving up and down the pyramid depending

## 6.1  IN THEIR WORDS  Dr. Brooke Ingersoll, *Department of Psychology, Michigan State University*

Although they differ in their theoretical foundations, the developmental and naturalistic behavioral models share a number of intervention techniques. Both follow the child's lead and teach within daily routines, such as play, dressing, feeding, and bathing. They also both use techniques to elicit communication from the child. They also differ in their use of several techniques. Developmental interventions use a number of techniques to increase the parents' responsiveness to their child's behavior, including imitating the child, using heightened animation, and modeling and expanding language. Naturalistic behavioral interventions use prompting and reinforcement around the child's focus of interest to teach new skills. Thus, developmental interventions focus on developing joint engagement between the parent and child, but may not teach skills that are currently outside the child's current repertoire; naturalistic behavioral interventions focus on teaching new skills, but are less likely to develop joint interactions between the parent and child. Therefore, neither approach is sufficient for addressing the wide-ranging social-communication deficits found in ASD. However, a blended approach that takes the "best of both worlds" is likely to have more success. Given their many similarities, the approaches can be easily integrated with each other within a parent training model, yielding a potentially more powerful social-communication intervention for children with ASD.

Parents' interaction styles with their child coming into parent training make them naturally better at some intervention techniques than others. Some parents are very good at following their child's lead and joining their child in play, but have difficulty prompting their child for a more complex response. Other parents are skilled at using prompting and reinforcement to get their child to respond to them (although they might not know that is what they are doing), but have a harder time following their child's lead in play. The nice thing about using a blended approach is that most parents feel success with some of the treatment techniques because they match their natural interaction styles with their children. The challenge for the parent trainer is to help the parent learn to use the strategies that they are not naturally inclined to use. For this reason, we broke the intervention down into small steps, so that parents need to learn only one to two techniques at a time. This allows parents to develop a foundation in responsiveness strategies before learning how to prompt their child for more advanced skills. For most families, we have found that this approach makes them more effective at both being responsive to their child's behavior and prompting their child for more advanced skills.

on the progress made by the child and the success of the strategies. The parent manual is full of tips, or examples, of how to implement each of the strategies (Ingersoll & Dvortcsak, 2010a). The practitioner's guide includes suggestions of how to work most effectively in groups and during individual sessions, and includes forms for measuring fidelity of the intervention techniques addressed (Ingersoll & Dvortcsak, 2010b).

## Evidence for Project ImPACT

The model developers conducted research in order to evaluate the use of the developmental, social-pragmatic (DSP) strategies on the language skills of young children with ASD (Ingersoll, Dvortcsak, Whalen, & Sikora, 2005). Three boys ages 30 to 46 months with ASD participated in one-to-one sessions at a center with

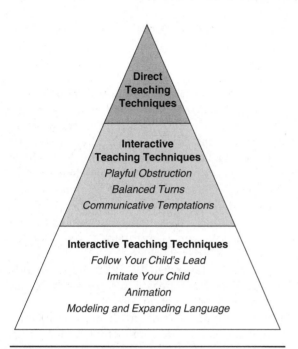

**FIGURE 6–2** The pyramid of Project ImPACT intervention techniques
*Source:* Ingersoll, B., & Dvortcsak, A. (2010). *Teaching social communication to children with autism: A practitioner's guide to parent training* (p. 68). New York: The Guilford Press. Used with permission.

the speech-language pathologist. A multiple-baseline design was used to evaluate the effect of the DSP intervention on the rate of spontaneous language. Fidelity of intervention was collected. The results revealed increases in the use of spontaneous language for all three boys over baseline levels supporting the implementation of the DSP strategies (Ingersoll et al., 2005).

Ingersoll and Dvortcsak (2006) designed, implemented, and evaluated the parent training program as part of an early childhood special education program in Oregon. They trained the teachers in the parent training model in 50 hours in multiple formats (workshops, group and individual sessions). Parents attended group sessions once a week for nine weeks and participated in three individual 1.5-hour sessions held at the school. Teachers were taught to build rapport, review information, model techniques, provide feedback, and build independence

(Ingersoll & Dvortcsak, 2006). Parents were taught both interactive and direct teaching techniques and given homework.

Results from the study included increases in parent knowledge on quizzes from preprogram scores that averaged 29% to post-program scores with an average of 75% correct on multiple-choice items. Both parents and teachers were satisfied on post-program survey items and indicated that the program benefited themselves and the children with autism spectrum disorders.

# Pivotal Response Treatment (PRT)

In 2006, Robert Koegel and Lynn Koegel published a book entitled *Pivotal Response Treatments for Autism*. In this text, the word *treatment* replaced *training* (see Chapter 4 for a description). The authors also describe pivotal response treatment (PRT) as a comprehensive service delivery model that uses both applied behavior analysis procedures and a developmental approach (Koegel, Openden, Fredeen, & Koegel, 2006). The introduction lists three core areas of motivation, social initiation, and self-regulation of behavior that, when addressed, produce large intervention gains (Koegel & Koegel, 2006). Five pivotal areas focused on in this approach are listed in this text: motivation, responsivity to multiple cues, self-management, self-initiations, and empathy (Koegel, Openden, et al., 2006).

## Strategies Based on Key PRT Concepts and Research Evidence

Many of the strategies used in PRT—such as arranging the environment to increase motivation; incorporating potential reinforcers; and using differential reinforcement, time delay, and reinforcing attempts—are based on applied behavior analysis and have been demonstrated as effective in multiple research studies. (See Chapter 4 in this text for a more detailed description of these strategies.) PRT was implemented in a group format in a 10-week program of 90-minute weekly sessions plus one individualized session for parents of children with autism (Minjarez, Williams, Mercier, & Hardan, 2011). Parents' use of the following six variables were scored: (1) presenting clear opportunities to respond, (2) interspersing maintenance tasks with acquisition tasks, (3) using shared control/child choice, (4) providing immediate contingent reinforcement, (5) using natural reinforcers, and (6) providing reinforcers following both expressive verbal attempts and correct responses. When mean fidelity scores were compared pre- and post-program, there was a significant difference in parent fidelity scores and the number of child utterances (Minjarez et al., 2011). The authors do not state which variables were not obtained from parents, but they do state that the study demonstrates that PRT can be administered effectively in group sessions with parents.

The pivotal skill with the least research evidence in pivotal response treatment is empathy. Research demonstrating that the strategies used to teach play and self-management are also effective in teaching empathy is needed. In addition, more research demonstrating that the identified focus areas are indeed pivotal (or that once used and exhibited by individuals with ASD, they lead to untaught or unplanned outcomes) would add support to the comprehensive model. For example, it makes sense that if a child with autism learns to initiate during play, there will be a generalization across settings; however, we know that such generalization is often a challenge for learners with ASD.

## The SCERTS Model

The SCERTS model is described as a comprehensive educational approach for individuals with autism spectrum disorders and related disabilities (Prizant, Wetherby, Rubin, Laurent, & Rydell, 2006a). The model is described by the authors as new and representative of the next generation of practice in the field (Prizant et al., 2006a). The SCERTS model was created by a multidisciplinary team (Prizant, Wetherby, Rubin,

Laurent, & Rydell, 2006b) for use by other multidisciplinary teams. Although publication of this model is relatively new, each of the authors has an extensive history of work in their respective areas with individuals with ASD and their families. For example, Dr. Prizant published an article on his Ph.D. research in 1981 on the topic of the function of echolalia for communication by individuals with autism. Dr. Wetherby has many publications in the area of speech and language development that have resulted in work with Prizant since the early 1980s. Together they have an edited volume that is part of the Communication and Language Intervention Series published by Brookes (Wetherby & Prizant, 2000).

The trademarked SCERTS model stands for the three main areas of the approach: social-communication, emotional regulation, and transactional supports (Prizant et al., 2006b). The model is based on developmental theory, learning theory, and family systems theory, and is reported to be dynamic in response to the interaction styles and needs of the individual, family, and professional team.

### Key Concepts of the SCERTS Model

The social-communication aspect of the approach has two key foci. Developing *joint attention* is the first. Individuals with ASD often have difficulty with joint attention, which is the foundation for engaging in reciprocal social interactions (Prizant et al., 2006a). This area is addressed in three aspects: sharing attention, sharing emotion, and sharing of intentions. The second key concept is symbol use. An understanding of abstract symbols is the basis for language development and communication.

The focus on emotional regulation has three key concepts. Self-regulation is the aim for all individuals. Assisting students with ASD to calm themselves in situations and environments that are stressful is one aspect of the model. If individuals are not able to regulate their emotions, it will be a continual challenge to learn new skills. Mutual regulation occurs when we get assistance from others to handle emotional situations. Sensory stimulation to aid with calming, or the use of music and topics of interest to foster motivation during activities, are examples of how others can assist the person with ASD with regulation. Finally, it is also important for individuals to learn how to recover from dysregulation. If someone becomes upset or engages in repetitive motor mannerisms as a response to a stressful environment, then having strategies to return to a regulated state that enables social interaction or on-task performance is important.

There are four key aspects to transactional supports. *Interpersonal supports* for individuals are extremely important. Interaction with a student with ASD in a style that facilitates communication and helps the student to regulate is a dynamic process. Parents and professionals need to be keen observers of the emotional states and preferences for interaction style of the individual with ASD. *Learning and educational supports* are often needed for individuals with ASD. Visual supports are commonly used (Hodgdon, 1995) with individuals with ASD. Pictures, photographs, adapted books, and other supports that facilitate learning are recommended.

*Support to families* is critical for the success of any model. Parents often request educational supports so that they can help to generalize the use of adapted curriculum to the home. Families may also have priorities for goals that they would like addressed that relate to home life. Emotional support for families is also important. *Support among professionals* is another key component to this model. Professionals who work in collaboration and as a team are far more likely to have success in meeting the goals established by the family. Family priorities guide the selection of educational goals (Prizant et al., 2006a). The functional needs of the student with ASD are also considered when selecting goals.

## Strategies Based on Key SCERTS Concepts

The SCERTS model emphasizes the use of functional communication in natural settings (Prizant et al., 2006b). Both verbal and nonverbal aspects of communication are developed.

Activities that occur in the daily routine are used to foster communication opportunities.

Teaching students with ASD to request assistance or respond to others' attempts to assist them to regulate are essential to developing emotional self-regulation (Prizant, 2006b). Team members should facilitate in stressful situations by providing strategies to help the student cope. Providing choices of activities or allowing the student to take a break when needed are strategies that can be helpful. The use of positive behavior supports is consistent with the SCERTS model. Teaching functional communication skills as replacements for problem behavior is an example of a strategy that facilitates regulation.

The design of activities and the educational environments should take into account what motivates individuals with ASD. A continuum of planned activity routines to naturally occurring activities should be included in the individual's schedule. Engineered activities and modified natural activities and environments are included along this continuum. Learning supports should be designed to foster communication and social interaction.

"Transactional supports are used to support active and independent participation in activities" (Prizant et al., 2006b, p. 4). Consistency and predictability are important for individuals with ASD. Interpersonal and learning supports that help students understand the purpose of activities and promote generalization are recommended.

The context for the successful implementation of these strategies is a collaborative, supportive relationship among professionals (Prizant et al., 2006b). Mutually respectful relationships enhance the family's sense of competence and trust. Family members are considered essential partners. In addition, the positive relationship between professionals and family members serves as a model for children with ASD. This relationship is a critical variable in the development of optimal social, emotional, and communication development for the individual with ASD.

Following an extensive assessment of social-communication and emotional regulation, goals and objectives are determined in one of three stages (Prizant et al., 2006a): (1) social partners stage, (2) language partner stage, and (3) conversational partner stage (Prizant et al., 2006a). During the social partner stage, adults are more active social and communicative partners and aim for interactions with a range of communicative functions that incorporate conventional gestures and vocalizations within social exchanges (Prizant et al., 2006b). During the language partner stage, partners become more persistent in communicating for a range of intentions, including requesting assistance, greeting others, showing off, taking turns, and commenting about actions or events. The child's partners in the conversational partner stage are focused on more advanced language abilities and social awareness of others, including greater sensitivity to others' perspectives and emotional states. Extended communicative exchanges are supported during this stage (Prizant et al., 2006b).

When providing interpersonal support, the nature of the partner responsivity will vary depending on the developmental state of the child; however, the following characteristics are recommended (Prizant et al., 2006b): follow the child's focus of attention, attune to the child's emotions and pace, respond to the child's signals, recognize and support the child's behavioral and language strategies to regulate arousal, imitate the child's verbal and nonverbal behavior, offer breaks, and facilitate reengagement in activities. Research demonstrating its effectiveness is important prior to recommending the model as evidence-based practice.

## Key Concepts of the Developmental and Social-Relational Approaches Put into Practice

A model program based on the developmental and social-relational approaches would have an interdisciplinary team that includes speech-language pathologists and occupational therapists to assess and design individualized program plans. Play would serve as the context for cognitive and emotional development. Symbolic and pretend play activities would be fostered. Adults would follow the lead of the child and would be focused on responding to child initiations in a responsive manner that matched the communication level of the child. Turn-taking would be central to most interactions, and control of the focus and pace of activities would be shared.

Educators would have knowledge of typical child development across domains and would be fostering interaction with the potential to expand child interactions to the next level. Educators would have an idea of the zone of proximal development for each child so that the appropriate supports or scaffolding would be in place and expectations for the form and content of interactions would be matched to individual abilities. Parents would be critical team members, and the program would emphasize numerous effective parent–child interactions throughout the day. Embedding learning opportunities in daily routines would be a focus. Enhancing parents' skills as responsive communicators and facilitators of social interaction would be an aim of the program. Professional educational activities would take place in the home, either in part or for all of the service delivery.

An emphasis on social-emotional development would take priority. Social interaction would be considered the context for cognitive development. In other words, growth would occur as a result of effective adult–child social interaction. Attention to nonverbal aspects of communication would be emphasized in order to maintain interaction or to highlight the importance of an event in an activity. Visual cues such as photographs or picture symbols would be included to support children who have yet to develop speech. Activities would be designed to be fun and engaging for the child and would be likely to focus on symbolic play and on interactions with shapes and sizes of materials, and would include writing or drawing.

Children with autism spectrum disorders would have access to typical peers. Peer interaction would be considered an important component of social-emotional development. Peers would serve as the context for fostering social skills and as a model for communication. Routine peer play would be incorporated into the program as frequently as possible.

# Research on the Developmental and Social-Relational Approaches

In her well-thought-out comparison study, Brooke Ingersoll (2010) compares and contrasts models based on applied behavior analysis and those based on a developmental, social pragmatic approach. The programs described in this chapter were reviewed. She concludes that the main differences in these approaches is that the strategies focused on ABA incorporate explicit prompting strategies that vary according to the child's initiation and the developmental approach does not use these strategies, but unlike ABA focuses on facilitative strategies such as adult responsiveness (i.e., contingent imitation, indirect language stimulation, and affective attunement) (Ingersoll, 2010). The models described in this chapter that are based on both theoretical approaches use all of these strategies (e.g., ESDM, Project ImPACT, SCERTS). It would be important for researchers to identify if those models that do not use explicit prompting and reinforcement are as effective for all children with autism spectrum disorders. Perhaps facilitative strategies were effective alone for young children with minimal interest in toys, but were insufficient when parents had to compete with high interest in objects

(Carter et al., 2011). Additional research is needed on child outcomes when facilitative strategies are used with fidelity by parents. Models that include fidelity checklists for practitioners will be helpful in designing such studies (e.g., EDSM, Project ImPACT, and PLAY Project).

Educators are exposed to models and approaches through author-marketed workshops and training events. Prior to adopting a model, it is important to know if there is research on outcomes from implementation of the model promoted or presented. It is not uncommon for proponents of models based on the developmental, social-relational approaches to cite the research from other models based on the same theoretical approach. However, this research is not support for a particular set of strategies unless they are evaluated and positive outcomes are determined when used by both model developers as well as other researchers, professionals, and parents.

Some specific topics for future research might include determining which strategies and practices are most helpful for individuals with autism spectrum disorders in their development of self-regulation of emotion and/or reaction to environmental stimuli. In addition, it will be interesting to determine if the development of social referencing abilities in early childhood leads to a greater focus on adult and peer models as well as more typical social interaction patterns. The field eagerly awaits more research and publication in peer-reviewed sources to support the claims made by the talented promoters of these approaches.

## SUGGESTIONS FOR DISCUSSION

1. Identify some key concepts that are included across programs using the developmental or social-relational approach.

2. Discuss the role of parents in the programs that use the approach discussed in this chapter.

3. Conduct a debate with one side arguing for the importance of following the child's lead during all interactions to facilitate communication and social interaction skills, and the other side arguing that there are situations when you want to impose adult structure or redirect the individual with ASD.

4. Provide a rationale for embedding educational activities in the daily routines of individuals with autism spectrum disorders.

5. Comment on this statement: "Addressing social relationships is aiming at the heart of autism."

6. Describe the skills that are considered pivotal or key according to the authors of pivotal response treatment, and discuss whether you think these skills are indeed pivotal.

7. Select a key strategy that is used by practitioners who are influenced by the developmental or social-relational theorists and devise a research question that could be used in a study to determine the effectiveness of the strategy.

## ▌ RESOURCES

### Books

Greenspan, S. I., & Wieder, S. (2006). *Engaging autism: Using the floortime approach to help children relate, communicate, and think*. Cambridge, MA: De Capo Lifelong Books.

Gutstein, S. E., & Sheely, R. K. (2002a). *Relationship development intervention with young children: Social and emotional development activities for Asperger syndrome, autism, PDD, and NLD*. New York: Jessica Kingsley.

Gutstein, S. E., & Sheely, R. K. (2002b). *Relationship development intervention with children, adolescents and adults: Social and emotional development activities for Asperger syndrome, autism, PDD, and NLD*. New York: Jessica Kingsley.

Ingersoll, B., & Dvortcsak, A. (2010a). *Teaching social communication to children with autism: A manual for parents*. New York: Guilford.

Ingersoll, B., & Dvortcsak, A. (2010b). *Teaching social communication to children with autism: A practitioner's guide to parent training*. New York: Guilford.

Koegel, R. L., & Koegel, L. K. (2006). *Pivotal response treatments for autism: Communication, social, and academic development*. Baltimore: Brookes.

Mahoney, G., & MacDonald, J. (2007). *Autism and developmental delays in young children: The responsive teaching curriculum for parents and professionals*. Austin, TX: Pro-ed.

Prizant, B. M., Wetherby, A. M., Rubin, E., Laurent, A. C., & Rydell, P. J. (2006a). *The SCERTS model: A comprehensive educational approach for children with autism spectrum disorders: Volume I, Assessment*. Baltimore, MD: Brookes.

Prizant, B. M., Wetherby, A. M., Rubin, E., Laurent, A. C., & Rydell, P. J. (2006b). *The SCERTS model: A comprehensive educational approach for children with autism spectrum disorders: Volume II, Program planning and intervention*. Baltimore, MD: Brookes.

Rogers, S. J., & Dawson, G. (2010). *Early Start Denver Model for young children with autism: Promoting language, learning and engagement*. New York: Guilford.

Sussman, F. (1999). *More than words: Helping parents promote communication and social skills in children with autism spectrum disorder*. Montreal, CA: A Hanen Centre Publication.

### Websites

*icdl.com/dirFloortime/overview/index.shtml*

The Interdisciplinary Council on Developmental and Learning Disorders with DIR®/Floortime™ information

*psychology.msu.edu/AutismLab/Project%20Impact.html*

Project ImPACT information

*www.hanen.org/Home.aspx*

The Hanen Centre® information

*www.RDIconnect.com*

Learning community committed to giving individuals a second chance at dynamic thinking

*www.responsiveteaching.org*

Information on Responsive Teaching

*www.scerts.com*

SCERTS ® Model website

*www.ucdmc.ucdavis.edu/mindinstitute/research/esdm/*

Early Start Denver Model Lab

# CHAPTER SEVEN

# Cultural Approaches

## CHAPTER OBJECTIVES

The reader should be able to:

- Define the following key concepts or characteristics of the autism culture according to the TEACCH approach: focus on details, variability in attention, concrete thinking, impaired concept of time and sequencing skills, attachment to routines and difficulty with generalization, strength in and preference for visual information, and marked sensory preferences and aversions.

- Explain why it is important to have an understanding of one's own culture when working with families from diverse backgrounds.

- Describe the characteristics of an educator who practices culturally responsive teaching.

The cultural perspectives addressed in this chapter will begin with a description of how the TEACCH approach considers individuals with autism spectrum disorders as part of a culture with common characteristics that define them as a group. Suggestions for acting as a cultural interpreter for individuals with autism spectrum disorder (ASD) when using the TEACCH approach are described. Common to all of the approaches described in this book is an emphasis on establishing collaborative relationships with families. It is important for educators to obtain the self-awareness and sensitivity necessary to work effectively with families from diverse backgrounds, and suggestions for working with diverse families and teaching in a manner that is culturally responsive will be presented. Finally, suggestions for working effectively with individuals with ASD from diverse cultural backgrounds, including incorporating educational practices that promote self-identity and ethnic identity, will be addressed.

Culture denotes a complex integrated system of beliefs, values, and behaviors common to a large group of people and may include adaptive responses, a shared language and folklore, ideas and thinking patterns, and communication styles. (Utley & Obiakor, 2001, p. 11)

## Theoretical Basis for the TEACCH Approach

The TEACCH approach supports and values maintaining respect for the culture of disability as central to the philosophy that guides practice. Although autism is not truly a culture as defined by anthropologists because the shared patterns of behavior are not learned from others who share the same culture, some practitioners consider individuals with ASD as part of a culture because the neurological disorder affects the ways they think, dress, work, spend leisure time, and understand the world (Bogdashina, 2005; Mesibov, Shea, & Schopler, 2004). Autism yields characteristic and predictive patterns of thinking and behavior, and in this sense could be considered a culture (Mesibov et al., 2004) as described by Gary Mesibov, In Their Words 7.1. The role of the educator is to act as cross-cultural interpreter with the necessary understanding of the culture, strengths, and deficits associated with ASD (Mesibov et al., 2004).

According to the creators of the TEACCH approach, it is the educator's goal to assist students with ASD to adapt to the physical and social environment that is often a challenge for this culture: "to see the world through their eyes, and then to use this perspective to teach them to function in our culture as independently as possible" (Mesibov et al., 2004, p. 31). This is accomplished by working in collaboration with parents to assess students carefully in order to determine the individual's strengths and interests, and then incorporating these interests when addressing the common manifestations of the culture of autism, such as attachment to routines, limited social skills and emotional empathy, limited play skills, difficulty with initiation, tantrums, and noncompliant behavior (Marcus, Kunce, & Schopler, 2005; Mesibov et al., 2004). Adaptation is facilitated using the structured teaching approach that has been designed with an understanding of and respect for the culture of autism (Mesibov et al., 2004).

**7.1 ☞ IN THEIR WORDS**  Dr. Gary B. Mesibov, *Division TEACCH, Department of Psychiatry, University of North Carolina at Chapel Hill*

### Addressing the Culture of Autism

The cultural perspective has been very helpful for our work with people with ASD in the TEACCH program. First, it has highlighted the fact that people with ASD are different, rather than damaged in any way. Focusing on their differences has led to more productive intervention approaches and strategies that utilize their considerable strengths. This results in the development of more positive intervention strategies and a greater respect for the people we serve. Thinking about ASD as a culture also helps us to remember that our ultimate goal is their meaningful and productive participation in our society, which is the ultimate goal for each culture in any multicultural society. So respecting differences, identifying strengths, and seeing a meaningful and productive life for all are the main components of our multicultural approach.

## The Structured Teaching Approach

The **structured teaching** approach was designed to provide the environmental and instructional adaptations necessary for an individual with ASD to function well within the larger social structure. Similar to individuals with hearing impairments who use a hearing aid and individuals with physical disabilities who use a walker or wheelchair, individuals with ASD are considered to need environmental modifications to be successful (Van Bourgondien, Reichle, & Schopler, 2003). Those who use the structured teaching approach believe that, because autism spectrum disorders are a lifelong disability, the need for these modifications is not likely to go away and some form of support will always be needed.

The structured teaching approach is based on the assumption that individuals with autism spectrum disorders have behavioral difficulties when their environments and the teaching strategies used are not based on their individual needs. Structured teaching is designed to create meaningful environments where individuals with ASD can succeed and where their behavioral difficulties will be minimized (Mesibov, Schopler, & Hearsey, 1994).

## History of Structured Teaching

The structured teaching approach was developed as a result of a research project that began in 1966 under the Department of Psychiatry at the University of North Carolina's School of Medicine (Schopler, Mesibov, & Baker, 1982). A division in this department entitled TEACCH (Treatment and Education of Autistic and related Communication handicapped CHildren) was responsible for developing a program to serve individuals with autism and language impairments and their families. In response to parents, some of whom were dissatisfied with the lack of structure during psychoanalytic play therapy sessions, and some of whom were dissatisfied with the

highly structured activities used by therapists using operant conditioning, Schopler and colleagues conducted a study evaluating the level of structure on outcome variables such as attending, appropriate affect, vocalization, social relating, and psychotic behavior of preschoolers referred for treatment (Schopler, Brehm, Kinsbourne, & Reichler, 1971).

The structured sessions were defined as those where the adult determined the materials to use, the length of time the child worked with each item, and the form of the teaching interaction. In the unstructured sessions, the child selected the materials, determined the length of time for interaction with each item, and chose the manner in which the item was used (Schopler et al., 1971). The results revealed more favorable outcomes when individuals received the structured sessions compared with unstructured sessions from both clinicians and parents. Individual differences also occurred, with those children rated with a high developmental level showing less difference in outcomes between structured and unstructured sessions. The structured teaching approach that was created following the outcomes of this study was referred to as developmental therapy during the early 1970s (Schopler et al., 1971; Schopler & Reichler, 1971).

In 1972, the legislature in North Carolina broadened the mandate of Division TEACCH to cover the entire state (Schopler et al., 1982). Services in both assessment and treatment were developed. Parent involvement as co-therapists was included from the beginning. Between 1966 and 1977, 657 families were served by the TEACCH program for assessment, intervention, or both (Schopler et al., 1971). Developmental therapy was the method used by parents and clinicians, with the therapist typically demonstrating strategies as parents observed through a one-way screen (Schopler & Reichler, 1971). To foster human relatedness, the child was not allowed to move around or use any object without the mediation by an adult. The adult focused on making materials important for the child and increasing the child's competence with the materials. The main aim was the development of spontaneous, organized activity and play where the child was reinforced by his or her own success (Schopler & Reichler, 1971).

The importance of structure when educating students with ASD has remained a focus of the intervention strategies used by TEACCH. Currently referred to as structured teaching, these methods provide students with autism the necessary special instruction, in forms that they comprehend, and in individualized settings that minimize their deficits (Mesibov & Shea, 1996). Structured teaching is a system of organizing the classroom and using teaching processes and styles that match the different ways that individuals with ASD understand, think, and learn (Mesibov & Howley, 2003). The following concepts are considered key to structured teaching.

# Key Concepts

The key concepts for the TEACCH approach are those related to the characteristics that comprise the culture of autism. An understanding of the culture is the first step to addressing the needs of individuals with ASD.

## Focus on Details Rather Than Connections

The primary characteristic of the thinking of individuals with ASD is that they have difficulty imposing meaning on their experiences (Mesibov et al., 2004). Underlying themes, concepts, reasons, connections, or "the big picture" often elude them. They are good observers of detail but they may be focusing on irrelevant details that impede learning. For example, when shown two photos of relatives and asked to identify "sister," the student may be looking at the trees in the background or the buttons on the sweater. Individuals in the ASD culture often seek predictability and routine to compensate for the lack of ability to draw connections (Mesibov & Shea, 2010).

## Variability in Attention

People with ASD have great difficulty interpreting and prioritizing the importance of external stimuli (Mesibov et al., 2004). They are also distracted by internal stimulation, such as a desire for an object or repeating a commercial jingle heard earlier in the day. Teachers often describe students with ASD as unable to pay attention to lessons (Mesibov & Howley, 2003). At other times, individuals with ASD can be intensely focused, especially with favorite activities, and they have difficulty disengaging or switching attention to other activities (Mesibov & Shea, 2010). Creating an environment with few distractions, such as one with few items on the walls or dividers to separate work areas, helps to minimize this distractibility (Mesibov et al., 1994), and schedules assist with transitions between activities (Mesibov & Howley, 2003).

## Concrete versus Abstract Thinking

Individuals with ASD have difficulty with words that have multiple meanings. They take language literally. If you say that you will be there in a minute, the expectation is that you will arrive after 60 seconds have passed. It is difficult for individuals with ASD to understand how someone can feel multiple emotions at the same time—for example, to be sad when someone is leaving but happy for their good fortune (Grandin, 1999). Providing information about expectations, such as being clear about what will happen first and then what will follow, is one strategy used in structured teaching to address this concrete thinking (Mesibov & Howley, 2003).

## Impaired Concept of Time and Sequencing Skills

Individuals with ASD frequently have difficulty with the concept of time. They can be late for appointments because they were engrossed in an activity of interest. They have difficulty understanding when an activity is over and with the concepts of beginning, middle, and end (Mesibov et al., 2004; Mesibov & Shea, 2010). Clear expectations about what work needs to be done, in what order, and when the task is finished assists individuals with ASD to complete tasks in a timely manner (Mesibov & Howley, 2003).

Sequencing is also difficult. Incorporating schedules that are visual and reviewed early in the day can be of great benefit for individuals with ASD who like predictability but have difficulty sequencing the events of the day on their own. **Schedules** are an important feature of structured teaching. Independent work systems, described later, also provide information about the activity completion within a period of time.

### Attachment to Routines and Difficulty with Generalization

Individuals with ASD tend to become attached to routines and the settings in which they are established (Mesibov & Shea, 2010). Transferring, or generalizing from the original learning setting to another, is often a challenge. To generalize skills from one place to another or from one person to another, the individual with ASD must notice the similarity in the contexts or situations. Observing these patterns or these similarities is difficult for individuals with ASD. Establishing routines with visual organization of the environment assists students with generalization (Schopler, Mesibov, & Hearsey, 1995).

### Strength in and Preference for Visual Information

Individuals with ASD are visual learners (Grandin, 1999; Mesibov & Shea, 2010). They often have difficulty understanding auditory information, including speech. They can also become dependent on adults for prompts to

assist them with completing a task or responding correctly to a given situation (Mesibov et al., 2004). Providing visual structure embedded in the environment will assist the student with ASD and decrease prompt dependence on adults for direction in following routines or completing tasks.

### Marked Sensory Preferences and Aversions

Individuals with ASD may be hyper- or hyposensitive to sensory input, have unusual food preferences, and exhibit self-stimulatory behavior (Mesibov et al., 2004; Mesibov & Shea, 2010). Increasing the individual's ability to communicate, providing structure, and focusing on incorporating individual interests to maximize engagement are all strategies used in structured teaching to address these differences.

## Strategies Based on Key Concepts

### Physical Organization

Organizing the physical environment with visually clear areas and boundaries assists the student with autism spectrum disorder to attend to the relevant cues and avoid distraction by sights and sounds (Mesibov & Howley, 2003; Mesibov et al., 1994). Wall dividers can minimize visual and auditory distractions, and shelves and storage cabinets with materials should be easily accessible (Schopler et al., 1995). Rugs and tape on the floor can indicate where the activity will take place. Some areas of the room can be painted different colors to indicate the reading corner or snack table. If students are able to read, signs indicating the different areas may be posted.

The amount of physical structure used to assist with distractions can be adjusted or faded with the individual's needs. A student may start with a desk between two dividers facing a blank wall and then move to a desk near those of his peers as the student learns to work despite distractions (Schopler et al., 1995). Transitions are often difficult for individuals with ASD, and a transition area or location in the room where schedules are placed may be helpful (Mesibov et al., 1994).

## Schedules

The use of schedules accommodates difficulties with the concepts of an activity's timing and what the activity will be (Mesibov & Howley, 2003). Students with autism spectrum disorders like predictability, and the use of a schedule facilitates the ability to know what will happen next. It is also difficult for some individuals with autism spectrum disorders to have a sense of time, and preferred activities seem to last minutes while less preferred activities drag on. Schedules assist the student in understanding what time the activity will begin and when it will be finished (Hodgdon, 1995; Schopler et al., 1995).

Many classrooms have a general schedule that is posted for all to view. This is helpful for the student with ASD. Individual schedules help the students to understand what will be happening during the time that is labeled more generally, such as "Work Session" or "Reading Period." Although a variety of schedule forms may be used, it is important that the schedule is meaningful for the student (Mesibov et al., 1994).

Picture schedules are commonly used in classrooms for young children. If the room is organized by color-coded areas, the picture or photograph can be placed on the same color background as the area where the activity will take place. Some teachers have the student take the picture or photo from the schedule and place it in a pocket near the activity area to indicate that the activity is occurring and that part of the schedule is finished. Objects can be used to facilitate transitions between activities by handing an object representing the next activity (a cup for snack time, for example) to the student to assist with the transition (Mesibov & Howley, 2003).

**FIGURE 7–1**   Sample schedule with an embedded unknown or choice activity

Some students with ASD experience difficulty when their schedule changes or is in some way different from the schedule presented at the beginning of the day. To facilitate a tolerance for change and unpredictability, the educator can place a picture of a question mark on the schedule (see Figure 7–1) and tell the student that this means he or she gets a choice of activities (Mesibov et al., 2004).

## Work Systems

**Structured work systems** (SWSs) assist the individual with autism spectrum disorder to learn to work independently. Work systems help students know exactly what is expected of them. In these systems, four pieces of information are communicated to the student (Carnahan, Harte, Schumacher-Dyke, Hume, & Borders, 2011; Carnahan, Hume, Clarke, & Borders, 2009; Mesibov & Howley, 2003):

- What work they are supposed to do or what activity to engage in

- How much work is required during the specific work period

- How the learner will know when progress is being made and the activity is finished

- What happens after the activity or work is completed

Work systems are set up prior to the student beginning the activities. Tasks can be numbered or color-coded and placed in boxes or lined up on shelves (or another means of visually indicating the tasks to be completed can be used) (Carnahan et al., 2011; Hume & Odom, 2007). A work-study box and its contents are always placed on the left with the contents visible (Mesibov et al., 1994). Students learn to work from left to right. When the materials in the work-study box have been processed, they are placed in a finished box to the right. When all the materials are gone, the students know they are finished with the task (see Figure 7–2).

Because the student will be completing all of the activities in the work system independently, the tasks must consist of those the student has already mastered. In other words, the independent work areas foster the maintenance of skills rather than the teaching of new skills (Carnahan et al., 2011). Typical tasks found in structured work systems are tasks with clear indications for completion such as worksheets, puzzles, and sorting or assembly of items. The

activities selected, and the visual format for the work system (pictures, objects, words), are individualized to match the comprehension level and skills of the student (Carnahan et al., 2011; Hume & Reynolds, 2010).

Many workstations indicate that there will be a reward following the completion of all the activities. Thus, students learn the routine of "first work, then play" (Mesibov et al., 1994). It is important to note, however, that working independently in an environment without social demands may be preferred to a social play situation for individuals with ASD. Completing routine tasks that are already mastered is usually a choice activity for individuals with ASD. Data collection on the student's use of work systems and on student behavior is an essential component of implementation (Hume & Reynolds, 2010).

## Task Organization

The organization of the materials for each task provides guidelines for task completion. It is helpful if activities are organized using visual clarity, visual organization, and visual instructions (Hume & Reynolds, 2010; Mesibov & Howley, 2003). Providing visual clarity in the classroom organization by color-coding areas for work, snack, and play or by highlighting relevant aspect of materials are examples of visual clarity (Hodgdon, 1995; Mesibov & Howley, 2003).

**Jigs** or blueprints can be developed to assist students in assembling parts or completing other tasks. Examples of jigs include a matching task with a color written on a page that is to be drawn in with a crayon (Mesibov et al., 1994), or a picture of an assembled item placed with its parts arranged in the order of assembly, or a drawing of a place setting for dinner with the items having a piece of velcro to match their spot in the setting. The type of visual organization needed depends on the skills of the individual. Displaying instructions visually and in order can facilitate the learning of the importance of moving from left to right, or from

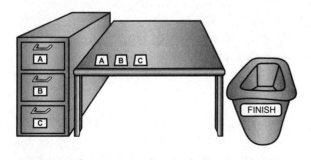

**FIGURE 7–2**  Independent workstation

top to bottom, as a strategy for completing tasks (Schopler et al., 1995).

Visual instructions are an essential component of structured teaching tasks (Mesibov & Howley, 2003; Mesibov et al., 2004). They help to clarify what the student is expected to accomplish, and they provide a mechanism for change when they include revisions of the written instructions that are typically followed by the student.

The TEACCH approach is child- and family-centered, and focused on the individual's strengths and interests. The teaching methods used by the TEACCH program are based on applied behavior analysis with an emphasis on cognitive-social learning theory (Mesibov et al., 2004). The use of prompts and reinforcers when teaching new tasks is promoted in several program descriptions (Mesibov et al., 1994; Schopler et al., 1995). However, making the environment and activities meaningful for the individual and facilitating the transfer of skills are part of the focus. Because social rewards are less meaningful, they are deemphasized and alternative reinforcers are selected. Consistent with good practice, it is important to individualize the type of reinforcer selected and to use the prompts and reinforcers found in the natural environment whenever possible.

Creating activities and experiences that are appropriate to the developmental level of the student is also incorporated in the TEACCH approach (Carnahan et al., 2011; Mesibov et al., 2004). Tasks and materials are individualized and visual information is incorporated when possible. In summary, the TEACCH approach incorporates widely used behavioral principles, cognitive-social learning theory, and developmental psychology, resulting in the eclectic model (Mesibov et al., 2004).

## Key Concepts Put into Practice

A model educational program based on the TEACCH approach would have the room physically organized to indicate clearly the activity that will take place in each area. This would be done by color-coding, labeling the areas, or marking the floor with tape. The educational goals and objectives would be individualized and determined through collaboration with families and as a result of assessment practices that provide important information for educators. The characteristics of the individual with ASD that are part of the culture of autism would be respected and considered when designing educational activities. Student interests and strengths, as well as family priorities, would be incorporated into the design of curriculum materials and activities.

Each student would have an individualized schedule that would be placed in a designated area or given to the student. The schedule would be in visual form, such as with pictures or in writing. Students would be taught to rely on their schedules to facilitate transitions between activities and, for some students, objects or icons would be used to indicate which activity is next.

State-of-the-art behavioral strategies such as errorless learning, effective prompting, and use of reinforcers would be used to teach new skills. Once the skills are mastered, students would work on the maintenance of skills using independent work systems where they could complete tasks with the guidance of visual cues alone. Person-centered planning would be used to determine the individualized goals for the future, and each student would be working toward these goals during daily educational activities.

## Research on Structured Teaching and the TEACCH Approach

Early publications focused on treatment outcomes of the TEACCH approach used parent satisfaction measures as a key variable. In 1978, Marcus, Lansing, Andrews, and Schopler (1978) demonstrated that 10 mothers could improve their teaching effectiveness—including increases in their ability to gain behavior control and use of language during instruction—following six to eight one-hour sessions with TEACCH staff members. Increasing family adaptations and reducing feelings of stress are considered two of the target outcomes for the TEACCH program. Parental satisfaction with this program was obtained for approximately half ($n$ = 348) of the families involved in TEACCH from 1966 through 1977 (Schopler et al., 1982; Schopler, Mesibov, DeVellis, & Short, 1981). The survey data suggest that the parents found the TEACCH program extremely helpful (Schopler et al., 1982), and the greater the contact a family had with the program, the higher the rating. Staff members also perceived the program as effective. The area rated as less effective was the reduction of bizarre behaviors. This area is not targeted as a goal for TEACCH staff members, who would rather focus on adaptations as a means of reducing these behaviors (Schopler et al., 1982). The authors indicate that they would like to expand the results obtained by this parent report measure by determining if their perceptions are accurate, what specific aspects of the program facilitate family adaptations, and how efforts can be individualized to better serve different children and their families (Schopler et al., 1981).

Improved adult outcomes for those individuals who attended the TEACCH program are also reported (Schopler et al., 1982; Schopler et al., 1981). In the early 1980s, fewer adults were placed in an institution following program participation compared with general reported outcomes during the prior 20 years. In the 1990s, some adolescents and adults lived in an experimental treatment program designed and operated by the Division TEACCH in North Carolina called the Carolina Living and Learning Center (CLLC). Outcomes for the participants living on this 79-acre farm with farming and landscaping as the main vocational curriculum were compared with adults living in a group home, institution, or family home (Van Bourgondien et al., 2003). The results indicated that the CLLC incorporated more communication adaptations,

visual structure, socialization programming, and preventive behavior management approaches compared with other settings (Van Bourgondien et al., 2003). Families were more satisfied with the CLLC placement compared with those in group homes, but there was no difference in families' satisfaction compared with the institutional setting. All groups were equally satisfied with peer interactions. The authors also state that those settings that reduced the use of visual systems, communication adaptations, or preventive approaches to address behavior problems over time experienced an increase in the frequency of negative behaviors in the adults with autism. The authors conclude that continued use of environmental adaptations is necessary (Van Bourgondien et al., 2003).

Another study revealed that eight (five from North Carolina) of 22 high-functioning individuals with autism, 18 years or older, who participated in a follow-up study were competitively employed full-time for at least six months (Venter, Lord, & Schopler, 1992). Such follow-up research of high-functioning individuals with autism provided a more optimistic view of outcomes compared with 20 years prior (Lord & Venter, 1992). Verbal IQ and reading and oral comprehension above the median differentiated adults who were competitively employed from those who were not (Venter et al., 1992).

Ozonoff and Cathcart (1998) compared outcomes for 11 subjects participating in a TEACCH-based home program for young children with a no-treatment control group. After four months of treatment, there were statistically significant differences for improvements of the treatment group as assessed on the Psychoeducational Profile-Revised (PEP-R) on the subtests of imitation, fine motor, gross motor, and cognitive performance, and on the total test score. The authors also state that mild autism scores determined by the Childhood Autism Rating Scale (CARS) (see Chapter 2 for a description) and good language skills predicted better progress in the home intervention.

Panerai and colleagues have completed a series of evaluations of a residential program in Italy for children and adolescents with autism that follows the TEACCH approach (Panerai, et al., 2009; Panerai, Ferrante, Caputo, & Impellizzeri, 1998; Panerai, Ferrante, & Zingale, 2002). Their first study evaluated the effects of the TEACCH approach used for 12 to 18 months with 18 children with autism via the Vineland Adaptive Behavior Scale (Sparrow, Balla, & Cicchetti, 1994), the PEP-R (Schopler, Reichler, Bashford, Lansing, & Marcus, 1990), the Echelle d'Evaluation Fonctionnelle des Comportements (a behavior scale) (Barthelemy, Hamenry, & Lelord, 1995), and structured observations. Program components that included schedules, tasks organized with visual work systems, and alternative communication systems incorporating objects, cards, and photographs resulted in improvements in communication with motor/gesture and objects, increases in the form of words used, and a reduction in self-injurious and stereotyped behaviors for this group of students (Panerai, Ferrante, Caputo, & Impellizzeri, 1998).

Outcomes from a group of eight students with a mean age of 9 years who attended the same residential program in Italy were compared with a matched group of peers who were included in the Italian school system with assigned support teachers (Panerai, Ferrante, & Zingale, 2002). Results indicated no differences reported on the Vineland Adaptive Behavior Scales (Sparrow et al., 1984), but significant improvements on the PEP-R (Schopler et al., 1990) for all areas but fine motor skills for the group attending the residential program based on incorporating structured teaching. The authors concluded that the integration system in Italy used at that time was not designed to meet the needs of individuals with ASD.

To evaluate the residential program further, Panerai, Ferrante, and colleagues compared outcomes for 11 individuals with autism attending this program, 13 individuals with autism who attended public school but whose parents were trained in the TEACCH approach and who used a TEACCH mediator who worked with the schools, and 10 students with autism who attended inclusive nonspecific programs for students with disabilities (Paneria et al., 2009). Results reveal significant differences between the outcomes for the children with autism who participated in each of the TEACCH-based programs compared with the inclusive programs on the measures of the Vineland Adaptive Behavior Scales (Sparrow et al., 1984) and the PEP-R (Schopler et al., 1990). There were no differences in gains between the two programs based on the TEACCH model. The authors conclude that attendance in a regular class was not sufficient to increase abilities in children with autism; however, the use of a TEACCH mediator in the schools and parents who follow the model at home demonstrated that positive outcomes can result in an inclusive context when these components are employed (Panerai et al., 2009).

Outcomes from 18 preschoolers participating in the TEACCH model adapted to the Chinese Heep Hong Society program in Hong Kong were compared to 16 preschoolers who attended a variety of non-TEACCH programs (Tsang, Shek, Lam, Tang, & Cheung, 2007). The researchers found significant differences for the experimental group for abilities such as imitation, fine motor, perception, eye-hand coordination, gross motor skills, and cognitive functioning (Tsang et al., 2007). Although the TEACCH model preschool resulted in comparatively positive outcomes, it is difficult to know what intervention occurred in the comparison programs due to a lack of description of the staff training or curriculum used.

Research evaluating the strategies proposed by the TEACCH approach to address the characteristics of the culture of autism is sparse. Mesibov and Shea (2010) write, "[T]here is clearly a need for additional research into both individual components of the TEACCH approach and overall program effectiveness" (p. 575). Hume and Odom (2007) evaluated the independent and on-task behaviors of three participants with autism following the implementation of an individual work system as developed by division TEACCH. All three participants increased their on-task and independent work (participant age 20) and play (participants ages 6 and 7) skills following instruction in the use of a work system. Using a single-case design, Carnahan and colleagues report that the use of an independent work system increased the on-task behavior of a high school student with ASD working in a library (Carnahan et al., 2009).

> Culture, like any other social or biological organism, is multidimensional and continually changing. . . . As manifested in expressive behaviors, culture is influenced by a wide variety of factors, including time, setting, age, economics, and social circumstances. (Gay, 2000, p. 10)

## Working in Collaboration with Diverse Families

Individuals with autism spectrum disorders are part of families that have an ethnic identity and participate to some degree in the customs of that ethnic community. The geographic location and society in which the individual lives also influences the beliefs and behaviors of the family and individual. Knowledge about how recently a family has immigrated to the United States and an understanding of the process of enculturation is also important (Rogers-Adkinson, Ochoa, & Delgado, 2003; York, 2006). In other words, a complex system of cultural influences affects an individual with autism spectrum disorder.

> All behaviors are culturally embedded. No behavior is ever independent of social or environmental contexts, even when these contexts are not easily identified. (Barrera & Kramer, 2009, p. xx)

Information about the beliefs and behaviors of these families is essential to an understanding of cultural differences and similarities among families from diverse heritages (Lynch, 2011a). It is important to get to know each family's culture and not make assumptions about any homogeneity of the experiences and behaviors of individuals within cultures (Hanson & Lynch, 2010; Kalyanpur & Harry, 1999). Urie Bronfenbrenner's (1979) ecolological model is helpful in illustrating the complexity of the influences on the child with autism spectrum disorder. Bronfenbrenner (1979) describes the influence of the interrelated systems as a series of embedded concentric circles, with the child in the middle, the family surrounding the child, the social structures (e.g., school, work) surrounding the family, and the cultural and policy influences as the outside circle that influences directly or indirectly each of the systems within the model (see Figure 7–3).

The families' priorities for goals, their desired rate for progress in skill areas, and their ability and willingness to facilitate the generalization of skills may be influenced by the culture of the family. Preference for the form and frequency of communication, the location of meetings with educators, and the format for discussions regarding students with ASD may be influenced by cultural considerations (Barrera & Kramer, 2009). In addition, information presented in the first language of the family is

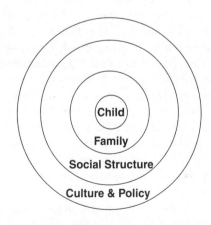

**FIGURE 7–3**  Bronfenbrenner's ecological model

important for communication with professionals (Dobson, Upadhyaya, McNeil, Venkateswaran, & Gilderdale, 2001; Hanson & Lynch, 2010).

Working collaboratively with families is considered best practice for educators of students with autism spectrum disorders (Dunlap, Iovannone, & Kincaid, 2008; National Research Council, 2001); consequently, the educator's ability to work with diverse families from varying cultural and socioeconomic backgrounds will determine the success of these collaborations. In their position statement, the Division of Early Childhood of the Council for Exceptional Children (2010) confirms a commitment to address explicitly implications for culturally and linguistically responsive practices and states their strong belief in the use of responsive, respectful, and evidence-based practices with children and families from culturally and linguistically diverse backgrounds. Awareness of cultural differences provides the scaffolding necessary for building collaborative relationships with families (Kalyanpur & Harry, 1999).

## A Posture of Cultural Reciprocity

Kalyanpur and Harry (1999) describe four steps that can be used to facilitate working with families with a **posture of cultural reciprocity**. The first step requires the educator to identify the cultural values embedded in their interpretation of a student's difficulty or a recommended practice. For example, if the strategy is aimed at increasing the independence of the student, it may reflect the value placed on independence by the professional staff. Is there an intervention proposed to address the comparatively active behavior of a student with autism? Who defines *active*? Are academic skills given more priority compared to social skills by program staff members? If professionals prefer to work on academic skills or skills to promote independence, they should be clear about their rationale for these goals so that this perspective can be shared with families. They should not assume that the family has the same perspective and priorities.

The second step is to determine if the family values the rationale given, and if not, how the family's view differs from that of the professional (Kalyanpur & Harry, 1999). Perhaps family members would prioritize social skills over academic competence, or they would prefer that their child eat more during lunch with assistance rather than eat less independently. The ability to understand a different perspective on priorities, or any issue, is an important skill for effective dialogue and collaboration with families (Barrera & Kraemer, 2009).

The third step is to acknowledge and respect any cultural differences identified and fully explain the cultural bias of the professional assumptions so that a discussion about the differing perspectives can occur (Barrera & Kramer, 2009; Kalyanpur & Harry, 1999). The aim of a discussion is to obtain clarity concerning how perspectives or priorities differ and to express a respect for differences in perspective. It is important for practitioners to be aware that what are usual customs, beliefs, and practices to them may be unusual for any given family.

The fourth step involves determining the most effective way of adapting professional interpretations or recommendations to the value system of the family through discussion and collaboration (Kalyanpur & Harry, 1999). Working out a goal or plan that is acceptable to all is more likely to have a positive outcome because all parties are motivated to work together toward the identified outcomes. In addition, working with families using a posture of cultural reciprocity ensures that both parents and professionals are empowered in the process. This process facilitates true collaboration because of the attention given to ensuring that families and professionals understand each other. Establishing reciprocity means that diverse worldviews, behaviors, and beliefs are considered legitimate (Barrera & Kramer, 2009).

> Learning about culture is a permanent journey of discovery, something to be learned from firsthand contacts with people from different places. (Kalyanpur & Harry, 1999, p. xiii)

To be able to work with a posture of cultural reciprocity, educators need to become aware of the influences of their own culture. "Everyone has a cultural, ethnic, linguistic, and racial identity" (Lynch, 2011a, p. 20). Knowledge of one's own values and behaviors that have been shaped by culture is a necessary first step to cultural competence in working with families that may not share the same cultural experiences (Byrd, 2002; Kea, Cartledge, & Bowman, 2002; Klein & Chen, 2001; Obiakor, 2002; Thompson, 2004). For example, educators from Anglo-European roots may not understand why a family does not feel pressure to toilet-train their young child or are less concerned with independence in general or independent self-feeding in particular (Lynch, 2011b). Young children in a Latino family may not be pushed to become more independent, and caregivers may continue to button clothes, tie shoes, and cut food, especially if the child has a disability (Zuniga, 2004).

Lynch (2011b) writes that educators can learn about other cultures (1) through books, the arts, and technology; (2) by talking, socializing, and working with individuals from the culture who act as guides or cultural mediators; (3) by participating in the daily life of the culture; and (4) by learning the language of the culture. Authors agree that self-evaluation followed by openness to different perspectives goes a long way toward learning about and working effectively with individuals from diverse backgrounds. They also state that in order to work effectively, the educator does not have to have the same cultural background as the learner (Gay, 2000; Kalyanpur & Harry, 1999).

Teaching is an increasingly cross-cultural phenomenon as the number of students from diverse backgrounds increases while the number of educators from multicultural backgrounds declines (Garcia, Arias, Murri, & Serna, 2010; Gay, 2003; Prater, 2002). As educators become aware of the influence of their own culture on their values and behaviors, they realize that beliefs and values that were once thought to be universal are, in fact, specific to one's own culture (Kalyanpur & Harry, 1999). What is important is a willingness to learn about how our own experiences have shaped us and to respect and accept the differences in experiences of the families with whom we are working (Hanson & Lynch, 2004; Kalyanpur & Harry, 1999).

Working in collaboration with families is essential to successful outcomes for individuals with disabilities (Salazar, 2010). Working effectively with families from diverse backgrounds is important for all educators (Freire, 1998), especially when the changing demographics of the United States are taken into consideration (Garcia et al., 2010; Gay, 2003; Lynch, 2011a; Utley & Obiakor, 2001). Learners with autism spectrum disorders are members of families from many ethnicities and cultures, and educators of these students are no exception when it comes to the importance of using cultural competence in all interactions.

One aspect of the possible cultural difference between families and educators, tutors, and therapists is the primary language spoken. There is a dearth of attention to the issue of the language of instruction when the family uses a language other than English. The lack of focus and research on this topic is especially surprising because individuals with autism spectrum disorder are primarily affected in the social-communication domain. According to Kremer-Sadlik (2005), parents are often advised to speak only one language, English, with their child, regardless of the parents' English proficiency or the language spoken with others in the home. This perspective could have negative ramifications, such as alienating the child from the family; lack of socialization opportunities in the home regarding family values, beliefs, and behaviors; and a general negative impact on the parent-child relationship (Kremer-Sadlik, 2005).

Barrera and Corso (2003) recommend using skilled dialogue to build successful relationships across diverse cultural and linguistic parameters. In their book on skilled dialogue, these authors have created a cultural data table, or survey, that can be used to collect information related to "potential culture bumps" (Barrera & Corso, 2003, p. 101). Sample items from this survey include pattern of language usage in child's primary caregiving environments, relative value placed on verbal and nonverbal communication, degree of acculturation to US culture, roles and rules associated with parenting and child rearing, and perceptions of identity and competence (Barrera & Corso, 2003). In addition, Barrera and Corso (2003) have created a Cultural Consonance Profile to assist in comparing the families' responses about beliefs and practices to that of the history for the practitioner.

Although there is no difference in the prevalence of ASD due to race (Fombonne, Simmons, Ford, Meltzer, & Goodman, 2001; Yeargin-Allsopp et al., 2003), there is a reported difference in the rates of service for families of children with autism from different ethnic groups (Dyches et al., 2004). Compared with mainstream culture in the United States, American Indian, Asian, and Latino cultures, which are focused on a collective or a group rather than the individual, have a greater emphasis on spiritual powers (Joe & Malach, 2004; Parette, Chuang, & Huer, 2004; Zuniga, 2004) and are more relaxed about child development or child progress (Zuniga, 2004), or are more accepting of "what is" (Joe & Malach, 2004). These cultural considerations may partially explain why families from these backgrounds are less eager to seek assistance from professionals outside the family who will focus on child progress for individuals with disabilities. Members of some cultural groups may consider self-disclosure as unsafe, or a sign of giving up control or independence (Barrera & Corso, 2003). In addition, some undocumented families from a Latino background may be reluctant to make contact with state and local agencies of any kind. Families living in poverty may not have the means to attend meetings, arrange for childcare, or communicate by email or cell phone.

Families from diverse backgrounds are likely to seek intervention based on their perceived cause of the disability (Kalyanpur & Harry, 1999). For example, a Hmong family might seek out a shaman, an African family might contact a traditional practitioner, and a Christian family might contact a priest or minister. Not all families from the same heritage follow the same belief system, and each family's understanding of medical and educational facilities is likely to vary. It is important for educators to aim for understanding of each family system and to avoid stereotyping by race, ethnicity, or socioeconomic status.

## Teaching in a Manner That Is Culturally Responsive

As previously mentioned, of primary importance for educators who wish to work in a culturally responsive (Gay, 2000) or culturally competent manner is self-evaluation of their own cultural beliefs, values, and behaviors (Gay, 2000; Kalyanpur & Harry, 1999; Lynch, 2011b). Certain aspects of our teaching style are covert—a hidden curriculum about our own cultural expectations (Kalyanpur & Harry, 1999). Our attitudes about time, frequency of verbal response, eye contact, activity level, and opportunity for problem solving in groups are all examples of culturally learned expectations (Hanson & Lynch, 2004). Without an understanding of how instructional strategies reflect cultural values, it is difficult to design curriculum and instruction that take into account the various cultural backgrounds of students with ASD.

Geneva Gay (2000) argues that educators who use culturally responsive teaching will achieve optimal outcomes for ethnically diverse students. She defines **culturally responsive teaching** as using the cultural knowledge, prior experiences, frames of reference, and performance styles of ethnically diverse learners. Culturally responsive teaching becomes evident through the instructional styles, methods of instruction, and curriculum materials used

**7.2** *IN THEIR WORDS*   Eleanor W. Lynch, *Professor Emeritus, San Diego State University*

## Considering Multicultural Issues and Autism

The study and understanding of disability is deeply rooted in the medical or disease model—a model that includes identifying disease based on a pattern of symptoms, searching for the cause, treating through prescription, determining strategies for prevention, and seeking a cure. Both education and special education are replete with examples of a focus on the characteristics of specific disabilities, prescriptive interventions, and strategies to prevent problems in both learning and behavior. This model is an important first step because it encourages a systematic approach to understanding problems that are new and/or complex. It provides initial understanding and solutions that lead to reduction of the problem and improvement in outcomes. Typically, the increased understanding and success with intervention enables researchers and practitioners alike to broaden their focus and incorporate additional data that enrich, and sometimes alter, their original perspectives.

Despite being described more than 60 years ago, the field of autism is in its infancy. The diagnostic criteria have recently changed. Multiple theories are put forward to explain the cluster of behaviors that underpins the diagnosis, and a variety of interventions, based on one's theoretical perspective, are being used throughout the world. The theories about autism, approaches to intervention, and beliefs about causation are argued vociferously in professional journals as well as the mass media. A great deal remains to be learned and applied through educational, medical, and biomedical research, but one area of study is largely missing from the dialogues and debates. Although finding effective interventions is a goal of all involved, much of what is currently in place is a "treatment of the disease" with little, if any, attention to the surrounding cultural context. The impact of culture, cultural beliefs, biases, and behaviors in all aspects of life is an understanding that came late in all professional areas, but increasing one's cultural competence is now a central theme in training and practice in education, medicine, allied health, social services, and business. It should be no less valued in diagnosing, providing effective educational interventions, managing the complex cluster of behaviors associated with autism, and designing the research studies that will lead to greater understanding. This is not the first call for a greater focus on multicultural perspectives in autism. Wilder, Dyches, Obiaker, and Algozzine (2004) and Dyches, Wilder, Sudweeks, Obiaker, and Algozzine (2004), citing the report from the Committee on Educational Interventions for Children with Autism (National Research Council, 2001), provide a call to action that focuses on multicultural issues in relation to teaching students with autism. They suggest that understanding diversity is critical in understanding and developing effective programs for students with autism.

For teachers, and all who are part of solving the mysteries of autism, understanding one's cultural beliefs, biases, and behaviors is the first step. We must recognize that almost all that is said or done is rooted in cultural mores and primary language. The second is learning more about the culture, ethnicity, race, language, and cultural identity of the children and families

*(continued)*

---

**7.2** *IN THEIR WORDS (continued)*

being served (Lynch & Hanson, 2011). We must learn how their view of the world may be different from our own and how that may affect their perceptions of the diagnosis and the intervention. The third step is integrating information about one's self and the children and families being served to develop interventions that are a better cultural match. What some may see as an added burden is, in fact, an added benefit. For, in fact, it is usually true that the better the data, the better the outcome.

---

by the educator. Each of these aspects will be considered separately.

## Adopting a Teaching Style for Diverse Learners

Teachers who practice culturally relevant methods see their teaching as an art (Ladson-Billings, 1994). They adapt their interaction style to be culturally congruent with the individual student (Ladson-Billings, 1994; Thompson, 2004). Instead of using a similar pace, method, and content of instruction for all students, the culturally responsive teacher uses a method that will be most effective with the individual student.

Maintaining high expectations for the learning potential of each student and maintaining a caring posture as a teacher are important attributes of a culturally responsive educator. According to Gay, caring means maintaining high performance expectations and providing the necessary supports to ensure that all learners meet their potential. "Failure is simply unacceptable to them" (Gay, 2000, p. 47). Teachers who practice culturally relevant methods believe that all of their students can succeed and not that failure is inevitable for some students (Ladson-Billings, 1994; Thompson, 2004).

Respecting each student as a valued individual is another attribute of a caring educator (Barrera & Kramer, 2009; Gay, 2000). Paulo Freire (1998) agrees that teaching requires

intellectual rigor, creativity, scientific competence, and the capacity to love. Genuine positive regard for students with cognitive disabilities is a trait of a competent teacher (Byrd, 2002). Providing resources and personal assistance as part of culturally responsive teaching is also empowering.

Gay (2000) also maintains that not all teaching styles are equally effective for all learners, and that culture influences the individual styles. She explains that when educators individualize their approach, they take into account the learning styles of the student and the preferences for pacing, sensory stimuli, environmental arrangements, and delivery of instruction and content.

## Culturally Responsive Methods of Instruction

An effective educator incorporates many learner characteristics when working with students with ASD. Because there is such variability in learners diagnosed with ASD, it is important that curriculum and instruction be individualized. "Culturally relevant caregiving and education means the willingness to bend, change, and revise in order to meet individual needs" (York, 2006, p. 120).

American Indian and Latino cultures along with Arab, Asian, and African American cultures are considered to be high-context cultures that rely less on verbal communication compared with low-context cultures such as Anglo-European cultures (Lynch, 2011a). In low-context cultures, social relationships are more impersonal and task specific (Hall, 1976). High-context cultures emphasize communication based on shared experience and implicit messages and on paralinguistic features of communication such as facial expression, voice tone, and proximity (Hall, 1976). The use of methods of instruction that deemphasize auditory information and provide support with visual cues is often recommended for individuals with autism spectrum disorders regardless of cultural background. Perhaps this issue is even more important to consider for students from high-context cultural heritages.

Several authors have addressed the issue that a field-dependent and field-sensitive teaching method may be more compatible with the learning style of individuals from some cultural backgrounds than the predominant field-independent style of teaching that occurs in typical public school classrooms (Daniels, 2002). The use of visual aids and concrete examples from relevant experiences is recommended for many students from diverse cultural backgrounds as well as for students with autism spectrum disorders (Garcia et al., 2010). For example, teach the concepts of big and little, near and far, counting, and so on, with objects that the individual experiences on a daily basis and that are more likely to have meaning than flashcards depicting objects rarely seen beyond the teaching session. Effective instructional methods for some students from culturally and linguistically diverse backgrounds include presenting information in a visual manner, relying more heavily on external cues and information, providing feedback and guidance, and using tactile and kinesthetic educational activities (California Department of Education, 2009; Ford, 1996).

Professionals who create a community of learners in the classroom and work collaboratively with the community are considered to be working in a manner that is responsive to students from diverse backgrounds (Garcia et al., 2010). It is challenging to create the collaborative educational activities and the community culture in a classroom that is recommended for students from some ethnic backgrounds (Kea et al., 2002; Ladson-Billings, 1994) because of the typical characteristics of students with autism spectrum disorders; however, the educator can work with staff members and families to create a sense of collective investment in the accomplishments of each student. Relaying a sense of pride about student outcomes and contribution to the classroom community facilitates a connection with families. Accomplishments should be celebrated (Kea et al., 2002) and talents should be showcased (Thompson, 2004).

Conducting educational activities in the community helps students with ASD make connections with the organizations and agencies in their neighborhoods. Through interactions with community members, educators can truly learn about the context in which their students live (Garcia et al., 2010). Barrera and Corso (2003) write that it is essential that educators engage in situated learning in order to go beyond knowing about diversity to obtaining an anchored understanding of diversity. School-to-work and service learning are both initiatives designed to connect students with their community and provide the opportunities to apply learned skills in real-life settings (Obiakor, 2002). Garcia and colleagues (2010) describe an instructional approach that respects and integrates students' beliefs, values, and histories, learned by interacting in and with the community, as **responsive pedagogy**. In addition, situated learning provides the opportunity for students with autism spectrum disorders and educators to learn about the expectations of the community members for participation in work and leisure activities (Byrd, 2002). Activities in the community assist with the development of citizenship literacy (Byrd, 2002), a concept found in many state curriculum objectives. Creating a welcoming environment for families and prioritizing home–school communication are supported by a focus on methods that build community connections (Kea et al., 2002; Prater, 2002).

## Culturally Valued Curriculum Materials

Using curriculum materials that reflect the ethnic identities of the learners has had a positive effect on skill acquisition for students from culturally and linguistically diverse backgrounds (Hoover, 2009; Gay, 2000). Designing educational activities that are relevant to the communities in which the students live and teaching in the community can be beneficial for students from diverse backgrounds (California Department of Education, 2009; Hoover, 2009). Stacey York's (2006) book contains suggested activities for young children that address cultural practices, ethnic identity, community membership, bias and stereotype, and social action.

Considering that students with autism spectrum disorders have difficulty with generalization, it may prove beneficial to incorporate images of individuals from a similar ethnic background in literacy activities. Demonstrating educational activities in situ or in real situations may be more effective than using verbal instruction alone (Garcia et al., 2010; Bogdashina, 2005). Designing curriculum materials that reflect cultural beliefs and practices should facilitate generalization as well as support the development of a positive ethnic identity.

## Encouraging Identity Development as an Educational Goal

It may seem like a farfetched goal to consider identity development as a goal for individuals with autism spectrum disorder. Individuals with ASD often lag behind their peers in the ability to understand their own gender identity (Krantz, 1996) and often have difficulty with peer and group interactions (Strain, Schwartz, & Bovey, 2008). However, it is important for educators to know the goals of any program, and this includes facilitating the development of ethnic or cultural identity.

It is a common educational goal to teach membership in a family and to facilitate social interaction with family members. Social skills with peers and co-workers are also common targets for educational programs of individuals with autism spectrum disorders. Developing a positive self-identity that includes statements about skills and talents would supplement the already common practices of teaching students with ASD to be successful. Fostering the development of a positive cultural identity—including identifying preferences of religious activities and describing common rituals and routines—can easily be included in an educational program. Teaching the knowledge and skills necessary for self-advocacy can result from a positive self-identity. Organizations such as People First provide a venue for networking and empowerment while encouraging individuals with disabilities to voice their important perspectives.

## Research Support for Practices Focusing on Culture

"The research base for the effects of cultural factors in autism is miniscule" (Brown & Rogers, 2003, p. 210). Relatively few researchers have focused on the cultural influences on ASD (Dyches et al., 2004), and much of the research outcomes neglect to report the ethnicity of the participants, or even if this data are reported, the researchers do not analyze results according to race, ethnicity, or culture as a factor.

It would seem that the behaviors of individuals with ASD would be influenced by the family culture. However, there remains a paucity of research addressing the effects of family values and behavior on the characteristics displayed by individuals with ASD. Gedney and Hall (2006) compared the reaction to touch and social proximity in students with ASD from Euro-American and Latino family backgrounds. Latinos typically touch and hold offspring often and highly value physical contact in the family. Perhaps a high amount of holding, touching, and physical displays of affection at a young age is correlated with a lack of difficulty in being touched by those individuals with autism spectrum disorders from Latino families. This is but one of the many questions that could be researched and have implications for practices with young children identified with ASD.

Research on the effects of including culturally similar curriculum materials for individuals with autism spectrum disorders was not found. Researchers must expand their inquiry to include cultural variables (Brown & Rogers, 2003). It is also very important to evaluate whether the recommended intervention services are equally effective beyond the current research centers located near universities and medical centers in metropolitan areas (Brown & Rogers, 2003). As previously argued, the generalization of any educational program will occur only if the family and other community members support the recommendations from educators. These communities include those found in rural areas, families from diverse ethnic and linguistic backgrounds, and families with diverse status in regard to immigration.

## SUGGESTIONS FOR DISCUSSION

1. Describe the role of the interventionist as cultural interpreter when using the TEACCH approach.
2. Identify the characteristics that create the culture of autism according to Mesibov and colleagues. Do you think that autism can be considered a culture?
3. Conduct a debate with one side arguing for the continued need for accommodations and systems of support when working with individuals with ASD and the other side arguing for the need to fade supplemental supports.
4. Identify some research studies that provide information about the evidence of the TEACCH approach.
5. Explain why it is important to understand one's own cultural perspectives when working with families from diverse backgrounds.
6. Discuss why taking a posture of cultural reciprocity is important when collaborating with families from diverse cultural and linguistic backgrounds.
7. Provide an illustration of how you would adapt curriculum and activities to suit the learning style of an individual with autism spectrum disorder.
8. Identify why it is beneficial to work in community settings and to address meaningful skills for community participation by learners with ASD.

## RESOURCES

### Books

Barrera, I., & Corso, R. M. (2003). *Skilled dialogue: Strategies for responding to cultural divesity in early childhood.* Baltimore, MD: Brookes.

Gay, G. (2000). *Culturally responsive teaching: Theory, research, and practice.* New York: Teachers College Press.

Kalyanpur, M., & Harry, B. (1999). *Culture in special education: Building reciprocal family-professional relationships.* Baltimore, MD: Brookes.

Lynch, E. W., & Hanson, M. J. (2011). *Developing cross-cultural competence: A guide for working with children and their families* (4th ed.). Baltimore, MD: Brookes.

Mesibov, G., & Howley, M. (2003). *Accessing the curriculum for pupils with autistic spectrum disorders*. London: David Fulton.

Mesibov, G. B., Shea, V., & Schopler, E. (2004). *The TEACCH approach to autism spectrum disorders*. New York: Springer.

## Websites

*cecerdll.fpg.unc.edu*
    Center for Early Care and Education Research—Dual Language Learners
*iris.peabody.vanderbilt.edu/resources.html*
    IRIS Center—modules on diversity
*nccc.georgetown.edu*
    National Center for Cultural Competence
*www.teacch.com*
    TEACCH Autism Program—University of North Carolina School of Medicine

## CHAPTER EIGHT

# Focus on Communication

## CHAPTER OBJECTIVES

The reader should be able to:

- Explain typical development of gestures, speech, and nonverbal behavior and describe the communication impairments associated with autism.
- Provide a rationale for why it is important to address communication as a priority goal and identify cultural considerations when selecting communication objectives.
- List five ways in which communication partners can facilitate interaction.

## Theories of Language Development

Psycholinguistic theorists hold that language acquisition is considered largely a process of children discovering the rules and regularities of their native language (Lue, 2001). Language acquisition has, at its foundation, a mental plan or structure in the human brain that is guided by an independent rule system (Lue, 2001). The environment plays a relatively minor role in language maturation in this theory compared with others. All native speakers of a language are assumed to know the rules without being explicitly taught. It is theorized that there is some universality or commonality to the rules followed in diverse languages (Owens, 1996).

Behaviorists focus on the stimuli that evoke a verbal response, the consequence of the performance, and the function of language (Lue, 2001). Speech is brought under the stimulus control of the environment through imitation, reinforcement, and successive approximations. Complex linguistic behaviors represent chains of various stimulus-response sequences (Owens, 1996). This theory serves as the foundation of many current language intervention techniques (Lue, 2001).

The interactionist, or constructivist, approach includes individual cognition as a fundamental factor that, along with the immediate linguistic environment, results in the development of complex language structures (Lue, 2001). This approach emphasizes the importance of experience in the contribution to language along with child development or maturation through stages (Lue, 2001; Piaget, 1950).

Social interactionists, or sociolinguists, view the social context as a critical factor in language development (Lue, 2001). Sociolinguists concentrate on the underlying reasons or social/communicative functions of language (Owens, 1996). Social interactionists state that language has a structure that follows certain rules, but that language is acquired only if the child has reason to talk (Snyder-McLean & McLean, 1978). According to this perspective, the social aspect of language cannot be separated from speech.

To facilitate communication with an individual with autism spectrum disorder, it is important to understand the typical pattern of communication development. Note the contributions of psycholinguistic theorists in the description of physical maturity of eye movement and vocal cords, behavioral theorists in the function of environment or caregiver response as shaper of communicative intent and vocal sounds, and social interactionists in the description of interaction for the purpose of social engagement with caregivers.

## Understanding Typical Communication Development

Language development occurs in conjunction with other aspects of child development (Lue, 2001). Speech-language pathologists refer to spoken language parameters and components with the following terms. **Phonology** refers to the sound system of language and the rules governing the structure of syllables and words; **morphology** refers to word formation and its effect on meaning; **syntax** is the word order of the language; **semantics** refers to the rules governing word meaning; and **pragmatics** refers to the customs for language use in specific contexts (Owens, 1996; Tager-Flusberg,

Edelson, & Luyster, 2011). The typical development of language in young children is divided into different periods with a range in age for when children use language to communicate.

The **prelinguistic period** of language development precedes the vocalization of first words (Lue, 2001). Infants are communicating even though they are not using spoken language. Infants coo, cry, and make facial movements that adults may interpret as communicative (Colorado Health Sciences, 1987; Yoder, Warren, McCathren, & Leew, 1998). Contingent responses to these behaviors may enhance communication through cause-and-effect learning. Caregiver responses help infants to acquire generalized expectations that their behavior has an effect on the world (Yoder et al., 1998).

During the first year, infants produce a variety of vocal sounds and some resemble speech sounds (Stoel-Gammon, 1998). Sounds such as cries, coughs, and burps that appear to be automatic responses to a physical state are considered **reflexive vocalizations** (Bates, 1979; Stoel-Gammon, 1998). Babbling, cooing, and playful yelling that contain phonemic features are nonreflexive vocalizations and begin to appear around 2 to 3 months of age. From 4 to 6 months, infants begin to explore their vocal capabilities with sounds from "raspberries" and squeals to consonant-vowel syllables (Heflin & Alaimo, 2007; Stoel-Gammon, 1998). During the first 6 months, vowel sounds tend to predominate. By this age, infants are able to discriminate between and recognize both photographs and their associated real objects (Rosinski, 1977).

**Canonical babbling**, or utterance of syllables that alternate between consonants and vowels, begins around 6 or 7 months. There is a marked shift from vowels alone to use of front consonants such as *m*, *b*, and *d*. Multisyllabic utterances during this period are characterized as reduplicated, or strings of identical syllables (e.g., *mamama*), or variegated, which contain varying consonants and vowels (e.g., *bago*) (Stoel-Gammon, 1998). Research across linguistic environments has revealed that consistent patterns in which babies articulate consonants with nasals (*m, n, ng*) are acquired first, followed by glides (*w, y*) (Lue, 2001). By 32 months of age, 90% of typical children can use certain sounds (*n, m, p, t, k*) in all positions of a word, with others (*f, w, b, g, d, j, h*) added by 36 months (Lue, 2001).

Two major transitions occur between ages 1 and 2 years: (1) transition to linguistic communication and (2) transition to symbolic communication (Wetherby, Reichle, & Pierce, 1998). Intentionality in communicative behavior becomes evident around 9 months of age, with the typical child averaging one communicative act per minute (Wetherby, Cain, Yonclas, & Walker, 1988). During this prelinguistic period (9 to 15 months), children use gestures in about 75% of their communicative signals, and about half of the gestures are accompanied by vocalizations (Wetherby, Reichle et al., 1998).

**Gestural vocabulary** appears several months prior to approximations of spoken words. Pointing is the most prevalent gesture (Wetherby, Reichle et al., 1998). In typically developing children, there is an alternating eye gaze between a person and an object around this period of time (Wetherby, Reichle et al., 1998). This form of communication is referred to as **coordinated joint attention** (Adamson & Chance, 1998). As babies increase their use of pointing with accompanying gaze shifts, care-givers become more responsive, attending to 100% of pointing gestures by 15 months of age (Lock, Young, Service, & Chandler, 1990). Around 11 months of age, referential gestures that mimic the actions produced by an object are used, and by 12 to 16 months of age, typical children are using representational gestures that are context-bound, such as in response to adult questions (e.g., using a hand like a cup in response to "Do you want a drink?").

First words are initially based on episodic associations such as waving bye-bye or saying "uh-oh" when a tower is knocked down (Bloom, 1993). A child repeats words heard as part of the sequence of events or episode. In this early **one-word stage**, or first word period,

acquisition of new words is slow, averaging about one word per week (Wetherby, Reichle et al., 1998).

Researchers have evaluated how many of the first 50 words are nominal (referring to names of objects, animals, and people) and have reported that the majority are nominals for English-speaking children (Vihman & McCune, 1994), but verbs may dominate for Mandarin-speaking babies (Tardif, 1996). "It is clear that there is much individual variation across children in the proportion of nominals and nonnominals used" (Wetherby, Reichle et al., 1998, p. 207).

Jargon babbling begins to occur around 12 months (Stoel-Gammon, 1998). The intonation of the babbling resembles adult speech but the content is not real words (Colorado Health Sciences, 1987). By the end of the first year, typical babies can say a few words followed by a vocabulary burst (three new words per week) after the first 20 to 50 words. By age 2, they are speaking in short sentences and have a vocabulary of approximately 300 words (Stoel-Gammon, 1998).

Patricia Kuhl's (2007) research with typically developing infants demonstrates that language is learned through social interaction. When 9-month-old infants from English-speaking backgrounds were exposed to Mandarin through frequent story reading by native Mandarin speakers, they maintained their recognition of the sounds important in Mandarin, similar to babies from Mandarin-speaking homes but significantly different from babies who were not read to in Mandarin. These skills were not repli-cated if the story reading was done by auditory means alone or a taped version of the story read-ing (Kuhl, 2007). Kuhl concludes that the social aspect of language learning is at the forefront and may account for why some individuals with autism spectrum disorders have difficulty with both social interaction and language acquisition (Kuhl, 2007).

By the end of the second year (**multiword stage**), gestures alone account for 10% of communicative signals, vocalizations alone account for approximately 40%, and gestures with vocalizations account for 50% (Wetherby, Reichle et al., 1998). Young children are averaging five communicative acts per minute (Wetherby, Reichle et al., 1988), and even at this age are able to select the mode of communication by evaluating the best form for the audience (Wetherby, Reichle et al., 1988). Typical children are able to switch communication modes as a repair strategy for a miscommunicated original message (Wetherby, Alexander, & Prizant, 1998) when the anticipated consequence of their cries or vocalizations are not met (Schuler, 1980). This ability to repair communicative breakdowns is a clear indication of the intention to communicate (Wetherby, Alexander, et al., 1998). Golinkoff (1986) sampled the communicative attempts in young children at age 1 and in 2-month intervals until age 2 years,

4 months, and found that 49% of interactions were negotiated episodes where the mother failed to understand the meaning initially and helped the child to clarify intentions, 38% were immediately successful, and 13% were missed attempts. The proportion of immediately successful communicative messages increased as children aged (Golinkoff, 1986). The communication partners of these young communicators were making an effort to clarify the meaning of the messages.

When children are about 2½ years old, they begin to combine two words, decrease jargon and babbling, and increase vocabulary growth (Lue, 2001). Grammatical morphemes begin to be included, and two-word utterances begin to show signs of syntax (Lue, 2001). By 24 months of age, some prepositions and word endings are used. Table 8.1 depicts the

**TABLE 8.1**  The explorer: 12 to 24 months

| Age (Months) | Motor | Cognition | Socialization | Communication |
|---|---|---|---|---|
| 15 | Enjoys unceasing activity; walks with rapid runlike gait<br>Walks a few steps backward and sideways<br>Carries objects in both hands or waves while walking<br>Throws ball with elbow extension<br>Takes off shoes and socks<br>Scribbles lines | Imitates small motor acts | Looks for adults when left alone<br>Likes music and dancing<br>Pushes toys<br>Imitates housework<br>Plays in solitary manner<br>Begins make-believe play | Points to clothes, persons, toys, and animals named<br>Uses jargon and words in conversation<br>Has four- to six-word vocabulary |
| 18 | Walks up stairs with help<br>Walks smoothly, runs stiffly<br>Drinks unassisted<br>Throws ball with whole arm<br>Throws and catches without falling<br>Jumps with both feet off floor<br>Turns pages<br>Scribbles in circles<br>Has muscle control for potty training | Recognizes pictures<br>Recognizes self in mirror<br>Remembers places where objects are usually located<br>Uses a stick as a toy<br>Imitates adult object use | Explores reactions of others; tests others<br>Enjoys solitary play, engages in increased cooperative play from here on<br>Pretends to feed doll | Begins to use two-word utterances<br>Has approximately 20-word vocabulary<br>Identifies some body parts<br>Refers to self by name<br>"Sings" and hums spontaneously<br>Plays question-and-answer with adults |

**TABLE 8.1 continued**

| Age (Months) | Motor | Cognition | Socialization | Communication |
|---|---|---|---|---|
| 21 | Walks up and down stairs with help of railing or hand<br>Jumps, runs, throws, climbs; kicks large ball; squats to play<br>Puts shoes on partway<br>Unzips<br>Fits things together, such as the pieces of an easy puzzle<br>Responds rhythmically to music with whole body | Knows shapes<br>Sits alone for short periods with book<br>Notices little objects and small sounds | Hugs spontaneously<br>Plays near but not with other kids<br>Likes toy telephone, doll, and truck for play | Likes rhyming games<br>Pulls person to show something<br>Tries to "tell" experiences<br>Understands some personal pronouns<br>Uses *I* and *mine* |
| 24 | Walks smoothly, watching feet<br>Runs rhythmically but unable to start or stop smoothly<br>Walks up and down stairs alone without alternating feet<br>Tiptoes for a few steps<br>Pushes tricycle<br>Eats with fork | Matches familiar objects<br>Comprehends *one* and *many* | Can role-play in limited manner<br>Imagines toys have life qualities; engages in pretend play that is constrained by the objects<br>Enjoys parallel play predominately<br>Prefers action toys<br>Cooperates with adults in simple household tasks<br>Orders others around<br>Communicates feelings, desires, and interests | Has 200- to 300-word vocabulary; names most common everyday objects<br>Uses short, incomplete sentences<br>Uses some prepositions (*in*, *on*) and pronouns (*I, me, you*) but not always correctly<br>Uses some regular verb endings (*-s, -ed, -ing*) and plural *s* |

*Source*: Owens, Robert E., *Language Development: An Introduction*, 4th Edition, © 1996. Reprinted by permission of Pearson Education, Inc., Upper Saddle River, NJ.

sequence of typical language development for young children ages 15 to 24 months of age (Owens, 1996).

Eve Clark (1977) studied the use of self-referents in typical children. The first personal pronoun used is the first-person form of *me, I, my,* or *mine*. It may be part of a set phrase such as *me, too* or *I do it* or *ia/wannit*. Use of one of these self-referents occurs by age 2½. The next pronoun used is *you* (Fay, 1980a). It is hypothesized that the relationship and uses of *I* and *you* may be learned from their previous pairing with gestures indicating attention to an object or action (Clark, 1977; Fay, 1980a). This referential labeling is challenging even for typical children (Fay, 1980a) and is facilitated by practice with caregivers. Communication competence not only requires skills of the speaker, but successful interactions also require skills of the communication partner (Light, 2003).

# Communication Issues and Delays in Autism

The communicative abilities of individuals with autism spectrum disorders are quite varied (Ogletree & Oren, 2006). For many, this impairment is manifested at a very young age when infants with autism do not follow the gaze of their caregiver, or they do not engage in a shared focus on objects and social partners, which is referred to as coordinated joint attention (Adamson & Chance, 1998). By 18 months of age, typical children are sharing attention with caregivers (Adamson & Chance, 1998), and the lack of these behaviors (sharing gaze and protodeclarative pointing) are two of the identifying factors used in the Checklist for Autism in Toddlers (CHAT) screening tool (Baron-Cohen, Allen, & Gillberg, 1992) for autism spectrum disorders. In addition, failure to attend to speech is an early and strong predictor of autism (Osterling & Dawson, 1994; Paul & Sutherland, 2005). Parents are most often concerned about issues of communication and speech of their children with autism spectrum disorder (ASD) in the second year of life (Prelock, Paul, & Allen, 2011).

Learners with ASD have overall reduced rates of communication (Paul & Sutherland, 2005). Speech may be used in an idiosyncratic manner, as in **echolalia**, or the immediate or delayed repetition of language (Fay, 1980b). If asked, "Do you want a book or music?" the child may respond, "book or music" (immediate echolalia) or the child may repeat a television commercial heard days prior (delayed echolalia) without comprehension of the content (Fay, 1980b). Immediate and delayed echolalia may serve different functions for some individuals with autism (Prizant & Rydell, 1984, 1993).

It is not uncommon for learners with autism to have difficulty with the use of pronouns. When referring to himself, the student may say, "He wants toy," or "Jack wants toy," instead of using *I* or *me* correctly (Tager-Flusberg et al., 2011). Correct use of pronouns requires an understanding of the changing referents of a speaker obtained through observational learning or practice (Fay, 1980b). Confusion with gender and the use of *he, she*, and *it* is likely to be an issue for individuals with autism.

If speech is used, the prosody, pitch, or volume (Fay, 1980b) of the sentence may be unusual.

The intonation of individuals with ASD has been described as "mechanical," "wooden," or "arrhythmic" (Fay, 1980b; Tager-Flusberg et al., 2011). There may be a lack of understanding of word boundaries and a tendency to comprehend phrases as single chunks of speech (Fay, 1980a). Individuals with ASD often have difficulty answering *wh-* questions, most likely due to their focus on irrelevant aspects of the question instead of on the key *wh-* word used (Koegel & Koegel, 1995; Krantz, Zalenski, Hall, Fenske, & McClannahan, 1981). When asked, "Who took you for a car ride?" the students may respond, "to the store" or "red car."

Vocalizations can be self-stimulatory when they occur independently of the presence of another person or a social context (Schuler, 1980). In addition, one of the forms that repetitive patterns of interest can take is repeated discussion of favorite topics. For example, a student with autism may ask a question about the type of car you drive not necessarily to converse with you but as a way to begin talking about cars in a stereotypic manner and regardless of the reaction of the conversation partner.

Individuals with autism often fail to generalize the meaning of words or the range of forms that a label such as "chair" can have, or that it refers to a variety of items that you sit on (Fay, 1980b; Grandin, 1999). They may repeatedly use word-chunk associations initially learned in relation to one object or event, such as "going-home-now" related to closing a car door. Pragmatics, or knowing the context in which to use language, or how to interact in a conversation is often a challenge for individuals with autism spectrum disorders (Tager-Flusberg et al., 2011). In addition, some individuals with autism will not understand the nuances of pragmatics and will take the words spoken literally (Bogdashina, 2005; Myles & Simpson, 2001). If a person with ASD is told to "hop to it," the response may be hopping from one place to the next. Or the person with autism may respond to a comment like "She is hot!" by touching the person and denying this fact.

## Communication Strengths

Some individuals with autism spectrum disorders do not have issues with the form and use of communication skills. For most individuals with autism spectrum disorders, there are no problems with the physical form or function of the mouth, vocal cords, or other parts of the anatomy involved in speech and communication (Lue, 2001). Individuals with ASD can have strengths that can be incorporated into any plan to increase communication. Visual spatial abilities are frequently strengths for individuals with ASD, and incorporating the visual modality when addressing language stimulation capitalizes on this strength (Charlop, Greenberg, & Chang, 2011; Goldstein, 2002; Schlosser, Sigafoos, & Koul, 2009). Vocabulary size also is a relative strength (Prelock et al., 2011).

Some individuals are good text readers and some are considered hyperlexic with highly developed word recognition skills and precocious reading development (Kupperman, Bligh, & Barouski, 1992; Patti & Lupinetti, 1993). Text-based communication systems facilitate interaction with learners preferring and skilled with the written word. Advanced skills with memorizing chunks of language, including songs, can be used to facilitate communication when incorporated in social scripts or stories. Some individuals with autism spectrum disorders are motivated by activities that involve others, such as by hugs, tickles, and swings in the air, and that can be incorporated into a communication strategy.

## The Importance of Communication

Communication is a basic human power that allows people to articulate their personal, educational, vocational, and social goals and to achieve their full potential. As a person develops communication competence, he or she meets this human need, realizes this human right, and attains this human power (Light, 2003, p. 3).

Individuals who have a difficult time with communication, such as those with cerebral palsy, autism spectrum disorders, and other disabilities, are often assumed to be less competent across domains than those who speak clearly with an adequate vocabulary in those cultures that place a high value on speech and language. When poor speech skills are equated with low cognitive ability, **expectations** for skill acquisition and performance are set way too low, and an unfortunate outcome may be that the individuals with disabilities only strive to meet these limited expectations for achievement (Koppenhaver, Pierce, Steelman, & Yoder, 1995). Educators need to have realistic yet challenging expectations for all students, including those with speech and communication delays.

It is important for educators to have realistic yet high aims for the potential of learners with autism spectrum disorders. "Rudimentary language skills can make a tremendous difference in the ability of children to control their environment" (Goldstein, 2002, p. 392). Even the acquisition of basic communication skills (gestures and oral) creates important opportunities, such as making choices and having wants and needs met. Through communication, we share our interests and preferences with others, or we share who we are and what makes us individuals. Educators who learn to respond to the initial communicative attempts and shape these into more elaborate systems of communication are not only facilitating the learners' ability to acquire many new skills, but also have worked to enhance the overall quality of life.

## The Verbal Behavior Approach

In Skinner's (1957) publication *Verbal Behavior*, he described how language could be categorized by the function of the expression. Individuals become listeners when they respond to the vocal verbal speech of others, and they become speakers when they use various forms (sign, pictures, vocalizations) to convey their feelings, affect others' behavior, and change their own circumstances (Greer & Ross, 2008). Skinner identified six speaker verbal functions, called verbal operants, that can occur through oral language or with signs (Greer & Ross, 2008). For example, one can say the same word *car*, but the context in which it is said differs according to the function. If it is a request, the word functions as a **mand** (e.g., "car, please"). If it is a label, it is a **tact** (e.g., the child points to a car and says, "Car"). If it is an imitation of a verbally expressed word, it is considered an **echoic** (e.g., "Say, car") and if it is expressed as part of an interaction or conversation it is considered an **intraverbal** (e.g., in response to the question, "What do we ride in?"). The **autoclitic** modifies the effect of the verbal operants just described (e.g., saying, "I have had nothing to eat since breakfast" before a mand for food). The sixth operant, **textual responding**, is verbal behavior under the control of the printed word (e.g., seeing the word *car* in print).

Educators who incorporate the applied verbal behavior approach typically begin with a focus on teaching students to request, or mand for, activities and to make choices (LeBlanc, Esch, Sidener, & Firth, 2006). Following a preference assessment to determine preferred objects or activities, the learner is required to sign as a communicative act prior to receiving the item or activity. Physical prompts are used to assist the student to shape the sign until the student independently initiates the sign or an approximation of it as a request.

Following the consistent use of mands, students then learn to label or **tact** items, to model or imitate vocal language (echoics), and to respond to questions by others (intraverbals). Advocates for this focus also intersperse requests for already established behavior (clap hands, touch nose) with the teaching of new skills. A component of the ABLLS-R assessment, described in Chapter 2, focuses on the student's current use of verbal behavior (Partington, 2006).

In a review of the research on verbal behavior, Sautter and LeBlanc (2006) found 60 articles published between 1989 and 2004, with the majority focused on mands and tacts.

Green (2006) reviewed the research on verbal behavior with individuals identified with ASD and found 16 published articles that included a total of 41 individuals who participated in the research. Most of these studies also focused on mands (requests) and tacts (labels). Additional research, published in a wide range of peer-reviewed journals, on the development of intraverbals that require attending to a social partner and demonstrations of the generality of skill acquisition across people and contexts is recommended (Green, 2006; LeBlanc et al., 2006).

## Cultural Similarities and Differences

All typical children begin to acquire language at about the same age, and caregivers use language to interact with their children and to support learning (Wilcox & Shannon, 1998). Cultures differ in their beliefs about how children learn language, the value placed on speech, and the appropriate social contexts for interaction (Wilcox & Shannon, 1998). For example, Mexican American adults engage in dyadic interactions less frequently than Anglo Americans, with adult–child interactions in Mexican American culture consisting of triads more frequently (van Kleeck, 1994). The Inuit consider a child who is "talkative" to be a potential problem compared with English-speaking Anglo cultures that place a high value on oral communication skills. For Anglo cultures, words are the focus of communication, even though a great deal of nonverbal language is communicated during any interaction (Owens, 1996).

Typical children become aware of cultural conventions as they acquire language (Rice, 1993). They learn about status and how to interact and communicate respect with individuals of different status and gender roles, how to resolve disputes, and to recognize acceptable expressions of affection (Grinker, Yeargin-Allsopp, & Boyle, 2011). Examples include Samoan children who make requests only of someone with a higher rank, who in turn will respond through a third party, and the Korean language, which requires the use of suffixes to denote levels of respect (Grinker et al., 2011). Typical children also are sensitive to differences in how other children communicate and learn which style of interaction is appropriate for which context (Rice, 1993). It is important for educators to be aware of these cultural differences in communication style when targeting goals and working with learners with ASD and their families.

Nonverbal behavioral repertoires vary across cultures, with Mexican American mothers using nonverbal instruction to communicate a directive (Garcia-Coll, 1990). Mexican American mothers also use tactile stimulation more often than vocalization with young infants compared with Anglo American mothers (Garcia-Coll, 1990). In addition, following the child's lead or providing a verbal model may be in conflict with the families' cultural practices. Using specific gestures such as thumbs down or thumbs up, or looking at a learner with prolonged eye contact may be misunderstood by individuals with ASD from diverse cultural backgrounds (Mirenda & Bopp, 2003), and communicative partners need to be aware of these differences when working with augmentative systems. Parents from diverse cultural backgrounds may have different perceptions of their roles as communication partners and facilitators of language (Kayser, 1995). These perceptions need to be considered when designing any intervention plan. See Chapter 7 for a thorough discussion of working with families from diverse backgrounds.

### Working with Families to Select Communication Goals

Assessment methods and instruments are selected in consultation with families that will address the area of communication, including current skills and performance. It is important to consider whether any identified communication objectives are functional (Bogdashina, 2005; Prizant, Wetherby, Rubin, Laurent, & Rydell, 2006b). Functional objectives are those that the learner can use across environments to facilitate communication about what is important.

If a speech-language pathologist is a member of the educational team, then part of any assessment will be conducted by this team member. Recommendations for communication goals and objectives will be the outcomes of assessments from all team members, including informal observations from educators and family members. During discussions about the selection of objectives, family priorities and consistency with cultural values and practices will be discussed (Kalyanpur & Harry, 1999).

It is in everyone's best interest to have the speech-language pathologist work as a team member and to provide information that is implemented by all educators involved with the learner with ASD, including family members. Speech-language pathologists who work with schools have been exploring alternatives to pull-out therapy sessions, including addressing language goals in the classroom (Cirrin & Penner, 1995). Concerns for pull-out sessions alone are lack of efficacy with language goals, lack of generalization, reduced naturalness of pull-out sessions, and negative effects of removing children from the classroom (Cirrin & Penner, 1995).

## Enhancing Educator Skills as Communication Partners

Because communication involves at least two people, a communicator and a partner, knowledge of strategies that communication partners can use is of great benefit for educators. It is also important for communication partners to identify those strategies that are effective for use with individuals with autism spectrum disorders. Eight of the 11 established treatments (antecedent interventions, behavioral packages, comprehensive behavioral treatment, joint attention, naturalistic teaching, pivotal response training [PRT], peer training, modeling) as identified by the National Standards Project (National Autism Center, 2009a) include studies focused on increasing communication skills of individuals with ASD across ages.

## Communication Partners Make a Difference

Fundamental to the successful use of any strategy is the knowledge that the behaviors and skills of the communication partner can make a difference for the individual with a disability and that the effective use of communication strategies is related to increases in communication of students (Hall & Macvean, 1997). Often, communication partners attribute a decrease in communication attempts to the student having a "bad day" rather than to their own skills and behavior as a communication partner. However, Hall and Macvean (1997) demonstrated a functional relationship between the communicative partners and communicative acts by their students.

Prizant and colleagues (2006a) state that adult communication partners must be self-aware of the most effective interpersonal strategies and styles to support the individual child's learning. Siegel-Causey and Guess (1989) agree that sensitivity to the various forms that communication attempts can take and to the effect of partner actions on future communicative interactions is one of their five guidelines for effective communication partners.

> The desire to communicate is strongest and the communication is easiest in the context of a relationship with a responsive partner. (Kaiser, Nietfeld, & Roberts, 2010, p. 43)

In addition to awareness (a cognitive term), Prizant and colleagues (2006a) state that a communication partner must accept that his or her behavior plays a critical role in supporting the learning of a child with autism spectrum disorder, and that the partner should be willing to assess the effect of his or her own behavior on the child's learning. Assessing the relationship between intervention and behavior change, or strategies used on student progress, is a hallmark of applied behavior analysis.

## Providing Frequent Opportunities Is Important

Providing frequent and varied opportunities for communication is necessary for practicing new skills so that they become fluent (Goldstein, 2002;

Prizant et al., 2006b). Sussman (1999) provides an acronym to assist parents with providing frequent opportunities for communication, ROCK (Repeat, Opportunities, Cue, and Keep it fun!), as part of the More Than Words Program. In a randomized, controlled trial study of a program for parents and their young children with autism, and based on strategies similar to the More Than Words program, the researchers found that outcomes were greatest for the parent's synchronous response to the child, the child's initiation to the parent, and for parent–child shared attention (Green, Charman, McConachie, Alfred, et al., 2010). In other words, the greatest gains were made for the parent–child interaction.

Hart and Risley (1995) describe the outcomes of their years of study of the communication interactions occurring between young children and their caregivers in family homes. One of the important conclusions of their work was that the amount of language the young child heard in the early years was related to the extent of vocabulary and general academic performance in later years. Practicing communication skills during speech sessions alone or during one designated activity at school, such as during snack time or lunch, provides insufficient opportunity for practice of new communication skills.

Coleen Sparkman describes a program where the opportunities for communication are embedded throughout the school day at high rates In Their Words 8.1.

## Working with Learner Motivation

Any theorist who considers the environment as a factor in the occurrence of a communication act would agree that an environment that stimulates an individual's motivation to communicate is important, and especially so for an individual with autism. Motivation may be critically important for those individuals who use augmentative or alternative communication systems (Light, 2003). Identifying what is motivating is a first step and can be done with a formal or informal reinforcer assessment.

## 8.1 IN THEIR WORDS
Coleen Sparkman, *M.A. CCC-SLP Director, Therapeutic PATHWAYS, Inc.*

## Our Job as Educators of Children with ASD

Each child should be looked at in terms of his deficits or the "barriers" that are impeding his progress—keep in mind the "core deficits" of autism as you are evaluating the child, including inability to imitate, poor attending, lack of functional communication, and absent initiation.

The goal of working with young children with autism should be maximizing potential and pushing them on to an accelerated trajectory of progress. The role of a speech-language pathologist can be very beneficial, or it can be obstructive—I would recommend that you take a step back and look at the child in a broader perspective than "syntax, phonology, morphology, semantics, and pragmatics." Instead, ask yourself "What barriers are present that prevent this child from developing skills rapidly?" Then ask, "How should we prioritize his skill development to accelerate his progress?" These questions should help keep the focus on the importance of the basics, including generalized imitation skills—necessary prior to being able to teach expressive language; attending skills—necessary to improve social referencing, articulation, and receptive language. This should also prevent the "tug of war" I often witness at IEPs [individualized education programs] when the speech-language pathologist is trying to "carve out a piece" of the child's program for therapy time. I would propose that one could use the speech-language pathologist as a consultant for the developmental norms for sound production, as well as for the appropriate language structures and social skills to teach. It is unlikely that the best use of this professional is in traditional therapy, identified as working with the child in a one-on-one or small-group setting.

Our job as educators of children with autism is one of prioritizing—if the child is an "early learner" and/or doesn't have generalized imitation skills yet, what relative contribution do any articulation problems present? Probably very little. What about the relative contribution of his length of utterance if he is demonstrating no initiation? Again, I would say, very little. It is critical for the speech-language pathologist to keep the child's skill repertoire in mind so that a common trap is avoided—the "secondary diagnosis"—which often occurs when different professionals identify the deficits they see within their treatment area and don't look at the child as a whole. Many young children with a diagnosis of autism have an inaccurate diagnosis of "apraxia" placed on them by well-meaning speech-language pathologists. When, in fact, if they had looked at the core deficits—lack of imitation, poor attending—and waited for the child to receive the benefits of some behavioral treatment, they would quickly see that, when the child gained an imitative repertoire, his verbal skills improved rapidly.

It is important that all people who come into contact with the child be aware of his level of communication skill and respond appropriately to him. At the center-based program I codirect with a Board Certified Behavior Analyst, we strive for 100 to 150 learning opportunities per hour—with many of these being language-related. This means teaching each instructional assistant, teacher, and parent how to set up the environment (including people as part of the environment)

*(continued)*

## 8.1 IN THEIR WORDS (continued)

and expectations to require eye contact, initiation, social referencing (looking at instructor before being given wanted item), and communicative intent (knock on closed door, verbal request to open door). At Therapeutic Pathways and the Kendall School, we have many children who come in with the same profile: nonverbal, not toilet-trained, significant self-stimulatory behaviors, no imitation skills, poor attending—who leave here able to carry on conversations with their peers, attend typical elementary schools independently, and get invited to birthday parties. Looking at all skill-building activities in terms of their relationship to the long-term goal—an independently functioning, communicatively competent individual—helps to steer the work we do with these individuals with autism.

A fundamental aspect of the diagnosis is that individuals with autism spectrum disorders are less likely to be motivated to communicate for social reasons, or less likely to initiate communication for social interaction alone. Consequently, many planned strategies involve arranging the environment so that the individual must communicate in order to gain access to preferred items or activities, including food, toys, or outside play. Working with the motivation of individuals with autism spectrum disorder can be crucial to the acquisition, maintenance, and generalization of skills (Koegel & Mentis, 1985).

### Acknowledge Communication Attempts

It is important for communication partners to be good observers of individuals with ASD and to acknowledge communication attempts from eye gaze, vocalizations, or motor movements (Koegel & Koegel, 2006; Siegel-Causey & Guess, 1989). Effective partners are responsive to the child's nonverbal and motor actions as acts of communication (Bogdashina, 2005). Research has revealed that partners of communicators with developmental disabilities often miss opportunities to respond to communicative overtures (Blockberger & Sutton, 2003;

Reichle, Hidecker, Brady, & Terry, 2003). When telegraphic speech is used by voice or augmentative and alternative communication (AAC) system output, greater demands are made of the conversational partner to interpret and respond to communicative intent and meaning (Blockberger & Sutton, 2003). In addition, educators often do not use communication devices and tend to dominate the content and sequence of interactions, ask many questions that require short responses, and focus on end products such as giving the right answer (Koppenhaver et al., 1995).

### Embed Communication in Ongoing Routines

Frequency is facilitated if opportunities are embedded in an ongoing or naturally occurring routine. Researchers from all theoretical perspectives advocate the use of routines for facilitating communication. Routines have the benefits of being sequential (McClannahan & Krantz, 1999; Siegel-Causey & Guess, 1989; Yoder & Davies, 1992), and predictable (Prizant et al., 2006b; Snyder-McLean, Solomonson, McLean, & Sack, 1984), with a clear beginning and ending (Mesibov, Schopler, & Hearsey, 1994; Prizant et al., 2006b), and are found in the natural environment (Pretti-Frontczak &

Bricker, 2004; Sussman, 1999). Routine patterns may result in individuals with autism feeling safe in an environment that is predictable (Bogdashina, 2005). Oral communication can be facilitated by using verbal routines to accompany familiar actions, such as "ready, set, go" or "one, two, three" and then waiting for the child to complete the phrase (Koegel & Koegel, 2006; Sussman, 1999; Yoder & Davies, 1992). Daily routines in the home are sustained by ecocultural influences and provide natural opportunities to promote children's learning (Sze & Koegel, 2006). Although children with autism were excluded from their study, Yoder and Davies (1992) found that more frequent language and more diverse vocabulary was exhibited by young children during routines compared with nonroutines.

Beisler and Tsai (1983) demonstrated an increase in the communication skills of preschoolers with autism through intense modeling of verbal responses and reinforcement based on responding to the communicative intent of the child during joint activity routines. McClannahan and Krantz (1999) embed opportunities for communication ("Ask teacher for book" or "Give Mom a hug") as part of a sequence of events (e.g., build train set, read book, use treadmill for 5 minutes) outlined in the individualized activity schedules used by learners with autism spectrum disorders.

## Incorporate Affect and Enjoyment

Regardless of theoretical approach, authors recommend that an effective partner is emotionally attached and enjoys interaction (Koegel & Koegel, 2006; Prizant et al., 2006b; Schreibman, Kaneko, & Koegel, 1991; Sussman, 1999). Researchers suggest that it is helpful to be animated and playful when working with young children (MacDonald & Mitchell, 2002). Research supporting the use of positive affect by educators is scarce. Lamers and Hall (2003) found that preschoolers with autism spectrum disorders could discriminate the prosody (rhythm and pacing) of voice used by their teachers.

## Elaborating Communication Duration and Complexity

Guided by the knowledge of the typical development of language, communication partners facilitate the increased sophistication of communication by assisting young children to use more elaborate language. Regardless of the theoretical perspective, it is agreed that communication partners need to be aware of the current level of skills of the child. Using overly complex speech to communicate to the child, or requiring too elaborate communication from the child, often results in an unsuccessful interaction.

Opinions vary regarding the most effective way to begin to facilitate communication. Authors of curriculum guides for use with the discrete trial format (based on applied behavior analysis) indicate that some compliance training, or the ability to follow adult instruction, and the ability to attend to the adult are prerequisites for language teaching (Leaf & McEachin, 1999; Lovaas, 2003; Maurice, Green, & Luce, 1996). The learner may begin with motor imitation as an easier skill to master, prior to vocal imitation.

Other authors recommend following the child's lead and interests as a way to begin and maintain interaction (Hancock & Kaiser, 2002; Koegel & Koegel, 2006; MacDonald & Mitchell, 2002; McGee, Morrier, & Daly, 2001). Incidental teaching (McGee et al., 2001), pivotal response treatment (Koegel & Koegel, 2006), and enhanced milieu teaching (Hancock & Kaiser, 2002) are approaches based on applied behavior analysis that include following the child's lead. These strategies require that educators be good observers and competent in their abilities to arrange the environment and capture the interests of the learner with autism spectrum disorder so that opportunities for communication are frequent and address targeted objectives.

Following the child's lead is also important in the SCERTS model (Prizant et al., 2006b), where strategies based on applied behavior analysis and social interactionist theories are combined. MacDonald and Mitchell (2002) take a social interactionist approach and note in their book for parents that interactions should involve shared control, in which the lead for the activity shifts between child and communication partner. During interactions, comments and reflections would outnumber questions and directives (MacDonald & Mitchell, 2002). They also suggest that communication by an adult should match the child in ways that are clearly understood by the child. It is important to match the pace of the communication and movements of the child (MacDonald & Mitchell, 2002). Although using comments and reflecting vocalizations may be an effective way to foster communication with language-delayed children, learners with autism spectrum disorders may ignore or move away from adults who only comment or reflect. Research demonstrating the effectiveness of reflecting child-led activities by imitation of child behavior as a strategy to increase communication with young learners with ASD is needed.

Turn-taking as a way to maintain communication and social interaction is considered a pivotal skill by some educators (Hancock & Kaiser, 2002; Koegel & Koegel, 2006; MacDonald & Mitchell, 2002; Prizant et al., 2006b; Quill, 2000; Snyder-McLean et al., 1984; Sussman, 1999). By initiating interactions, responding to the child, and giving the child an opportunity to respond on the part of the communication partner, the communicative interactions can become longer in duration. Shared control during interactions involve turn-taking in leading activities (MacDonald & Mitchell, 2002).

In their comparison of prelinguistic milieu teaching and the Picture Exchange Communication System (PECS) (described below), Yoder and Stone (2006) determined that milieu teaching strategies resulted in comparatively more generalized turn-taking and initiation of joint attention by preschoolers with ASD. Incorporating turn-taking as a method of teaching the back-and-forth aspect of conversations and as a method of expanding the duration of interactions has theoretical appeal, but it needs to be confirmed as an important skill-building strategy through research.

Many individuals with ASD are not motivated by social communication or by interacting with others. This defining characteristic of autism spectrum disorders provides the greatest challenge to strategies based on the social interactionist approach. Some young learners show a clear preference for interacting with a toy alone compared with interacting with that toy if an adult is in proximity and initiates any interaction (MacDonald et al., 2006). Ingersoll, Schreibman, and Stahmer (2001) found a relationship between avoiding social interaction with peers in an inclusive preschool program and producing significantly less language after 6 months compared with children with ASD who did not avoid their peers. Creating an environment that fosters social motivation is currently one of the greatest challenges for researchers and practitioners (Turan & Halle, 2006).

## Focusing on Oral Language

### From First Sounds to Paragraphic Speech

Strategies based on the principles of behavior analysis have been used extensively to teach speech and language skills to learners with autism spectrum disorders. Discrete trial instruction involves the educator modeling an oral sound that, when imitated exactly or in approximation, is immediately reinforced.

The discrete trial format has been used to teach beginning words such as labeling of objects, naming colors, and identification of familiar people from photographs. Discrete trial teaching is considered an evidence-based strategy for teaching communication skills (Brunner & Seung, 2009; Goldstein, 2002; Odom, Collet-Klingenberg, Rogers, & Hatton, 2010). Oral requests for items or activities have been placed on prerecorded language master cards that serve as a model for the learner with autism spectrum disorder. Even young children can learn to run the card through the machine, listen to the words "Book, please," and then repeat the recorded message to an educator (McClannahan & Krantz, 1999, 2005). Using cues other than adult models helps to avoid prompt dependency on teacher instruction.

McGee and Morrier (2005) report that 95% of the learners with autism spectrum disorders who complete their toddler and preschool programs transition with vocal language. Incidental teaching, an evidence-based naturalistic language (Brunner & Seung, 2009; Odom, Collet-Klingenberg, Rogers, & Hatton, 2010), was used in this program. Educators follow the child's lead and arrange for frequent opportunities to communicate. The physical layout of the classroom includes a gate between areas that requires a request to open for entrance and participation in fun activities such as songs, painting, or exercise games. Because building communication skills is a focus of the program, each child's language goals are placed on the wall in an abbreviated format so that all educators know which language skills to target with which child (McGee, et al., 2001). Research indicates that incidental teaching has been used to increase the use of adjectives or descriptors in typical preschoolers (Hart & Risley, 1975), and to increase the use of prepositions (McGee, Krantz, & McClannahan, 1985) and labels of items for making sandwiches (McGee, Krantz, Mason, & McClannahan, 1983) by individuals with autism. Published research verifying the claims that incidental teaching results in the development of vocal language skills in young children with autism spectrum disorders would provide needed evidence.

Pivotal response treatment (PRT), an evidence-based strategy (Odom, Collet-Klingenberg, et al., 2010), has also been used to teach communication and language skills. The authors claim that 90% of young children with autism who participate in PRT programs acquire words (Koegel & Koegel, 2006). Similar to incidental teaching, this approach begins with child initiation or interest in an object or activity. Tasks are varied to keep the child's interest, maintenance tasks are interspersed throughout the session to create behavioral momentum, and natural reinforcers (toys requested) are used (Koegel, Bruinsma, & Koegel, 2006).

## Research on Second-Language Learning and Autism

In spite of strong recommendations for increased research in the area of second language learning and autism spectrum disorders (Brown & Rogers, 2003), there were no publications of research found when "autism," "English-language learners," and "second language learners" were used together in a database search. There is a belief among educators that bilingualism is difficult and not accessible for learners with a language delay or impairment (Kayser, 1995). Most professionals focus on English-only interventions, even though outcomes from research in speech-language pathology in the United States support the hypothesis that the native language may be instrumental in helping learners with language impairments develop skills in both native and majority languages (Kayser, 1995). The lack of bilingual clinicians may be an important factor for not working with the home language when targeting skills (Kayser, 1995).

Fragoso and Hall (2006) used a stimulus-equivalence procedure to teach three boys with autism to (a) identify a picture, (b) label the picture, and (c) read the written word in both English and Spanish. A computer program was designed to provide the sequence of matching-to-sample tasks needed to teach, test, and probe for learning. All three boys were able to identify the correct response for each of the words in both Spanish and English with 100% accuracy, even though the picture-to-written-Spanish-words, English-written-word-to-Spanish-written-word, and English-word-spoken-to-English-word-written associations were never directly taught. The results of this study are encouraging because this procedure, if replicated, could address the second language learning issues of some learners with ASD. Clearly, research in this area is well overdue.

## Using Augmentative and Alternative Communication (AAC) Systems

Approximately 14% to 25% of children have little or no functional speech when they are diagnosed with ASD (Wendt, 2009). Augmentative systems to supplement or enhance speech or writing and the use of systems as an **alternative** to spoken language are frequently used with individuals with ASD who have characteristic delays in language development (Ogletree & Oren, 2006). **Augmentative systems** are frequently used to support or supplement communication at the same time that speech goals are being addressed (Charlop, et al., 2011). Research has shown that augmentative systems do not deter the development of speech as long as educators continue to target vocal language (Charlop et al., 2011; Ogletree & Oren, 2006; Schlosser et al., 2009). Speech-generating devices, computer-aided instruction, the Picture Exchange Communication System, and visual supports are each considered evidence-based practices for use with individuals with ASD (Odom, Collet-Klingenberg, et al., 2010).

> Functional communication is achieved when children spontaneously use the skill in naturally occurring settings and situations. Functional communication should be our goal with AAC systems. (Charlop et al., 2011, p. 1139)

Once it has been determined that use of an augmentative system would be beneficial, the challenge of selecting the form arises: Should the individual use pictures, photographs, tangible symbols, voice output devices, or sign language? At this time, "there is no evidence indicating that any one AAC approach is superior to any other in yielding higher rates of spontaneous and generative communication or optimizing generalization" (Wendt, 2009, p. 103). An assessment of the learner's current skills in the areas of

contingency awareness, presymbolic intentional communication, and understanding of levels of symbolic representation is recommended (Rowland & Schweigert, 2000). Rowland and Schweigert (1993) suggest that the system selected should be one that can be used by the individual, one that is as abstract as possible, and one that is as portable as possible. A system designed with black-and-white drawings that are not understood by the student would be useless, as would a voice output device that stays in the corner of a classroom and is not used in other environments.

Some students with ASD may need to be taught intentional communication that can be used to have their wants and needs met. Students may have a history of being reinforced for crying or screaming in order to get what they want, or taking the hand of an adult and moving that person toward the object or activity that they prefer as a means of communicating wants and needs. They may not have learned a system of getting their needs met through a communicative act.

## Pictures, Photographs, and 3D Objects

Frost and Bondy (2002) have put together a method based on applied behavior analysis to teach children with developmental disabilities to begin to communicate, or use intentional communication, through the exchange of a picture, photograph, or 3D small component of the preferred item. The **Picture Exchange Communication System (PECS)** is an augmentative system that has been widely adapted for students without, or with minimal, oral communication skills (Bondy & Frost, 2001, 2009). In the early phases of this program, students learn about the act of approaching an adult and exchanging a picture or a photograph for what they want. Two adults are needed for the initial phases, one to act as the *prompter* and one to act as the *communicator*, or to respond to the initiations of the student with autism spectrum disorders. Later phases include teaching discrimination of items to select preferred

**FIGURE 8–1**   Phase 1 - The PECS model
*Source:* Illustration from the L. Frost M.S, CCC/SLP, and Andy Bondy, Ph.D book titled: *The Picture Exchange Communication System Training Manual*, Second Edition. New York, DE. 19713. Used with permission from Pyramid Educational Products, Inc. p. 71 All rights reserved.

ones, requesting in sentence form, and then commenting on what the student observes in the environment (see Figure 8–1). Many PECS programs are designed using picture symbols (PICS) from the Mayer-Johnson Company (Johnson, 1995).

PECS is considered an evidence-based practice according to the National Professional Development Center on ASD (Odom, Collet-Klingenberg, et al., 2010). In their book chapter, Bondy and Frost (2009) identified 33 publications regarding PECS. Some examples include two studies that demonstrated that the three participating children with autism in each of the studies could make communication and social gains using PECS and that all three children increased their use of verbal speech (Charlop-Christy, Carpenter, Le, LeBlanc, & Kellet, 2002; Ganz & Simpson, 2004). In their study of 18 preschoolers with significant disabilities, Schwartz and Garfinkle (1998) found that increases in spontaneous speech were greater for those children who had at least five words when they began the PECS program. PECS was established as a viable alternative communication system for three

of five participating nonverbal adults with developmental disabilities (Stoner et al., 2006). Yoder and Stone (2006) found that the use of PECS facilitated more generalized requests in preschoolers with autism compared with prelinguistic milieu teaching. Research outcomes have demonstrated gains with the use of PECS, such as promotion of speech acquisition, reduction of problem behaviors, and increases in social approach behaviors (Bondy & Frost, 2009). The duration of PECS training varies for each child, but when they are taught correctly, individuals with autism can easily acquire PECS in the training environment through phase III or higher (Charlop et al., 2011).

When working with any symbolic system, it is important to assess the learner's knowledge of the relationship between symbol and referent (Quill, 2000; Rowland & Schweigert, 1993). The learner's understanding of true symbolic behavior occurs when he or she is capable of understanding the dual representation of a picture, that it is a photograph and at the same time a referent for the object in the picture (Mollica, 2003). Educators may need to teach picture/object correspondence. A sequence of activities to teach this skill is found in *Activity Schedules for Children with Autism: Teaching Independent Behavior*, by McClannahan and Krantz (2010). Educators begin by pairing a photograph with a preferred food item or activity. When the learner correctly identifies the item from the photo, he or she is rewarded with access to the item for a brief period of time.

Students with severe cognitive impairments or who have poor memory, or who do not understand abstract symbols may need to use systems that are constant in visual or auditory form (Charlop et al., 2011). For example, in the Picture Exchange Communication System (PECS), the picture of the object remains in sight and the individual using the system does not have to recall what it is he or she requested. Another example is a **tangible object system** (Rowland & Schweigert, 2000), in which three-dimensional objects that are similar to or are parts of the object or activity that they represent (part of a palette and paintbrush to represent art class) are used. Advantages of this system for individuals with severe cognitive disabilities include the following: They are easily manipulated, require fewer memory skills, and are a clear representation of the object.

When using an augmentative communication system such as a photo or picture exchange, it is important to arrange the environment so that the student is motivated to communicate (Quill, 2000). For example, a student may have several racing magazines that he enjoys reading. These magazines can be placed on a high shelf so that the student needs to ask for assistance to get them. He then could be asked to describe the cover of the magazine he wants or to tell the teacher what articles are included in the magazine he would prefer. The curriculum published by Kathleen Quill (2000) provides a sequence of activities to teach initial communication skills. If the student is using the PECS (Bondy & Frost, 1994), there must be access to the picture book and facilitation of its use throughout the classroom.

## Signs and Gestures

Manual signs can refer to the signs used as part of language systems (e.g., American Sign Language) or any manual signs used to represent spoken language (Wendt, 2009). "Manual signing and gestures are very effective communication options for individuals with ASDs" (Wendt, 2009, p. 93). Early research by Creedon (1973) demonstrated that a simultaneous communication system that includes signs could increase the language skills of nonverbal learners with autism ages 4 to 9 years old. Following an intervention program based on applied behavior analysis, the learners increased their vocabulary from 101 to 370 words, mastered personal pronouns, and generated sentences comparable to 2- and 3-year-olds; some began to mouth words and use oral approximations for words; and three children could verbalize hi and bye. Additional positive collateral effects are reported (Creedon, 1973).

*Makaton* sign language consists of approximately 350 language concepts that are presented accompanied by grammatical speech and facial expressions (Bogdashina, 2005). This system is used with individuals with disabilities in England and Australia, among other countries. In a survey of 23 establishments in England that reported to be using Makaton peer tutors, 15 establishments reported an increase in sign use as a means of making needs known, and eight reported more general enjoyment and interaction in communication sessions (Hooper & Walker, 2002).

Buday (1995) evaluated the inclusion of music to teach manual signs to 10 children with autism. Signs were presented under two conditions: (1) music and speech and (2) rhythm and speech. The music-and-speech condition resulted in significantly more signs imitated correctly and spoken words imitated correctly, compared with the rhythm-and-sign condition. The author speculates that the music condition held the students' attention better, facilitated the recall of the signs, and was more enjoyable for this group of students compared with rhythm alone (Buday, 1995).

Interventionists who use the verbal behavior approach frequently select sign language as a preferred form for an augmentative system due to the availability and potential for complex expression (Greer & Ross, 2008). Although some practitioners consistently begin teaching communication augmented with signs, others do not recommend the use of signs with some individuals with ASD. For example, students with poor fine motor skills or difficulty with imitation (Mesibov, Shea, & Schopler, 2004) should be able to choose an alternative to sign language (Mirenda & Erickson, 2000). In his study comparing sign language and PECS with two school-age students with autism spectrum disorders, Tincani (2004) found that PECS resulted in more mands for one of the students who had weak motor imitation skills, and sign language resulted in more mands for the other student who had moderate motor imitation skills. However, the use of sign language produced more word vocalization for both participants.

### Voice-Output Communication Aids (VOCAs)

Speech-generating devises, also referred to as voice-output communication aids (VOCAs) can also be used as an augmentative system for students with ASD who have no functional speech, or who speak but who have poor articulation or a meager vocabulary. VOCAs are portable devices with speech output that is either recorded from human speech (digitized) or created from a synthesizer (Ogletree & Oren, 2006). Text-to-speech devices enable the user to type words and sentences that are converted to vocal output. The output from the best synthesizers approaches that of natural speech (Schlosser et al., 2009). Only a few studies evaluated the use of VOCAs with individuals with ASD, and they focused on using a device for making requests (Charlop et al., 2011).

Currently, most applications of AAC for expressive communication using visual-spatial symbols are used with strategies based on the principles of applied behavior analysis

(Mirenda, 2001). Bock, Stoner, Beck, Hanley, and Prochnow (2005) emphasize the importance of considering the individual child when selecting an AAC system. In the outcomes of their study comparing VOCAs and PECS for six nonspeaking preschoolers with developmental disability, three appeared to have a slight preference for PECS, two for VOCAs, and one had no clear preference (Bock et al., 2005). Learners are more likely to use the augmentative system(s) that they prefer (Schlosser et al., 2009).

When selecting any form of AAC with individuals who are learning English as a second language or who are bilingual, it is important to incorporate the language used at home when selecting and designing symbols so that the negative effects of ignoring the cultural values and language of the family are not experienced (Lund & Light, 2001). In addition, illustrations of people should be representative of the diversity found in the community where the learner lives.

## Addressing Deficits in Nonverbal Communication

Although it is recommended that educators and other adults model appropriate gestures, facial expression, posture, proximity, and voice intonation when communicating with learners with autism (Prizant et al., 2006b), modeling alone is often not enough, and the use of nonverbal behavior may need to be taught directly (Taylor & McDonough, 1996). Individuals with autism spectrum disorders are typically not good observational learners of the behavior of others for a variety of reasons; for example, they may be uninterested in people, they may attend to irrelevant cues, or they may not match the communicative act with the context (e.g., smiles at birthday parties).

Teaching children to point as a functional skill has been accomplished successfully through most-to-least prompting and reinforcement (McClannahan, & Krantz, 1999). The use of pointing and other gestures to accompany speech (e.g., "Over there!") has been taught to young children with autism in preparation for transition to kindergarten (Buffington, Krantz, McClannahan, & Poulson, 1998).

McGee and colleagues (Feldman, McGee, & Mann, 1993) evaluated the facial expressions used by preschoolers with autism spectrum disorders and their typical peers and found that there was no difference in the amount of smiling, laughing, or crying between the two groups. However, the children with ASD used facial expressions that were not related to the context. For example, the children with autism spectrum disorders were likely to laugh if a classmate was hurt or crying.

Using the applied behavior analysis strategies of discrimination training and matching-to-sample tasks, elementary school students with autism spectrum disorders were taught to match the appropriate facial expression of emotion to a videotaped context (Hall & Russell, 2000). The ability to recognize facial expressions for happy, sad, and angry generalized to the faces of their classroom teachers. Although research has shown that learners with autism can discriminate the vocal prosody of their teachers (Lamers & Hall, 2003), research focused on teaching appropriate vocal prosody was not found.

# Functional Communication to Replace Challenging Behavior

Research has demonstrated that when individuals with challenging behaviors, including those with autism spectrum disorders, learn communication skills that serve the same function as the challenging behavior, the problem behaviors decrease (Carr & Durand, 1985) because they now have a more appropriate and effective means of getting their needs met. Even authors who describe the unusual behaviors of individuals with autism spectrum disorders as a different language (Bogdashina, 2005) or as the expression of a different cultural perspective

(Bogdashina, 2005; Mesibov, et al., 2004) would support the importance of teaching more acceptable and effective means of communication. Authors who state that autism is its own culture would agree that by understanding the function of the behavior, educators are fulfilling their role as a cultural interpreter (Mesibov, et al., 2004).

**Functional communication training** has been identified as an evidence-based strategy (Odom, Collet-Klingenberg, et al., 2010). The first step in the process of functional communication training is to determine the purpose or function of the challenging behavior. (See Chapter 5 for a description of a functional analysis of behavior.) The principles of behavior analysis are used to determine the function of the challenging behavior (Brady & Halle, 1997).

Once the function has been determined, an educator would then select a communication skill that is **functionally equivalent**, or serves the same function as the problem behavior, and teach it. For example, if the child stands in front of the refrigerator and has a tantrum when he wants something inside, teaching him to point to the refrigerator and then to the item that he wants should replace these tantrums. It is critical that the new communication forms be more efficient than the problem behaviors they replace (Carr et al., 1994). If the learner who has tantrums has difficulty with fine motor coordination and finds pointing difficult, then tantrums may be more efficient for him. If the form of the communicative behavior is already in the person's repertoire, then it is clear that this form of communication can be taught to be used functionally (Carr et al., 1994); otherwise, the new behavior must be taught.

The replacement behavior also must be recognizable to others (Durand & Merges, 2001). If the learner's pointing is so unclear that it does not result in the desired response from caregivers, then it is not a good choice of communicative act. It is important that the consequence for using the replacement communication skill is reinforced or that the learner meets with success (Heflin & Alaimo, 2007), increasing the probability that the individual will use the new behavior in lieu of the problem behavior. While teaching the replacement communication skill in context, strategies, such as extinction, should be put into place to make the previous behavior nonfunctional (Durand, Bertotti, & Weiner, 1993).

Systematic instruction using evidence-based strategies such as stimulus and response prompting, prompt fading, and differential reinforcement are recommended to teaching replacement behaviors (Sigafoos, O'Reilly, & Lancioni, 2009). Commonly taught replacement behaviors include teaching pointing, saying "I want," or giving a photo or picture of the desired object as an indication of wanting a tangible item; teaching the use of the statement "I need a break" or touching or using a "take a break" card or icon (Martin, Drasgow, Halle, & Brucker, 2005) to escape from a demanding situation; and teaching greetings and opening lines such as "Let's talk about . . ." to initiate social attention.

To determine if the selected communication skill is serving the same function, data must be collected (Carr et al., 1994). Data must be collected in the context where the communicative acts occur, and by educators who have the skills to take valid and reliable data. Once it has been determined that the new communicative behavior is useful and helpful for the learner with autism spectrum disorder, educators can focus their efforts on ensuring that the strategy is used consistently and generalizes across people and contexts (Durand et al., 1993). In other words, it is not good enough for the child to point to get the item that he or she wants from the refrigerator with Mom alone or only in his or her own kitchen.

Functional communication training is more likely to be successful in environments that encourage making choices (Durand et al., 1993; Moes, 1998). Providing choices to individuals with autism spectrum disorders is a way of teaching them that they can influence others without problem behavior (Sigafoos et al., 2009). Embedding choice opportunities in teacher-assigned homework activities increased the accuracy, productivity,

and affect of individuals with autism and reduced their disruptive behaviors (Moes, 1998). Making choices teaches students that they have an active role in their daily routine. It is important that they begin learning to adjust to changes in their routines at a young age so that they will not have difficulty with change in future community and vocational settings. Additional research is needed to identify effective methods of combining functional communication training and choice-making interventions (Sigafoos et al., 2009).

Public school classrooms where students with challenging behaviors are grouped together create an environment where functional communication training can be difficult because of the burden on staff members to address the many issues in the group, and the challenge of finding the time for the training needed to implement sophisticated behavioral interventions such as functional communication training (Durand et al., 1993). Designing communication strategies with home–school collaboration and with training for the entire support team is recommended.

## Strategies to Teach Complex Language

Research evidence supports the use of strategies based on applied behavior analysis to teach complex language skills to children with autism spectrum disorders. For example, Krantz, Zalenski, Hall, Fenske, and McClannahan (1981) taught learners with autism to use adjectives as descriptors for various objects (e.g., *big pencil*; *blue car*). They also designed a home–school communication program aimed at teaching students to increase the use of multiple words and sentences, recall remote events that occurred in the past at school or at home, and provide a method of communication between school and home (Krantz et al., 1981). Following an established practice session held at the end of the day when students received modeling and reinforcement for accurate responses to questions about occurrences at school, three boys with autism began to report their activities at school to their parents at home accurately and with increasingly complex language, including the use of multiple sentences.

Brinton and Fujiki (1995) report in a case study that they used a journal with a learner who was a member of the Church of Jesus Christ of the Latter-Day Saints to recall and then report remote events. The learner reported the events verbally and the clinician wrote the information in the journal (all church members are encouraged to keep a journal). The authors reported an increase in the use of complex sentences during the 18-month period of intervention; however, they did not report on the accuracy of the learner's reporting these events to others (Brinton & Fujiki, 1995).

Applied behavior analysis has been used effectively to teach assertive statements and responses during games and conversations. Using modeling, behavioral rehearsal, and a token reinforcement system, three adolescents with autism were taught positive statements such as "Great play!" and "Isn't this fun?" and negative assertions such as "Please pay attention" and "It's my turn now" during card and ball games (McGee, Krantz, & McClannahan, 1984). Spontaneous positive statements were most frequently recorded during card games (McGee et al., 1984). Additional strategies used to teach conversational skills, including script following and fading, are addressed in Chapter 9.

# Designing an Evidence-Based Classroom to Facilitate Communication

An educational environment that incorporates evidence-based strategies for teaching communication skills would begin with a meaningful assessment of communication and language skills. Following multiple forms of assessment that included observations of learner behavior across contexts, objectives would be selected by the IEP team. Family input regarding the selection of skills is essential so that any communication skills targeted could be addressed across environments. All educators working with individuals with autism spectrum disorders would have knowledge of the objectives and strategies, and these strategies would be implemented across environments and not exclusively in any one setting (such as a pull-out session). All educators would understand that it is important to address communication skills frequently and that their behavior as communication partners has a direct effect on skill increases by learners with autism spectrum disorders.

Strategies implemented would be those that are evidence-based or identified through research with individuals with autism spectrum disorders. Classroom activities would include routines that are predictable, and each student would have an individualized schedule in written or picture form. Changes in targets would be data-driven so that new skills are introduced only when previous skills have been mastered, rather than determined by weekly themes such as words that begin with the letter *b*. Nonverbal as well as oral language skills would be targeted, and if augmentative systems are introduced, then oral language skills would continue as a focus. If oral language skills are too difficult for effective communication, then total communication would be attempted while using an alternative system such as a sign or VOCA.

Learners would be given choices and asked to communicate their preferences throughout the day. Motivational activities would be used with objectives embedded or as a reward for completion of less preferred tasks. Some learners would be taught to request breaks. The environment would be rich with opportunities for the development of new communication skills and for practice of those skills that are recently acquired. Educators would know how to expand or elaborate on communicative acts, and all educators would be competent shapers of verbal and nonverbal skills.

## SUGGESTIONS FOR DISCUSSION

1. Describe why it is relevant to understand the typical development of communication and language when designing programs for learners with autism spectrum disorders.
2. Devise a list of the opportunities that can be used or created to practice communication skills.
3. Debate how you would select the form of augmentative communication for a young child with ASD who has not developed speech, with one side arguing in favor of using PECS and the other side arguing in favor of a total communication approach that includes sign language.
4. Provide the rationale for speech-language therapists working with learners with autism spectrum disorders in the educational environment, where they can practice target skills.
5. Describe the criteria you would use in determining when to introduce an augmentative system of communication for an individual with ASD.
6. Discuss why there is so little research on second language learners with autism spectrum disorders.
7. Identify creative ways to maintain home–school communication that involves the learner with autism spectrum disorder.
8. How would you design a study to evaluate the effects of the use of the expression of affect on skill acquisition for students with ASD?

## RESOURCES

### Books

Bondy, A. S., & Frost, L. A. (2001). *A picture's worth: PECS and other visual communication strategies in autism.* Bethesda, MD: Woodbine.

Freeman, S., & Dake, L. (1997). *Teach me language: A language manual for children with autism, Asperger's syndrome and related developmental disorders.* Langley, British Columbia: SKF Books.

Mirenda, P., & Iacono, T. (2009). *Autism spectrum disorders and AAC.* Baltimore, MD: Brookes.

Quill, K. A. (2000). *Do-watch-listen-say: Social and communication intervention for children with autism.* Baltimore, MD: Brookes.

### Websites

*www.mayer-johnson.com*
   Resource materials including picture symbols and the PECS manual
*www.pecs.com*
   Pyramid Group Management Services, Inc. Contains webcasts, resources, and information about the Picture Exchange Communication System

# CHAPTER NINE

# Building Social Skills and Social Relationships

## CHAPTER OBJECTIVES

The reader should be able to:

- Describe the typical sequence of development of joint attention and social referencing.
- Identify two of the earliest signs of autism spectrum disorders that involve interaction with caregivers.
- Provide an example of the three strategies used in at least half of the empirical studies targeted to increase social skills from the review by Hwang and Hughes (2000).

## Theories of Social Development

The theoretical perspectives that guide interventions to address social and emotional areas were reviewed in Chapter 4 (applied behavior analysis) and Chapter 6 (developmental, cognitive, social-constructivist, and transactional). Behaviorists would address acquisition of social skills as they would any other behaviors—by arranging environmental variables, ensuring that individual motivation is high, and reinforcing approximations of social interaction, including proximity to peers. Accountability would be ensured through data collection on educator intervention (fidelity of treatment) and student behavior. Selection of socially valid and culturally relevant behavior would be targeted.

Generalization across settings, materials, and social partners would be the aim of any program, and strategies for generalization would be designed at the beginning of any program. The sequence of typical development would guide the practice of all theorists; however, practitioners using applied behavior analysis may elect to teach areas of relative strength so that the children with autism are beyond their peers in some skills. For example, children may be taught to read early so that they can focus on the more challenging skills in the social-emotional domain.

Developmentalists would ensure that any targeted social-emotional skills were age-appropriate and taught in a sequential manner consistent with typical development. Developmentally appropriate materials and activities would be introduced as children mature. The environment would be arranged so that children have the opportunity for experiences that stimulate learning. Social constructivists would include peers in any program, provide supports and scaffolding for new skills, and ensure that educational experiences were embedded in ongoing activities. Play would be an important educational context for young children. Modeling of socially appropriate behavior would be included as part of all theoretical approaches.

## Understanding Typical Social-Emotional Development

One of the earliest interactions between infant and caregiver is a sharing of emotional states, which includes face-to-face interactions involving sharing and regulation of mutual attention and affective expression (Kasari, Sigman, Yirmiya, & Mundy, 1993). Sharing emotions during the 3- to 6-month period is a main contributor to interpersonal development (Rogers & Bennetto, 2000). According to Adamson and Chance (1998), this is the first phase in the development of shared attention and begins with an initial period when the infant attends to social partners or caregivers. Around 5 to 6 months, this interest wanes and the focus of attention shifts to objects and nearby events (Adamson & Chance, 1998). Sometime between 6 and 18 months of age, the infant begins to maintain a shared attentional focus on objects and events with a variety of social partners. This ability to coordinate attention to people and objects, or **coordinated joint attention**, marks a pivotal point in early social-communication development. It is not until around 13 months of age that most infants maintain periods of sustained coordinated joint attention with caregivers,

and even later with peers or unfamiliar adults (Bakeman & Adamson, 1984).

Infants may initiate coordinated joint attention for several functions. They may use a pointing gesture and look to see if the partner is looking at the object or event, they may request help in obtaining a desired object, or they may seek information about an event or object when there is uncertainty (Adamson & Chance, 1998). The process of seeking information from a partner is called **social referencing**.

Several skills facilitate or inhibit social referencing (Walden, 1993). Wariness in the approach of new objects would facilitate social referencing because children who are wary look for the emotional cues of their caregivers prior to touching new or unfamiliar objects. The ability to sustain and move attentional focus is also important for social referencing (Walden, 1993). The young child must be able to inhibit behavior (refrain from touching an object) before a caregiver is referenced, and this skill is less likely in children who are developmentally delayed (Walden, 1993). Social referencing also requires an understanding that another's interpretation can be inferred from his or her behavior and that this information has value (Walden, 1993).

Meltzoff and Moore (1989) revealed that infants as young as 72 hours old will mimic caregiver behaviors in the forms of tongue protrusion and mouth opening. Replications of this study met with varying results (Rogers, 2006). **Mimicry** is defined as the spontaneous, or automatic, and rapid matching of the observed rudimentary action of a model (Moody & McIntosh, 2006). Research has also revealed that mimicry of mouth and tongue movements declines between 2 and 4 months of age and that there is a variety in the frequency in which infants mimic oral, motor, and vocal behaviors during the first 6 months (Rogers, 2006).

Infants are exposed to models of cultural norms and are also prompted and guided to "do as I do" (Hart & Risley, 1999). Imitation of behaviors that involve an understanding of both the goals and means of the model is likely to begin by the end of the first year. By the end of the second year, there is increasing growth in infants' use of imitation, which begins to include vocal imitation of the caregiver (Carpenter, 2006). Currently there is no information regarding the relationship between effortful imitation and mimicry (Rogers, 2006). It is known that when someone attempts to imitate novel movements, the subject tends to perform a more simplified version of the action that is within the current behavioral repertoire until the behaviors become so well practiced that they have a level of automaticity (Rogers, 2006). "If mimicry follows mastery, this would support the idea that automaticity of perception-action responses is a result of advanced learning and practice rather than a starting-state capacity" (Rogers, 2006, p. 17).

Social games such as turn-taking during pat-a-cake begin between 6 and 12 months of age (Warren, Yoder, & Leew, 2002). These games involve observing others and imitation of actions. Infants are able to determine the demonstrator's goals and intentions toward objects by sharing the same goals as the demonstrator during joint attentional activities (Carpenter, 2006). Following the coordinating of joint attention is a transitional period out of infancy when the child begins to understand symbols, including language, and begins to include symbols in social interaction (Adamson & Chance, 1998).

Research has shown that infants engage in meaningful joint attention activities prior to producing conventional language (Carpenter, Nagell, & Tomasello, 1998), and that new words were more likely to occur during activities when joint attention between infant and caregiver was occurring (Adamson & Chance, 1998). The rate of language acquisition and the frequency of joint activities are influenced by culture. In their longitudinal study of language development, Hart and Risley (1999) found that, in some cultures, conversation between adults and children is considered inappropriate and that it is expected that children will learn from listening. When the researchers compared a sample

of the most talkative young children and the most taciturn, they described all the taciturn youngsters as African American. None of the most talkative were African American (Hart & Risley, 1999).

The expression of emotions in children as young as 3 months of age can serve to regulate interaction (Oatley & Jenkins, 1996). Between 12 and 18 months, young children are learning to repair miscommunications by evaluating the consequences of their own communicative acts (Golinkoff, 1986). By 18 to 24 months, they are asking questions such as "What's that?" or "Where's that?" (Chapman & Miller, 1980).

By the time infants are 3 months old, they smile in response to attention and invitations to play (Oatley & Jenkins, 1996). By 7 months, babies can match vocal and facial expressions (Oatley & Jenkins, 1996). Infants older than 10 months are beginning to look at a caregiver's face for emotional information more often than other parts of the body (Oatley & Jenkins, 1996). During the first 2 years of life, typical young children have learned to differentiate between anger and joyful expressions in others (Kasari, Sigman, Yirmiya, & Mundy, 1993). They also show fearful avoidance of a visual cliff and of strangers (Oatley & Jenkins, 1996), and they express anger. Between 1 and 2 years of age, children respond to another's distress, and by the time children are age 3, they offer comfort appropriate to the needs of others (Oatley & Jenkins, 1996).

## Peer and Sibling Interaction

Play behavior typically begins with exploring and manipulating toys. Mouthing of objects and kicking mobiles are common occurrences for infants. Infants as young as 8 weeks old have been noted to smile as they interact with objects, such as when moving a mobile (Watson, 1976). Through repeated actions, babies learn the cause and effect of their body movements on objects. Exploring object properties by twisting knobs or banging objects together is also a characteristic of early manipulative play.

By the end of the first year, infants are engaging in functional play, or using objects appropriately, such as rolling a car on a surface or placing a peg in a hole. Symbolic pretend play or make-believe play emerges between 2 and 3 years of age. There are three fundamental forms of symbolic play (Leslie, 1987): (1) substituting one object for another (pretending a block is a truck), (2) attributing absent or false properties (pretending a pot is very hot), and (3) using imaginary objects as present (pretending there is dinner on an empty plate).

Early social play occurs when infants interact with caregivers by imitating vocalizations; using objects in turn-taking, such as shaking a rattle; and playing games like peek-a-boo. Toddlers begin to interact with peers through play such as parallel play with similar toys or sharing materials. Peer interactions become more prominent during the preschool years (Goldstein & Morgan, 2002). Approximately 75% of preschoolers have been described as having friends, although relationships at this age can change from day to day. Asher, Parker, and Walker (1996) describe friendship as a dyadic construct that includes mutual liking between two individuals. Around age 8 or 9 years, friendships become deeper and are characterized by less egocentrism and a greater sensitivity to others (Goldstein & Morgan, 2002).

# Social-Emotional Issues in Autism Spectrum Disorders

Persistent deficits in social communication and social interaction are aspects of one of the defining characteristics for the diagnosis of autism spectrum disorder (American Psychiatric Association, 2012). Social impairments can include deficits in social-emotional reciprocity; deficits in the use of nonverbal communicative behaviors used for social interaction, such as eye gaze, gestures, body postures, and facial expressions; and deficits in developing and

maintaining relationships, including an absence of symbolic or imaginative play activities and making friends (www.dsm5.org). This core impairment has led some to identify social deficits as the "heart" of autism spectrum disorders (Gutstein, 2005).

Two of the factors that appear to be predictive of the diagnosis of autism spectrum disorder (ASD) on the Checklist for Autism in Toddlers (CHAT) (Baron-Cohen, Allen, & Gillberg, 1992) screening tool for infants involve a social component: (1) lack of joint attention skills or lack of protodeclarative pointing, and (2) lack of eye gaze with a caregiver that is found in joint attention and social referencing. The initial level of responding to joint attention in younger siblings of children with ASD also strongly predicted the level of responding to joint attention at 34 months of age (Yoder, Stone, Walden, & Malesa, 2009). Research has revealed that children diagnosed with autism rarely pointed to external events, followed points, or alternated their gaze between objects and people during infancy (Wetherby & Prutting, 1984). They were also found to be impaired in their ability to direct or share attention with the experimenter compared with typical peers and those with mental retardation (Mundy, Sigman, Ungerer, & Sherman, 1986). Compared with children with Down syndrome and typical peers, children with autism displayed fewer orienting responses to stimuli, and this lack of responding was more severe for social stimuli (Dawson, Meltzoff, Osterling, Rinaldi, & Brown, 1998). Children with autism have been shown to display relatively few deictic gestures, or gestures used for social reasons such as in joint attention (Attwood, Firth, & Hermelin, 1988).

One hypothesis is that, because of possible problems with overselectivity of stimuli (Schreibman & Lovaas, 1973) and an inability to select relevant stimuli, infants and young children with ASD may not attend to caregiver facial expression or consider eye gaze as important. Other researchers state that specific deficits in imitation skills may be fundamental (Rogers & Bennetto, 2000). The tendency of children with autism not to imitate others may be due to impairment with identifying with others (Carpenter, 2006).

Dawson (2008) proposes a social motivation hypothesis where the infant who might be having difficulty forming and generalizing the reward value of social stimuli spends less time paying attention to, and socially engaged with, people and has a stronger focus on objects. This reduced attention to people, including their faces, gestures, and speech, or less experience with social stimuli, results in a failure of the specialization of the cortical regions of the brain that mediate social cognition. In addition, there is less efficient functioning of the brain.

When researchers asked adults to interact with their children with ASD, it was found that the children with autism engaged in similar amounts of looking, vocalizing, and smiling compared with their peers; however, they tended not to show objects or point out events to caregivers (Sigman, Mundy, Sherman, & Ungerer, 1986). Another study showed that children with autism displayed the same amount of pride, or smiling, when they completed a puzzle, but were less likely to seek attention for the achievement by showing the finished puzzle to someone else (Kasari, Sigman, Baumgartner, & Stipek, 1993). Children with autism are also less likely to exhibit an empathy response to situations when others display fear or pain compared with typical peers and those with Down syndrome (Sigman & Ruskin, 1999).

Researchers have found that children with autism spectrum disorders display facial expressions for the same amount of time as their peers (McGee, Feldman, & Chernin, 1991; Mundy et al., 1986), but that the expressions may not match the context—for example, children with ASD may show a negative facial expression in a context that typically elicits a positive one (McGee et al., 1991; Mundy et al., 1986). Children with ASD may be insensitive to faces. Studies have found that children with autism showed a preference for matching photographs based on accessories rather than facial expression (Weeks & Hobson, 1987).

In general, students with autism spectrum disorders may need to learn to attend and respond appropriately to nonverbal social cues. Taking turns (Koegel, Koegel, & Carter, 1999), reading facial expressions of emotion (Taylor & McDonough, 1996), and accurately interpreting voice tone (Lamers & Hall, 2003) are some of the social skills that are likely weak or lacking for students with autism spectrum disorders.

The defining characteristics also include lack of varied, spontaneous make-believe play and a failure to develop peer relationships. It is rare for a child with autism to spontaneously produce pretend play such as object substitution (Lewis & Boucher, 1988). It is not uncommon for learners with ASD to be uninterested in any social interaction with peers and to avoid sharing toys or activities with peers. Even when individuals with ASD have specific social behaviors, they engage in social interaction less often (Lord & Magill, 1989).

Some individuals with autism spectrum disorders have good social skills and may even seek out interaction with adults but rarely initiate interaction with peers (Fredeen & Koegel, 2006). Compared with their typical peers, children with ASD infrequently initiate bids to play with peers or initiate social interaction with siblings (Fredeen & Koegel, 2006). Lack of social initiation with peers results in a decrease in learning opportunities from peers.

The play behavior of children with ASD also differs from that of their peers. They are often content to play with toys alone and do not seek out adults in order to share toy play (Sigman & Mundy, 1989). In addition, the restricted patterns of interest may manifest as using toys in a repetitive manner for purposes other than using the toy as it was intended (Schuler & Wolfberg, 2000). For example, a child with autism spectrum disorder may line up cars in a row in the same order each time, or spend time spinning the wheels of the car in the air. Overall, children with autism spectrum disorders engage in fewer different functional play acts and produce less diverse functional play compared with peers of a similar maturational age (Sigman & Ungerer, 1984).

Individuals with ASD often have difficulty engaging in the complexities of a sustained conversation. An individual with ASD might dominate the topic of conversation with a repetitive pattern of interest, may lack the ability to initiate a topic, or may not respond to others consistent with a topic introduced by a conversation partner (Mesibov, Shea, & Schopler, 2004). Craig and Evans (1989) revealed that students with language impairments had difficulty obtaining a turn in a conversation by interrupting others compared with peers.

## The Importance of Relating to Others

Attending to caregivers, peers, siblings, and educators is important because so many opportunities to learn new skills and obtain information about the world in which the child with autism spectrum disorder operates are lost if fundamental attention and observational skills are lacking. If children with autism do not attend to others and imitate the behavior of others (Rogers & Williams, 2006), they do not learn how to pick up subtle social cues or how to do the culturally relevant "social dance" with others (Hart & Risley, 1999).

Social skills are important for functioning within a society. Lack of knowledge of how to interact with others or which behaviors are tolerated in a specific context can lead to individuals being asked to leave classrooms or resign from jobs. Lack of social skills may result in placement in schools that are restricted from classmates and peers.

Most cultures value social skills, and many people believe that relationships, including friendships, enrich the quality of life. This belief may not be held by some individuals with autism spectrum disorders, who find social interaction uncomfortable or unpleasant. However, prior to assuming that learners with autism spectrum disorders do not want to have friends, it is important to ensure that they have the skills to develop friendships so that they can truly make a choice regarding the extent of their social relationships. By targeting foundational social skills, educators can assist learners with ASD in obtaining the skills necessary for functioning in a social world and the ability to choose social relationships with others.

Some individuals with autism spectrum disorders are interested in social interaction and participation in activities with peers and community members (Mesibov et al., 2004). Some choose to get married. In the area of social skills, similar to other domains, it is important to individualize any goals and programs. The review of the literature from the National Standards Project revealed that all of the established treatments, except for schedules, has been used to target interpersonal skills, and six of the established practices (antecedent interventions, comprehensive behavioral treatment, naturalistic teaching, pivotal response training (PRT), peer training, and modeling) have targeted increases in play skills (National Autism Center, 2009a).

## Enhancing Educator Skills as Social Partners

Typical children probably do not develop the ability to shift and sustain attentional focus without assistance from those around them (Walden, 1993). Therefore, children with autism spectrum disorders clearly need assistance from caregivers and educators. Learning depends on caregivers' sensitivity to the child's attentional and motor abilities. Parents may contribute to the development of social referencing by reliably providing information and affect during interactions (Walden, 1993). They attempt to scaffold referential looks by providing unsolicited messages (Walden, Knieps, & Baxter, 1991).

In their review of research, McCollum and Hemmeter (1997) found that those who attempt to interact with individuals who find it difficult to interpret communication acts often use directive styles, including parents of children with disabilities, who were found to be more directive than parents of typically developing children during social referencing situations (Walden et al., 1991). A style that is directive and responsive may enhance communication development (Iacono, 2003). Parents of children with autism tend to keep their children on task more than other caregivers (Kasari, Sigman, Mundy, & Yirmiya, 1988). In a study comparing Anglo and Hispanic clinicians, Hispanic clinicians were found to use more varied facial expressions, more eye gaze, and more touch to control behavior, and to give more compliments and directives compared with their Anglo colleagues (Kayser, 1995).

Parents of typical children encourage imitation.

> Learning to talk is about becoming a partner in a culture's dances. Imitation, modeling, prompting, and consequences are each a small part of learning to dance, of learning to perform socially approved steps (words) in culturally determined sequences (utterances, sentences). Practice can then make performance more perfect and fluent. (Hart & Risley, 1999, p. 199)

Research has revealed that parents and educators may not provide sufficient opportunities for communication and social interaction (Keen, Sigafoos, & Woodyatt, 2005) or ask the type of questions that would enable a conversation if the individual is using an AAC system (Koppenhaver, Abraham, & Yoder, 1994). Interactions with individuals who use an AAC system tend to be dominated by the communicative partner. One way to increase participation in social interaction is to teach responses to nonobligatory turns during conversations, such as "cool," "right on," and "uh-huh" (Light, Arnold, & Clark, 2003). There is a need to investigate AAC interventions focused on social interaction with individuals with ASD due to the fact that "AAC approaches have largely focused on the communication of needs and wants; less attention has been paid to the development of social interaction skills" (Drager, Light, & Finke, 2009, p. 271).

## Addressing Joint Attention and Social Referencing

Addressing joint attention as an early identifiable deficit associated with ASD is essential because it may be a foundational skill for social interaction. Researchers have successfully taught young children with ASD to initiate bids for attention from adults. Sharing attentional focus on an object or activity for three or more seconds may be an active ingredient in joint attention (Lawton & Kasari, 2010). In a randomized wait-list control study, Kasari and colleagues (Kasari, Gulsrud, Wong, Kwon, & Locke, 2010) demonstrated that caregiver-mediated sessions could result in increased responsiveness to joint attention and diversity of functional play acts that was maintained one year post-intervention. A combination of behavioral and developmental procedures was used in coaching sessions with caregivers of preschoolers with ASD for 24 sessions (three sessions per week for eight weeks). Increases in responses to joint attention and functional play skills were related to scores on a level of comfort rating scale completed by experimenters on the implementation of the intervention by caregivers. Increases in initiations for joint attention did not improve significantly, indicating that initiating joint attention may be particularly difficult for preschoolers with ASD (Kasari et al., 2010).

McClannahan and Krantz (2005) arranged the environment to facilitate engagement and provided a reinforcer natural to the context to teach joint attention. They used an audio script prerecorded on a device to prompt the word *look* when passing novel items in a hallway. When children pressed the play button on the audio recording and imitated the words, they were rewarded with access to a favorite toy or edible item. Children were also taught to orient to the adult when saying "look." The audio scripts were faded and the children were able to generalize across new items and people (Krantz & McClannahan, 1998). Whalen and Schreibman (2003) used reinforcers natural to the context and interspersed maintenance tasks when targeting new skills to teach five preschoolers with autism gaze following. The intervention was clearly delineated. Four of the five children who completed training also initiated joint attention. Taylor and Harris (1995) used time delay to teach children with autism to ask, "What's that?" when presented with novel items.

> Teaching only the behaviors (or forms) of joint attention may not be sufficient to enhance motivation to the degree needed for children with autism to spontaneously and consistently enter a joint attention interaction. (Vismara & Lyons, 2007, p. 215)

Vismara and Lyons (2007) used objects related to the perseverative interests of young children with ASD in an alternating treatment design with preferred objects and evaluated the requests for joint attention from adults. PRT techniques were used during play sessions. The results revealed that joint attention initiation generalized from perseverative objects to nonperseverative stimuli over time for two of the three participants. The number of joint attention initiations was higher for the nonperseverative interest items throughout the treatment session for the third child. The authors conclude that motivation may serve as a pivotal variable for acquisition and maintenance of initiations for joint attention.

The early goals of the SCERTs model focus on joint attention (Prizant, Wetherby, Rubin, Laurent, & Rydell, 2006b). This model describes child goals, partner goals, and supports needed for each target skill. In this model, the communication partner arranges the environment, embeds varied learning opportunities, and ensures that the activities are sufficiently motivating for the child. Other authors have suggested that the inclusion of motivating activities may lead to joint attention (Koegel, Openden, Fredeen, & Koegel, 2006). Currently there is a lack of empirical evidence that caregivers and educators can be taught to increase joint attention through SCERTs.

**Joint activity routines** have been described as an effective context for teaching joint attention (Reichle, Cooley Hidecker, Brady, & Terry, 2003). The eight critical elements of joint activity routines are (1) an obvious theme or purpose, (2) requirement for joint focus and interaction, (3) limited number of clearly defined roles, (4) exchangeable roles, (5) logical sequence, (6) structure for turn-taking in a predictable sequence, (7) planned repetition, and (8) plan for controlled variation (Snyder-McLean, Solomonson, McLean, & Sack, 1984). Examples include peek-a-boo, Frisbee, and simple meal preparation. These routines are also referred to as social routines (Warren et al., 2002). Research on joint activity routines or social routines used with individuals with autism spectrum disorders is lacking (Simpson, 2005).

Ingersoll, Lewis, and Kroman (2007) taught five preschool-age children with autism to imitate gestures using contingent imitation, linguistic mapping, following the child's lead, physical prompting, and contingent reinforcement. All children increased their use of gestures (e.g., arms raised for "big," hands on face with "oh, no," finger making a circle pattern for "spin") and generalized spontaneous gesture use to some novel situations. Learners with autism were also taught to use relevant gestures when communicating, such as saying "over there" and pointing when responding to a question about the location of an item (Buffington, Krantz, McClannahan, & Poulson, 1998). Children with autism have been taught to attend to an adult's comments, such as "I am feeling tired, or sick" and respond appropriately to this expressed affect (e.g., "That's too bad") (Gena, Krantz, McClannahan, & Poulson, 1996).

Gutstein and Sheely (2002a, 2002b) have designed a curriculum of social and emotional development activities that begin with Novice (Level 1) skills of attending to speakers and following the eye gaze of a partner, through Partner (Level VI) skills that focus on family, friendship, and intimate relationships. Educators or coaches support individuals with autism spectrum disorders who are learning to share activities with adults and with peers. The authors suggest that coaches work on skills in a systematic progression so that one set of skills serves as scaffolding for the next. Coaches should keep objectives simple and keep activities joyful, lively, and meaningful, with a focus on competence (Gutstein & Sheely, 2002a).

Early activities in the relationship development intervention (RDI) curriculum aim for gaining the child's attention by using unexpected labels, putting a novel item (such as a shoe) on one's head, or creating a tunnel where the child crawls through and is greeted by a coach making a silly face at the other end. Another suggested activity is to release the air of a balloon on the neck of a child and then place the balloon near your face so that the child looks at the face when requesting a repeat of the activity. A third activity in the first level of the program is a modified version of Mother May I, in which the child must look at the adult prior to making the next step toward a goal. If the child does not reference the adult, he or she must return to the start line (Gutstein & Sheely, 2002a). Although some of the previously described activities appear to have face validity, there are no published studies on the effectiveness of these activities or information confirming that success in one activity leads to generalized social referencing (Simpson, 2005).

Greenspan and Wieder (2000) state that the Developmental Individual-differences Relationship-based (DIR) model addresses functional emotional processes because of the emphasis on early emotional interactions between young children and caregivers. "If the child is spinning the wheels of a car, the practitioner using the DIR approach would draw on the child's interest and, warmly smiling, spin the wheels in the opposite direction to get reciprocal, affective interaction started" (Greenspan & Wieder, 2000, pp. 289–290). As the practitioner follows the child's lead, he or she helps the child attend and engage by looking for opportunities for a visceral sense of pleasure and intimacy that results in the child wanting to relate to the human world (Greenspann & Wieder, 2000). These authors state that it is important to relate to the child with ASD when he or she

is displaying strong affect. Without published research on outcomes, it is difficult to know how often children with ASD attend to adults when they are warmly smiling or if they ignore adults regardless of their displayed affect.

# Teaching Social and Play Skills with Young Peers

## Incorporating Behavioral Strategies

Placing students alongside peers is likely to be insufficient in initiating social interaction because children with autism are likely to lack the behaviors of initiation and responding to social bids with peers and may need to be taught these skills directly (Strain, Schwartz, & Bovey, 2008). Identifying the preferred peer of the student with autism spectrum disorder and including that peer in social activities may increase the generalization of social interaction across settings (Hall & Smith, 1996).

In their review, Hwang and Hughes (2000) identified behavioral strategies that have been demonstrated to increase social skills. Three of these strategies were incorporated in at least half of the published studies they reviewed and include using natural reinforcement, time delay, and arranging the environment to facilitate engagement (see Chapter 4 for a description of these strategies). Each of these strategies is considered evidence-based according to the National Professional Development Center (NPDC) on ASD (Odom, Collet-Klingenberg, Rogers, & Hatton, 2010). **Parent-implemented interventions** and **peer-mediated interventions** are also included in the 24 identified evidence-based strategies by the NPDC on ASD.

In a review of parent-implemented home-based strategies aimed at promoting social and communicative behavior in young children with ASD, researchers found that all 12 of the studies demonstrated that parents were able to implement new strategies in natural environments, such as routines at home, with positive outcomes for their children (Meadan, Ostrosky, Zaghawan, & Yu, 2009). Only two of the studies reported fidelity of the parent education program, and half assessed social validity of the strategies. The authors recommend that future research on parent-implemented interventions identify and include strategies that support generalization of skills at the beginning of the program and report on the success of these strategies. Stahmer & Gist (2001) compared outcomes from two groups implementing PRT and basic behavioral techniques with young children with ASD. One group of parents received information and education, and the other also received support in the form of group process and a focus on relationship building. Their findings were that both groups met criteria for learning the PRT strategies that resulted in increases in the social communicative skills for their child; however, the group members with the support component "were more likely to master the techniques at a higher level" (Stahmer & Gist, 2001, p. 81).

Peer-mediated strategies usually involve typical peers and an adult who reviews strategies that can be used to facilitate social interaction with a peer with autism spectrum disorders and provides feedback and reinforcement to both peers. "Peer mediated approaches represent the largest and most empirically supported type of social intervention for children with autism" (Kasari & Locke, 2011, p. 1160). Laushey and Heflin (2000) evaluated a peer-mediated strategy of a buddy system in which peers in a kindergarten class were taught to stay, play, and talk to their buddy. Compared with proximity to peers alone, this strategy increased the social skills of the students with autism, such as asking for an object, getting the attention of a peer, waiting for a turn, and looking in the direction of the speaker. Arranging for motivating activities and reinforcement procedures has been used to increase the social initiation of children with autism (Oke & Schreibman, 1990). Additional strategies of arranging affection activities (McEvoy et al., 1988); priming with a low-demand, high-reinforcement session prior

to the regular school activity (Zanolli, Daggett, & Adams, 1996); and the use of a tactile prompting device (Shabani et al., 2002) have all resulted in increased social initiations by children with autism toward typical peers. When designing a social skills strategy, it may be important to include extra time for the student to initiate and respond to others. Because oral communication may be difficult, students with ASD may need more time than their typical peers to answer any questions or to formulate their own comment or question.

Imitation of peers has also been the target of behavioral interventions. A training session that included prompts and praise was used to teach children with autism to follow an adult and then a peer model, which was effective in getting the children with autism to participate in a follow-the-leader game that occurred in a different setting (Carr & Darcy, 1990). Small-group imitation training that incorporated a least-to-most prompting strategy and praise for imitating a peer was successful for preschoolers with autism during the training session, but it was maintained into the follow-up period for only one of the participants (Garfinkle & Schwartz, 2002). Two children with autism were taught to imitate their peers when the peers used pivotal response training, and gains in language, communication, and joint attention (although not targeted) were maintained at a two-month follow-up (Pierce & Schreibman, 1995).

Play has been used as a context for teaching play skills and social interaction with peers. Lifter (2008) argues that play should be considered a developmental domain and that individualized play targets for children with ASD should be informed by developmental assessment and should capitalize on the child's interests embedded in activities that are on the leading edge of play development. Stahmer, Ingersoll, and Carter (2003) provide a thorough review of the research using behavioral strategies to promote play. They cite research publications that have incorporated the following behavioral strategies to teach play and peer interaction involving children with autism spectrum disorders:

discrete trial teaching (Lifter, Sulzer-Azaroff, Anderson, & Cowdery, 1993), pivotal response training, imitation training, differential reinforcement of appropriate play, self-management (Stahmer & Schreibman, 1992), video modeling (Jahr, Eldevik, & Eikeseth, 2000), and the use of play scripts (Goldstein & Cisar, 1992). Incidental teaching has been used by typical peers to increase the play and social interaction skills of classmates with autism (McGee, Almeida, Sulzer-Azaroff, & Feldman, 1992). Photographic activity schedules, along with embedded scripts (Betz, Higbee, & Reagon, 2008), and correspondence training (Morrison, Sainato, Benchaaban, & Endo, 2002) have been used to increase peer engagement and play.

The social skills curriculum manual developed by the LEAP Outreach Project (2003b) includes a guide for educators of preschool-age children with ASD in inclusive classrooms. Some of the skills addressed are getting your friend's attention, sharing, play organizing, and accepting compliments. Posters to support the curriculum and data sheets for recording the social skills of participants are included in the manual.

Advanced play skills such as symbolic play have been taught to children with autism spectrum disorders using pivotal response training or using clear instructions, child choice, turn-taking, direct reinforcement, and reinforcing attempts and interspersing maintenance tasks with skill acquisition (Schreibman, Stahmer, & Pierce, 1996; Stahmer, 1995; Thorp, Stahmer, & Schreibman, 1995). During play activities, social competence is targeted by educators who encourage and extend conversation, use exaggerated positive affect, model social statements, and redirect inappropriate behavior (Schreibman, et al. 1996). Graduated time delay was used to teach play sequences (zoo keeper and circus train) that included requesting peer assistance to three boys with autism ages 6, 7, and 9 years old (Liber, Frea, & Symon, 2008).

Kamps, Kravits, and Ross (2002) have outlined the steps needed to implement social skills groups and play groups that incorporate

behavioral principles and strategies such as reinforcement, progress monitoring, self-monitoring, and self-instruction.

Taylor and Jasper (2001) designed behaviorally based programs that can be used to increase social interaction with peers that include beginning skills (eye contact, greetings, requesting items), intermediate programs (follows directions, pretends, offers information), and advanced skills (comments about play, expresses empathy, responds to changes in conversational topic). The description of each target skill in the curriculum includes the suggested prerequisite skills; procedures for implementing the teaching strategy, including any prompts; and instructions for peers.

Strain, Schwartz, and Bovey (2008) have identified the following variables that affect social competence intervention efficacy: fidelity of intervention, functionality of behavioral targets, access to peers who are typically developing, dosage (intensity or amount), strategies to promote generalization and maintenance, and social validity. These authors state that, "without understanding and controlling for these variables, the most elegant and well-designed intervention may be rendered ineffective" (p. 262).

## Play Dates

Research has revealed that mother-reported frequency of play dates with their young child having high-functioning ASD in their home correlated with the child with ASD spending greater amounts of time engaged in conversing with, taking turns, and sharing objects with peers on the playground (Frankel, Gorospe, Chang, & Sugar, 2011). The authors state that they do not know if play dates in the home promote better peer relationships on the playground or if the reverse is true. The researchers did not note if the interactions occurred with the same children on the playground who participated in the play dates.

R. L. Koegel and his colleagues evaluated the social interaction between two children with autism and their typical peers during play dates with and without contextual support (Koegel, Werner, Vismara, & Koegel, 2005). Increases in reciprocal social interaction and positive affect occurred during the contextual support condition when a facilitator selected mutually reinforcing activities and structured the play activities so that cooperation between peers was critical to the activity (e.g., arranging for one child to hold the measuring cup while the other poured ingredients). The authors state that more research is needed on the effects of contextual support on the facilitation of play between peers (Koegel et al., 2005).

Greenspan and Wieder (2000) suggest that once a child is fully interactive and engaged with an adult, then play with one other peer should begin. Parents can act as mediators to encourage engagement and interaction. A peer who is interactive and verbal and who can model play and encourage the child with ASD is best to invite. It is good to select natural play partners who will pursue and interact with the child and respond to adult coaching. The number of play dates a week should match the age of the child, so 3-year-olds would have three play dates (Greenspan & Wieder, 2011).

Gutstein and Sheely (2002b) recommend that when groups of peers with and without autism spectrum disorder are created, any peers should share the same level of competence so that one learner does not feel less capable than another. The authors state, "[M]atching persons with equal development and then placing them together in dyads or groups to help each other learn, leads to the development of intensely powerful emotional bonds" (Gutstein & Sheely, 2002b, p. 29).

Without research outcomes, it is difficult to know which learners with which characteristics are most likely to benefit from play dates. Wolfberg (2003) suggests that groups are comprised of more capable typical peers. Greenspan and Wieder (2000) agree that the play partner should be more capable but suggest starting with one peer. Gustein and Sheely (2002b) suggest that peers should be at the same competence level. Which configuration

for a group works best, for which skills? How does the role of a coach, mediator, or play guide differ, and which aspects do they share? It is recommended that educators look to research for evidence regarding these questions.

## Integrated Play Groups: Using a Social-Constructivist Approach

Pam Wolfberg (2003, 2009) has designed a curriculum for encouraging play between peers with and without autism spectrum disorders. The integrated play-groups model aims to maximize the potential of every child with autism to socialize and play with peers within a jointly constructed play culture (Wolfberg, 2003). By including typical peers, ideally from the same community as the child with autism, the learner becomes acquainted with peer culture and the expectations of a cultural member (Rogoff, 1990).

Influenced by multiple theorists, Dr. Wolfberg states that Vygotsky was a major source of inspiration. Vygotsky emphasized the importance of peers in the development of socialization and introduction to a peer culture (Vygotsky, 1978). The notion of guided participation from Vygotsky is also included as the key role of the educator facilitating the groups (Wolfberg, 2003). It is recommended that the integrated play groups are comprised of a higher ratio of expert players (those without disabilities) to novice players (children with autism spectrum disorder) and a play guide (e.g., special education teacher) and assistant who meet twice a week or more for 30 minutes to an hour for 6 to 12 months (Wolfberg, 2003). Play guides facilitate the play by monitoring play initiations, scaffolding play, and using social-communication guidance to elicit and sustain joint engagement in activities that are enjoyed by the interacting group members (Wolfberg, 2003). Pam Wolfberg describes how educators can facilitate play In Their Words 9.1.

Wolfberg (2003) includes an assessment system as part of the curriculum and recommends that sessions be recorded and analyzed

**9.1  IN THEIR WORDS**  Dr. Pamela Wolfberg, *Autism Spectrum Program, Department of Special Education, San Francisco State University*

## Teaching Educators to Use Guided Participation and Scaffolding during Play

The practice of scaffolding play is central to guiding children effectively in Integrated Play Groups, an established research-based model designed to promote social, communication, and play development in children with autism while building relationships with typical peers (Wolfberg, 2009). By definition, **scaffolding** refers to the provision of adjustable and temporary support structures. Applied to Integrated Play Groups, scaffolding involves building on the child's play initiations by systematically adjusting assistance to match or slightly exceed the level at which the child is able to engage independently in play with peers—within the child's "zone of proximal development." The idea of scaffolding is to avoid being so lax that the play falls apart or so intrusive that it ruins the moment. The key is to find that ever-so-delicate balance of allowing the play to unfold in genuine ways while sustaining child engagement. That means knowing when to step in, when to step out, and, especially, when to be quiet.

Scaffolding play sometimes involves providing children with a high degree of support. The role of the play guide is akin to that of a stage director when the actors are first learning their parts. The play guide physically steps in and shows the children how to play together using directing and modeling techniques. These strategies may take different forms and incorporate physical, verbal, nonverbal, and visual supports. . . . As the children become more engaged, adult support becomes less intensive. Hence the role of the play guide shifts from that of director to coach. The adult essentially steps out and away from the group, offering verbal and/or visual cues from the sidelines. The emphasis is on redirecting the children to look to one another rather than the adult for directions and cues to carry out play scripts. . . . As the children become fully engaged in play activities, adult support is at a minimum. The play guide withdraws to the periphery of the group, remaining on "stand by" [and] ready to jump in on a moment's notice (Wolfberg, 2003, pp. 172–178).

to evaluate progress. Table 9.1 describes the symbolic and social dimensions of play that can be evaluated over time.

Publications describing outcomes from Integrated Play Groups are included in the 33 studies comprising the evidence-based practice of a peer training package (National Autism Center, 2009b). Researchers from San Francisco State University have reported increases in functional and symbolic play, less isolated and stereotypic play, and more diverse play following the integrated play groups (O'Connor, 1999; Wolfberg & Schuler,

1993; Zercher, Hunt, Schuler, & Webster, 2001), with skills generalizing to other peers, settings, and social contexts for at least three novice players (Wolfberg & Schuler, 1993). The results from replications of integrated play groups include a case study reported by Lantz, Nelson, and Loftin (2004) and increasingly sophisticated play skills for two children with autism in two play groups piloted in Taiwan (Yang, Wolfberg, Wu, & Hwu, 2003). Wolfberg (2003) states that the first decision to be made by the stakeholder team is whether or not an integrated play group is a good

**TABLE 9.1** Framework for observing children's developmental play patterns (symbolic and social dimensions) in integrated play groups

| Symbolic Dimension of Play | Social Dimension of Play |
|---|---|
| **Not Engaged** | **Isolate** |
| Child does not touch objects or toys or act out roles in play. Child may enact self-stimulatory behavior that does not involve play materials (e.g., gazes at own hand, rocks body, waves or flaps arms and hands, glances at toys). | Child appears to be oblivious or unaware of others. May wander without looking at peers, occupy self by watching anything of momentary interest, play with own body or play alone (e.g., lies on floor, gets on and off chair, sits quietly gazing into space, plays with back to peers) |
| **Manipulation-Sensory** | **Orientation-Onlooker** |
| Child explores and manipulates objects or toys but does not use them in conventional ways. There is an apparent motivation to obtain sensory input and exert control over the physical world. Play schemes include: | Child shows an awareness of the other children by looking at them or in the direction of their play materials and activities. Child does not enter into play with peers (e.g., quietly watches peers, turns body to face peers, peripherally gazes at peers, imitates peers while watching from distance) |
| 1. Simple actions with single objects (e.g., mouth, gaze, shake, bang, drop) | |
| 2. Simple action sequences combining objects (e.g., line up, fill and dump, twist and turn) | **Parallel-Proximity** |
| 3. Performing difficult feats with objects (e.g., balance a coin, spin a plate) | Child plays independently beside rather than with other children. There is simultaneous use of the same play space or similar materials as peers. Child may occasionally imitate, show objects, or alternate actions with peers (e.g., child plays beside peers at water table; child pushes a truck beside a peer who builds a roadway; child lines up animal figures next to peer who lines up animal figures; child brushes a doll's hair near a child pushing a doll carriage) |
| **Functional** | |
| Child demonstrates conventional use of an object or association of two or more objects. Child responds to logically related physical properties of objects. There is a quality of delayed imitation that may reflect simple pretense. Play schemes include: | |
| 1. Uses object/toy as intended (e.g., roll car on floor, press buttons on cash register) | **Common Focus** |
| 2. Combines two or more related objects (e.g., stack blocks, connect pieces of train track, place cup on saucer) | Child plays by interacting with one or more peers. There is joint attention on the play as child and peer engage in joint action, mutual imitation, or reciprocal social exchanges. The play may include taking turns, giving and receiving assistance and directives, active sharing of materials, sharing of emotional expression (e.g., child and peer exchange blocks, take turns brushing a doll's hair, pretend to talk to each other on telephone, engage in peek-a-boo, talk and laugh with one another) |
| 3. Follows simple scripts/familiar routines with realistic props directed to self, dolls, or peers (e.g., hold telephone to ear, place bottle in doll's mouth, brush peer's hair) | |
| **Symbolic-Pretend** | |
| Child acts as if doing something or being someone else with an intent that is representational. Play scripts vary in complexity and cohesion. Play schemes include: | **Common Goal** |
| 1. Object substitutions, using one object to represent another (e.g., hold banana to ear as if it were a telephone) | The child engages in play with peers, which is structured for the purpose of attaining a common goal or making a product. Child and peers explicitly plan and carry out a common agenda by defining specific rules and roles, negotiating behavior exchanges, and compromising around divergent interests. The efforts of one child supplement those of another. There is a sense of cooperation and belonging to a group (e.g., child and peers plan and build a block tower to a specified height, plan and act out eating in a restaurant each with an assigned role, plan in advance to take turns being first to play a game) |
| 2. Attribution of absent or false properties (e.g., hold teapot over cup, make slurping sounds while drinking from empty cup) | |
| 3. Imaginary objects as present (e.g., move hand to mouth as if holding a cup) | |
| 4. Role-playing scripts (real or invented) with dolls, self, peers, and/or imaginary characters (e.g., tea party with teddy bears, telephone conversation with make-believe person, acting out bedtime sequence with doll in reciprocal roles of mother and baby, acting out space fantasy with peers and invented creatures) | |

*Source:* From P. Wolfberg (2003), *Peer play and the autism spectrum: Integrated play groups field manual,* p. 121. Shawnee Mission, KS: Autism Asperger Publishing Company. Used with permission.

choice of intervention. Additional research that includes the characteristics of participants, fidelity of intervention measures, and generalization of play skills would assist in determining which learners with autism spectrum disorder would benefit from engaging in integrated play groups.

In the TEACCH approach, the most important priority is making social interactions enjoyable, and the best way to do this is to incorporate the interests and understanding of the participants (Mesibov et al., 2004). Highly structured groups are used with the visual supports needed to facilitate learning, such as charts, checklists, and scripts. Instead of prompting or scaffolding by educators, the group members are assisted with participation through the use of visual structure. Positive social experiences are arranged in contexts that are highly motivating to the learners with autism spectrum disorders (Mesibov et al., 2004).

## Friendship

Parents report that more than half of children, adolescents, and adults with autism spectrum disorders do not have friends, even if the individuals themselves state that they do (Kasari & Locke, 2011). Friendships are defined as companionship, support, conflict, and closeness. Two of the three proposed criteria for deficits in social communication and social interaction for the DSM-5 (www.dsm5.org) are deficits in social-emotional reciprocity and deficits in developing and maintaining relationships, or key aspects of friendship.

There is a paucity of research on the issue of social-emotional reciprocity. Weiss and Harris (2001) recommend three strategies to teach perspective taking that include the goals of identification of emotions of others in context, of emotions of self in context, and multiple emotions of one person. These strategies include field of vision task (own and other person's perspective), perception versus nonperception (can and cannot see something), and pretending. However, it is unclear whether social-emotional reciprocity is a necessary criterion for friendship. Temple Grandin describes her friendships as the sharing of mutual interests and activities with less of a focus on disclosure and social-emotional reciprocity (Grandin & Barron, 2005).

In their study comparing dyads of friends that included high-functioning children with ASD with dyads of typical peers, Bauminger and colleagues (2008) found that there were significantly lower frequencies of goal-directed behaviors, sharing, and positive affect in the dyads including children with high functioning autism spectrum disorder (HRASD). The dyads with HFASD also spend a higher frequency of time in parallel play, unoccupied, and with less coordinated play. These dyads also rated themselves as lower on dimensions of help, intimacy, and closeness (Bauminger et al., 2008). Their self-perceptions are realistic; however, the question remains as to whether they are bothered by less intimacy, closeness, and sharing of affect.

There is research on strategies to promote social interaction and sharing during play and social activities. How the development of social skills and time with peers leads to friendship development for individuals with ASD is less known. Additional information on the contribution that friendship has on the quality of life for individuals with ASD would be helpful for those who are designing interventions to offer foundational skills and systems of support.

> When individuals on the spectrum engage in improved social interactions, loneliness and isolation are likely to be reduced, sexual victimization and perpetration resulting from naivete may become less frequent. That is, intervention may act as a potential barrier against the development of comorbid conditions, including depression and anxiety. (Koegel, Fredeen, Koegel, & Lin, 2011, p. 1105)

## Cognitive-Behavior Therapy to Address Anxiety

According to the proposed DSM-5, several comorbid diagnoses can exist with ASD, including depression and anxiety disorders, such as general anxiety disorder, obsessive-compulsive disorder, and social anxiety disorder. Estimates of anxiety and/or depression in individuals with ASD are found to be as high as 65% (Klin, 2011). It is hypothesized that there may be a common genetic link between ASD and other psychiatric disorders that increases the risk of each (Wood, Fujii, & Renno, 2011). For those higher functioning individuals who can talk about their thoughts and behavior, cognitive-behavior therapy has been used to address anxiety and increase socially appropriate behavior.

Cognitive-behavior therapy (CBT) was developed by Aaron T. Beck in the 1960s as a short-term, structured psychotherapy for depression focused on modifying dysfunctional thinking and behavior (Beck, 1995). The premise behind the cognitive model is that distorted or dysfunctional thinking is common to psychological disturbances and that a realistic evaluation and modification of thinking can produce improved mood and behavior. The therapist focuses on underlying dysfunctional beliefs. CBT is a well-supported intervention for otherwise typically developing youth with anxiety disorders (Wood et al., 2011).

There is a wide range of prevalence estimates (47% to 84%) for the rate of anxiety in young people with ASD (Sofronoff & Beaumont, 2009) and for social anxiety (20% to 57%) in youth with ASD (Wood et al., 2011). Research on CBT with individuals with ASD reveals that the typical age of participation is between 7 and 14 years old (Wood et al., 2011). CBT has been used effectively to increase daily living skills and decrease anxiety in children with high-functioning autism (Drahota, Wood, Sze, & Van Dyke, 2011), to control anger in children with Asperger syndrome (Sofronoff, Attwood, Hinton, & Levin, 2007), and (using the Building Confidence program) to reduce anxiety of children with autism according to parent report and diagnostic measures (Wood et al., 2009).

Lang and colleagues reviewed the publications through 2009 on CBT for the treatment of anxiety in autism spectrum disorders (Lang, Regester, Lauderdale, Ashbaugh, & Haring, 2010). They identified nine articles and concluded that there was evidence in support of CBT for anxiety in individuals diagnosed with Asperger syndrome, but there were not sufficient numbers of participants to draw conclusions for others on the spectrum. They also state that most intervention packages include CBT that is amended to include strategies based on applied behavior analysis (e.g., reinforcement, prompting, self-management) and that emphasize teaching practical skills and deemphasize introspection. Some programs include the use of visual supports such as coping cards with written strategies for "when I am anxious" or "when I want to ask the professor for help" (Beck, 1995). The authors recommend that future research analyze the components in order to determine the active mechanisms in these interventions (Lang et al., 2010).

Much of the implementation of CBT is conducted in a group format rather than with a modular and individualized approach (Wood, et al., 2011). The effectiveness of format and context for the intervention (clinic versus in vivo) should be addressed in future studies of CBT (Wood, Fujii, & Renno, 2011).

> CBT that emphasizes direct experiences in the child's social milieu and that is closely linked with conceptual training on others' perspectives and emotional states—especially when presented in an individualized format in a high-dose, high-density fashion in middle-childhood (and possible adolescent) age-group—appears to be a promising practice... However, the extent evidence is quite preliminary. (Wood et al., 2011, pp. 216, 219)

## Social Skills Curriculum for Adolescents, Young Adults, and High-Functioning Children with ASD

Social skills curriculum designed specifically for children with high-functioning autism that covers skills such as nonverbal communication, perspective taking, emotional regulation, and steps of prosocial behaviors are relatively new (Sofronoff & Beaumont, 2009). In their review of social skills interventions for high-functioning children with ASD, Rao, Beidel, and Murray (2008) found 10 articles that evaluated various social skills training programs, with seven of them reporting positive outcomes. In the discussion, they suggest that researchers come to a consensus on which social skills should be targeted because some programs focus on skills such as greetings and initiating conversation, and others target problem solving and self-control. The lack of generalization of skills taught in programs was also identified as an issue. For example, although there were positive outcomes from the SCORES Skills Strategy (Vernon, Shumaker, & Deshler, 1996) in demonstrated social skills in the classroom, skill mastery was not noticeable to parents (Webb, Miller, Pierce, Strawser, & Jones, 2004). Another study reporting positive outcomes from a social skills training program in terms of recognition of emotion and social problem-solving skills found that there was no increase in children's spontaneous dyadic and group interaction with peers at recess (Bauminger, 2007). The Program for the Evaluation and Enrichment of Relational Skills (PEERS) was designed to address some of these issues, including involving parents as an essential part of the program.

## The Program for the Evaluation and Enrichment of Relational Skills (PEERS)

PEERS is an adaption of a social skills program, Children's Friendship Training (CFT) (Frankel & Myatt, 2003), which is based on developmental research on how children form and maintain quality friendships (Laugeson & Frankel, 2010). Early research on the model supported the inclusion of parents as an essential component for generalization (Frankel, Myatt, Cantwell, & Feinberg, 1997). The CFT model, which included content on conflict training, was demonstrated as effective for teens with attention deficit hyperactivity disorder (ADHD) (Carpenter, Frankel,

Marina, Duan, & Smalley, 2004) and with fetal alcohol disorders (O'Connor et al., 2007).

The manualized curriculum for PEERS includes content covered in a 14-week program where teens meet with a facilitator in one room while their parents meet separately in another room (Laugeson & Frankel, 2010; Laugeson, Frankel, Gantman, Mogil, & Dillon, 2011). Following each session, teens and parents are given homework assignments and together they facilitate the generalization of the content focused on in the group sessions. The manual provides a guide for facilitators of the groups. Topics of the sessions include entering and exiting conversations with peers; using electronic forms of communication; how to be a good sport; and how to handle arguments, disagreements, and bullying (Laugeson, Frankel, Mogil, & Dillon, 2009). Training in PEERS is provided by the Semel Institute at the University of California at Los Angeles (UCLA) and is required prior to implementing the program.

The researchers are expanding the model with a focus on a manualized curriculum for teachers, and another for facilitators working with young adults ages 18 to 24. The young adult model involves caregivers who may or may not be parents. Outcomes from the implementation of PEERS with young adults indicate that, compared with a delayed treatment control, caregivers reported an overall improvement in social skills, including increases in cooperative social behavior with peers and caregivers, self-control, and social assertiveness (Gantman, Kapp, Orenski, & Laugeson, 2011). There were also changes in social responsiveness for participants with changes in autistic mannerisms (e.g., restricted interests and repetitive behaviors ) subscale of the Social Skills Rating System (Gresham & Elliot, 1990).

Research evaluating PEERS has revealed that, compared with a delayed treatment control, teens ages 13 to 17 with ASD improved their knowledge of the rules of social etiquette and reported a significant increase in hosted get-togethers and better quality of friendships, and their parents reported significant improvements in their teens' overall level of social skills (Laugeson et al., 2009). Evaluation at a 14-week follow-up revealed that these outcomes had been maintained (Laugeson et al., 2011). Additional research indicates that gains may be maintained for even longer. Evaluation of PEERS participants one to five years after program completion revealed that improvements that were made from baseline to post-intervention had been maintained in the overall social skills score on the Social Skills Rating Scale, the reduction in problem behaviors reported, the increased frequency of get-togethers, and in the knowledge of social skills (Mandelberg et al., 2011).

## Think Social!

Michelle Garcia Winner has designed and self-published an assessment and curriculum that focuses on providing students with mild to moderate disabilities, including ASD, with a cognitive behavioral framework to address social skills (Winner, 2008). Winner (2002, 2007) recommends an assessment that includes observing students with peers in different environments; interacting with the student informally; conducting a double interview where the student is interviewed first where verbal and nonverbal responses are noted, followed by the student interviews the assessor who takes note of the student's ability to generate questions and use appropriate nonverbal behavior; and responding to a pictorial sequence of the events of a social situation and social scenarios. Activities are suggested that follow the ILAUGH (initiation of language, listening with eyes and brain, abstract and inferential language/communication, understanding perspective, gestalt processing, humor and human relatedness) model of social cognition presented in a curriculum guide (Winner, 2008). Example activities from the 36 lessons included in the curriculum focus on physical reactions to events, becoming a detective while observing others, and identifying expected and unexpected behaviors in social situations.

In their book written for teens and young adults with disabilities, Winner and Crooke (2009) help navigate social situation and do so clearly and with humor. An example chapter title is "CSI: Curiously Social Investigations—Figuring out the 'Why' behind the Words." Michelle Garcia Winner is a dynamic speaker who uses creative means (e.g., working with a rubber chicken) to gain the attention of school-age students. Her curriculum has appeal to educators. However, there is little research in support of the outcomes, such as changes in social behavior, from the model or information about which concepts, lessons, and activities are essential to the effectiveness of the program.

The TEACCH approach uses structured groups that include individuals with ASD and typical peers to facilitate conversation skills (Mesibov et al., 2004). When social groups are organized by TEACCH, typical peers are paired with individuals with ASD who are approximately the same age so that they can discuss topics of mutual interest. Typical peers are well prepared to participate in activities with individuals with ASD. Conversational guidelines are used; for example, after three sentences about a topic you want to learn about, ask your partner about what he or she wants to talk about, or suggest that topics are changed every three minutes (Mesibov et al., 2004).

# Additional Strategies Used to Increase Social Skills and Social Interaction

## Scripts and Script Fading

Educators from several theoretical perspectives (behavioral, Vygotskian, and the TEACCH approach) suggest that scripts should be used to facilitate social interaction. The use of **scripts** has helped students with autism increase the quantity and quality of interactions with peers. Typically developing students learn social scripts by watching others in a social context. They learn when to say hello and good-bye and when and how to conduct, enter, and exit conversations.

McClannahan and Krantz (2005) have implemented and evaluated the use of scripts and script fading as a strategy that incorporates the principles of behavior analysis. A first script might incorporate an object or activity of interest and then have the learner with autism run a recorded sentence through a card reader and repeat this scripted sentence to an educator. Educators use manual guidance from behind to prompt use of the script. Access to the object or activity serves as a reinforcer for script following (McClannahan & Krantz, 2005). Pictorial scripts can be embedded in activity schedules and serve as cues for initiation of social interaction. (See Chapter 4 for description of photographic activity schedules.) If the learner is a reader, then text can be used to facilitate interaction with adults and peers.

Once scripts are used consistently and accurately as indicated by data, then the scripts are systematically faded using graduated guidance, from manual prompting to spatial fading, to shadowing (McClannahan & Krantz, 2005). Written scripts are faded by leaving off the last word or phrase until only the initial word remains. Figure 9–1 provides an example of fading text using plastic envelopes.

Once students memorize the basic script of a social interaction for a given context, they often add and change the script to make it more individualized and more like their own voice. When adults first learn the steps of a dance, they often look stiff and robotic until they are comfortable with the steps and can relax and dance them fluently; students with autism spectrum disorders learning a new social script may also appear stiff until they are comfortable with what to say given the social context.

It has been demonstrated through published research by behavior analysts that scripts and script fading can lead to unscripted social interaction between peers (Krantz & McClannahan, 1993; Ross, 2002; Sarokoff, Taylor, & Poulson, 2001). Figure 9–2 shows an example of a data sheet and script for a learner with autism who uses sentences. Some learners can put together their own scripts from a selected group of sentences that are known to

be understood or, if the learner can write, to produce their own scripts (McClannahan & Krantz, 2005).

Although Kamps, Potucek, Lopez, Kravits, and Kemmerer (1997) demonstrated the effectiveness of a social skills package that included scripts with students with autism, they call for more research on training educators to use scripts and to fade scripts systematically so that social interaction generalizes to additional peers and in nonintervention settings.

## Video Modeling

In their review of the literature on using video for instructing students with autism, Ayres and Langone (2005) identify social skills as one of the prime targets for this medium. **Video modeling** has been used successfully to teach students with autism to share toys and to make comments during play (Taylor, Levin, & Jasper, 1999), to increase social initiations with peers during play activities (Nikopoulos & Keenan, 2004); video-enhanced activity schedules were used to increase play and social skills (Kimball, Kinney, Taylor, & Stromer, 2004). Video modeling has been used to increase pretend play with figurines (MacDonald, Clark, Garrigan, & Vangala, 2005) and to teach pretend play with a sibling as model and play partner (Reagon, Higbee, & Endicott, 2006). Video modeling also has been used to teach conversational skills (Charlop & Milstein, 1989; Thiemann & Goldstein, 2001). Adults, peers, and (in some videos) the individuals themselves (Wert & Neisworth, 2003) serve as the models.

Once the video has been made, it should be shown to the learner with autism spectrum disorder at least once, or preferably several times, immediately before participating in the target activity (Ganz, Tapscott Cook, & Earles-Vollrath, 2006). As with other instructional strategies, watching these recordings may not be sufficient alone to result in imitation, and some additional structure may be needed as part of video modeling. (See Chapter 4 for a more extensive discussion of video modeling.)

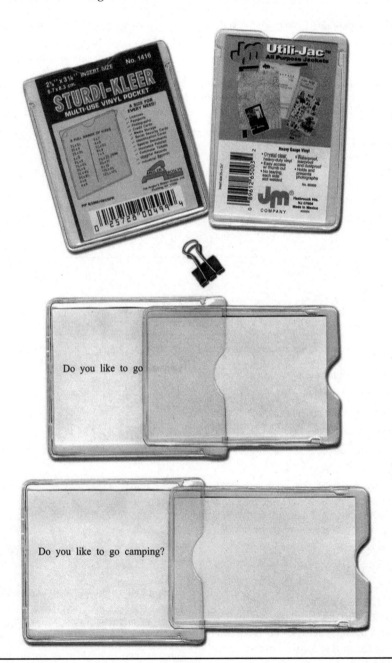

**FIGURE 9–1** Plastic envelopes used for fading steps of scripts
*Source:* From L. E. McClannahan & P. J. Krantz (2005), *Teaching conversation to children with autism: Scripts and script finding.* Bethesda, MD: Woodbine House, p. 81. Used with permission.

**Child:** _Abby_   **Observer:** _Moriah_   **Date:** _7/1/05_   **Script Set:** _40_   **Fading Step:** _2_

| Script | Said Script | Number of Unscripted Statements |
|---|---|---|
| I make my school lunch every day. | + | \|\| |
| Sometimes I make sandwiches for Dad. | − | \| |
| Salads are great on hot days. | + | \|\|\|\|\|\| |
| Lean Cuisine meals are pretty good. | + | \|\| |
| What did you bring for lunch today? | + | \|\|\| |

n = _____4_____     n = _____14_____

**Fading Steps:**

1. Last words of scripts faded
2. Last two words of scripts faded
3. All but first two words of scripts faded
4. All but first words of scripts faded
5. Scripts cards are blank
6. Scripts cards are absent

---

**FIGURE 9–2**   Sample data sheet for a child who uses sentences
*Source:* From L. E. McClannahan & P. J. Krantz (2005), *Teaching conversation to children with autism: Scripts and script fading.* Bethesda, MD: Woodbine House, p. 88. Used with permission.

## Social Stories

An approach used with individuals with ASD to prevent problem behavior in social situations and increase initiation and maintenance of social interaction is the use of **social stories**. Carol Gray defined social stories in 1991 as a process that results in a product for a person with autism spectrum disorders (Gray, 2010). Social stories can be written by parents, teachers, therapists, neighbors, family members, or anyone who works or lives with a person with ASD. The goal of a social story is to improve social understanding (Gray & Garand, 1993). The story is written most frequently from the perspective of the person with ASD. It can be written in the third person like a newspaper article. It is recommended that it be written using positive language, keeping the self-esteem of the audience safe (Gray, 2010).

There are seven types of social story sentences, with ratios that define the frequency in which they are to be used (Gray, 2010). *Descriptive sentences* are statements of fact. It is the only required type of sentence for a social story and the most frequently used. Examples include "My name is ——" or "My house is on First Street." *Perspective sentences* are those that refer to the internal state of the person. These are used rarely because it is often difficult to know someone else's thoughts and feelings. An example of a perspective sentence is "Many children enjoy eating ice cream."

*Sentences that coach*, such as "I will try to follow directions during circle time," guide the behavior of the audience. It is important not to be too literal with these statements. Gray (2010) recommends that you write, "I will *try to . . . ,*" rather than, "I *will* sit quietly. . . ." There are three types of coaching sentences, suggestions for the person with ASD, responses for the team, and self-coaching statements. *Affirmative sentences* enhance the meaning of surrounding statements, such as "This is very important" or "This is a good idea," following the comment "One child slides down the slide at a time" (Gray, 2010). *Partial sentences* that encourage the student to fill in the blank can also be used.

The important ratio to consider when writing a social story is that there should be only one partial or complete coaching sentence for every two to five descriptive, perspective, and/or affirmative sentences, or the number of sentences that describe divided by the number of sentences that coach should be equal to or greater than 2 (Gray, 2010).

Here is a sample social story:

*Who shares at recess?*
Our school has many classrooms.
Our school has many students.
There is a big playground at our school.
There are swings, a grass field, and lots of
    toys to play with in the playground.
Some children have their favorite toys.
When it is nice weather, we usually play on
    the playground at recess time.
It is important to share toys with other
    children so everyone has a turn with their
    favorite toys.
If someone asks to play, you can say, "OK,
    let's play."

If someone says, "I want to play with you,"
    you can say, "OK, let's play together."
If someone wants to share a toy, you can say,
    "OK, let's share."
Who shares toys at recess?
We all share toys at recess.

Several guidelines are recommended when writing social stories. First, identify the goal, which should be to share accurate social information in a meaningful way (Gray, 2010). The author should gather information about the topic so that descriptions are accurate and so that a rationale for directives is clear. The third step is to tailor the text to the learning style, interests, needs, and abilities of the individual with ASD. Typically the title can ask a *wh-* question. The story is written from a first-person perspective; in positive language; with concrete, easy-to-understand text. Social stories can be illustrated for young children or individuals with more severe cognitive disabilities.

According to Gray (2010), when you introduce the social story, it should be in a relaxed setting with a comment that you want to share a story written for that individual. The social story should be reviewed in a positive, casual style. Others can read the social story to the person with ASD. Ideally, it is read close to the event depicted in the story. Individual knowledge about the person determines how much time can lapse between the story and the event (Gray, 2010). Stories are faded by rewriting and changing sentences or by placing the stories in a location where the student can read them when he or she wants but does not review them routinely (see Table 9.2).

Social stories have been identified as an evidence-based practice when grouped in the category of social narratives by the the National Professional Development Center on ASD (Odom, Collet-Klingenberg, Rogers, & Hatton, 2010) and as a story-based intervention package by the National Standards Project (National Autism Center, 2009a). However, this same literature was reviewed by researchers who completed a meta-analysis of 28 social story

**TABLE 9.2** The social story checklist

**Directions:** This checklist compares a story with the defining characteristics of a social story. The comparison helps to identify strengths and areas that may need revision.

Title of story                                                                                          Author

The story is written for

Carefully read the story aloud and place a checkmark in the appropriate blank:

|  | Yes | No |
|---|---|---|
| 1. Is there an introduction, body, and conclusion? | ____ | ____ |
| 2. Does the story answer the relevant *wh-* questions? Sometimes, many of these questions may be answered in a single (often opening) statement. | ____ | ____ |
| 3. If the story is written for a young student, is it written from a first-person perspective, as though the student is describing the event? If the story is for an older student or adult, is it written from a third-person perspective, similar to a newspaper article? | ____ | ____ |
| 4. Does the story have a positive tone? If negative information is included, is it stated carefully using a third person perspective? | ____ | ____ |
| 5. Does the story adhere to either the social story ratio (basic or complete)? (Zero to one partial or complete coaching sentences for every two to five partial or complete descriptive, perspective, affirmative, or cooperative sentences—the complete social story ratio) | ____ | ____ |
| 6. Is the story literally accurate? Can it be interpreted literally without altering the intended meaning? | ____ | ____ |
| 7. Is alternative vocabulary used in place of terms that may cause the person with ASD to become upset or nervous? | ____ | ____ |
| 8. Is the text written with consideration of the reading ability and attention span of the person with ASD, using visual supports to enhance the meaning of the story? | ____ | ____ |
| 9. If illustrations are used, are they developed and presented with consideration of the ability of the person with ASD? | ____ | ____ |
| 10. Has an effort been made to incorporate the student's interests into the format, content, illustrations, or implementation of the story? | ____ | ____ |
| 11. Overall, does the story have a patient and reassuring quality? | ____ | ____ |

*Source:* Adapted from C. Gray (2000). *The new social stories book.* Appendix A. Arlington, TX: Future Horizons, Inc. Used with permission.

studies published through 2007; they concluded that social stories should not be considered an evidence-based practice because of the weak research designs and lack of generalization and social validity data (Test, Richter, Knight, & Spooner, 2011).

Since 2007, additional studies with more robust designs have been published. Schneider and Goldstein (2010) revealed outcomes with a large effect size for on-task behavior following the reading of social stories. Quirmbach, Lincoln, Feinberg-Gizzo, Ingersoll, and Andrews (2009) used a randomized control group design to evaluate the effect of two types of social stories, (1) standard and (2) directive, compared with a control story on the game-playing skills of 45 children with ASD. Results revealed no difference between the standard and directive social stories on increases in game-playing skills, but both were significantly better than the control story. The researchers also found differences in outcomes dependent on the child's verbal comprehension, with social stories not rated as effective for the third of the children who had extremely low verbal comprehension skills. Even taking these studies into account, there is a need to isolate the effect of social stories in packages and evaluate their use with peers over time (Ferraioli & Harris, 2011).

## Comic Strip Conversations

Comic strip conversations, also created by Carol Gray (1994), were developed to provide a strategy for discussing social interaction and problem social situations using a visual media. Line drawings are used to describe real situations involving individuals with ASD. Balloon-shaped symbols represent types of interactions, for example, a symbol from the mouth of one person to the ear of another symbolizes listening, and two balloons intersecting symbolizes interrupting. The balloons can be colored to represent different emotions, such as red for anger, blue for sad, and green for happy, friendly ideas. It is recommended that a comic strip conversation is created to provide guidance following the identified problem social situation and then that conversation or story is read to the individual as a preventive approach.

Several publications from the same authors (Pierson & Glaeser, 2005, 2007) describe the use of comic strip conversations as a positive behavior support strategy for social situations (Glaeser, Pierson, & Fritschmann, 2003). In their qualitative study with three students with autism, Pierson and Glaeser (2007) state that, when comic strip conversations were used for six weeks, the teachers and paraprofessionals working with the three students reported improvements in targeted social skills (appropriate use of hands and feet, apologizing for actions, increasing social greetings). Other researchers used an A/B design to evaluate a combination of social stories and comic strip conversation with two participants with autism (Hutchins & Prelock, 2005). Additional research with more rigorous designs is needed in order to determine the effectiveness of this strategy.

## Superflex: A Superhero Social Thinking Curriculum

Also using comic drawings, Michelle Garcia Winner has created a set of characters to teach children in grades K through 5 to identify and manage social-emotional feelings and interaction with others. The curriculum includes a character that represents the hero in the program called Superflex (Madrigal & Winner, 2008). Superflex deals with his own emotional states well, behaves as expected, and interacts with others using his skills as an effective social detective. He learns to deal with opposing forces such as Glassman and Mean Jean. The comic strip characters appeal to this age group and to educators, but the approach lacks research evidence to support behavior changes related to implementation.

## Love and Marriage?

The PEERS model currently in development for individuals with ASD ages 18 to 24 includes sessions on dating and having appropriate get-togethers with friends (The Help Group, 2011). The more advanced level of the relationship development intervention curriculum has a focus on personal identity and relationships with others (through a circles diagram) (Gutstein & Sheely, 2002b). Coaching instructions are provided for each of these activities and include role-play, skits with video, and asking partners to make lists and set goals. Research on outcomes from these models is yet to be published.

Because similarity is one of the main criteria for selecting friends, it is not uncommon for young adults with Asperger syndrome to befriend someone with the same diagnosis or even to marry a similar individual (Attwood, 1998). Research on the percentage of individuals with autism spectrum disorders who marry and information about the structure or success of these marriages is scarce. One reason it is difficult to obtain this information is that some individuals with ASD who completed intervention programs successfully when they were young do not want to be identified when they are young adults and entering a marriage. Others, like Mr. Lopez (see In Their Words 9.2), were quite willing to share their perspectives on marriage. Mr. Lopez is an adult living with autism spectrum disorder and his wife has a developmental disability.

Howlin (2004) notes that the few descriptions of marriages between individuals with autism spectrum disorders display some of the issues expected, such as problems in communication, in expressing feelings and emotions, and with inflexibilities and routine patterns of behavior. She also states that many professionals working in the area of autism spectrum disorders indicate that one of the parents may share some of the same characteristics as their offspring. Educators working with families having individuals with ASD may find that they are not only assisting the child with developing the social skills to obtain social relationships, but that they are also assisting the family with establishing a system of support that benefits all family members. In working with families, it may be important to explore consistencies between expectations of the family with those held by the individual with ASD regarding love and marriage.

> There is a value judgment with the NT [neurotypical] world that emotional relatedness is a prerequisite to achieving happiness and success. The authors ask you to consider that this judgment may be actually preventing some ASD children from becoming happy, functioning adults. (Grandin & Barron, 2005, p. 114)

## Issues and Research Questions

In their article on social-communicative competence, Brown and Odom (1994) listed research questions, most of which remain relevant for educators of learners with autism spectrum disorder. What learning history is necessary and sufficient to produce sustained social interaction? What learning history and environmental supports are necessary and sufficient to produce children's meaningful social relationships and friendships? What environmental supports will be needed to facilitate generalization and maintenance of newly acquired social behavior to children's communities, homes, and schools? What social skills interventions will be perceived as useful and hence more likely to be used by interventionists (e.g., teachers)?

Schuler and Wolfberg (2000) point out that, if students learn social skills in an isolated setting away from peers and their peer culture, their social deficits may be aggravated. Similarly, when students with social disabilities, such as those with ASD, are continually introduced to a new group of students, they are placed in a situation that is difficult even for students without disabilities. The experience can be similar to one of being the new kid several times over. When students enter a new school, class, or group of peers, there is typically a period of adjustment and careful entry into the peer group. Students with ASD do not have the skills to enter such situations with finesse or even with the group entry skills learned by attention to subtle cues. It is important for educators to weigh the pros and cons of placing students with ASD in a series of exits and entrances with peers. Educators need to reconcile the need for structure and predictability with the benefits of cultural learning for students with ASD.

> In addition, we know little about which elements of existing interventions are essential to affect behavior change. Component analyses to identify these "active ingredients" would be helpful, especially when evaluating combination treatments or comparing multiple approaches. (Ferraioli & Harris, 2011, p. 182)

Individualizing evidence-based practices is also key to achieving positive outcomes. Skills in adapting or individualizing practices without compromising fidelity of intervention, or losing the essential or critical components of a program is a sophisticated skill set for practitioners. The long-term effects of any intervention need to be measured to ensure that outcomes are sustained (Kasari & Locke, 2011).

## 9.2    *IN THEIR WORDS*

### T. L. and C. L. Discuss Life as a Married Couple

**Interviewer:** Would you mind telling me a little bit about how you met?

**C:** Well, we met at a dance. When was that dance thing?

**T:** Eight years ago.

**Interviewer:** Then how long was it from when you met till you got married?

**T:** We got married six years later after we met but we didn't start dating till four years later after we met.

**Interviewer:** Okay. Then you dated for two years . . . and then decided, "Okay, let's do this. Let's get married?"

**C:** Yes.

> *(laughter amongst all)*

**Interviewer:** It's a big decision . . .

**C:** Oh yes.

**Interviewer:** . . . to get married.

**C:** Very big decision.

**T:** Big step.

**Interviewer:** And now it's been two years?

**T:** That we've been married.

**Interviewer:** You're now married. Is it something you thought that you always wanted or are you surprised: "Oh, I'm married now"? What were your thoughts about marriage?

**C:** My thoughts . . . .

**Interviewer:** When you were a little girl, did you think "oh, when I grow up I definitely want to get married"? Or did you think "no, I never want to get married"? And then you met T?

**C:** Yeah.

**Interviewer:** . . . and "everything changed."

> *(laughter amongst all)*

**C:** Everything changed, yes. I told you about that huh? I did?

**T:** Kinda.

**C:** Kinda told him.

**Interviewer:** Okay. So, what do you mean?

**C:** Well, everything, it changed because there's more responsibilities . . . and that's always gonna go on as long as you're married.

**Interviewer:** Definitely, yeah. Well, tell me what you mean by responsibilities. Like house chores or responsibilities for the relationship or what? What do you mean by responsibilities?

*(continued)*

**9.2**  *IN THEIR WORDS (continued)*

**C:**  Responsibilities for the marriage and . . . the house chores.

**T:**  And working at additional things together.

**C:**  Yeah.

**T:**  You know, making the relationship or the marriage work, which are additional responsibilities you don't have as a single person or before you're married.

**Interviewer:**  True.

**C:**  Yeah.

**T:**  So that's marriage as opposed to being single.

**Interviewer:**  What are the benefits?

**C:**  Benefits. What are the benefits?

**T:**  Taking turns on doing . . .

**C:**  Yes, taking turns.

**T:**  . . . on certain things.

**Interviewer:**  Okay. So you have two people to do the same thing that you might have had one person to do?

**T:**  Or sometimes doing a certain chore or task together instead of by ourselves.

**Interviewer:**  Okay. Okay. Are there times that you prefer to be alone? 'Cause in a lot of marriages, that is the case. That you have times together and times alone. Is that the case for the two of you as well?

**T/C:**  Yes.

**Interviewer:**  What do you do in those times?

**C:**  Well, when he's tired from work and stuff he relaxes in the bedroom and I'll watch TV . . . and it's like—leave him alone till he's more relaxed or ready to talk. 'Cause when he comes home from work he's stressed, so tired, so he wants to rest.

**Interviewer:**  Now, what about you T? Did you think that someday you'd get married? Or what were your thoughts? Do you remember what your thoughts were when you were younger?

**T:**  When I was little I used to have fantasies about getting married. And then, when I got older, in my mid-twenties, I sometimes couldn't help feeling kind of hesitant about it. There were times I wondered if I ever wanted to get married or not because of the big responsibilities that are involved in a marriage as well as a relationship. Many people fail to realize that marriage and relationships are not always buttercups and daisies.

**C:**  Yes.

**T:**  They have a flip side to it with a lot of work and responsibilities.

**C:**  Absolutely.

**T:**  But, however, I think part of the problem with our society is there's not enough people being honest about it. They tend to give you a false impression.

**Interviewer:** Romanticize it, you mean?

**T:** You know, thinking what it's like on TV and the movies and . . .

**C:** Exactly.

**T:** . . . romance novels, but it's really not like that.

**C:** But it's not. It's really not like that.

**T:** A lot more work and a lot more pressure involved . . . than what you see.

**Interviewer:** Yes. That's a very good point. So what do you do to cope together? What are your support systems?

**T:** Try to communicate with one another.

**Interviewer:** Great. That's the key I think.

**T:** Talk to people we confide in. Certain friends, certain relatives.

**C:** Yes.

**T:** And, ah, we started going to therapy earlier this year, which has opened new doors for us . . .

C: Ah huh.

**Interviewer:** That's great.

**T:** . . . for communication.

**C:** We found out that it really helps a lot.

**Interviewer:** That's good. I'm glad that you found someone who's helpful.

**C:** And we noticed it, too, it really, it changed a lot of things in our marriage, too, huh babe?

**T:** Mmm hmm.

**Interviewer:** That's great. I agree with you wholeheartedly that relationships take energy, take work . . .

**C:** Yes.

**T:** . . . marriage does too. Even more.

**C:** But it's worth it if you're with the right person. The right guy.

**Interviewer:** And C, you say it's worth it. . . . I'm asking again, what are the pros? What makes it good to be with T?

**C:** Well, it makes it good because I know he loves me. I know he's always gonna be there for me to support me, you know, the good things. And I know he'll—I don't know how to say it . . . I can't think of it right now. It'll come to me.

**Interviewer:** Perhaps you could just finish by stating what would be your advice about a good relationship or a good marriage. If someone were going to be entering into or making the decision about getting married, what would be your advice?

**T:** My advice is, don't get married until you know you are ready . . . and tell yourself that it's a big responsibility and that to not, remember that it's not always hunky dory, remember that it's going to have some down sides, too. And that it's important to have the right attitude but to always remember that it will have its share of ups and downs and to not be dishonest about it. Maybe not discourage somebody from marriage but not to encourage anybody to get married, at least not until they're ready.

*(continued)*

**9.2   IN THEIR WORDS (continued)**

**Interviewer:** Okay. Good advice.

**T:** And to not, you know, so they don't try to get married to feel accepted or to avoid feeling left out.

**Interviewer:** That's excellent advice.

**C:** And if they are to get married, they need to sit down and . . . talk things over to say they're having a problem with each other, they need to sit down and they need to talk about what that problem is. For instance, if one of them stays out late, and they might go "You know what, you came in late, I was worried, what happened?"

**T:** My other advice is that if you don't want to have to deal with the stress or responsibilities involved in a marriage or relationship then, ah, don't get married. And probably don't be in a relationship for that matter because there's nothing wrong with being single either.

**Interviewer:** Yeah, you were saying before, don't do it just to be accepted or think that that's what's expected by society.

**T:** Yes, but also remember that it's going to have its share of down sides and that it's important that there's going to be some headaches and some aches and pains involved at times. And if they don't want to have to work hard at it or work harder at it then the best thing to do is not get married and probably not be in a relationship.

**C:** Exactly.

**Interviewer:** Do you get the sense that there is a social pressure about marriage?

**T:** Yes. Because when I was growing up my home town, I was always being nagged about marriage and nagged about being in a relationship and . . .

**Interviewer:** From family? From peers? From . . .?

**T:** From friends, family, classmates . . . pretty much everywhere. So, especially my home town since it's a very small . . . is a very small community with basically nothing to do.

**C:** Mmm hmm. My thing was like, and his thing is, if you're ready to get married, get married. If you're not ready to get married, don't get married 'cause marriage is not for everyone. It's very true. It's not.

**Interviewer:** I agree with you. And what about you C? Did you feel that there were social pressures?

**C:** It's sometimes. It's true sometimes.

**T:** Some of them are not telling you . . . about the headaches and downfalls that they've gotta deal with. They want and expect you to believe that their courtship is always dandy, but that's not how it is.

**Interviewer:** Well, thank you. Thank you for your time.

(A little later a small child was running around our table and C was saying how cute he was. I [the interviewer] asked if they planned to have children and T responded.)

**T:** No. I could not handle the stress. I just could not.

## SUGGESTIONS FOR DISCUSSION

1. Describe joint attention and explain why it is a key deficit for children with ASD.

2. Discuss the role of imitation in the development of social-relational skills and how problems with imitation can affect social development.

3. Conduct a debate with one side arguing for the inclusion of typical peers from the beginning of any program, and the other side arguing for the teaching of prerequisite skills prior to entering social situations with peers.

4. Identify the strategies educators can use to teach social skills during play.

5. Identify an important topic of a social skills group for adolescents and explain why you chose that topic.

6. Pair with a partner and have your partner express an emotion without using any oral communication. Describe how you "read" the message expressed and discuss why the ability to understand nonverbal messages is important.

7. Describe what skills are needed to conduct a conversation with two or more peers and why conversing with others may be challenging for individuals with autism spectrum disorders.

8. Choose one of the research questions suggested by Brown and Odom (1994) (these questions were noted in this chapter), and state how you could conduct a study to provide information to address this question.

## RESOURCES

### Books

Gray, C. (2010). *The new social story book.* Arlington, TX: Future Horizons.

Laugeson, E. A., & Frankel, F. (2010). *Social skills for teenagers with developmental and autism spectrum disorders: The PEERS treatment manual.* New York: Routledge.

McClannahan, L. E., & Krantz, P. J. (2005). *Teaching conversation to children with autism: Scripts and script fading.* Bethesda, MD: Woodbine House.

Wolfberg, P. J. (2003). *Peer play and the autism spectrum: The art of guiding children's socialization and imagination.* Shawnee Mission, KS: Autism Publishing Company.

### Websites

*www.semel.ucla.edu/peers*
   Information on the Program for Education and Enrichment of Relationship Skills (PEERS)
*www.ttoolbox.com*
   Teacher's toolbox. Distributor for The LEAP Outreach Project manuals
*www.thegraycenter.org*
   The Gray Center for information on Social Stories[TM]

## CHAPTER TEN

# Transition to Adulthood

## CHAPTER OBJECTIVES

The reader should be able to:

- List the skills that foster self-determination.
- Identify the best predictor of future employment for youth with disabilities.
- Describe the various roles of parents and the importance of working with families in planning and implementing transition programs.

This chapter will focus on the transition from school to adult services and what we know about how best to prepare youth and their families for this period of life. Options for employment, residential opportunities, and post-secondary educational experiences will be described, along with systems of support that can foster success. Data from the National Longitudinal Transition Study will be used to describe the current state of transition for youth with autism spectrum disorder (ASD). A discussion about how communities of practice, including parents and professionals, can influence policy and create positive change will end the chapter and the book.

## Legislation Guiding Practice

The Individuals with Disabilities Education Improvement Act (IDEA, PL 108-446) of 2004 outlines the responsibilites of school districts for transition planning for youth with disabilites. This law requires that a coordinated set of activities are designed within an outcome-oriented process, with a focus on improving the academic and functional achievement of the student with a disability, to facilitate the student's movement from school to post-school activities, including post-secondary education, vocatonal education, and integrated employment (including supported employment, continuing and adult education, adult services, indpendent living, and community participation) (Yell, 2012).

It is also part of IDEIA that transition plans are based on the individual's needs, and that the strengths, preferences, and interests of the individual are taken into account. Transition education services are required and must include instruction; related services; community experiences; the development of employment and other post-school adult living objectives; and, when appropriate, acquisition of daily living skills and functional vocational evaluation. Statements describing these services are required by law to be included in the individualized education program (IEP) no later than when the student is age 16 and they must be updated annually. This plan is referred to as an individualized transition plan (ITP). During the IEP meeting, when transition goals are being considered, the school must invite the student and a representative of the agency likely to provide or pay for the transition services (Yell, 2012). If the agency cannot attend, the school must ensure that agency representatives participate in the planning process. If the student is unable to attend, then his or her interests and preferences are to be considered. The Carl D. Perkins Vocational and Applied Technology Education Act Amendments of 1990 (PL 101-392) require that assessments should factilitate placements in integrated environments and serve as the basis for transition planning. The measurable goals serve as the centerpiece for selecting appropriate transition assessments (Kraemer, 2008).

In 2010, President Obama released the reauthorization of the Elementary and Secondary Education Act entitled *The Blueprint for Reform.* One of the four priorities in this blueprint is as follows: "Implementing college- and career-ready standards and developing improved assessments aligned with those standards" (U.S. Department of Education, 2010, p. 3). Part of this priority is raising standards so all students graduate from high school ready for college or a career, regardless of disability status. The National Governors Association and the Council of Chief State School Officers, have been working to establish a set of

educational standards that address this priority which, as of January 2011, have been adopted by 38 states and the District of Columbia (Yell, 2012).

When the students, including those with a diploma, exit the school system, they are required to have a summary of performance (SOP). The SOP describes the academic achievement of each student and provides recommendation for support in order to obtain post-secondary goals (Yell, 2012). Once individuals with ASD turn 22 or graduate from high school with a diploma, they no longer have a legal right to appropriate transition services. Individuals may apply for vocational rehabilitation services.

> There is no federal mandate governing adult services for adults with autism, and matters are complicated by procedures for determining eligibility that vary greatly across different agencies. (Bruey & Urban, 2009, p. 91)

The Rehabilitation Act of 1973 was amended in 1998 (PL 105-220) and provides federal grants for states to provide and operate comprehensive vocational rehabilitation (VR) services for individuals with disabilites (Revell & Miller, 2009). In addition to providing training and job placement services, VR also provides counseling and guidance. One must be eligible for services, according to the following criteria: (1) the presence of a disability that is an impairment to employment, and (2) the expectation that VR services will result in the individual obtaining employment. Once eligible, an individualized plan for employment (IPE) is created with the VR counselor (Revell & Miller, 2009). The Workforce Investment Act of 1998 established One Stop Career Centers that can serve as a key resource for finding access to vocational training and job placement for individuals with disabilites.

It is important for anyone with a disability seeking employment to be aware of the Americans with Disabilies Act of 1990, which prohits private employers, state and local governments, employment agencies, and labor unions from discriminating against qualified individuals with disabilities in job applications procedures; hiring; firing; advancement;

compensation; job training; and other terms, conditions, and privileges of employment. A qualified employee or applicant with a disability is an individual who, with or without reasonable accommodation, can perform the essential functions of the job. Reasonable accomodation may include, but is not limited to, making existing facilities used by employees accessible and usable; job restructuring; modifying work schedules; reassignment to a vacant position; and acquiring or modifying equipment or devices, adjusting or modifying examinations, training materials, or policies, and providing qualified readers or interpreters. The employer is required to make an accommodation to the known disability of a qualified applicant or employee but is not required to lower quality or production standards to make an accommodation (Yell, 2012).

When an individual with ASD reaches age 18, he or she may qualify for Supplemental Security Income (SSI) from the Social Security Administration (SSA) to assist with living expenses, even if he or she continues to live at home (Gabriels, 2011). Although SSI provides a monthly check and health insurance benefits, this income can be a deterant to seeking paid employment (Revell & Miller, 2009). The individual with ASD can apply for SSI when he or she reaches age 18 to determine eligibility, regardless of whether funds were received prior to reaching adult status. When their child reaches adolescence or adulthood, it is not uncommon for parents to consider creating a special needs trust to ensure that he or she is cared for after the parents pass away. Self-suffiency trusts are an option that enable famlies to set aside resources without interfering with the benefits of the individual with ASD (Zager, 2005).

# Best Practice in Developing the Individualized Transition Plan (ITP)

In a review of the transition plans of 94 high school students with disabilities published in 1997, the authors found that the vocational goals received the highest ratings, with 45% receiving the top score; educational goals were equally divided between adequate and minimal ratings; and the majority of the goals in the areas of recreation and residential living received minimal ratings for quality (Grigal, Test, Beattie, & Wood, 1997). Adult services were not involved in the planning for transition. Individuals with autism were not a category evaluated in this study.

In their book, *Autism and the Transition to Adulthood*, Wehman, Smith, and Schall (2009) suggest a set of questions that the IEP team should consider when planning for transition. Examples include "What is the student's or caregiver's vision for the student's future?" "Will the student need additional training or education after high school to be able to realize his or her vision?" and "What experiences does this student need to better inform his or her decision making to prepare for life beyond high school?" (Wehman et al., 2009, p. 47).

## Preparing for the ITP Meeting

It is recommended that the form and focus of assessment be considered as part of an overall plan involving all stakeholders, including the individual with ASD (Sax, 2002). Person-centered planning would be ideal for considering options for the periods during and after secondary education.

## Person-Centered Planning

The focus of person-centered planning is the collaboration of stakeholders (family, friends, teachers) who develop a plan with the individual with ASD that is focused on the desired future outcomes. An important aspect of the person-centered planning approach is that the involvement of family and friends, along with the individual with ASD, is ensured. One person does not dominate the meeting, whose focus remains on the interests and preferences of the individual with ASD. Several frameworks are available for completing such plans, including the McGill Action Planning System (MAPS) and Choosing Outcomes and Accommodations for Children (COACH) approaches discussed in Chapter 2, and the Planning Alternative Tomorrows with Hope (PATH) (Pearpoint, O'Brien, & Forest, 1993). Because the planning process is focused around the strengths, interests, and preferences of the individual with ASD, the plans are often creative, individualized, and sensitive to the individual's wishes (Bruey & Urban, 2009). "Person centered planning requires equal participation, positive and clear communication, and active involvement of the focus individual" (Sax, 2002, p. 15).

If the individual with ASD brings skills in self-advocacy to the meeting, she or he will be more likely to get the outcomes that meet her or his interests and needs (Sicile-Kira, 2006). The Self-Advocacy for Education and Transition Planning program (Van Reusen, Bos, Schumaker, & Deshler, 1994) guides the student toward the goals of conducting a student-directed transition plan with accompanying self-advocacy instruction. The program is comprised of a series of lesson plans that provides information about transition plans and uses the IPLAN (Inventory your strengths, goals and choices, Provide your inventory, Listen and respond, Ask questions, and Name your goals) formula to guide the student (Wehmeyer, 2002). Another self-advocacy curriculum, the Integrated Self-Advocacy Curriculum, was created by Valerie Paradiz. It assists adolescents and young adults with learning to speak for themselves, asking for what they need, negotiating, knowing their rights and responsibilities, and being able to explain their disability to others. People First is an organization that is founded on the principle of self-advocacy; this organization may be a source of support and inspiration for youth with ASD.

Next S.T.E.P. (Student Transition and Educational Planning) is another program with the goal of facilitating self-directed transition planning (Halpern et al., 1997). The curriculum consists of 16 lessons, including content focusing on an introduction to transition planning, self-evaluation, goal identification, and preparation for the transition plan meeting (Wehmeyer, 2002). The Choicemaker Self-Determination Transition Curriculum (Martin & Marshall, 1995) is another guide to a self-directed IEP that is comprised of three sections: choosing goals, expressing goals, and taking action. Transition planning has eleven steps that students can follow as the leader of their own IEP meetings, including introduce everyone, state your own transition goals, deal with differences in opinion, state the support you need, and work on IEP goals all year (Martin, Marshall, Maxson, & Jerman, 1996). The Transition Planning Inventory (Clark & Patton, 1997) has a student form that can be used to guide the transition planning process. The student is asked to identify his or her preference for employment or further education as well as for living arrangements after graduation. In addition, a checklist of 46 items is used to self-evaluate current knowledge and skills in the areas of employment, further education/training, leisure activities, community participation, daily living, health, communication, interpersonal relationships, and self-determination.

## Planning for Career Options

It is important to have some guiding principles when considering vocational and career assessment. For example, individuals and their families should be involved, varied assessments should be used, information should be collected under natural conditions, and the focus should be on successful functioning with the necessary services and supports (Rogan, Grossi, & Gajewski, 2002).

The assessment may include an interest survey where students identify preferred tasks and potential occupations. The Reading-Free Vocational Interest Inventory: 2 (Becker, 2000) is a tool that can be used with nonreaders. It requires the individual to select preferred tasks from a group of three drawings depicting different occupational activities (e.g., auto repair, carpentry, office work). Readers at the ninth-grade level could complete the Self-Directed Search (Holland, 1994), a career self-assessment that identifies the match between job personalities and key characteristics of different occupations

(Kraemer, 2008). The Brigance® Employability Skills Inventory (Brigance, 1995) identifies basic skills of career awareness and job preparation such as job-seeking knowledge, interviewing skills, preemployment writing, self-concept, motor coordination, and work experience (Kraemer, 2008).

An assessment of the work environment most suited for successful performance on the job, and an assessment that considers the student's interests and preferences, would be important information for career planning. The completion of an ecological assessment would provide this information. The ecological assessment includes the identification of a targeted environment, a description or task analysis of the job, and a record from an observation of student performance as she or he completes relevant tasks (Rogan et al., 2002). A discrepancy analysis between the skills needed in the targeted environment and those observed in the individual with ASD can be made with the aim of addressing any essential missing skills. A situational assessment of job sampling is another strategy where the individual is asked to perform tasks in the potential workplace (Rogan et al., 2002). A lot can be learned from a situational assessment, including aspects of the environment that are problematic (noise level, social demands), aspects that are supportive, and any missing job-related or social skills that could be addressed. In addition, the situational assessment allows the student to see if the job met expectations. Student satisfaction with the job site through a survey or interview can be obtained (Rogan et al., 2002).

## Working with Families

Family members are essential partners in the development of the transition plan. Planning for the future of the student with ASD involves preparing for the time when she or he is no longer supported by the educational system and IDEA. Families are also transitioning to working with a new system and facing the unknown regarding post-secondary outcomes for their child. This transition period can be stressful for families. Compared with mothers of toddlers with ADS, mothers of adolescents reported higher levels of anger and higher levels of behavioral disengagement (Smith, Seltzer, Tager-Flusberg, Greenberg, & Carter, 2008). Compared with mothers of typical adolescents, mothers of adolescents and adults with ASD who were interviewed by telephone regarding daily diaries reported lower levels of positive affect and days with more arguments, significantly more fatigue (50% of days compared to 25%), significantly more time caring for their children and doing household chores, and significantly more time giving emotional support (Smith et al., 2010).

Caregivers of children and adolescents with ASD have concerns about the individual's social and communication deficits, behavior problems, and dependency needs that can restrict family activities (Gabriels, 2011). Almost half of the parents who responded to a national survey about educational services indicated that one of the highest levels of dissatisfaction was with their children's preparation for life after high school (Turnbull, Zuna, Turnbull, Poston, & Summers, 2007). In response to the interviews conducted by Bonnie Kraemer (see In Their Words 10.1), parents report a heightened sense of worry and stress related to the future of their son or daughter with ASD.

## Cultural Considerations

The degree of independence expected from adolescents and young adults varies depending on the cultural background of the family (Lynch & Hanson, 2011). In some cultures, the family members would be considered negligent if they placed their child in an apartment or group home, and living outside the family home is not even considered. The same holds true for employment options and expectations. Therefore, it is necessary to explore the hopes, dreams, and expectations for each family and not make assumptions about post-school goals or preferences.

In their review of parent involvement in transition planning for 308 African American, Hispanic American, Native American, and

# 10.1 IN THEIR WORDS

**Bonnie R. Kraemer,** *Ph.D., Associate Professor,*
*Department of Special Education,*
*San Diego State University*

The period of transition from school to adult life is a critical stage of the lifespan for youth with autism spectrum disorder (ASD) and their families. Although many more services are being provided for young children with ASD and children are being identified at a younger age, there exists a gap in specific programming for this population at the high-school level and beyond. As discussed in this chapter, it is important that transition programming for youth with ASD be comprehensive in nature and that it begin early. For many individuals on the spectrum, age 16 is not early enough to begin planning for the future. It must begin much earlier.

Recent data from the National Longitudinal Transition Study 2 (June 2011) indicate that the post-school employment rates for young adults with autism are the third lowest among IDEA eligibility groups. Post-school community living outcomes and social networks are also limited. By planning early, involving youth and families in the process, and connecting with key adult stakeholders, we can improve the post-school outcomes for youth with autism.

There are multiple components to effective transition programming, including a person-centered assessment process to determine student strengths, needs, and interests. Transition programming must also be driven by the post-school outcomes that are desired by the student and his or her family. For some individuals, competitive employment and independent living might be priorities; for others, it may be a focus on family and social relations. The annual IEP goals and short-term objectives for students with autism should be aligned with their post-school outcomes and must drive the educational program.

Involving parents in the transition planning of their son or daughter is considered best practice and allows them to have more control during this critical period of the lifespan. In my ongoing work examining the period of transition for young adults with ASD between the ages of 16 and 25, families routinely express their desire for increased involvement. In my research, families are interviewed to determine how they are involved in the transition process and how they are affected during this period of the lifespan. Data from nearly 100 families interviewed indicate that the majority feel they do not have knowledge of adult services/programming options and that services are limited. They overwhelmingly have a desire to be actively involved in their son's or daughter's life planning, with nearly 40% of the families wanting more involvement than they currently have. Families also report that they are significantly affected by the transition from school to adult life. They frequently worry about where the young adult will work and live, as well as her or his access to friends and social activities. Moreover, 60% of parents report that worries "spill over" and affect their personal well-being. These families also have heightened stress compared to families of transition-age youth with intellectual disability with no autism diagnosis.

It can been seen that parents of youth with autism have significant concerns regarding vocational options, future residential environments, social networks, and needs for assistance when compared to other disability groups. These concerns may reflect a realistic view of the post-school world that often offers limited adult services and greater uncertainty than the public school years. It is conceivable that if families are more involved in the transition process and are given more opportunities to play an active role, their feelings regarding post-school outcomes would be more favorable, and even the outcomes themselves would be more positive.

European American families from a large urban school district in the western United States, Greenen, Powers, and Lopez-Vasquez (2001) found that there was a discrepancy between the reported involvement of families from non-European backgrounds and the perception of professionals working in schools. In other words, professionals described culturally and linguistically diverse parents as less involved than European Americans, primarily because the families whose cultures and languages differed from European Americans were less likely to participate in school-based planning. However, families themselves felt very involved with transition planning because they reported high rates of involvement in activities such as teaching the child cultural values of the family, talking about transition, teaching their child how to use transportation, and teaching their child to care for his or her disability—activities considered significantly more important compared with European American families (Greenen et al., 2001). The results from this study underline the need for educators to work with families in a culturally responsive manner, as described in Chapter 7.

## Collaborating with Adult Agencies

In their 1997 study of transition plans written for individuals with disabilities other than ASD, Grigal and colleagues (1997) noted that adult services personnel were rarely involved in developing the transition plans. Although the quality of direct care staff has an impact on the quality of the services provided by adult agencies, the U.S. Department of Heath and Human Services reported a high turnover rate for these positions of 50% annually (Gerhardt, 2009).

One program that aims to work in collaboration with adult agencies by providing a series of internships with identified adult programs is called Project Search (www.projectsearch.us). Developed in 1996 by Erin Riehle in Cincinnati, Project SEARCH is a high school transition program that is currently available in 39 states for students with significant disabilities. The goal is competitive employment achieved through classroom instruction, career exploration, and on-the-job training with a host business liaison. Students are referred to the program through their schools or vocational rehabilitation counselor.

# Research on Best Practices for Adults with ASD

In the published reviews of evidence-based practices (see Chapter 3 for a full description), it is noted that there are fewer studies conducted with adolescents and adults with ASD compared with younger individuals (National Autism Center, 2009a; Odom, Collet-Klingenberg, et al., 2010). The only identified established treatment by the National Standards Project where research was conducted with individuals between the ages of 19 to 21 was behavioral packages. The additional established treatments that involved participants with ASD ages 15 to 18 included self-management and modeling (National Autism Center, 2009a). Specific behavioral strategies that have a research base with this age range include reinforcement, prompting, task analysis, differential reinforcement, and time-delay (Odom, Collet-Klingenberg, et al., 2010).

# Implementing Evidence-Based Practices

Among the likely reasons for the continued poor outcomes for adults on the spectrum are minimal professional attention to evidence-based practice in transition planning and intervention. (Gerhardt & Lainer, 2011, p. 38)

## Self-Management

Self-management is an important skill for addressing the organization and completion of tasks and for coping with social-emotional challenges. Individuals with ASD often respond well to the structure of self-management and the control and independence that results from the use of this strategy. A complete description of self-management, and the components of self-instruction, self-recording, and self-reward, is found in Chapter 5.

Three adolescents with autism were taught to self-manage a token system delivered for conversational statements and responses following the reading of a short story (Newman, Buffington, & Hemmes, 1996). Initially the adolescents received a token delivered by staff members, for comments and responses; then they were taught to self-deliver tokens. The percentage of appropriate conversation increased for all three boys, and these increases were maintained by self-reinforcement of tokens (Newman et al., 1996).

## Modeling

Modeling has been used by job coaches who demonstrate or model tasks as a component of teaching a new skill on the job site. Video modeling has been used to aid with transitions, to provide an example for job interviews, and to assist with the development of social skills. In fact, many social skills training programs incorporate modeling and role-play of social situations.

## Additional Behavioral Packages and Strategies

Examples of behavioral packages are the use of photographic activity schedules to teach independent completion of job skills, with each photograph representing a different task or task component (McClannahan & Krantz, 2010). Scripts have been used to teach social conversation at dinner in a group home. Incidental teaching has been used to teach sandwich making for residents with ASD (McGee, Krantz, Mason, & McClannahan, 1983). Correspondence training was used to teach accurate reporting and completion of exercise routines in a gym. See Chapter 4 for other examples of behavioral strategies that can be used with adolescents and young adults.

# Preparing for Post-School Outcomes

## Addressing Social Skills and Relationships

Adolescents and young adults with ASD continue to have significant social problems as reflected by

having limited to no friendships or acquaintances and difficulties understanding and engaging in romantic relationships. (Gabriels, 2011, p. 1169)

Authors agree that a lack of social skills can hinder success with job interviews and interpersonal aspects of employment (Neuhring & Sitlington, 2003; Smith, Belcher, & Juhrs, 1995). Heightened expectations may result in less tolerance of awkward and maladaptive behaviors displayed during interactions with community members (Gabriels, 2011). Educators and clinicians commonly use social skills groups to address the social issues experienced by individuals with ASD.

The first social skills intervention program for adolescents with ASD reported in the literature used the TEACCH approach (Mesibov, 1984). The groups typically start with assisting in the identification of topics for conversation by having all group members put topics of interest into a hat and holding a brief conversation on each topic after it is drawn. Sometimes a homework assignment in which the adolescent is required to phone three peers and talk about one of the topics is used to assist the students with recall of conversation details (Mesibov, Shea, & Schopler, 2004). Group members also practice taking turns in conversations, staying on the topic, and avoiding persistent questioning or monologues. Adults engage in these groups as participants to provide support and external reinforcement if needed. Although the social skills groups used by the TEACCH approach have been described in various publications (e.g., Mesibov, Shea, & Adams, 2001; Schopler, Mesibov, & Kunce, 1998), research on the generalization of these skills beyond these groups, such as at home, was not found.

Behavioral strategies that have been used to increase the conversation skills of students with autism have focused on adolescents. Peers were used to prompt each other and maintain the topic of sports during dyad and group conversations (Krantz, Ramsland, & McClannahan, 1989). McGee, Krantz, and McClannahan (1984) used practice and reinforcement to teach three adolescents with autism to respond to peers and maintain conversations during game activities, and self-reinforcement was used to maintain ongoing conversations among three males with autism in another study (Newman, Buffington, & Hemmes, 1996).

Grandin and Barron (2005), two adults with autism, list 10 unwritten rules of social relationships that were very helpful for them. Some examples are rule number 4: Honesty is different than diplomacy, rule number 5: Being polite is appropriate in any situation, rule number 8: Know when you are turning people off. Grandin and Duffy (2008) state that individuals must develop strategies for controlling anger because outbursts are not tolerated in the workplace. See Chapter 8 for a more thorough review of social skills strategies, models, and programs.

Chantal Sicile-Kira (2006), a parent of a youth with autism writes, "Even if your young adult is not interested in relationships or intimacy and sex, these topics need to be addressed" (p. 107). For many, the goal of sexuality education will be to protect the individual from sexual exploitation, to increase self-esteem, and to teach healthy sex habits (Koller, 2000). It may be important to explain why following people may frighten them; why it is not okay to remove clothes in public; and the importance of good hygiene, privacy, and rules regarding masturbation.

## Circles®: Intimacy and Relationships Education

If individuals with ASD would benefit from visual supports when addressing social relationships and related behaviors, then the color-coded circles concept may be helpful. Using concentric circles of different colors, Walker-Hirsch and Champagne (1991) describe in part 1 of their curriculum the social behavior associated with each level. For example, the center circle is the self (purple), and no one should touch you unless you want to be touched; the next circle (blue) is the hug circle for family and close friends; and an outer circle, or wave circle (orange), is for an acquaintance and for children. During adolescence, issues

of personal safety and sexual maltreatment become an increasing concern. Part 2 of this curriculum focuses on relationship building and making choices about intimacy.

## Self-Determination

Self-determination is a set of skills that enables an individual to be the causal agent in life (Wehmeyer, 2005). Included in this set of skills is being able to identify when and by whom support is needed (Wehman et al., 2009). Component elements of self-determined behavior include making choices, decision making, goal setting and attainment, problem solving, self-regulation, student-directed learning skills, self-advocacy, perceptions of efficacy and control, self-awareness, and self-knowledge (Wehmeyer, Shogren, Smith, Zager, & Simpson, 2010). The recommended process of obtaining these skills (Field, Sarver, & Shaw, 2003) occurs when the individual knows him- or herself and the environment, including his or her own strengths, weaknesses, and preferences, and options for support; values themselves; and plans, acts, and learns from the outcome.

The ARC's Self-Determination Scale (Wehmeyer & Kelchner, 1995) is a 72-item self-report measure that provides information about the characteristics of self-determination. The items address four subscales, or aspects of self-determination: (1) student autonomy; (2) student self-regulation, including problem solving, goal setting, and task performance; (3) psychological empowerment; and (4) self-realization (Wehmeyer, 2002). This self-determination scale is used as part of the measures in the National Longitudinal Transition Study. The U.S. Office of Special Education Programs (2005) published a fact sheet about self-determination of youth with disabilities that reported results of this scale. Youth were classified into 12 disability categories, and autism was one. Scores on each of the subscales (personal autonomy, autonomy in career planning, self-realization, psychological empowerment) were grouped into high, medium, and low ranges. Youth with autism consistently had the lowest percentages in the high category for all four of the subscales compared with the other 11 disability categories (U.S. Office of Special Education Programs, 2005).

In a proposed ecological approach to self-determination that considers person-specific and ecology-specific variables, specific practices are recommended to increase self-determination (Wehmeyer et al., 2010). These practices include educating stakeholders about self-determination, promoting making choices, maximizing experiences leading to determining preferences, maximizing opportunities to practice skills, ensuring access to universal design, and design of systems to promote greater choice making and control. Focusing on these strategies is a start in facilitating successful transition planning (Held, Thoma, & Thomas, 2004). As Wehmeyer and his colleagues (2010) state, "[T]hough there is an emerging evidence base for practices to promote self-determination of students with ASD, there remains much to be done with regard to both research and intervention development and evaluation" (p. 484).

## Focusing on Life Skills

Life skills can be described as the adaptive and positive behaviors necessary for an individual to deal with the demands of life; they include decision making, problem solving, goal setting, communication, self-awareness, assertiveness, interpersonal skills, and the ability to cope with stress (Gabriels, 2011). More specifically, life skills for individuals with ASD can include behavior life skills, such as understanding emotions; self-regulation skills and safety; social life skills, such as relationship skills; and self-care skills, including diet and meal preparation, money management, exercise routines, and hygiene (Gabriels, 2011). An important interpersonal skill to address is grooming. As Grandin and Duffy (2008) explain, "If you are talented, you can often get away with being eccentric at work, but you usually can't get away with poor grooming—a very important part of social skills" (p. 29).

## Providing Opportunities for Prevocational Training

One key to success in employment is having previous work experience. (Schall & Wehman, 2009, p. 13)

There is agreement that individuals with ASD are employable in multiple occupations (Grandin, 1999; Lattimore, Parsons, & Reid, 2002; Smith et al., 1995). Positions that require maintaining a system, accuracy, memory, attention to detail, and repetition are well suited to the typical strengths of individuals with ASD (Hendrickx, 2009). What is important is to begin to prepare for vocational skills early in the educational process (McClannahan, MacDuff, & Krantz, 2002; Neuhring & Sitlington, 2003) and to arrange for the necessary support during the initial aspects of employment. Temple Grandin and Kate Duffy (2008) recommend cultivating talents early, including building on perseverative interests, because extreme talents in a vocation make up for challenges in social skills.

When should you start planning for transition? You can never begin too early. (Bruey & Urban, 2009, p. xii)

Wehman and colleagues (2009) outline the skills for preparing students with disabilities for future career options, beginning with developing the image of self as worker and providing opportunities for completing odd jobs, school work around career options, and field trips to visit community members at work in the elementary grades. They recommend that, by middle school, students become familiar with the characteristics of various jobs and that internships in different positions, with mentoring from adults, takes place. By high school students should be learning about the skills needed for a particular job or field, completing internships, and having paid work experiences. Following graduation, the focus of the preparation shifts to searching for employment and the skills needed to find and retain work, such as preparing a résumé, completing applications, and practicing the social-communication skills needed for a successful interview.

In their handbook entitled *Opening Doors to Postsecondary Education and Training,* the Wisconsin Department of Public Instruction has a checklist for planning and preparing that can be completed by youth (Burmaster, 2007). The checklist begins with pre–high school activities (develop a list of interests, develop study skills) and outlines steps that can be taken during each year of high school (e.g., 10th grade: continue or develop self-advocacy skills, visit colleges and other post-secondary education training options).

A systematic review of the secondary transition literature yielded four predictors of post-school employment with a moderate level of evidence: paid employment/work experience, inclusion in general education, vocational education, and work study (Test et al., 2009). The implication of this research is that providing opportunities for youth with ASD with vocational training and work experiences during high school is important for obtaining employment after graduation.

Adults with ASD often describe the importance of a mentor and attribute success to the relationship with this person (Bruey & Urban, 2009). A mentor could be someone from the job setting, including someone with ASD, and could serve as part of the transition team. The role of the mentor may be to discuss ideas and thoughts or to provide another perspective on a situation (Hendrickx, 2009).

## Community-Based Instruction

Community-based instruction occurs when educational objectives are taught in natural community settings. These objectives can be implemented across domains, such as pre-vocational experiences, math concepts while shopping, social skills during recreational activities, and transportation skills to address increased independence and quality of life.

A major advantage of community-based instruction is that it enables students with autism to generalize what they have learned. Students often do not carry over classroom instruction into the community, which makes instruction nonfunctional. (Hendricks, Smith & Wehman, 2009, p. 113)

It is important that IEP objectives that are addressed in community settings are worked on with at least the rigor they are given in the classroom. The valuable time spent in the community should not be used as a field trip for the group or be a wasted opportunity to work on functional and valuable skills. Scheduling and transporting students for community-based instruction is often the greatest challenge for educators. Possible solutions include using public transportation, organizing the teaching schedule with the school bus schedule, using parents' cars with mileage reimbursement, and walking to sites (Hendricks et al., 2009).

## Mobility and Transportation

Mobility, the ability to travel from one point to another, is important to students' independence. Traveling safely by foot, bus, train, or car, however, can present special challenges for students with autism. (Smith & Targett, 2009, p. 211)

The ability to use public transportation can be a very important skill that will facilitate many post-secondary activities. Independent transportation may be required for certain jobs, may mean access to recreational activities, can provide a means to meet with peers, and is a skill that enables self-determination. It is a foundational skill for providing access to the community.

## Leisure and Recreation

The ability to enjoy a range of activities can influence the quality of life for anyone. It may be advantageous to introduce youth with ASD to new activities when they have support so that they can cultivate new interests or expand preferred interests. High schools have many clubs and sports teams and often sponsor recreational activities, so the school is the first place to look for a student's recreation and leisure opportunities (Smith & Targett, 2009). If the high school does not have a club or organization focused on the special interest of the student with ASD, perhaps he or she could start one.

Some schools require the completion of volunteer hours of service to the community. In such circumstances, parents or educators could inquire if this requirement may be satisfied by accompanying a student with ASD to activities typical for peers outside school hours (Bruey & Urban, 2009). The community recreation center is likely to offer events that could be attended by individuals with ASD, and some communities have support services if needed.

## Incorporating Technology

> The striking lack of literature on adults with ASDs and complex communication needs that are associated with ID [intellectual disability] is indicative that this group has largely been forgotten. (Iacono, Johnson, & Forster, 2009, p. 468)

There is a lack of research on effective practices for accommodating adolescents and young adults who use AAC, perhaps reflecting that they often have few opportunities to receive intervention to address their social and communication needs (Iacono et al., 2009). It is known that the social networks of individuals with intellectual disability (ID) are typically small and comprised mainly of family members and paid staff. Adults with ASD and ID are among those with the poorest outcomes in terms of employment. More attention is clearly needed to identify means of using technology to provide access to opportunities in the community.

Increasingly mobile and user-friendly devices enable the use of technology as a source of support and information for individuals with ASD. Research demonstrated how an iPod with an individualized video modeling sequence resulted in transitions during classes and activities for four elementary-age students with autism (Cihak, Fahrenkrog, Ayres, & Smith, 2010). The same use of this evidence-based practice (video modeling) could be used to facilitate the transition for high schoolers and employees. iPads with embedded activity schedules have been used to facilitate the

successful use of public transportation to a worksite. iPads and iPods are carried by same-age peers, and their use may not even be noticeable in the community. The field awaits future research that demonstrates how technology can increase independence and quality of life for individuals with autism spectrum disorders.

## Adult Services and Supports

> [A] looming crisis of unprecedented magnitude [is coming] for adults with autism, their families, and the ill-prepared and underfunded adult service system charged with meeting their needs. (Gerhardt & Lainer, 2011, p. 37)

### Employment

Mark Romoser (2000), an adult with ASD, writes in his article "Malemployment in Autism," "[t]hose of us who fail the social services triage test are pretty much left to fend for ourselves in an employment market that prizes 'people skills' above all else, even competence" (p. 246). He continues by arguing that there are benefits to hiring individuals with autism that include the possibility of longevity in one position, attention to detail, preference for repetitive tasks, and the lack of interference of social behaviors such as phone calls with job performance.

Data collected in 2005 from wave 3 from the National Longitudinal Transition Study (www.nlts2.org) reveals that individuals with autism were reported as employed at a job for over 12.5 months at a higher percentage than for most of the other disability categories. The types of jobs that were held according to the categories used by the researchers at the highest percentages were for food service, cleaning, stocking, shipping and receiving, and assembling and sorting.

In her review of outcome studies, Howlin (2004) reports that the average proportion of adults with ASD in the United Kingdom finding work is 20%, with most employed in menial and poorly paid jobs. Employment stability was also found to be poor. Among the reported difficulties were a failure to appreciate social rules and mistreatment by co-workers in the form of teasing and bullying. "The vast majority of adults with autism are either unemployed or underemployed" (Gerhardt & Lainer, 2011).

McClannahan, MacDuff, and Krantz (2002) report that 73% of the adults with autism in their Adult Life-Skills program have been in supported employment for 64% to 100% of the months that they have received services. Using applied behavior analysis to address social and vocational skills at an early age, this program has successfully transitioned young adults to employment situations in positions of data entry, laundry work, hotel housekeeping, filing and collating, merchandise receiving, grounds maintenance, and kitchen work. In this program, employment situations are individualized to match the interests and skills of the young adult, and then a job coach is assigned to work alongside the new employee until supports can be faded.

Hagner and Cooney (2005) identify common job modifications that were helpful for individuals with ASD during employment. One modification was to maintain a consistent schedule for the employee with ASD and a consistent position if working with a team. Reducing the social demands of the role and responsibilities was another modification that was helpful. Design and implementation of organizers to structure and keep track of work and structure downtime were other suggestions. In addition to job modification, other key strategies used by supervisors to support employees with ASD included using a supervision style that was direct and specific, and checking for understanding following any communication; assisting the employee to learn social cues encountered on the job; encouraging co-workers to initiate interaction; identifying some key co-workers to keep an eye out for the employee, with the aim of transferring relationships and supports to company employees; and providing support services, such as maintaining a liaison role for nonwork issues that affect the job, and remaining on call in case problems arise. "It seems likely that supervisory

and management style has a great deal to do with the success or failure of an employment experience for an individual with autism" (Hagner & Cooney, 2005, p. 97).

## Employment Options

> Work is more than just a livelihood or a paycheck; it is the key to a satisfying and productive life. For me and many of my spectrum peers, work is the superglue that holds our lives together in an otherwise confusing world. (Grandin, 2005, p. 29)

Various types of employment options available for adults with disabilities are described in the *Transition Tool Kit* available from Autism Speaks™ (2011).

**Competitive Employment:** In competitive employment, individuals are employed full- or part-time with market wages and responsibilities, and no long-term support is provided.

**Supported Employment:** In supported employment, individuals are employed in competitive jobs with ongoing support services while they are on the job. The support can be funded through state developmental disability or vocational rehabilitation agencies (Autism Speaks, 2011). Over the last decade, provider agencies have moved away from center-based models to more appropriate service models such as supported employment (Gerhardt & Lainer, 2011).

**Customized Employment:** In customized employment, the strengths and abilities of the individual with ASD with signficant disabilities is taken into consideration as job tasks and duties are negotiated with businesses. The job is uniquely created for the individual (Autism Speaks, 2011). Person-centered planning is at the core of customized the job description (Gerhardt & Lainer, 2011).

**Self-Employment:** Tailoring a job to match the interests and strengths of the individual with ASD so she or he can have an income but work on her or his own terms is the focus of self-employment. Lazar and Kraemer (2007) conducted a pilot survey to determine how many adults with autism spectrum disorders are self-employed in the United States and what type of work provides the opportunity for self-employment. The majority of the 52 respondents identified themselves with Asperger syndrome and were able to complete the survey without assistance. Most respondents were employed in a service-based business (91%), such as computer work, work in the arts or writing, taxi driver, dog trainer, carpet cleaner, caterer, housepainter, mechanic, respite worker, and sales. Most respondents stated that their self-employment incorporated a special interest, talent, or hobby and that the major advantages were independence, control over the environment, use of individual interests and talents, and personal enjoyment. The areas where the respondents needed most assistance were record keeping and finances, and the most challenging aspect of being self-employed was reported to be financial difficulty.

**Segregated Employment:** Segregated employment occurs in a segregated environment: only with other workers with disabilities. Contract work is often obtained that involves tasks such as assembling parts, collating, or packaging, and individuals may receive an income from the job.

**Sheltered Employment:** In sheltered employment, jobs are completed in a protected or separate environment that typically includes training and assistance with tasks (Autism Speaks, 2011).

**Day Programs:** Day programs are designed to teach preemployment skills and skills of daily living. Those who attend are

individuals with disabilities who work with staff members in a high staff-to-client ratio (Gerhardt & Lainer, 2011).

## Residential Options

Data from the National Longitudinal Transition Study 2 published in 2007 indicated that 72.6% of young adults with disabilities continued to live with their parents after high school, 9.9% lived alone, and 0.5% lived in a group home or assisted living facility. In an outcome study of adolescents and young adults with ASD, it was determined that the percentage of individuals age 23 and older living independently was 64% of those with Asperger syndrome, but only 8% for the autism group, and all depended on caregivers for some degree of support (Cederlund, Hagberg, Billsted, Gillberg, & Gillberg, 2008). When individuals with ASD do not have the skills to live independently, alternative options, although limited, may be available. Some adult services offer supervised apartments, a staff member who lives in residence with several adults with ASD, or group homes.

Authorized by the Rehabilitation Act of 1973, each state in the United States has at least one center for independent living (CIL) that provides support services to individuals with disabilities. CILs use a model of consumer control and "encourage people who themselves have been successful at establishing independent, self-sufficient lives to assist others with severe disabilities to do the same" (Wilson, 1998, p. 248). Some centers also provide transition services through collaborations with multidisciplinary teams. The focus of the CILs is to provide and improve services for youth in transition in local communities.

Depending on the location, families may have a choice of different models, but not all models are available in all states (Gerhardt & Lainer, 2011). Transition models offer a brief residential experience with the plan of transitioning to that environment in the future. Supported living programs provide residential services to adults with developmental disabilities who are living in self-owned or leased homes in the community. Supervised living is a residential model where individuals with ASD are provided supervision on a regular basis, such as from a staff member assigned to work with adults sharing an apartment. Group homes are residential facilities that are staffed 24 hours a day by trained agency staff members. Instruction in daily living and self-help skills is usually provided. Intermediate-care facilities, an optional Medicaid service, are the most intensive option and provide residential services for larger numbers of individuals with disabilities. Typically, one facility has several group-home-size residences. Each state has at least one such facility (Autism Speaks, 2011).

In the 1960s, the National Institute of Mental Health provided grants that funded research by behavioral psychologists working with the Achievement Place Research Project at the University of Kansas. This research defined the residential treatment model known as the teaching-family model (TFM). The first group home in the United States for adolescents and young adults with autism based on the teaching-family model was developed by the Princeton Child Development Institute in New Jersey. The teaching-family model has a core teaching team that typically includes a married couple who live in the house, rent-free, with the residents with disabilities (Gerhardt & Lainer, 2011). Staff training, support from consultants and administrators, and systematic evaluation by stakeholders are features of this model. Staff turnover in the teaching-family model is reported to be significantly less than that of other models where staff members work in shifts (Gebhardt & Lainer, 2011).

The National Association of Residential Providers for Adults with Autism (www.narpaa. org) has a website that assists with locating residential programs in states (most are on the East Coast) and provides a forum for exchanging information and obtaining funding for this "national crisis in services to adults with developmental disabilities." Autism Speaks (2011) recommends that families start early in identifying and choosing the right residential option. They suggest some key questions to ask: "Where would the individual with ADS be happiest

and feel safest?" "What supports does he or she need?" "What setting can help expand upon his or her strengths and abilities?" Questions to consider asking regarding different types of facilities include: "What kind of training does the staff receive?" "How often are they on duty?" "What is the turnover rate?" "How structured is the schedule?" "Can I speak with other families about their experiences?"

## Post-Secondary Education

In their study on the predictors of outcomes in transition, Test and colleagues (2009) found four moderate-level predictors for post-school education: inclusion in general education, paid employment/work experience, transition program, and vocational education. Experiences in new environments, such as taking vocational education courses at a technical college, prior to high school graduation was helpful for youth.

When planning post-secondary education, it is important to consider the options that are available. Students may choose to attend a traditional two- or four-year college, a technical or vocationally focused school, or a rehabilitation program. Bruey and Urban (2009) outline the skills needed and other considerations for each of these settings in their transition guide. For example, they suggest that considerations for attending a technical school include whether or not the individual can structure time, set priorities, organize work independently, accept not being perfect, and take transportation to and from the school independently.

Some four-year universities offer college internship programs (CIP) for college-age students with ASD. Internship programs currently exist at Berkeley, California; Lee, Massachusetts; Melbourne, Florida; and Bloomington, Indiana. For the high tuition rate, students get a curriculum designed to meet their needs (Blackwelder-Williams, 2009). It is recommended that students entering post-secondary education contact the campus services to get the accommodations and supports they need to be successful.

Grandin and Duffy (2008) recommend taking a lighter load of classes and continuing with work experience because work experiences are how one learns to get along with others. Erik Weber, a recent graduate with an M.A. degree, shares his insights about the factors that made his post-secondary education a success (see In Their Words 10.2).

## Advocating for Policy Change

> Improving outcomes for job seekers with ASD is an important goal for our nation.—Kathleen Martinez, Assistant Secretary for Disability Employment Policy (2011, p. 16)

It is clear that improving adult services and outcomes for adolescents and adults with ASD will take families and professionals working together to raise awareness, advocate for policy change, and improve service quality by implementing evidence-based practices across contexts. In July 2010, Executive Order 13548, "Increasing the Federal Employment of Individuals with Disabilities," was signed by President Obama; it requires federal agencies to develop and implement action plans for increasing the number of individuals with disabilities employed in their workforce (Martinez, 2011). On July 29, 2011, Peter Bell, executive vice-president of Autism Speaks, and the father of Tyler, a young adult with ASD, was interviewed by Alison Steward of PBS. He stated, "We can make some major differences today that will improve the future for those who will become adults." One of the actions he described was the creation of a national consortium, Advancing Futures for Adults with Autism, that will focus on creating policy, increasing awareness, and ensuring opportunities for adults to find jobs and places to live.

---

**10.2    IN THEIR WORDS**    Erik N. Weber,  *M.P.A., San Diego State University,*
*Adult with Autism*

### Ready, Set, Go to College

When I was 5 years old and still nonverbal, after a year of intense therapy, professionals told my parents to find an institution for me to live out my life. That institution was college. Here are some things that helped me transition:

- Before I graduated from high school, I applied to a local community college. Some community colleges allow high school students to take classes after completing the sophomore year. Summer college classes are also a great option to earn college units while getting comfortable with the environment and workload.

- I also made an appointment with a counselor in Disabled Student Services. Prior to the meeting, I submitted my high school IEP that stated accommodations. The counselor set up my file and composed comparable accommodations for college. I signed a permission document for my mom to have access to my information or to be allowed to advocate on my behalf, if necessary. It is important to consider that you may have to file the same permission slip with *every* administrative office, so make multiple photocopies to distribute as needed, including your parents.

- Filing the FAFSA (financial aid forms) is necessary for financial aid and scholarships. I also found it is prudent to research options for disabled student assistance and for related scholarships available through LDA.

*(continued)*

## 10.2   *IN THEIR WORDS (continued)*

- I made an appointment with the college career center to take placement tests that helped identify personal interests, values, and preferences for potential career areas. The strengths and weaknesses displayed through test results can be translated into possible career paths, a step that helps to define what majors to pursue. It is advisable to research appropriate jobs based on the testing. In addition, I enrolled in a "personal development" course called College and Career Success that prepares new students with college study and survival tools.

- Once I had a realistic career path based on testing and Internet follow-up research, I met with an academic counselor to map out coursework toward a degree, a certificate, or later transfer to a four-year institution. Disabled students can have nine units designated as full-time status once they are officially enrolled as freshmen (after high school graduation). Most scholarships require students to be full-time. Courses taken at college prior to high school graduation can be used just for college later, or to satisfy high school coursework with a special permission form.

- Attending the new student orientation workshop is an important preparation for transition in education. Learning to ask for, and accept, **help** so that success would be assured was an important verification means for self-advocacy.

- When selecting classes for college, I started with subjects in my major area that were familiar and interesting to me. I checked www.ratemyprofessor.com to read about potential instructors. Likewise, I asked the academic and disabilities counselors if they had course/professor recommendations. The counselors were reluctant to respond but often revealed who had historically been more "disability friendly." I found it advisable to contact professors ahead for introduction by email and disclose a learning difference needing accommodation. My advice to aspiring college students is:

Do not hesitate to express your enthusiasm for taking each class. Be sure to introduce yourself in person on the first day. You will be surprised how willing most of them are to be helpful.

I advise that when the time comes and you are in class, *communicate* (speak up if you need help or a tutor); schedule testing appointments *early* with the teacher/ test center based on the class syllabus; participate verbally in class whenever appropriate; take advantage of free tutoring offered at most colleges for each class; keep an appointment book that documents *all due dates for assignments, all tests*, and when to turn in any related paperwork. Keep a list of phone numbers and email addresses for professors, counselors, the registrar, and financial offices. Make sure everyone has permission to speak with each other on your behalf.

If you are intending to transfer from a two-year to a four-year college, also go to that institution to find out their requirements so that any courses you take will be transferable. Some two-year colleges have "articulation agreements" with universities that ensure the courses will be accepted. This is very important to research ahead so that you don't waste time or tuition funds. Decide the "end game" and plan accordingly.

Historically, family members have been instrumental in advocating for children with disabilities, resulting in policy development and change. Their motivation is clear—wanting the best quality of education and quality of life for their loved ones. Alone they can make a difference for their family, and together they can make a difference for the community at large. Families who belonged to the Pennsylvania Association for Retarded Citizens took action against the Commonwealth of Pennsylvania because they felt that their children were not receiving the benefits of an education. Out of this action, legislation requiring a free, appropriate public education (FAPE) was created (Turnbull, Turnbull, Erwin, Soodak, & Shogren, 2011).

The pattern of families organizing to create policy and systems change, support each other, provide information, support professionals, and raise money for funds to conduct research of all kinds, including determining the best educational practices, continues through today. A few examples of organizations formed through the work of families include the Autism Society of America (ASA), the Medical Investigation of Neurodevelopmental Disorders (MIND) Institute, Autism Speaks, and the National Foundation for Autism Research (NFAR).

The history of the ASA is described on its website (www.autism-society.org). It was founded in 1965 by Bernard Rimland. Dr. Rimland was a parent of a son with autism and author of a key book that changed the perspective of professionals from blaming parents to considering a biological cause. The ASA, the oldest and largest grassroots organization within the autism community, is a leading source of information on autism. Supporters are connected through a working network of nearly 200 chapters nationwide, in almost every state. Each of the chapters, with parent and professional volunteer members, provides information, resources, support, and local grassroots advocacy. The organization holds a national conference and some local chapters arrange regional conferences. "The Autism Society firmly believes that employment is the first step toward meaningful engagement in one's community and in advancing one's economic security" (Sell, 2011, p. 8); thus, it is actively engaging in policy reform promoting Employment First as a service delivery strategy. Employment First supports the development of policies, practices, and procedures that lead to integrated employment.

The Medical Investigation of Neurodevelopmental Disorders (MIND) Institute at the University of California at Davis was started with funds that were received by a group of parents who lobbied the California legislature. The MIND's website states, "The M.I.N.D. Institute is an international, multidisciplinary research organization committed to excellence, collaboration and hope, striving to understand the causes and develop better treatments and ultimately cures for neurodevelopmental disorders. Standing shoulder to shoulder, families, scientists, physicians, educators, and administrators are working together to unlock the mysteries of the mind."

Autism Speaks was initiated by Suzanne and Bob Wright in 2005, as they describe on their website:

> In 2004, our grandson was diagnosed with autism. Helpless, we watched him slip away into the cruel embrace of this disorder. There seemed to be nothing we could do. But that heartbreaking moment was the beginning of what has become a very public and heartfelt mission. We launched **Autism Speaks** in February 2005 to help find a cure for autism by raising the funds that will facilitate and quicken the pace of research, to raise public awareness of autism, and to give hope to all those who suffer from this disorder.

The National Foundation for Autism Research (NFAR) is a San Diego–based organization that was started by Juan and Sharon Leon. The group organizes a Race for Autism each year and raises funds to support small research grants that benefit learners with ASD as well as a teacher's fund to provide materials for educators who work with students with autism spectrum disorders. Sharon and Juan Leon explain how and why they started this organization in In Their Words 10.3.

## 10.3 IN THEIR WORDS Sharon and Juan Leon, *Founders of the National Foundation for Autism Research*

## Doing So Much More than "Making Lemonade out of Lemons"

**Author (Laura J. Hall):** I've told you multiple times that I'm very impressed with the work that you do—the energy behind it, the professionalism, and your contribution certainly here in San Diego. What leads you to say "Okay, let's start an organization and put all that extra energy into the field"?

**Juan:** Ten years ago, when our son Michael received a diagnosis of autism, there was not a lot of concrete support systems either by the scientific or medical community or parent groups that could give you a lot of guidance or direction for treatment. There still is a huge need to make progress and have better answers on how to help our children do better and reach their potential.

**Sharon:** At the time, applied behavior analysis (ABA) therapy was not a mainstream form of behavioral intervention readily available for a child with autism. For the most part, it was up to the parent to research, to determine, and to fund what they thought was the best approach for their child. And this could feel quite overwhelming when you may not be a medical expert, behavioral expert, or an educator.

**Juan:** The first five to seven years, we focused on Michael and his needs. We spent a lot of time and energy understanding what was available in terms of different alternative programs, and what was available from the mainstream community. Sometimes we had to seek legal action to get services. There's a lot of pressure on a parent to try everything to help your child. And there's also that guilty feeling when, if you don't do it, you're not doing enough for your child.

Since Michael's diagnosis in 1995, we saw the number of children being diagnosed with autism exponentially grow. And we wondered, "Does anyone outside the autism community know what's going on? What is happening on a community level to address their growing needs?"

In 2003, I started looking at the money being raised for autism and at how much money is raised per child with autism. By comparison, the funds raised by the autism community are much, much lower than other conditions. The autism community in 2003 raised between $20 or $30 million a year. Other organizations for diseases like cancer or muscular dystrophy raise over $200 million. Do you know how many requests for money we received in the mail during the eight years we had been directly affected by autism? Only a handful. I saw the need to have more people asking for donations for autism. And that's how NFAR came about. Autism needed more public awareness and more opportunities to raise the funds needed for research and development of pilot programs. We needed to do something positive in the world of autism—to make lemonade out of lemons.

I spent a lot of time looking for a name with the right elements before coming up with the National Foundation for Autism Research. The name tries to convey the mission and scope of the organization. Obviously, autism is an important one. My view at the time, and still is, is that we need an organization raising $50 or $100 million a year. And the only way to get that is to be *national*. We believe that the only way to make positive traction is through *research*, and that takes time and money. The only way to make this kind of progress is to do the hard work of raising money and investing in research—that is the *foundation* part.

**Sharon:** In San Diego, we wanted to look at "What are the needs of the community? What are the programs and services that are missing here? What are the programs and services that need to grow?" That's why the San Diego Race for Autism was initiated—to raise funds to benefit children living with autism in San Diego.

**Author:** Why did you create a grant for teachers?

**Juan:** With the growing epidemic of autism, teachers just don't have enough resources. Teachers are often caught between the parents' and the district's demands, especially in trying and evaluating emerging innovative programs. The San Diego Autism Teacher's Fund gives teachers opportunities to apply for funding for specialized programs, materials, and technology, and it allows us to get materials into their hands and into the hands of the students. A very important part of our grant making is funding research and pilot programs that can demonstrate results and that can be quickly duplicated in other sites. If a program is shown to work in one classroom, then the school district will be much more motivated to expand that program to other classrooms. The investment we make in one teacher and his or her students will be multiplied many times over.

**Sharon:** The teachers have all demonstrated a real love for teaching, and a lot of times they're put into difficult situations, particularly in special education where you have so many IEPs. Parents are interested in what's happening with their child and the time and resources given to their child. But a teacher has a full caseload, right, and needs to give time and effort to each one of her students. Sometimes the support systems within the classroom are good and sometimes they're not so good, and what we want to do is figure out "How can we best support the teachers so that they can most effectively teach the students?" Our ultimate goal is for the student to receive the resources he or she needs to be successful in life.

**Juan:** And when the students are making progress, everybody wins.

At the initiation of parents, or in collaboration with parents, some of the more renowned programs for learners with autism spectrum disorders were organized (Handleman & Harris, 2006). Some programs started in church basements (McClannahan & Krantz, 2006; Meyer et al., 2006), and today these programs are models for the implementation of evidence-based practices, or those based on applied behavior analysis. Families remain essential partners.

## Call for Optimism and Action in the Creation of Communities of Practice

The good news is that we do have evidence-based practices, practices based on applied behavior analysis that we know are effective

in increasing the quality of life for individuals with autism spectrum disorders. We know the most effective forms of training for educators involve didactic information from knowledgeable sources, then on-site coaching from someone knowledgeable and skilled in evidence-based practice, and opportunity for modeling and feedback. Many more educators can become increasingly skilled and increasingly effective in their work.

We know that implementation of evidence-based practices takes years and that systems change, and we know that the support of administrators is important for sustained change. Systems change takes a lot of knowledge and effort. However, we have seen how groups of parents and groups of parents and professionals, when working in partnership, have changed policy and practices; have raised funds for research; and have created state-of-the-art schools, and meaningful communities of practice. Creating partnerships and focusing our work as educators on evidence-based practices is clearly the direction for positive change.

## SUGGESTIONS FOR DISCUSSION

1. Identify the potential benefits and possible barriers to completing person-centered planning.
2. Find the location of the center for independent living (CIL) in your state and describe the type of services provided to the local community.
3. Conduct a debate with one side arguing for the importance of embedding life skills into the high school curriculum of students with ASD and the other side arguing for the need to maintain a focus on high academic standards.
4. Reflect on your expectations for parent involvement in planning meetings, including the development of transition plans.
5. Define self-determination and identify how you are developing related skills in your practice.
6. You are a high school teacher and want to maximize the success of your students with ASD. Considering the factors that predict future employment and post-secondary education, what will you embed in the curriculum?
7. List the ways we can maximize the possibility of employment success for individuals with ASD.
8. Discuss why there are fewer published research studies with adults with ASD.

## RESOURCES

### Books

Autism Speaks™. (2011). *Transition tool kit: A guide to assist families on the journey from adolescence to adulthood.* Autism Speaks, Inc. Available from : http://www.autismspeaks.org/family-services/tool-kits/transition-tool-kit.

Grandin, T., & Duffy, K. (2008). *Developing talents: Careers for individuals with Asperger syndrome and high-functioning autism.* Shawnee Mission, KS: Autism Asperger Publishing Co.

Wehman, P., M. D., Smith, M. D., & Schall, C. (2009). *Autism and the transition to adulthood: Success beyond the classroom.* Baltimore, MD: Brookes.

### Websites

*www.autism-society.org*
   Autism Society of America
*www.autismspeaks.org*
   Autism Speaks
*www.narpaa.org*
   National Association of Residential Providers for Adults with Autism
*www.nfar.org*
   National Foundation for Autism Research
*www.nlts2.org*
   National Longitudinal Transition Study 2

*www.peoplefirstca.org*

People First® of California, Inc.: Self-Advocates Training Self-Advocates ("We are people first, our disability is second!")

*www.projectsearch.us*

Project SEARCH (internships and employment)

*www.researchautism.org*

Organization for Autism Research

*www.teaching-family.org*

Description of the teaching-family model for residential services

*www.ucdmc.ucdavis.edu/mindinstitute*

MIND Institute at the University of California at Davis

# References

Abrahams, B. S., & Geschwind, D. H. (2008). Advances in autism genetics: On the threshold of a new neurobiology. *Nature Reviews Genetics, 9,* 341–355.

Adamson, L. B., & Chance, S. E. (1998). Coordinating attention to people, objects, and language. In A. M. Wetherby, S. F. Warren, J. Reichle (Eds.) *Transitions in prelinguistic communication,* (pp. 15–37). Baltimore, MD: Brookes.

Akshoomoff, N., Corsello, C., & Schmidt, H. (2006). The role of Autism Diagnostic Observation Schedule in the assessment of autism spectrum disorders in school and community settings. *The California School Psychologist, 11,* 3–14.

Akshoomoff, N. A., & Stahmer, A. (2006). Early intervention programs and policies for children with autism spectrum disorders. In H. E. Fitzgerald, B. M. Lester, & B. Zuckerman (Eds.), *The crisis in youth mental health: Crisis issues and effective programs* (pp. 109–131). Westport, CT: Praeger.

Alberto, P. A., & Troutman, A. C. (2009). *Applied behavior analysis for teachers* (8th ed.). Upper Saddle River, NJ: Pearson Education.

Alcantara, P. R. (1994). Effects of videotape instructional package on the purchasing skills of children with autism. *Exceptional Children, 61,* 40–55.

Allen, K. D., & Cowan, R. J. (2008). Naturalistic teaching procedures. In J. K. Luiselli, D. C. Russo, W. P. Christian, & S. M. Wilczynski (Eds.), *Effective practices for children with autism: Educational and behavioral support interventions that work* (pp. 213–240). New York: Oxford University Press.

American Psychiatric Association. (1980). *Diagnostic and statistical manual of mental disorders* (3rd ed.). Washington, DC: Williams & Wilkins.

American Psychiatric Association. (1987). *Diagnostic and statistical manual of mental disorders* (3rd ed. rev). Washington, DC: Williams & Wilkins.

American Psychiatric Association. (1994). *Diagnostic and statistical manual of mental disorders* (4th ed.). Washington, DC: Williams & Wilkins.

American Psychiatric Association. (2000). *Diagnostic and statistical manual of mental disorders* (4th ed. – text revised). Washington, DC: Williams & Wilkins.

American Psychiatric Association. DSM5 development. *http://www .dsm5.org/Pages/Default.aspx.* Retrieved January 26, 2012.

American Speech-Language-Hearing Association. (2005). *Evidence-based practice in communication disorders* [Position Statement]. *www.asha .org/policy. doi: 10.1044/policy. PS2005-00221*

Anderson, J. L., Albin, R. W., Mesaros, R. A., Dunlap, G., & Morelli-Robbins, M. (1993). Issues in providing training to achieve comprehensive behavioral support. In J. Reichle & D. P. Wacker (Eds.), *Communicative alternatives to challenging behavior: Integrating functional assessment and intervention strategies* (pp. 363–406). Baltimore, MD: Brookes.

Anderson, S. R., & Romanczyk, R. G. (1999). Early intervention for young children with autism: Continuum-based behavioral models. *Journal of the Association for Persons with Severe Handicaps, 24*(3), 162–173.

Anderson, S. R., Taras, M., & Cannon, B. O. (1996). Teaching new skills to young children with autism. In C. Maurice, G. Green, & S. Luce (Eds.), *Behavioral intervention for young children with autism: A manual for parents and professionals* (pp. 181–193). Austin, TX: Pro-ed.

Anzalone, M. E., & Williamson, G. G. (2000). Sensory processing and motor performance in autism spectrum disorders. In A. M. Wetherby & B. M. Prizant (Eds.), *Autism spectrum disorders: A transactional developmental perspective* (pp. 143–166). Baltimore, MD: Brookes.

Apple, A. L., Billingsley, F., & Schwartz, I. S. (2005). Effects of video modeling alone and with self-management on compliment-giving behaviors of children with high- functioning ASD. *Journal of Positive Behavior Interventions, 7*(1), 33–46.

Asher, S. R., Parker, J. G., & Walker, D. L. (1996). Distinguishing friendship from acceptance: Implications for intervention and assessment. In W. M. Bukowski, A. F. Newcomb, & W. W. Hartup (Eds.), *The company they keep: Friendship in childhood and adolescence* (pp. 366–405). New York: Cambridge University Press.

Aspy, R., & Grossman, B. G. (2007). *The Ziggurat model: A framework for designing comprehensive interventions for individuals with high-functioning autism and Asperger syndrome.* Shawnee Mission, KS: AAPC.

Association for Children's Mental Health. (2004). *Evidence based practices for families: Beliefs, definitions, suggestions.* Lansing, Michigan: Author.

Attwood, T. (1998). *Asperger's syndrome: A guide for parents and professionals.* London: Jessica Kingsley.

Attwood, T., Firth, U., & Hermelin, B. (1988). The understanding and use of interpersonal gestures by autistic and Down syndrome children. *Journal of Autism and Developmental Disorders, 18*(2), 241–257.

Autism Research Institute. (2009). Parent ratings of behavioral effects of biomedical interventions. ARI Publication 34/March 2009. San Diego, CA.

Autism Society of America, Retrieved June 1, 2011, from *http://www .autismsociety.org/site/PageServer? pagename=about_whatis_home.*

Autism Speaks™ (2011). *Transition tool kit: A guide to assist families on the journey from adolescence to adulthood. www.AutismSpeaksorg:* Author.

Ayllon, T. (1999). *How to use token economy and point systems* (2nd ed.). Austin, TX: Pro-ed.

Ayres, A. J. (1972). *Sensory integration and learning disabilities.* Los Angeles, CA: Western Psychologiccal Services.

Ayres, K. M., & Langone, J. (2005). Intervention and instruction with video for students with autism: A review of the literature. *Education and Training in Developmental Disabilities, 40*(2), 183–196.

Baer, D. M., Wolf, M. M., & Risley, T. (1968). Current dimensions of applied behavior analysis. *Journal of Applied Behavior Analysis, 1,* 91–97.

Baer, D. M., Wolf, M. M., & Risley, T. R. (1987). Some still-current dimensions of applied behavior analysis. *Journal of Applied Behavior Analysis, 20,* 313–327.

Bagnato, S. J., Neisworth, J. T., & Munson, S. M. (1997). *Linking assessment and early intervention: An authentic curriculum-based approach.* Baltimore, MD: Brookes.

Bailey, J., & Burch, M. (2011). *Ethics for behavior analysis.* New York: Routledge.

Bailey, A., Le Couteur, A., Gottesman, I., Bolton, P., Simonoff, E., Yuzda, F., et al. (1995). Autism as a strongly genetic disorder: Evidence from a British twin study. *Psychological Medicine, 25,* 63–77.

Baird, G., Charmon, T., Baron-Cohen, S., Cox, A., Swettenham, J., Wheelwright, S., et al. (2000). A screening instrument for autism at 18 months of age: A 6-year follow-up study. *Journal of the American Academy of Child and Adolescent Psychiatry, 39,* 694–702.

Bakeman, R., & Adamson, L. B. (1984). Coordinating attention to people and objects in mother-infant and peer-infant interaction. *Child Development, 55,* 1278–1289.

Baker, S. K., Plasencia-Pienado, J. & Lezcano-Lytle, V. (1998). The use of curriculum-based measurement with language-minority students. In M. R. Shinn (Ed.), *Advanced applications of curriculum-based measurement* (pp. 175–213). New York: Guilford Press.

Baker-Ericzen, M. J., Stahmer, A. C., & Burns, A. (2007). Child demographics associated with outcomes in a community-based pivotal response training program. *Journal of Positive Behavior Interventions, 9,* 52–60.

Bambara, L. M., Nonnemacher S., & Kern, L. (2009). Sustaining school-based individualized positive behavior support: Perceived barriers and enablers. *Journal of Positive Behavior Interventions, 11,* 161–176.

Banda, D. R., & Grimmett, E. (2008). Enhancing social and transition behaviors of persons with autism through activity schedules. A review. *Education and Training in Developmental Disabilities, 43,* 324–333.

Bandura, A. (1977). *Social learning theory.* Upper Saddle River, NJ: Prentice-Hall.

Baranek, G. T. (2002). Efficacy of sensory and motor interventions for children with autism. *Journal of Autism and Developmental Disorders, 32*(5), 397–422.

Baron-Cohen, S., Allen, J., & Gillberg, C. (1992). Can autism be detected at 18 months? The needle, the haystack and the CHAT. *British Journal of Psychiatry, 161,* 839– 843.

Baron-Cohen, S., Cox, A., Baird, G., Sweettenham, J., Nightingale, N., Morgan, K., Drew A., & Charman, T. (1996). Psychlological markers in the detection of autism in infancy in a large population. *British Journal of Psychiatry, 168,* 158– 163.

Barrera, I., & Corso, R. M. (2003). *Skilled dialogue: Strategies for responding to cultural diversity in early childhood.* Baltimore, MD: Brookes.

Barrera, I., & Kramer, L. (2009). *Using skilled dialogue to transform challenging interactions: Honoring identity, voice, & connection.* Baltimore, MD: Brookes.

Barry, L. M., & Singer, G. H. S. (2001). A family in crisis: Replacing the aggressive behavior of a child with autism toward an infant sibling. *Journal of Positive Behavior Interventions, 3*(1), 28–38.

Barthelemy, C., Hamenry, L., & LeLord, G. (1995). *L'autisme de enfant: La therapie d'echange et de developpement.* Paris: Expansion Scientifique Francaise.

Bates, E. (1979). Intentions, conventions, and symbols. In E. Bates, L. Benigni, I. Bretherton, L. Camaioni, & V. Volterra (Eds.), *The emergence of symbols* (pp. 33–42). New York: Academic Press.

Bauminger, N. (2007). Brief report: Group social-multimodal intervention for HFASD. *Journal of Autism and Developmental Disabilities, 37,* 1605–1615.

Bauminger, N., Solomon, M., Aciezer, A., Heung, K., Gazit, L., Brown, J., & Rogers, S. J. (2008). Children with autism and their friends: A multidimensional study of friendship in high-functioning autism spectrum disorder. *Journal of Abnormal Child Psychology, 36,* 135–150.

Beck, J. S. (1995). *Cognitive therapy: Basics and beyond.* New York: Guilford Press.

Becker, R. L. (2000). *Reading-free vocational interest inventory (second edition).* Columbus, OH: Elbern Publications.

Behavior Analyst Certification Board. (2010). Guidelines for responsible conduct. Retrieved June 5, 2011, from *http://www.bcab.com.*

Beisler, J. M., & Tsai, L. Y. (1983). A pragmatic approach to increase expressive language skills in young autistic children. *Journal of Autism* and *Developmental Disorders, 13*(3), 287–303.

Ben-Arieh, J., & Miller, H. J. (2009). *The educator's guide to teaching students with autism spectrum disorders.* Thousand Oaks, CA: Corwin.

Berument, S. K., Rutter, M. L., Lord, C., Pickles, A., & Bailey, A. (1999). Autism screening questionnaire: Diagnostic validity. *British Journal of Psychiatry, 175,* 444–451.

Betz, A., Higbee, T. S., & Reagon, K. A. (2008). Using joint activity schedules to promote peer engagement in preschoolers with autism. *Journal of Applied Behavior Analysis, 41,* 237–241.

Beukelman, D. R., & Mirenda, P. (1998). *Augmentative and alternative communication: Management of severe communication disorders in children and adults.* Baltimore, MD: Brookes.

Birnbrauer, J. S., & Leach, D. J. (1993). The Murdock early intervention program after 2 years. *Behavior Change, 10,* 63–74.

Blackwelder-Williams, S. (2009). Bridging the gap: Students on the spectrum find hope after high school. *Autism Advocate, 57*(4), 27–30.

Blair, K. C., Lee, I., Cho, S., & Dunlap, G. (2011). Positive behavior support through family-school collaboration for young children with autism. *Topics in Early Childhood Special Education, 31*(1), 22–36.

Blankenship, K., Erickson, C. A., Stigler, K. A., Posey, D. J., & McDougle, C. J. (2011). Psychopharmacological treatment of autism. In D. G. Amaral, G. Dawson, & D. H. Geschwind (Eds.), *Autism spectrum disorders* (pp. 1196–1214). New York: Oxford University Press.

Blockberger, S., & Sutton, A. (2003). Toward linguistic competence: Language experiences and knowledge of children with extremely limited speech. In J. Light, D. Beukelman, & J. Reichle (Eds.), *Communicative competence for individuals who use AAC: From research to effective practice* (pp. 63–106). Baltimore, MD: Brookes.

Bloom, L. (1993). *The transition from infancy to language: Acquiring the power of expression.* New York: Cambridge University Press.

Bock, S. J., Stoner, J. B., Beck, A. R., Hanley, L., & Prochnow, J. (2005). Increasing functional communication in non-speaking preschool children: Comparison of PECS and VOCA. *Education and Training in Developmental Disabilities, 40,* 264–278.

Bogdashina, O. (2005). *Communication issues in autism and Asperger syndrome: Do we speak the same language?* London: Jessica Kingsley.

Bondy, A. S., & Frost, L. A. (1994, August). The picture exchange communication system. *Focus on Autistic Behavior, 9*(3), 1–18.

Bondy A. S., & Frost, L. A. (2001). *A picture's worth: PECS and other visual communication strategies in autism.* Bethesda, MD: Woodbine House.

Bondy, A. S., & Frost, L. A. (2009). The Picture Exchange Communication System: Clinical and research applications. In P. Mirenda & T. Iacono (Eds.), *Autism spectrum disorders and AAC* (pp. 279–302). Baltimore, MD: Brookes.

Bonggat, P., & Hall, L. J. (2010). Evaluation of the effects of sensory integration-based intervention by a preschool special education teacher. *Education and Training in Autism and Developmental Disabilities, 45,* 294–302.

Boreen, J., Johnson, M. K., Niday, D., & Potts, J. (2009). *Mentoring beginning teachers: Guiding, reflecting, coaching.* Portland, ME: Stenhouse.

Boutot, E. A., & Bryant, D. P. (2005). Social integration of students with autism in inclusive settings. *Education and Training in Developmental Disabilities, 40*(1), 14–23.

Bradshaw, C. P., Mitchell, M. M., & Leaf, P. J. (2010). Examining the effects of schoolwide positive behavioral interventions and supports on student outcomes: Results from a randomized controlled effectiveness trial in elementary schools. *Journal of Positive Interventions, 12,* 133–148.

Brady, N. C., & Halle, J. W. (1997). Functional analysis of communicative behaviors. *Focus on Autism, 12*(2), 95–104.

Bricker, D., Capt, B., & Pretti-Frontczak, K. (2002). *Assessment, Evaluation, and Programming System for infants and children: Vol. 2 Test birth to three years and three to six years.* Baltimore, MD: Brookes.

Bricker, D., Pretti-Frontczak, K., Johnson, J. J., & Straka, E. (2002). *Assessment, Evaluation, and Programming System for infants and children: Vol. 1 Administration guide.* Baltimore, MD: Brookes.

Bricker, D., & Waddell, M. (2002a). *Assessment, Evaluation, and Programming System for infants and children: Vol. 3 AEPS curriculum for birth to three years.* Baltimore, MD: Brookes.

Bricker, D., & Waddell, M. (2002b). *Assessment, Evaluation, and Programming System for infants and children: Vol. 4 AEPS curriculum for three to six years.* Baltimore, MD: Brookes.

Brigance, A. H. (1995). *BRIGANCE® employability skills inventory.* North Billerica, MA: Curriculum Associates.

Brinton, B., & Fujiki, M. (1995). Conversational intervention with children with specific language impairment. In M. Fey, J. Windsor, & S. Warren (Eds.), *Language intervention: Preschool through the elementary years* (pp. 183–212). Baltimore, MD: Brookes.

Brock, S. E., Jimerson, S. R., & Hansen, R. L. (2006). *Identifying, assessing and treating autism at school.* New York: Springer Science+Business Media, Inc.

Bronfenbrenner, U. (1979). *The ecology of human development.* Cambridge, MA: Harvard University Press.

Browder, D. M. (2001). Curriculum and assessment for students with moderate and severe disabilities. New York: Guilford Press.

Brown, J. R., & Rogers, S. J. (2003). Cultural issues in autism. In S. Ozonoff, S. J. Rogers, & R. L. Hendren (Eds), *Autism spectrum disorders: A research review for practitioners* (pp. 209–226). Washington DC: American Psychiatric Publishing, Inc.

Brown, W. H., & Odom, S. L. (1994). Strategies and tactics for promoting generalization and maintenance of young children's social behavior. *Research in Developmental Disabilities, 15*, 99–118.

Bruey, C. T., & Urban, M. B. (2009). *The autism transition guide: Planning the journey from school to adult life.* Bethesda, MD: Woodbine House.

Brunner, D. L., & Seung, H. K. (2009). Evaluation of the efficacy of communication-based treatments for autism spectrum disorders: A literature review. *Communication Disorders Quarterly, 31*, 15–41.

Buday, E. M. (1995). The effects of signed and spoken words taught with music on sign and speech imitation by children with autism. *Journal of Music Therapy, 32*, 189–202.

Buffington, D. M., Krantz, P. J., McClannahan, L. E. & Poulson, C. L. (1998). Procedures for teaching appropriate gestural communication skills to children with autism. *Journal of Autism and Developmental Disorders, 28*(6), 535–545.

Buggey, T. (1995). An examination of the effectiveness of videotaped self-modeling in teaching specific linguistic structures to preschoolers. *Topics in Early Childhood Special Education, 15*, 434–458.

Buggey, T. (2005). Video self-modeling applications with students with autism spectrum disorder in a small private school setting. *Focus on Autism and Other Developmental Disabilities, 20*, 52–63.

Buggey, T. (2009). Seeing is believing: Video self-modeling for people with autism and other developmental disabilities. Bethesda, MD: Woodbine House.

Buie, T., Fuchs, G. J., Furuta, G. T., Kooros, K., Levy, J., Lewis, J. D., Wershil, B. K., & Winter, H. (2010). Recommendations for evaluation and treatment of common gastrointestinal problems in children with ASDs. *Pediatrics, 125*, Supplement 1, 19–29.

Burmaster, E. (2007). *Opening doors to postsecondary education and training: Planning for life after high school.* Madison: Wisconsin Department of Public Instruction.

Byrd, H. B. (2002). Instructional strategies for African American learners with cognitive disabilities. In F. E. Obiakor & B. A. Ford (Eds). *Creating successful learning environments for African American learners with exceptionalities* (pp. 55–66). Thousand Oaks, CA: Corwin.

California Department of Education. (2009). Preschool English learners: Principles and practices to promote language, literacy, and learning—A resource guide (2nd ed.). Sacramento, CA: Child Development Division, California Department of Education.

Callahan, K., & Rademacher, J. A. (1999). Using self-management strategies to increase the on-task behavior of a student with autism. *Journal of Positive Behavior Interventions, 1*(2), 117–122.

Campbell, J. M. (2003). Efficacy of behavioral interventions for reducing problem behavior in persons with autism: A quantitative synthesis of single-subject research. *Research in Developmental Disabilities, 24*, 120–138.

Carnahan, C., Harte, H., Schumacher-Dyke, K., Hume, K, & Borders, C. (2011). Structured work systems: Supporting meaningful engagement in preschool settings for children with autism spectrum disorders. *Young Exceptional Children, 14*(1), 2–16.

Carnahan, C. R., Hume, K., Clarke, L., & Borders, C. (2009). Using structured work systems to promote independence and engagement for students with autism spectrum disorders. *TEACHING Exceptional Children, 41*(4), 6–14.

Carpenter, E. M., Nagell, K., & Tomasello, M. (1998). Social cognition, joint attention, and communicative competence from 9 to 15 months of age. *Monographs of the Society for Research in Child Development, 63*(4), 1–176.

Carpenter, M. (2006). Instrumental, social, and shared goals and intentions in imitation. In S. J. Rogers and J. S. G. Williams (Eds.), *Imitation and the social mind: Autism and typical development* (pp. 48–70). New York: Guilford Press.

Carpenter, M., Frankel, F., Marina, M., Duan, N., & Smalley, S. L. (2004). Internet treatment delivery of parent-adolescent conflict training for families with an ADHD teen: A feasibility study. *Child and Family Behavior Therapy, 26*(3), 1–20.

Carr, E. G. (1977). The motivation of self-injurious behavior: A review of some hypotheses. *Psychological Bulletin, 84*, 800–816.

Carr, E. G. (2011). Positive behavior support and problem behavior. In D. G. Amaral, G. Dawson, & D. H. Geschwind (Eds.), *Autism spectrum disorders* (pp. 1144–1155). New York: Oxford University Press.

Carr, E. G., & Darcy, M. (1990). Setting generality of peer modeling in children with autism. *Journal of Autism and Developmental Disorders, 20*(1), 45–59.

Carr, E. G., Dunlap, G., Horner, R. H., Koegel, R. L., Turnbull, A. P., Sailor, W., Anderson, J., Albin, R. W., Koegel, L. K., & Fox, L. (2002). Positive behavior support: Evolution of an applied science. *Journal of Positive Behavior Interventions, 4*, 4–16, 20.

Carr, E., & Durand, M. (1985). Reducing behavior problems through functional communication training. *Journal of Applied Behavior Analysis, 18*, 111–126.

Carr, E. G., Levin, L., McConnachie, G., Carlson, J. I., Kemp, D. C., & Smith, C. E. (1994). *Communication-based intervention for problem behavior: A user's guide for producing positive change.* Baltimore, MD: Brookes.

Carr, J., Nicolson, A., & Higbee, T. (2000). Evaluation of a brief multiple-stimulus preference assessment in a naturalistic context. *Journal of Applied Behavior Analysis, 33*, 353–357.

Carter, A. S., Messinger, D. S., Stone, W. L., Celimli, S., Nahmias, A. S., & Yoder, P. (2011). A randomized controlled trial of Hanen's "More Than Words" in toddlers with early autism symptoms. *Journal of Child Psychology and Psychiatry, 52,* 741–752.

Case-Smith, J., & Arbesman, M. (2008). Evidence-based review of interventions for autism used in or of relevance to occupational therapy. *American Journal of Occupational Therapy, 62,* 416–429.

Causton-Theoharis, J. N., & Malmgren, K. W. (2005). Increasing peer interactions for students with severe disabilities via paraprofessional training. *Exceptional Children, 71*(4), 431–444.

Cederland, M., Hagberg, B., Billsted E., Gillberg, J. C., & Gillberg, C. (2008). Asperger syndrome and autism: A comparative longitudinal follow-up study more than 5 years after original diagnosis. *Journal of Autism and Developmental Disorders, 38,* 72–85.

Chakrabarti, S., & Frombonne, E. (2001). Pervasive developmental disorders in preschool children. *Journal of the American Medical Association* [Special Issue], *285*(24), 3093–3099.

Chambless, D. L., Baker, M. J., Baucom, D. H., Beutler, L. E., Calhoun, K. S., Crits-Christoph, P., . . . Woody, S. R. (1998). Update on empirically validated therapies, II. *The Clinical Psychologist, 51*(1), 3–15.

Champagne, M. P., & Walker-Hirsch, L. Circles curriculum: Intimacy & relationships. Santa Barbara, CA: John Stanfield.

Chance, P. (2008). The teacher's craft: The 10 essential skills of effective teaching. Long Grove, IL: Waveland Press.

Chandler, L. K., & Dahlquist, C. M. (2006). *Functional assessment: Strategies to prevent and remediate challenging behavior in school settings.* Upper Saddle River, NJ: Pearson Education.

Chapman, R., & Miller, J. (1980). Analyzing language and communication in the child. In R. Schiefelbusch (Ed.), *Nonspeech language and communication.* Baltimore, MD: University Park Press.

Charlop, M. H., Greenberg, A. L., & Chang, G. T. (2011). Augmentative

and alternative communication systems. In D. G. Amaral, G. Dawson, & D. H. Geschwind (Eds.), *Autism spectrum disorders* (pp. 1129–1143). New York: Oxford University Press.

Charlop, M. H., & Milstein, J. P. (1989). Teaching autistic children conversational speech using video modeling. *Journal of Applied Behavior Analysis, 22,* 275–285.

Charlop, M. H., & Walsh, M. (1986). Increasing autistic children's spontaneous verbalizations of affection through time delay and modeling procedures. *Journal of Applied Behavior Analysis, 19,* 307–314.

Charlop-Christy, M. H., Carpenter, M., Le, L., LeBlanc, L. A., & Kellet, K. (2002). Using the Picture Exchange Communication System wth children with autism: Assessment of PECs acquisition, speech, social-communicative behavior, and problem behavior. *Journal of Applied Behavior Analysis, 35,* 213–231.

Charlop-Christy, M. H., & Daneshvar, S. (2003). Using video modeling to teach perspective taking to children with autism. *Journal of Positive Behavior Interventions, 5,* 12–22.

Charlop-Christy, M., & Haymes, L. K. (1998). Using objects of obsession as token reinforcers for children with autism. *Journal of Autism and Developmental Disorders, 28,* 189–198.

Cihak, D., Fahrenkrog, C., Ayres, K. M., & Smith, C. (2010). The use of video modeling via a video iPod and a system of least prompts to improve transitional behaviors for students with autism spectrum disorders in the general education classroom. *Journal of Positive Behavior Interventions, 12,* 103–115.

Cihak, D. F., & Schrader, L. (2008). Does the model matter? Comparing video self- modeling and video adult modeling for task acquisition and maintenance by adolescents with autism spectrum disorder. *Journal of Special Education Technology, 23*(3), 9–20.

Cirrin, F. M., & Penner, S. G. (1995). Classroom-based and consultative service delivery models for language intervention. In M. Fey, J. Windsor, & S. Warren (Eds.), *Language*

*Intervention: Preschool through the Elementary Years* (pp. 333–362). Baltimore, MD: Brookes.

Clark, E. (1977). From gesture to word: On the natural history of deixis in language acquisition. In J. S. Bruner & A. Garton (Eds.), *Human growth and development*. Oxford, England: Oxford University Press.

Clark, G. M., & Patton, J. R. (1997). *Transition planning inventory*. Austin, TX: Pro-ed.

Cohen, H., Amerine-Dickens, M., & Smith, T. (2006). Early intensive behavioral treatment: Replication of the UCLA Model in a community setting. *Developmental and Behavioral Pediatrics, 27*(2), 145–155.

Coleman, M. (2005). A neurological framework. In M. Coleman (Ed.), *The neurology of autism* (pp. 40–74). New York: Oxford University Press.

Coleman, M., & Betancur, C. (2005). Introduction. In M. Coleman (Ed.), *The neurology of autism* (pp. 3–39). New York: Oxford University Press.

Colorado Health Sciences (1987). Communicating with preverbal and young children [video].

Conroy, M. A., Asmus, J. M., Sellers, J. A., & Ladwig, C. N. (2005). The use of an antecedent-based intervention to decrease stereotypic behavior in a general education classroom: A case study. *Focus on Autism and Other Developmental Disabilities, 20*(4), 223–230.

Constantino, J. N. (2005). *Social Responsiveness Scale: Parent form*. Los Angeles: Western Psychological Services.

Cook, E. H. (1998). Genetics of autism. *Mental Retardation and Developmental Disabilities Research Reviews, 4,* 113–120.

Coonrod, E. E., & Stone, W. L. (2005). Screening for autism in young children. In F. Volkmar, R. Paul, A. Klin, & D. Cohen (Eds.), *Handbook of autism and pervasive developmental disorders* (pp. 707–729). Somerset, NJ: John Wiley.

Cooper, J., Heron, T., & Heward, W. (2007). *Applied behavior analysis* (2nd ed.). Columbus, OH: Pearson, Education.

Council for Exceptional Children. (2010). *Special education professional ethical principles*. Alexandria, VA: Author.

Courchesne, E. (2011). "Neurodevelopmental Studies of Autism: From MRI and fMRI to Neurons and Gene Pathways." Keynote Address: 10th International Meeting for Autism Research conference, May, San Diego, CA.

Courchesne, E., Townsend, J., Akshoomoff, N. A., Saitoh O., Yeung-Courchesne, R., & Lincoln, A. J. (1994). Impairment in shifting attention in autistic and cerebellar patients. *Behavioral Neuroscience, 108*, 848–865.

Courchesne, E., Webb, S. J., & Schumann, C. M. (2011). From toddler to adults: The changing landscape of the brain in autism. In D. G. Amaral, G. Dawson, & D. H. (Eds.), *Autism spectrum disorders* (pp. 611–631). New York: Oxford University Press.

Cox, A. L., Gast, D. L., Luscre, D., & Ayres, K. M. (2009). The effects of weighted vests on appropriate in-seat behaviors of elementary-age students with autism and severe to profound intellectual disabilities. *Focus on Autism and Other Developmental Disabilities, 24*, 17–26.

Craig, H. K., & Evans, J. L. (1989). Turn exchange characteristics of SLI children's simultaneous and nonsimultaneous speech. *Journal of Speech & Hearing Disorders, 54*(3), 334–347.

Creedon, M. P. (1973). Language development in nonverbal autistic children using a simultaneous communication system. Paper retrieved on June 20, 2006, from ERIC database.

Crone, D. A., Hawken, L. S., & Bergstrom, M. K. (2007). A demonstration of training, implementing, and using functional behavior assessment in 10 elementary and middle school settings. *Journal of Positive Behavioral Interventions, 9*, 15–29.

Crosland, K. A., Zarcone, J. R., Lindauer, S. E., Valdovinos, M. G., Zarcone, T. J., Hellings, J. A., & Schroeder, S. R. (2003). Use of functional analysis methodology in the evaluation of medication effects. *Journal of Autism and Developmental Disorders, 33*(3), 271–279.

Daniels, V. I. (2002). Maximizing the learning potential of African American learners with gifts and talents. In F. E. Obiakor & B. A. Ford (Eds). *Creating successful learning environments for African American learners with exceptionalities* (pp. 95–106). Thousand Oaks, CA: Corwin.

Dawson, G. (2008). Early behavioral intervention, brain plasticity, and the prevention of autism spectrum disorder. *Developmental and Psychopathology, 20*, 775–803.

Dawson, G., Meltzoff, A. N., Osterling, J., Rinaldi, J., & Brown, E. (1998). Children with autism fail to orient to naturally occurring social stimuli. *Journal of Autism and Developmental Disorders, 28*(6), 479–485.

Dawson, G., & Osterling, J. (1997). Early intervention in autism. In M. J. Guralnick (Ed.) *The effectiveness of early intervention* (pp. 307–326). Baltimore, MD: Brookes.

Dawson, G., Rogers, S., Munson, J., Smith, M., Winter, J., Greenson, J., Donaldson, A., & Varley, J. (2010). Randomized, controlled trial of an intervention for toddlers with autism: The Early Start Denver Model. *Pediatrics, 125*, e17–e23.

Dawson, G., & Watling, R. (2000). Interventions to facilitate auditory, visual, and motor integration in autism: A review of the evidence. *Journal of Autism and Developmental Disorders, 30*, 415–421.

DEC/NAEYC. (2009). *Early childhood inclusion: A summary*. Chapel Hill: The University of North Carolina, FPG Child Development Institute.

DeGangi, G. A., & Greenspan, S. I. (2001). Research on the FEAS: Test development, reliability, and validity studies. In S. I., Greenspan, G. DeGangi, & S. Wieder (Eds). *The Functional Emotional Assessment Scale (FEAS) for infancy and early childhood* (pp. 167–191). Bethesda, MD: Interdisciplinary Council on Developmental and Learning Disorders.

DeLeon, I., & Iwata, B. (1996). Evaluation of multiple-stimulus presentation format for assessing reinforcer preferences. *Journal of Applied Behavior Analysis, 29*, 519–533.

Devlin, S. D., & Harber, M. M. (2004). Collaboration among parents and professionals with discrete trial training in the treatment of autism. *Education and Training in Developmental Disabilities, 39*(4), 291–300.

Dietz, C., Swinkels, S., van Daalen, E., van Engeland, H., & Buitelaar, J. K. (2006). Screening for autism spectrum disorder in children aged 14–15 months. II. Population screening with the Early Screening of Autistic Traits (ESAT) questionnaire. Design and general findings. *Journal of Autism and Developmental Disorders, 36*, 713–722.

Division of Early Childhood of the Council for Exceptional Children. (2010). Position Statement: Responsiveness to ALL children, families, and professionals: Integrating cultural and linguistic diversity into policy and practice. Missoula, MT: Author.

Dobson, S., Upadhyaya, S., McNeil, J., Venkateswaran, S., & Gilderdale, D. (2001). Developing an information pack for the Asian careers of people with autism spectrum disorders. *International Journal of Language and Communication Disorders, 36*, 216–221.

Dodge, D. T., Colker, L. J., & Heroman, C. (2006). *The creative curriculum for preschool* (4th ed,). Washington, DC: Teaching Strategies.

Dombro, A. L., Colker, L. J., & Dodge, D. T. (2003). *The creative curriculum for infants & toddlers* (rev. ed.). Washington, DC: Teaching Strategies.

Dowrick, P. W., & Dove, C. (1980). The use of self-modeling to improve swimming performance of spina bifida children. *Journal of Applied Behavior Analysis, 13*, 51–56.

Dowrick, P. W., & Hood, M. (1981). Comparison of self-modeling and small cash incentives in a sheltered workshop. *Journal of Applied Behavior Analysis, 66*, 394–397.

Drager, K. D. R., Light, J. C., & Finke, E. H. (2009). Using AAC technologies to build social interaction with young children with autism spectrum disorders. In P. Mirenda & T. Iacono (Eds.), *Autism spectrum disorders and AAC* (pp. 247–278). Baltimore, MD: Brookes.

Drahota, A., Wood, J. J., Sze, K. M., & Van Dyke, M. (2011). Effects of cognitive behavior therapy on daily living skills in children with high-functioning autism and concurrent anxiety disorders. *Journal of Autism and Developmental Disorders, 41,* 257–265.

D'Souza, Y., Fombonne, E., & Ward, B. J. (2006). No evidence of persisting measles virus in peripheral blood mononuclear cells from children with autism spectrum disorder. *Pediatrics, 118,* 1664–1675.

Duchnowski, A. J., & Kutash, K. (1997). Future research in special education: A systems perspective. In J. L. Paul, M. Churton, H. Rosselli-Kostoryz, W. C. Morse, K. Morfo, C. Lavely, & D. Thomas (Eds.), *Foundations of special education: Basic knowledge informing research and practice in special education* (pp. 236–246). New York: Brookes/Cole.

Dunlap, G., & Fox, L. (1999). A demonstration of behavioral support for young children with autism. *Journal of Positive Behavior Intervention, 1*(2), 77–87.

Dunlap, G., Iovannone, R., & Kincaid, D. (2008). Essential components for effective autism educational programs. In J. K. Luiselli, D. C. Russo, W. P. Christian, & S. M. Wilczynski (Eds.), *Effective practices for children with autism: Educational and behavioral support interventions that work* (pp. 111–135). New York: Oxford University Press.

Dunn, W. (1999). *Sensory profile.* San Antonio, TX: Psychological Corporation.

Dunst, C. J., Raab, M., Trivette, C. M., & Swanson, J. (2010). Community-based everyday child learning opportunities. In R. A. McWilliam (Ed.), *Working with families of young children with special needs* (pp. 60–92). New York: Guilford Press.

Durand, V. M. (1988). The Motivation Assessment Scale. In M. Hersen & A. Bellack (Eds.), *Dictionary of behavioral assessment techniques* (pp. 309–310). Elmsford, NY: Pergamon Press.

Durand, V. M. (1990). Severe behavior problems: A functional communication training approach. New York: Guilford Press.

Durand, V. M., Bertotti, D. & Weiner, J. (1993). Functional communication training: Factors affecting effectiveness, generalization and maintenance. In J. Reichle & D. Wacker (Eds.), *Communication approaches to the management of challenging behavior* (pp. 317–340). Baltimore, MD: Brookes.

Durand, V. M., & Carr, E. G. (1987). Social influences on "self-stimulatory" behavior: Analysis and treatment application. *Journal of Applied Behavior Analysis, 20,* 119–132.

Durand, V. M., & Crimmins, D. B. (1987). Assessment and treatment of psychotic speech in an autistic child. *Journal of Autism and Developmental Disorders, 17*(1), 17–28.

Durand, V. M., & Merges, E. (2001). Functional communication training: A contemporary behavior analytic intervention for problem behavior. *Focus on Autism and Other Developmental Disorders, 16*(2), 110–119.

Dworzynski, K., Happe, F., Bolton, P., & Ronald, A. (2009). Relationship between symptom domains in autism spectrum disorders: A population based twin study. *Journal of Autism and Developmental Disorders, 39,* 1197–1210.

Dyches, T. T., Wilder, L. K., Sudweeks, R., Obiakor, F. E., & Algozzine, B. (2004). Multicultural perspectives on autism. *Journal of Autism and Developmental Disorders, 34,* 211–222.

Dyer, K. (1987). The competition of autistic stereotyped behavior with usual and specially assessed reinforcers. *Research in Developmental Disabilities, 8,* 607– 626.

Dyer, K. (1989). The effects of preference on spontaneous verbal requests in individuals with autism. *Journal of the Association for Persons with Severe Handicap, 14,* 184–189.

Dykens, E. M., & Lense, M. (2011). Intellectual disabilities and autism spectrum disorder: A cautionary note. In D. G. Amaral, G. Dawson, & D. H. (Eds.), *Autism spectrum disorders* (pp. 263–284). New York: Oxford University Press.

Edelson, S. M., Edelson, M. G., Kerr, D. C. R., & Grandin, T. (1999). Behavioral and physiological effects of deep pressure on children with autism: A pilot study evaluating the efficacy of Grandin's Hug Machine. *American Journal of Occupational Therapy, 53*(2), 145–152.

Eikeseth, S. (2009). Outcomes of comprehensive psycho-educational interventions for young children with autism. *Research in Developmental Disabilities, 30,* 158–178.

Elder, J. H., Shankar, M., Shuster, J., Theriaque, D., Burns, S., & Sherrill, L. (2006). The gluten-free, casein-free diet in autism: Results of a preliminary double blind clinical trial. *Journal of Autism and Developmental Disorders, 36*(3), 413–420.

Eldevik, S. Eikeseth, S., Jahr, E., & Smith, T. (2006). Effects of low-intensity behavioral treatment for children with autism and mental retardation. *Journal of Autism and Developmental Disorders, 36*(2), 211–224.

Eldevik, S., Hastings, R. P., Hughes, J. C., Jahr, E., Eikeseth, S., & Cross, S. (2009). Meta-analysis of early intensive behavioral intervention for children with autism. *Journal of Clinical Child and Adolescent Psychology, 38,* 439–450.

Erbas, D., Tekin-Iftar, E., & Yucesoy, S. (2006). Teaching special education teachers how to conduct functional analysis in natural settings. *Education and Training in Developmental Disabilities, 41*(1), 28–36.

Escalona, A., Field, T., Singer-Strunck, R., Cullen, C., & Hartshorn, K. (2001). Brief report: Improvements in the behavior of children with autism following massage therapy. *Journal of Autism and Developmental Disorders, 31*(5), 513–516.

Esch, B. E., & Carr, J. E. (2004). Secretin as a treatment for autism: A review of the evidence. *Journal of Autism and Developmental Disorders, 34,* 543–556.

Fay, W. H. (1980a). Aspects of language. In W. H. Fay & A. L. Schuler (Eds.), *Emerging language in autistic children* (pp. 51–85). Baltimore, MD: University Park Press.

Fay, W. H. (1980b). Aspects of speech. In W. H. Fay & A. L. Schuler (Eds.), *Emerging language in autistic children* (pp. 19–50). Baltimore, MD: University Park Press.

Feldman, R. S., McGee, G. G., & Mann, L. (1993). Nonverbal affective decoding ability in children with autism and in typical preschoolers. *Journal of Early Intervention, 17*(4), 341–350.

Fenske, E. C., Zalenski, S., Krantz, P. J. & McClannahan, L. E. (1985). Age at intervention and treatment outcome for autistic children in a comprehensive intervention program. *Analysis and Intervention in Developmental Disabilities, 5,* 49–58.

Ferraioli, S., & Harris, S. L. (2011). Treatments to increase social awareness and social skills. In B. Reichow, P. Doehring, D. V. Cicchetti, & F. R. Volkmar (Eds.), *Evidence-based practices and treatments for children with autism* (pp. 171–196). New York: Springer.

Field, T., Lasko, D., Mundy, P., Henteleff, T., Kabat, S., Talpins, S., & Dowling, M. (1997). Brief report: Autistic children's attentiveness and responsivity improve after touch therapy. *Journal of Autism and Developmental Disorders, 27*(3), 333–338.

Field, S., Sarver, M., & Shaw, S. (2003). Self-determination: A key to success in postsecondary education for students with learning disabilities. *Remedial and* Special Education, 24, 339–349

Findley, M., & Cooper, H. M. (1983). Locus of control and academic achievement: A literature review. *Journal of Personality and Social Psychology, 44*(4), 419–427.

Fiore, J. A. (2000). Core skills curriculum. In K. Quill (Ed.), *Do-Watch-Listen-Say: Social and communication intervention for children with autism* (pp. 191–394). Baltimore, MD: Brookes.

Fixsen, D. L., Naoom, S. F., Blase, K. A., Friedman, R. M., & Wallace, F. (2005). *Implementation research: A synthesis of the literature.* Tampa: University of South Florida, Louis

de la Parte Florida Mental Health Institute, the National Implementation Research Network (FMHI Publication #231).

Fombonne, E., Quirke, S., & Hagen, A. (2011). Epidemiology of pervasive developmental disorders. In D. G. Amaral, G. Dawson, & D. H. (Eds.), *Autism spectrum disorders* (pp. 90–111). New York: Oxford University Press.

Fombonne, E., Simmons, H., Ford, T., Meltzer, H. & Goodman, R. (2001). Prevalence of pervasive developmental disorders in the British Nationwide Survey of Child Mental Health. *Journal of the American Academy of Child & Adolescent Psychiatry, 40*(7), 820–827.

Fombonne, E., Zarakarian, R., Bennett, A., Meng, L., & McLean-Heywood, D. (2006). Pervasive developmental disorders in Montreal, Quebec, Canada: Prevalence and links with immunizations. *Pediatrics, 118,* e139–e150.

Ford, D. Y. (1996). *Reversing underachievement among gifted black students: Promising practices and programs.* New York: Teachers College Press.

Fovel, J. T. (2002). *The ABA program companion: Organizing quality programs for children with autism and PDD.* New York: DRL Books.

Fox, L., Benito, N., & Dunlap, G. (2002). Early intervention with families of young children with autism and behavior problems. In J. M. Lucyshyn, G. Dunlap, & R. W. Albin (Eds.), *Families and positive behavior support: Addressing problem behavior in family contexts* (pp. 251–267). Baltimore, MD: Brookes.

Fox, L., Dunlap, G., & Buschbacher, P. (2000). Understanding and intervening with children's challenging behavior: A comprehensive approach. In A. Wetherby & B. Prizant (Eds). *Autism spectrum disorders: A transactional developmental perspective* (pp. 307–331). Baltimore, MD: Brookes.

Fragoso, C., & Hall, L. J. (2006, May). *Stimulus equivalence as a second language teaching strategy for children with autism spectrum disorder.* Paper

presented at the 32nd Annual Convention of the Association for Behavior Analysis, International. Atlanta, Georgia.

Frankel, F. D., Gorospe, C. M., Chang, Y. C., & Sugar, C. A. (2011). Mothers' reports of play dates and observation of school playground behavior of children having high-functioning autism spectrum disorders. *Journal of Child Psychology and Psychiatry, 52,* 571–579.

Frankel, F., & Myatt, R. (2003). *Children's friendship training.* New York: Brunner- Routledge.

Frankel, F., Myatt, R., Cantwell, D. P., & Feinberg, D. T. (1997). Parent assisted children's social skills training: Effects on children with and without attention-deficit hyperactivity disorder. *Journal of the Academy of Child and Adolescent Psychiatry, 36,* 1056–1064.

Frea, W. D., & McNerney, E. K. (2008). Early intensive applied behavior analysis intervention for autism. In J. K. Luiselli, D. C. Russo, W. P. Christian, & S. M. Wilczynski (Eds.), *Effective practices for children with autism: Educational and behavioral support interventions that work* (pp. 83–110). New York: Oxford University Press.

Fredeen, R. M., & Koegel, R. L. (2006). The pivotal role of initiations in habilitation. In R. L. Koegel and L. K. Koegel (Eds.), *Pivotal response treatments for autism: Communication, social, and academic development* (pp. 141–164). Baltimore, MD: Brookes.

Freeman, B. J. (1997). Guidelines for evaluating intervention programs for children with autism. *Journal of Autism and Developmental Disorders, 27,* 641–651.

Freeman, B. J., Ritvo. E., & Miller, R. (1975). An operant procedure to teach an echolalic, autistic child to answer questions appropriately. *Journal of Autism and Childhood Schizophrenia, 5,* 169–176.

Freeman, S., & Dake, L. (1997). *Teach me language.* Langley, British Columbia: SKF.

Freire, P. (1998). Teachers as cultural workers: Letters to those who dare teach. Boulder, CO: Westview Press.

French, N. K., & Picket, A. L. (1997). Paraprofessionals in special education: Issues for teacher educators. *Teacher Education and Special Education, 20*(1), 61–73.

Frey, A. J., Park, K. L., Browne-Ferrigno, T., & Korfhage, T. L. (2010). The social validity of program-wide positive behavior support. *Journal of Positive Behavior Interventions, 12,* 222–235.

Frost, L. A., & Bondy, A. S. (2002). *The picture exchange communication system: Training manual* (2nd ed.). Newark, DE: Pyramid Educational Consultants.

Gabriels, R. L. (2011). Adolescent transition to adulthood and vocational issues. In D. G. Amaral, G. Dawson, & Geschwind, D. H. (Eds.), *Autism spectrum disorders* (pp. 1167–1181). New York: Oxford University Press.

Gantman, A., Kapp, S. K., Orenski, K., & Laugeson, E. A (2011 ). Social skills training for young adults with high-functioning autism spectrum disorders: A randomized controlled pilot study. *Journal of Autism and Developmental Disorders,* PubMed.gov, Epub ahead of print. *http://www.ncbi .nlm.nih.gov/pubmed/21915740*

Ganz, G. B., Tapscott Cook, K., & Earles-Vollrath, T. L. (2006). *How to write and implement social scripts.* Austin, TX: Pro-ed.

Ganz, J. B., & Sigafoos, J. (2005). Self-monitoring: Are young adults with MR and autism able to utilize cognitive strategies independently? *Education and Training in Developmental Disabilities, 40*(1), 24–33.

Ganz, J. B., & Simpson, R. L. (2004). Effects on communicative requesting and speech development of the Picture Exchange Communication System in children with characteristics of autism. *Journal of Autism and Developmental Disorders, 34,* 395–409.

Ganz, G. B., Tapscott Cook, K., & Earles-Vollrath, T. L. (2006). *How to write and implement social scripts.* Austin, TX: Pro-ed.

Garcia, E., Arias, M. B., Harris Murri, N. J., & Serna, C. (2010). Developing responsive teachers: A challenge for a demographic reality. *Journal of Teacher Education, 61,* 132–142.

Garcia-Coll, C. T. (1990). Developmental outcome of minority infants: A process-oriented look into our beginnings. *Child Development, 61,* 270–289.

Garfinkle, A., & Schwartz, I. S., (2002). Peer imitation: Increasing social interactions in children with autism and other developmental disabilities in inclusive preschool classrooms. *Topics in Early Childhood Special Education, 22*(1), 26–38.

Gay, G. (2000). *Culturally responsive teaching: Theory, research, & practice.* New York: Teachers College Press.

Gay, G. (2003). *Becoming multicultural educators.* San Francisco, CA: Jossey-Bass.

Gedney, G. & Hall, L. J. (2006, May). *The effects of culture on touch avoidance in children with autism.* Presentation at the 32nd Annual Convention for the Association for Behavior Analysis. Atlanta, Georgia.

Gena, A., Couloura, S., & Kymissis, E. (2005). Modifying the affective behavior of preschoolers with autism using in-vivo or video modeling and reinforcement contingencies. *Journal of Autism and Developmental Disorders, 35,* 545–556.

Gena, A., Krantz, P. J., McClannahan, L. E., & Poulson, C. L. (1996). Training and generalization of affective behavior displayed by youth with autism. *Journal of Applied Behavior Analysis, 29,* 291–304.

Gerhardt, P. F. (2009). *The current state of services for adults with autism.* Arlington, Virginia: Organization for Autism Research.

Gerhardt, P. F., & Lainer, I. (2011). Addressing the needs of adolescents and adults with autism: A crisis on the horizon. *Journal of Contemporary Psychotherapy, 41,* 37– 45.

Gersten, R., Fuchs, L. S., Compton, D., Coyne, M., Greenwood, C., & Innocenti, M. S. (2005). Quality indicators for group experimental and quasi-experimental research in special education, *Exceptional Children, 71,* 149–164.

Geschwind, D. H. (2011). Autism genetics and genomics: A brief overview and synthesis. In D. G. Amaral, G. Dawson, & Geschwind, D. H. (Eds.), *Autism spectrum disorders* (pp. 812–824). New York: Oxford University Press.

Ghezzi, P. M., & Bishop, M. R. (2008). Generalized behavior change in young children with autism. In J. K. Luiselli, D. C. Russo, W. P. Christian, S. M. Wilczynski (Eds.), *Effective practices for children with autism: Educational and behavioral support interventions that work* (pp. 137–158). New York: Oxford University Press.

Giangreco, M. F. (2010). One-to-one paraprofessionals for students with disabilities in inclusive classrooms: Is conventional wisdom wrong? *Intellectual and Developmental Disabilities, 48,* 1–13.

Giangreco, M. F., Broer, S. M., Suter, J. C. (2011). Guidelines for selecting alternatives to overreliance on paraprofessionals: Field-testing in inclusion-oriented schools. *Remedial and Special Education, 32,* 22–38.

Giangreco, M. F., Cloninger, C. J., & Iverson, V. S. (1998). *Choosing outcomes and accommodations for children (COACH): A guide to educational planning for students with disabilities* (2nd ed.). Baltimore, MD: Brookes.

Giangreco, M. F., Edelman, S. W., Luiselli, T. E., & MacFarland, S. Z. (1997). Helping or hovering? Effects of instructional assistant proximity on students with disabilities. *Exceptional Children, 64*(1), 7–18.

Giangreco, M. F., Suter, J. C., & Doyle, M. B. (2010). Paraprofessionals in inclusive schools: A review of recent research. *Journal of Educational and Psychological Consultation, 20,* 41–57.

Gibson, S. A. (2005). Developing knowledge of coaching. *Issues in Teacher Education, 14*(2), 63–74.

Gilliam, J. E. (1995). *Gilliam Autism Rating Scale (GARS).* Austin, TX: Pro-ed.

Gilliam, J. E. (2001). *Gilliam Asperger's Disorder Scale (GADS).* Austin, TX: Pro-ed.

Gilliam, J. E. (2005). *Gilliam Autism Rating Scale (GARS2).* Austin, TX: Pro-ed.

Girolametto, L., Sussman, F., & Weitzman, E. (2007). Using case study methods to investigate the effects of interactive intervention for children with autism spectrum disorders. *Journal of Communication Disorders, 40,* 470–492.

Glaeser, B. C., Pierson, M. R., & Fritschmann, N. (2003). Comic strip conversations: A positive behavioral support strategy. *TEACHING Exceptional Children, 36*(2), 14–19.

Glasberg, B. A. (2005). *Functional behavior assessment for people with autism: Making sense of seemingly senseless behavior.* Bethesda, MD: Woodbine House.

Glasberg, B. A. (2008). Stop that seemingly senseless behavior! *FBA-based intervention for people with autism.* Bethesda, MD: Woodbine House.

Goldstein, H. (2002). Communication intervention for children with autism: A review of treatment efficacy. *Journal of Autism and Developmental Disorders, 32,* 373–396.

Goldstein, H., & Cisar, C. L. (1992). Promoting interaction during sociodramatic play: Teaching scripts to typical preschoolers and classmates with disabilities. *Journal of Applied Behavior Analysis, 25,* 265–280.

Goldstein, H., & Morgan, L. (2002). Social interaction and models of friendship development. In H. Goldstein, L. Kaczmarek, & K. English (Eds.), *Promoting social communication* (pp. 5–26). Baltimore, MD: Brookes.

Golinkoff, R. M. (1986). "I beg your pardon?" The preverbal negotiation of failed messages. *Journal of Child Language, 13,* 455–476.

Gotham, K. Bishop, S. L., & Lord, C. (2011). Diagnosis of autism spectrum disorders. In D. G. Amaral, G. Dawson, & D. H. (Eds.), *Autism spectrum disorders* (pp. 30–43). New York: Oxford University Press.

Gotham, K., Risi, S., Pickles, A., & Lord, C. (2007). The Autism Diagnostic Observation Schedule: Revised algorithms for improved diagnostic validity. *Journal of Autism*

*and Developmental Disorders, 37,* 613–627.

Grandin, T. (1992). An inside view of autism. In E. Schopler and G. B. Mesibov (Eds.), *High-functioning individuals with autism* (pp. 105–126). New York: Plenum Press.

Grandin, T. (1999). *Visual thinking of a person with autism* [Video Presentation]. Arlington, TX: Future Horizons.

Grandin, T. (2005). My world is what I do. In T. Grandin and S. Barron (Eds), *Unwritten rules of social relationships: Decoding social mysteries through the unique perspectives of autism* (pp. 1–54). Arlington, TX: Future Horizons.

Grandin, T., & Barron, S. (2005). *Unwritten rules of social relationships: Decoding social mysteries through the unique perspectives of autism.* Arlington, TX: Future Horizons.

Grandin, T., & Duffy, K. (2008). *Developing talents: Careers for individuals with Asperger syndrome and high-functioning autism.* Shawnee Mission, KS: Autism Asperger Publishing Co.

Gray, C. (1994). *Comic strip conversations: Colorful, illustrated interactions with students with autism and related disorders.* Arlington, TX: Future Horizons.

Gray, C. (2010). *The new social story book.* Arlington, TX: Future Horizons.

Gray, C., & Garand, J. D. (1993). Social stories: Improving responses of student with autism with accurate social information. *Focus on Autistic Behavior, 8*(1), 1–10.

Green, G. (1996). Evaluating claims about treatment in autism. In C. Maurice, G. Green, & S. Luce (Eds.), *Behavioral intervention for young children with autism: A manual for parents and professionals* (pp. 15–28). Austin, TX: Pro-ed.

Green, G. (2001). Behavior analytic instruction for learners with autism: Advances in stimulus control technology. *Focus on Autism and Other Developmental Disabilities, 16,* 72–86.

Green, G. (2006, June). "Verbal behavior" and autism: A review and call for research. Paper presented for Arbutus Coast Presentations, Vancouver, British Columbia.

Green, J., Charman, T., McConachie, H., Alfred, C., et al. (2010). Parent-mediated communication-focused treatment in children with autism (PACT): A randomized controlled trial. *The Lancet, 375,* 2152–2161.

Green, V. A., Pituch, K. A., Itchon, J., Choi, A., O'Reilly, M., & Sigafoos, J. (2006). Internet survey of treatments used by parents of children with autism. *Research in Developmental Disabilities, 27,* 70–84.

Green, G., & Shane, H. C. (1994). Science, reason, and facilitated communication. *Journal of the Association for Persons with Severe Handicaps, 19,* 151–172.

Greenan, S., Powers, L. E., & Lopez-Vasquez, A. (2001). Multicultural aspects of parent involvement in transition planning. *Exceptional Children, 67,* 265–282.

Greenspan, S. (1990). How emotional development relates to learning [Video program guide]. In S. Greenspan (Ed.), *Floor Time: Tuning in to each child (supplement).* New York: Scholastic.

Greenspan, S. I., & DeGangi, G. (2001). *The Functional Emotional Assessment Scale administration and scoring form.* Bethesda, MD: Interdisciplinary Council on Developmental and Learning Disorders.

Greenspan, S. I., DeGangi, G., & Wieder, S. (2001). *The Functional Emotional Assessment Scale (FEAS) for infancy and early childhood.* Bethesda, MD: Interdisciplinary Council on Developmental and Learning Disorders.

Greenspan, S. I., & Lewis, D. (2002). *The affect-based language curriculum (ABLC): An intensive program for families, therapists and teachers.* Bethesda, MD: Interdisciplinary Council on Developmental and Learning Disorders.

Greenspan, S. I., & Wieder, S. (1997). Developmental patterns and outcomes in infants and children with disorders in relating and communicating: A chart review of 200 cases of children with autistic spectrum diagnoses. *Journal of Developmental and Learning Disorders, 1,* 87–141.

Greenspan, S. I., & Wieder, S. (1998). *The child with special needs: Encouraging intellectual and emotional growth.* Reading, MA: Perseus Books.

Greenspan, S. I., & Wieder, S. (1999). A functional developmental approach to autism spectrum disorders. *Association for Persons with Severe Handicaps, 24*(3), 147–161.

Greenspan, S. I., & Wieder, S. (2000). A developmental approach to difficulties in relating and communicating in autism spectrum disorders and related syndromes. In A. Wetherby & B. Prizant (Eds). *Autism Spectrum Disorders: A transactional developmental perspective* (pp. 279–306). Baltimore, MD: Brookes.

Greenspan, S. I., & Wieder, S. (2001). The clinical application of the FEAS. In S. I., Greenspan, G. DeGangi, & S. Wieder (Eds). *The Functional Emotional Assessment Scale (FEAS) for infancy and early childhood* (pp. 75–113). Bethesda, MD: Interdisciplinary Council on Developmental and Learning Disorders.

Greenspan, S. I., & Wieder, S. (2005a). Can children with autism master the core deficits and become empathetic, creative and reflective? A ten to fifteen year follow-up of a subgroup of children with autism spectrum disorders (ASD) who received a comprehensive Developmental, Individual Difference, Relationship-Based approach (DIR). *Journal of Developmental and Learning Disorders, 9,* 39–61.

Greenspan, S. I., & Wieder, S. (2005b). Floor time DVD training guide. Bethesda, MD: Interdisciplinary Council on Developmental and Learning Disorders.

Greenspan, S. I., & Wieder, S. (2006). *Engaging autism: Using the floor time approach to help children relate, communicate, and think.* Cambridge, MA: De Capo Lifelong Books.

Greenspan, S. I., & Wieder, S. (2011). Relationship-based early intervention approach to autistic spectrum disorders: The developmental, individual difference, relationship-based model (the DIR model). In D. G. Amaral, G. Dawson, & D. H. Geschwind (Eds.), *Autism spectrum disorders* (pp. 1068–1080). New York: Oxford University Press.

Greer, R. D., & Ross, D. E. (2008). *Verbal behavior analysis: Inducing and expanding new verbal capabilities with language delays.* Boston: Pearson Education.

Gresham, F. M., & Elliott, S. (1990). *The social skills rating system.* Circle Pines, MN: American Guidance Service.

Griffin-Shirley, N., Matlock, D. (2004). Paraprofessionals speak out: A survey. *RE:View, 36*(3), 127–36.

Grigal, M., Test, D. W., Beattie, J., & Wood, W. M. (1997). An evaluation of transition components of individualized education programs. *Exceptional Children, 63,* 357–372.

Grinker, R. R., Yeargin-Allsopp, M., & Boyle, C. (2011). Culture and autism spectrum disorders: The impact on prevalence and recognition. In D. G. Amaral, G. Dawson, & D. H. Geschwind (Eds.), *Autism spectrum disorders* (pp. 112–136). New York: Oxford University Press.

Gutstein, S. (2004). Going to the heart of autism: The Relationship Development Intervention program. [Brochure] Houston, TX: The Connections Center.

Gutstein, S. (2005, October). Going to the heart of autism. Presented at a two-day introductory workshop, San Diego, CA.

Gutstein, S. (2009). Empowering families through Relationship Development Intervention: An important part of the biopsychosocial management of autism spectrum disorders, *Annals of Clinical Psychiatry, 21,* 174–182.

Gutstein, S. E., Burgess, A. F., & Montfort, K. (2007). Evaluation of the Relationship Development Intervention program, *Autism, 11,* 397–411.

Gutstein, S. E., & Sheely, R. K. (2002a). *Relationship development intervention with young children.* New York: Jessica Kingsley.

Gutstein, S. E., & Sheely, R. K. (2002b). *Relationship development intervention with children, adolescents and adults: Social and emotional development activities for asperger syndrome, autism, PDD, and NLD.* New York: Jessica Kingsley.

Gutstein, S., & Sheely, R. K. (2004). *Going to the heart of autism: The Relationship Development Intervention program.* [DVD] Houston, TX: The Connections Center. http://www .rdiconnect.com/RDI/intro.asp.

Gutstein, S. E., & Whitney, T. (2002). Asperger syndrome and the development of social competence. *Focus on Autism and Other Developmental Disabilities, 17*(3), 161– 171.

Hackenberg, T. D. (2009). Token reinforcement: A review and analysis. *Journal of the Experimental Analysis of Behavior, 91,* 257–286.

Hagerman, R. J., Narcisa, V., & Hagerman, P. J. (2011). Fragile X: A molecular and treatment model for autism spectrum disorders. In D. G. Amaral, G. Dawson, & D. H. Geschwind (Eds.), *Autism spectrum disorders* (pp. 801–811). New York: Oxford University Press.

Hagner, D., & Cooney, B. F. (2005). "I do that for everybody": Supervising employees with autism. *Focus on Autism and Other Developmental Disabilities, 20,* 91–97.

Hall, E. T. (1976). *Beyond culture.* Garden City, NY: Doubleday.

Hall, L. J., Grundon, G. S., Pope, C., & Romero, A. B. (2010). Training paraprofessionals to use behavioral strategies when educating learners with autism spectrum disorders across environments. *Behavioral Interventions, 25,* 37–51.

Hall, L. J., & Macvean, M. L. (1997). Increasing the communicative behaviour of students with cerebral palsy through feedback to, and the selection of goals by integration assistants. *Behaviour Change, 14,* 174–183.

Hall, L. J., McClannahan, L. E. & Krantz, P. J. (1995). Promoting independence in integrated classrooms by teaching aides to use activity schedules and decreased prompts. *Education and Training in*

*Mental Retardation and Developmental Disabilities, 30,* 208–217.

Hall, L. J. & Russell, A. (2000, May) "Social interaction and communication strategies for children with moderate to severe cognitive disabilities". Contemporary Forums: The child with special needs, San Fransisco, CA.

Hall, L. J., & Smith, K. L. (1996). The generalisation of social skills by preferred peers with autism. *Journal of Intellectual and Developmental Disability, 21,* 313–330.

Halle, J. W. (1987). Teaching language in the natural environment: An analysis of spontaneity. *Journal of the Association for Persons with Severe Handicaps, 12,* 28–37.

Halle, J., Brady, N. C., & Drasgow, E. (2004). Enhancing socially adaptive communicative repairs of beginning communicators with disabilities. *American Journal of Speech-Language Pathology, 13,* 43–54.

Halpern, A. S., Herr, C. M., Wolf, N.K., Lawson, J. D., Doren, B., & Johnson, M. D. (1997). *Next S.T.E.P.: Student transition and education planning: Teacher manual.* Eugene: University of Oregon.

Hancock, T. B., & Kaiser, A. P. (2002). The effects of trainer-implemented enhanced milieu teaching on the social communication of children with autism. *Topics in Early Childhood Special Education, 22,* 39–54.

Handleman, J. S., & Harris, S. L. (2001). *Preschool education programs for children with autism.* Austin, TX: Pro-ed.

Handleman, J. S., & Harris, S. L. (2006). *School-age education programs for children with autism.* Austin, TX: Pro-ed.

Hanna, S., & Wilford, S. (1990). *Floor Time: Tuning in to each child.* New York: Scholastic.

Hanson, M. J., & Lynch, E. W. (2004). *Understanding families: Approaches to diversity, disability and risk.* Baltimore, MD: Brookes.

Hanson, M. J., & Lynch, E. W. (2010). Working with families from diverse backgrounds. In R. A. McWilliam (Ed.), *Working with families of young children with special needs* (pp. 147–174). New York: Guilford Press.

Haring, T. G., Breen, C. G., Pitts-Conway, V., & Gaylord-Ross, R. (1986). Use of differential reinforcement of other behavior during dyadic instruction to reduce stereotyped behavior of autistic students. *Journal of Mental Deficiency, 90*(6), 694–702.

Harris, S. L., Handleman, J. S., Gordon, R., Kristoff, B., & Fuentes, F. (1991). Changes in cognitive and language functioning of preschool children with autism. *Journal of Autism and Developmental Disorders, 21*(3), 281–290.

Harris, S. L., & Weiss, M. J. (2007). *Right from the start: Behavioral intervention for young children with autism.* Bethesda, MD: Woodbine House.

Harris, S. L., & Wolchik, S. A. (1979). Suppression of self-stimulation: Three alternative strategies. *Journal of Applied Behavior Analysis, 12,* 185–198.

Harrower, J. K., & Dunlap, G. (2001). Including children with autism in general education classrooms. *Behavior Modification, 25*(5), 762–784.

Hart, B., & Risley, T. R. (1974). The use of preschool materials for modifying the language of disadvantaged children. *Journal of Applied Behavior Analysis, 1,* 253–256.

Hart, B. & Risley, T. R. (1975). Incidental teaching of language in the preschool. *Journal of Applied Behavior Analysis, 8,* 411–420.

Hart, B., & Risley, T. R. (1995). *Meaningful differences in the everyday experience of young American children.* Baltimore, MD: Brookes.

Harvard Business Essentials. (2004). *Coaching and mentoring: How to develop top talent and achieve stronger performance.* Boston, MA: Harvard Business School Press.

Heflin, L. J., & Alaimo, D. F. (2007). *Students with autism spectrum disorders: Effective instructional practices.* Upper Saddle River, NJ: Pearson Education.

Held, M. F., Thoma, C. A., & Thomas, K. (2004). "The John Jones show": How one teacher facilitated self-determined transition planning for a young man with autism. *Focus on Autism and Other Developmental Disabilities, 19,* 177–188.

Hemmeter, M., & Kaiser, A. (1994). Enhanced milieu teaching: An analysis of parent- implemented language intervention. *Journal of Early Intervention, 18,* 269–289.

Hendricks, D. R., Smith, M. D., & Wehman, P. (2009). Teaching youth success: From classroom to community. In P. Wehman, M. D. Smith, & C. Schall (Eds.), *Autism and the transition to adulthood: Success beyond the classroom* (pp. 111–138). Baltimore, MD: Brookes.

Hendrickx, S. (2009). *Asperger syndrome & employment: What people with Asperger syndrome really really want.* London: Jessica Kingsley Publishers.

Henry, S., & Smith Myles, B. (2007). *The comprehensive autism planning system (CAPS) for individuals with Asperger syndrome, autism and related disabilities: Integrating best practices throughout the student's day.* Shawnee Mission, Kansas: Autism Asperger Publishing Co.

Hertz-Picciotto, I. (2011). Environmental risk factors in autism: Results from large-scale epidemiologic studies. In D. G. Amaral, G. Dawson, & D. H. Geschwind (Eds.), *Autism spectrum disorders* (pp. 827–862). New York: Oxford University Press.

Hilton, J. C., & Seal, B. C. (2007). Brief report: Comparative ABA and DIR trials in twin brothers with autism. *Journal of Autism and Developmental Disorders, 37,* 1197– 1201.

Hine, J. F., & Wolery, M. (2006). Using point-of-view video modeling to teach play to preschoolers with autism. *Topics in Early Childhood Special Education, 26,* 83– 93.

Hodgdon, L. A. (1998). *Visual strategies for improving communication.* Troy, MI: Quirk Roberts.

Holland, J. L. (1994). *The self-directed search: A guide to educational and vocational planning.* Odessa, FL: Psychological Assessment Resources.

Hooper, H., & Walker, M. (2002). Makaton peer tutoring evaluation: 10 years on. *British Journal of Learning Disabilities, 30,* 38–42.

Hoover, J. J. (2009). *Differentiating learning differences from disabilities.* Upper Saddle River, NJ: Pearson.

Horner, R. H., Albin, R. W., Sprague, J. R. & Todd, A. W. (2000). Positive behavior supports for students with severe disabilities. In M. E. Snell & F. Brown (Eds.), *Instruction of students with severe disabilities* (pp. 207–243). Columbus, OH: Merrill.

Horner, R. H., Carr, E. G., Halle, J., McGee, G., Odom, S., & Wolery, M. (2005). The use of single-subject research to identify evidence-based practice in special education. *Exceptional Children, 71*(2), 165–179.

Horner, R. H., Sugai, G., Smolkowski, K., Eber, L., Nakasato, J., Todd, A. W., & Esperanza, J. (2009). A randomized, wait-list controlled effectiveness trial assessing school-wide positive behavior support in elementary schools. *Journal of Positive Behavior Interventions, 11*, 133–144.

Houston, R., & Frith, U. (2000). *Autism in history: The case of Hugh Blair of Borgue.* Oxford: Blackwell.

Howard, J. S., Sparkman C. R., Cohen, H. G., Green, G. & Stanislaw, H. (2005). A comparison of intensive behavior analytic and eclectic treatments for young children with autism. *Research in Developmental Disabilities, 26*, 359–383.

Howlin, P. (2004). *Autism and Asperger syndrome: Preparing for adulthood.* London: Routledge.

Howlin, P., Magiati, I., & Charman, T. (2009). Systematic review of early intensive behavioral interventions for children with autism. *American Association on Intellectual and Developmental Disabilities, 114*, 23–41.

Hubbard, A. (2005). Academic modifications. In B. S. Myles (Ed). *Children and youth with Asperger syndrome* (pp. 35–58). Thousand Oaks, CA: Corwin.

Hudson, A., Melita, B., & Arnold, N. (1993). Brief report: A case study assessing the validity of facilitated communication. *Journal of Autism and Developmental Disorders, 23*(1), 165–173.

Hume, K., Bellini, S., & Pratt, C. (2005). The usage and perceived outcomes of early intervention and early childhood programs for young children with autism spectrum disorder. *Topics in Early Childhood Special Education, 25*(4), 195–207.

Hume, K., & Odom, S. (2007). Effects of an individual work system on the independent functioning of students with autism. *Journal of Autism and Developmental Disorders, 37*, 1166–1180.

Hume, K., & Reynolds, B. (2010). Implementing work systems across the school day: Increasing engagement in students with ASD. *Preventing School Failure, 54*, 228–227.

Hutchins, T. L., & Prelock, P. A. (2005). Using social stories and comic strip conversations to promote socially valid outcomes for children with autism. *Seminars in Speech and Language, 27*(1), 47–59.

Hwang, B., & Hughes, C. (2000). The effects of social interactive training on early social communicative skills of children with autism. *Journal of Autism and Developmental Disorders, 30*(4), 331–343.

Hyman, S. L., & Levy, S. E. (2011). Dietary, complementary and alternative therapies. In B. Reichow, P. Doehring, D. V. Cicchetti, & F. R. Volkmar (Eds.), *Evidence-based practices and treatments for children with autism* (pp. 275–293). New York: Springer Science+Business Media.

Iacono, T. A. (2003). Pragmatic development in individuals with developmental disabilities who use AAC. In J. Light, D. Beukelman, & J. Reichle (Eds.), *Communicative competence for individuals who use AAC: From research to effective practice* (pp. 323–360). Baltimore, MD: Brookes.

Iacono, T., Johnson, H., & Forster, S. (2009). Supporting the participation of adolescents and adults with complex communication needs. In P. Mirenda & T. Iacono (Eds.), *Autism spectrum disorders and AAC* (pp. 443–474). Baltimore, MD: Brookes.

Ingersoll, B. R. (2010). Teaching social communication: A comparison of naturalistic behavioral and development, social pragmatic approaches for children with autism spectrum disorders. *Journal of Positive Interventions, 12* (1), 33–43.

Ingersoll, B., & Dvortcsak, A. (2006). Including parent training in the early childhood special education curriculum for children with autism spectrum disorders. *Topics in Early Childhood Special Education, 26*, 179–187.

Ingersoll, B., R., & Dvortcsak, A. (2010a). *Teaching social communication to children with autism: A manual for parents.* New York: Guilford Press.

Ingersoll, B., & Dvortcsak, A. (2010b). *Teaching social communication to children with autism: A practitioner's guide to parent training.* New York: Guilford Press.

Ingersoll, B., Dvortcsak, A., Whalen, C., & Sikora, D. (2005). The effects of a developmental, social-pragmatic language intervention on rate of expressive language production in young children with autistic spectrum disorders. *Focus on Autism and Other Developmental Disabilities, 20*, 213–222.

Ingersoll, B., Lewis, E., & Kroman, E. (2007). Teaching the imitation and spontaneous use of descriptive gestures in young children with autism using a naturalistic behavioral intervention. *Journal of Autism and Developmental Disorders, 37*, 1446–1456.

Ingersoll, B., Schreibman, L. & Stahmer, A. (2001). Brief report: Differential treatment outcomes for children with autism spectrum disorder based on level of peer social avoidance. *Journal of Autism and Developmental Disorders, 31*, 343–349.

Interagency Autism Coordinating Committee. (2011). *Summary of advances in autism spectrum disorder research: 2010.* Bethesda, MD: Department of Health and Human Services.

Iwata, B. A., Dorsey, M. F., Slifer, K. J., Bauman, K. E., & Richman, G. S. (1982). Toward a functional analysis of self-injury. *Analysis and Intervention in Developmental Disabilities, 2*, 3–20.

Iwata, B. A., Pace, G. M., Dorsey, M. F., Zarcone, J. R., Vollmer, T. R., Smith, R. G., Rodgers, T. A., Lerman, D. C.,

Shore, B. A., Mazaleski, J. L., Goh, H., Cowdery, G. E., Kalsher, M. J., McCosh, K. C., & Willis, K. D. (1994). The functions of self-injurious behavior: An experimental-epidemiological analysis (reprinted). *Journal of Applied Behavior Analysis, 27,* 215–240.

Jahr, E. (1998). Current issues in staff training. *Research in Developmental Disabilities, 19*(1), 73–87.

Jahr, E., Eldevik, S., & Eikeseth, S. (2000). Teaching children with autism to initiate and sustain cooperative play. *Research in Developmental Disabilities, 21,* 151–169.

Joe, J. R., & Malach, R. S. (2004). Families with American Indian roots. In E. W. Lynch & M. H. Hanson (Eds.) *Developing cross-cultural competence: A guide for working with children and their families* (pp. 109–140). Baltimore, MD: Brookes.

Johnson, R. M. (1995). *The picture communication symbol guide.* Solana Beach, CA: Mayer-Johnson.

Johnston, S. S., & O'Neill, R. E. (2001). Searching for effectiveness and efficiency in conducting functional assessments: A review and proposed process for teachers and other practitioners, *Focus on Autism and Other Developmental Disabilities, 16*(4), 205–214.

Joyce, B., & Showers, B. (2002). *Student achievement through staff development* (3rd ed.). Alexandria, VA: Association for Supervision and Curricular Development.

Kaiser, A. P., & Hester, P. P. (1994). Generalized effects of enhanced milieu teaching. *Journal of Speech and Hearing Research, 37,* 1320–1340.

Kaiser, A. P., Nietfeld, J. P., & Roberts, M. Y. (2010). Applying evidence-based practices to support communication with children who have autism spectrum disorders. In H. H. Schertz, C. Wong, & S. L. Odom (Eds.), *Young Exceptional Children: Monograph Series No. 12 Supporting young children with autism spectrum disorders and their families* (pp. 39–53). Missoula, MT: Division of Early Childhood of CEC.

Kalyanpur, M., & Harry, B. (1999). *Culture in special education: Building reciprocal family-professional relationships.* Baltimore, MD: Brookes.

Kamps, D. M., Kravits, T., & Ross, M. (2002). Social-communicative strategies for school-age children. In H. Goldstein, L. Kaczmarek, K. English (Eds.), *Promoting social communication* (pp. 239–277). Baltimore, MD: Brookes.

Kamps, D. M., Potucek, J., Lopez, A. G., Kravits, T., & Kemmerer, K. (1997). The use of peer networks across multiple settings to improve social interaction for students with autism. *Journal of Behavioral Education, 7*(3), 335–357.

Kasari, C., Gulsrud, A. C., Wong, C., Kwon, S., & Locke, J. (2010). Randomized controlled caregiver mediated joint engagement intervention for toddlers with autism. *Journal of Autism and Developmental Disorders, 40,* 1045–1056.

Kasari, C., & Locke, J. (2011). Social skills interventions for children with autism spectrum disorders. In D. G. Amaral, G. Dawson, & D. H. Geschwind (Eds.), *Autism spectrum disorders* (pp. 1156–1166). New York: Oxford University Press.

Kasari, C., Sigman, M., Baumgartner, P., & Stipek, D. J. (1993). Pride and mastery in children with autism. *Journal of Child Psychology and Psychiatry, 34,* 353–362.

Kasari, C., Sigman, M., Mundy, P. & Yirmiya, N. (1988). Caregiver interactions with autistic children. *Journal of Abnormal Child Psychology, 16,* 45–56.

Kasari, C., Sigman, M., Yirmiya, N., & Mundy, P. (1993). Affective development and communication in young children with autism. In A. Kaiser and D. Gray (Eds.), *Enhancing children's communication: Research foundations for intervention* (pp. 201–222). Baltimore, MD: Brookes.

Kaymakcalan, H., & State, M. W. (2011). Rare genetic variants and autism spectrum disorders. In D. G. Amaral, G. Dawson, & D. H. Geschwind (Eds.), *Autism spectrum disorders* (pp. 722–736). New York: Oxford University Press.

Kayser, H. (1995). Intervention with children from linguistically and culturally diverse backgrounds. In M. Fey, J. Windsor, & S. Warren (Eds.) *Language Intervention: Preschool through the Elementary Years* (pp. 315–332). Baltimore, MD: Brookes.

Kea, C. D., Cartledge, G., & Bowman, L. J. (2002). Interventions for African American learners with behavioral problems. In F. E. Obiakor & B. A. Ford (Eds.) *Creating successful learning environments for African American learners with exceptionalities* (pp. 79–94). Thousand Oaks, CA: Corwin.

Keen, D., Sigafoos, J., & Woodyatt, G. (2005). Teacher responses to communicative attempts by children with autism. *Journal of Developmental and Physical Disabilities, 17*(1), 19–33.

Keenan, M. (2006). Empowering parents with science. In M. Keenan, M. Henderson, K.P. Kerr, & K. Dillenburger (Eds.), *Applied behaviour analysis and autism: Building a future together* (pp. 18–52). London: Jessica Kingsley.

Keenan, M., Henderson, M., Kerr, K. P., and Dillenburger, K. (2006). *Applied behaviour analysis and autism: Building a future together.* London: Jessica Kingsley.

Kennedy, C. H., & Itkonen, T. (1993). Effects of setting events on the problem behavior of students with severe disabilities. *Journal of Applied Behavior Analysis, 26,* 321–327.

Kern, J. K., Miller, V. S., Evans, P. A., & Trivedi, M. H. (2002). Efficacy of porcine secretin in children with Autism and Pervasive Developmental Disorder. *Journal of Autism and Developmental Disorders, 32*(3), 153–160.

Kern, J. K., Trivedi, M. H., Grannemann, B. D., Garver, C. R., Johnson, D. G., Andrews, A. A., Savla, J. S., Mehta, J. A., & Schroeder, J. L. (2007). Sensory correlations in autism. *Autism, 11,* 123–134.

Kimball, J. W., Kinney, E. M., Taylor, B. A., & Stromer, R. (2004). Video enhanced activity schedules for children with autism: A promising package for teaching social skills. *Education and Treatment of Children, 27*(3), 280–298.

Kimball, J. G., Lynch, K. M., Stewart, K. C., Williams, N. E., Thomas, M. A., & Atwood, K. D. (2007). Using salivary cortisol to measure the effects of a Wilbarger protocol-based procedure on sympathetic arousal: A pilot study. *American Journal of Occupational Therapy, 64,* 406–413.

Kise, J. A. G. (2006). *Differentiated coaching: A framework for helping teachers change.* Thousand Oaks, CA: Corwin.

Klein, M. D., & Chen, D. (2001). *Working with children from culturally diverse backgrounds.* Clifton Park, NY: Delmar.

Klin, A. (2011). Asperger's syndrome: From Asperger to modern day. In D. G. Amaral, G. Dawson, & D. H. Geschwind (Eds.), *Autism spectrum disorders* (pp. 44–59). New York: Oxford University Press.

Knoblauch, B., & Sorenson, B. (1998). IDEA's definition of disabilities. *ERIC Digest,* Reston VA: ERIC Clearinghouse on Disabilities and Gifted Education.

Koegel, L. K., Camarata, S. M., Valdez-Manchaca, M. C., & Koegel, R. L. (1998). Teaching children with autism to use a self-initiated strategy to learn expressive vocabulary. *American Journal on Mental Retardation, 102,* 358–369.

Koegel, L. K., Carter, C., & Koegel, R. L. (2003). Teaching children with autism self- initiations as a pivotal response. *Topics in Language Disorders, 23,* 134–145.

Koegel, L. K., Fredeen, R. M., Koegel, R. L., & Lin, R. (2011). Relationships, independence, and communication in autism and Asperger's disorder. In D. G. Amaral, G. Dawson, & D. H. Geschwind (Eds.), *Autism spectrum disorders* (pp. 1095–1112). New York: Oxford University Press.

Koegel, L. K., Koegel, R. L., Boettcher, M. A., Harrower, J., & Openden, D. (2006). Combining functional assessment and self-management procedures to rapidly reduce disruptive behaviors. In R. L. Koegel

& L. K. Koegel, (Eds.), *Pivotal response treatments for autism: Communication, social, and academic development* (pp. 245–258). Baltimore, MD: Brookes.

Koegel, L. K., Koegel, R. L., & Dunlap, G. (1996). *Positive behavioral support: Including people with difficult behavior in the community.* Baltimore, MD: Brookes.

Koegel, L. K., & LaZebnik, C. (2004). *Overcoming autism: Finding the answers, strategies, and hope that can transform a child's life.* New York: Viking.

Koegel, L. K., Stiebel, D., & Koegel, R. L. (1998). Reducing aggression in children with autism toward infant or toddler siblings. *Journal of the Association for Persons with Severe Handicaps, 23*(2), 111–118.

Koegel, R. L., Bruinsma, Y. E. M., & Koegel, L. K. (2006). Developmental trajectories with early intervention. In R. L. Koegel, & L. K. Koegel (Eds). *Pivotal response treatments for autism: Communication, social, and academic development* (pp. 131–140). Baltimore, MD: Brookes.

Koegel, R. L., Firestone, P. B., Kramme, K. W., & Dunlap, G. (1974). Increasing spontaneous play by suppressing self-stimulation in autistic children. *Journal of Applies Behavior Analysis, 7,* 521–528.

Koegel, R. L., & Frea, W. D. (1993). Treatment of social behavior in autism through modification of pivotal social skills. *Journal of Applied Behavior Analysis, 26,* 369–377.

Koegel, R. L., Frea, W. D., & Surratt, A. V. (1994). Self-management of problematic social behavior. In E. Schopler & G. B. Mesibov (Eds.), *Behavioral issues in autism* (pp. 81–97). New York: Plenum Press.

Koegel, R. L., & Koegel, L. K. (1990). Extended reductions in stereotypic behavior of students with autism through a self-management treatment package. *Journal of Applied Behavior Analysis, 23*(1), 119–127.

Koegel, R. L., & Koegel, L. K. (1995). *Teaching children with autism: Strategies for initiating positive interactions and improving learning opportunities.* Baltimore, MD: Brookes.

Koegel, R. L., & Koegel, L. K. (2006). *Pivotal response treatments for autism: Communication, social, and academic development.* Baltimore, MD: Brookes.

Koegel, R. L. Koegel, L. K. & Carter, C. M. (1999). Pivotal teaching interactions for children with autism. *School Psychology Review, 28,* 576–594.

Koegel, R. L., & Mentis, M. (1985). Motivation in childhood autism: Can they or won't they? *Journal of Child Psychology and Psychiatry, 26,* 185–191.

Koegel, R. L., Openden, D., Fredeen, R. M., & Koegel, L. K. (2006). The basics of pivotal response treatment. In R. L. Koegel & L. K. Koegel (Eds.), *Pivotal response treatments for autism: Communication, social, and academic development* (pp. 3–30). Baltimore, MD: Brookes.

Koegel, R. L., & Schreibman, L. (1977). Teaching autistic children to respond to simultaneous multiple cues. *Journal of Experimental Child Psychology, 24,* 299– 311.

Koegel, R. L., Schreibman, L., Good, A. Cerniglia, L., Murphy, C., & Koegel, L. K. (1989). *How to teach pivotal behaviors to children with autism: A training manual.* Unpublished manuscript, University of California, Santa Barbara.

Koegel, R. L., Werner, G. A., Vismara, L. A., & Koegel, L. K. (2005). The effectiveness of contextually supported play date interactions between children with autism and typically developing peers. *Research and Practice for Persons with Severe Disabilities, 30,* 93–102.

Koller, R. (2000). Sexuality and adolescents with autism. *Sexuality and Disability, 18,* 125–135.

Koppenhaver, D. A., Abraham, L. M., & Yoder, D. E. (1994). *Social and academic organization of composition lessons for AAC users.* Unpublished manuscript.

Koppenhaver, D. A., Pierce, P. L., Steelman, J. D., & Yoder, D. E. (1995). Contexts of early literacy intervention for children with developmental disabilities. In M. Fey, J. Windsor, & S. Warren (Eds.), *Language intervention: Preschool through the elementary years* (pp. 241–274). Baltimore, MD: Brookes.

Kraemer, B. (2008). Assessment for transition education and planning. In J. A. McLoughlin & R. B. Lewis (Eds.), *Assessing students with special needs* (7th ed., pp. 532–561). Upper Saddle River, NJ: Pearson.

Krantz, P. J. (Speaker). (1996). *The child who could not play.* [Video Presentation] Canadian Broadcast Corporation.

Krantz, P. J., & McClannahan, L. E. (1993). Teaching children with autism to initiate to peers: Effects of a script-fading procedure. *Journal of Applied Behavior Analysis, 26,* 121–132.

Krantz, P. J., & McClannahan, L. E. (1998). Social interaction skills for children with autism: A script adding procedure for beginning readers. *Journal of Applied Behavior Analysis, 31*(2), 191–202.

Krantz, P. J., Ramsland, S. E., & McClannahan, L. E. (1989). Conversational skills of autistic adolescents: An autistic peer as prompter. *Behavioral Residential Treatment, 4*(3), 171–189.

Krantz, P. J., Zalenski, S., Hall, L. J., Fenske, E., & McClannahan, L. E. (1981). Teaching complex language to autistic children. *Analysis and Intervention in Developmental Disabilities, 1,* 259–257.

Kratochwill, T. R., Sheridan, S. M., Carlson, J., & Lasecki, K. L. (1999). Advances in behavioral assessment. In C. R. Reynolds & T. B. Gutkin (Eds.), *The handbook of school psychology* (3rd ed., pp. 350–382). New York: Wiley.

Kremer-Sadlik, T. (2005). To be or not to be bilingual: Autistic children from multilingual families. In J. Cohen, K.T. McAlister, K. Rolstad, & J. MacSwan (Eds.), *Proceedings of the 4th International Symposium on Bilingualism* (pp. 1225–1234). Somerville, MA: Cascadilla Press.

Krug, D. A., Arick, J. R., & Almond, P. J. (1993). Autism Screening Instrument for Educational Planning (2nd ed.). Austin, TX: Pro-ed.

Kuhl, P. (2007). Is speech learning gated by the social brain? *Developmental Science, 10,* 110–120.

Kupperman, P., Bligh, S., & Barouski, K. (1992). The syndrome of hyperlexia vs. high functioning autism and Asperger's syndrome. Center for Speech and Language Disorders, 1–3. Paper retrieved June 20, 2006, from ERIC database.

Ladson-Billings, G. (1994). *The dreamkeepers.* San Fransisco: Jossey-Bass.

Lamb, J. A. (2011). Whole genome linkage and association analyses. In D. G. Amaral, G. Dawson, & D. H. Geschwind (Eds.), *Autism spectrum disorders* (pp. 669–689). New York: Oxford University Press.

Lamers, K., & Hall, L. J. (2003). The response of children with autism to preferred prosody during instruction. *Focus on Autism and Other Developmental Disabilities, 18*(2), 95–104.

Lang, R., Regester, A., Lauderdale, S., Ashbaugh, K., & Haring, A. (2010). Treatment of anxiety in autism spectrum disorders using cognitive behavior therapy: A systematic review. *Developmental Neurorehabilitation, 13,* 53–63.

Lantz, J. F., Nelson, J. M., & Loftin, R. L. (2004). Guiding children with autism in play: Applying the integrated play group model in school settings. *TEACHING Exceptional Children, 37*(2), 8–14.

Lattimore, L. P., Parsons, M. B., & Reid, D. H. Geschwind (2002). A prework assessment among adults with autism beginning a supported job. *Journal of Applied Behavior Analysis, 35,* 85–88.

Laugeson, E., & Frankel, F. (2010). *Social skills for teenagers with developmental and autism spectrum disorders: The PEERS treatment manual.* New York: Routledge.

Laugeson, E., Frankel, F., Gantman, A., Dillon, A., & Mogil, C. (2011). Evidence-based social skills training for adolescents with autism spectrum disorders: The UCLA PEERS Program. *Journal of Autism and Developmental Disorders,* PubMed.gov: EPub ahead of print. *http://www.ncbi.nlm.nih.gov/ pubmed/21858588*

Laugeson, E. A., Frankel, F., Mogil, C., & Dillon, A. R. (2009). Parent-

assisted social skills training to improve friendships in teens with autism spectrum disorders. *Journal of Autism and Developmental Disorders, 39,* 569–606.

Laushey, K. M., & Heflin, J. (2000). Enhancing social skills of kindergarten children with autism through the training of multiple peers as tutors. *Journal of Autism and Developmental Disabilities, 30*(3), 183–193.

Lavie, T., & Sturmey, P. (2002). Training staff to conduct a paired-stimulus preference assessment. *Journal of Applied Behavior Analysis, 10,* 197–205.

Lawton, K., & Kasari, C. (2010). Social development and intervention in young children with autism spectrum disorders. In H. H. Schertz, C. Wong, & S. L. Odom (Eds.), *Young Exceptional Children Monograph Series No. 12 Supporting young children with autism spectrum disorders and their families* (pp. 66–74). Missoula, MT: The Division of Early Childhood of the Council for Exceptional Children.

Lazar, M., & Kraemer, B. (2007). Self-employment in adults with autism spectrum disorder. Manuscript submitted for publication.

Leaf, R. (2008). Coaches primer: Assessing, benefitting, collaborating. In R. Leaf, M. Taubman, & J. McEachin (Eds.), *It's time for school: Building quality ABA educational programs for students with autism spectrum disorders* (pp. 93–135). New York: DRL Books.

Leaf, R., & McEachin, J. (1999). *A work in progress: Behavior management strategies and a curriculum for intensive behavioral treatment of autism.* New York: DRL Books.

LEAP Outreach Project. (2003a). *Classroom management in the inclusive classroom.* Teacher's Toolbox, *www.ttoobox.com.*

LEAP Outreach Project. (2003b). *Nurturing social skills in the inclusive classroom.* Teacher's Toolbox, *www.ttoobox.com.*

Leblanc, L. A., Esch, J., Sidener, T., & Firth, A. M. (2006). Behavioral language intervention for children with autism: Comparing applied verbal behavior and naturalistic teaching approaches. *Analysis of Verbal Behavior, 22,* 49–60.

Leblanc, M. P., Ricciardi, J. N., & Luiselli, J. K. (2005). Improving discrete trial instruction by paraprofessional staff through an abbreviated performance feedback intervention. *Education and Treatment of Children, 28*(1), 76–82.

LeCouteur, A., Lord, C., & Rutter, M. (2003). *The Autism Diagnostic Interview: Revised* (ADI-R). Los Angeles: Western Psychological Services.

Leekam, S. R., Libby, S. J., Wing, L., Gould, J. & Taylor, C. (2002). The Diagnostic Interview for Social and Communication Disorders: Algorithms for ICD-10 childhood autism and Wing and Gould autistic spectrum disorder. *Journal of Child Psychology and Psychiatry, 43*(3), 327–342.

Lerman, D. C., Vorndran, C. M., Addison, L., & Kuhn, S. C. (2004). Preparing teachers in evidence-based practices for young children with autism. *School Psychology Review, 33*(4), 510–526.

Leslie, A. M. (1987). Pretense and representation: The origins of "Theory of Mind." *Psychological Review, 94*(4), 412–426.

Lewis, L. S. (2002). Dietary intervention for the treatment of autism: Why implement a gluten and casein free diet? In W. Shaw (Ed.), *Biological treatments for autism and PDD* (pp. 159–178). Lenexa, KS: Great Plains Laboratory.

Lewis, T. J., & Sugai, G. (1999). Effective behavior support: A systems approach to proactive school-wide management. *Focus on Exceptional Children, 31*(6), 1–24.

Lewis, V., & Boucher, J. (1988). Spontaneous, instructed and elicited play in relatively able autistic children. *British Journal of Developmental Psychology, 6*(4), 325–339.

Liber, D. B., Frea, W. D., & Symon, J. B. G. (2008). Using time-delay to improve social play skills with peers for children with autism. *Journal of Autism and Developmental Disorders, 38,* 312–323.

Lifter, K. (2008). Developmental play assessment and teaching. In J. K. Luiselli, D. C. Russo, W. P. Christian, & S. M. Wilczynski (Eds.), *Effective practices for children with autism: Educational and behavioral support interventions that work* (pp. 299–324). New York: Oxford University Press.

Lifter, K., Sulzer-Azaroff, B., Anderson, S., & Cowdery, G. (1993). Teaching play activities to preschool children with disabilities: The importance of developmental considerations. *Journal of Early Intervention, 17,* 139–159.

Light, J. C. (2003). Shattering the silence: Development of communicative competence by individuals who use AAC. In J. Light, D. Beukelman, & J. Reichle (Eds.), *Communicative competence for individuals who use AAC: From research to effective practice* (pp. 3–38). Baltimore, MD: Brookes.

Light, J. C., Arnold, K. B., & Clark, E. A. (2003). Finding a place in the "social circle of life": The development of sociorelational competence by individuals who use AAC. In J. Light, D. Beukelman, & J. Reichle (Eds.), *Communicative competence for individuals who use AAC: From research to effective practice* (pp. 361–397). Baltimore, MD: Brookes.

Linder, T. (2008). *Transdisciplinay play-based assessment (second edition) (TPBA2).* Baltimore: Brookes.

Lock, A., Young, A., Service, V., & Chandler, P. (1990). Some observations on the origins of the pointing gesture. In V. Volterra & C. J. Erting (Eds.), *From gesture to language in hearing and deaf children* (pp. 42–55). New York: SpringerVerlag.

Lord, C., & Corsello, C. (2005). Diagnostic instruments in autistic spectrum disorders. In F. Volkmar, R. Paul, A. Klin, & D. Cohen (Eds.), *Handbook of autism and pervasive developmental disorders* (pp. 730–771). Somerset, NJ: Wiley.

Lord, C., & Magill, J. (1989). Methodological and theoretical issues in studying peer directed behavior and autism. In G. Dawson (Ed.), *Autism: Nature, diagnosis, and treatment* (pp. 326–345). New York: Guilford Press.

Lord, C., Rutter, M. L., DiLavore, P. C., & Risi, S. (2001). *The autism diagnostic observation schedule.* Los Angeles: Western Psychological Services.

Lord, C., Rutter, M., & Le Couteur, A. (1994). Autism Diagnostic Interview—Revised: A revised version of a diagnostic interview for caregivers of individuals with possible pervasive developmental disorders. *Journal of Autism and Developmental Disorders, 24,* 659–685.

Lord, C., & Venter, A. (1992). Outcome and follow-up studies of high-functioning autistic individuals. In E. Schopler & G. B. Mesibov (Eds.), *High-functioning individuals with autism* (pp. 187–199). New York: Plenum Press.

Losardo, A., & Notari-Syverson, A. (2001). *Alternative approaches to assessing young children.* Baltimore, MD: Brookes.

Lovaas, O. I. (1981). *Teaching developmentally disabled children: The me book.* Austin, TX: Pro-ed.

Lovaas, O. I. (1987). Behavioral treatment and normal educational and intellectual functioning in young autistic children. *Journal of Consulting and Clinical Psychology, 55,* 3–9.

Lovaas, O. I. (2003). *Teaching individuals with developmental delays: Basic intervention techniques.* Austin, TX: Pro-Ed.

Lovaas, O. I., Koegel, R. L., & Schreibman, L. (1979). Stimulus overselectivity in autism: A review of research. *Psychological Bulletin, 86,* 1236–1254.

Lucyshyn, J. M., Horner, R. H., Dunlap, G., Albin, R. W., & Ben, K. R. (2002). Positive behavior support with families. In J. M. Lucyshyn, G. Dunlap, & R. W. Albin (Eds.), *Families and positive behavior support: Addressing problem behavior in family contexts* (pp. 3–43). Baltimore, MD: Brookes.

Lucyshyn, J. M., Kayser, A. T., Irvin, L. K., & Blumberg, E. R. (2002). Functional assessment and positive behavior support at home with families. In J. M. Lucyshyn, G. Dunlap, & R. W. Albin (Eds.), *Families and positive behavior support: Addressing problem behavior in family contexts* (pp. 97–132). Baltimore, MD: Brookes.

Lue, M. S. (2001). *A survey of communication disorders for the classroom teacher.* Nedham Heights: MA: Allyn & Bacon.

Lund, S., & Light, J. (2001). *Fifteen years later: An investigation of the long-term outcomes of augmentative and alternative communication interventions.* (Student-Initiated Research Grant HB24B990069). University Park: Pennsylvania State University.

Lynch, E. W. (2011a). Conceptual framework: From culture shock to cultural learning. In E. W. Lynch & M. J. Hanson (Eds). *Developing cross-cultural competence: A guide for working with children and their families* (pp. 20–40). Baltimore, MD: Brookes.

Lynch, E. W. (2011b). Developing cross-cultural competence. In E. W. Lynch, M. J. Hanson (Eds.), *Developing cross-cultural competence: A guide for working with children and their families* (pp. 41–75). Baltimore, MD: Brookes.

Lynch, E. W., & Hanson, M. J. (Eds.). (2011). *Developing cross-cultural competence: A guide for working with children and their families* (4th ed.). Baltimore, MD: Brookes.

MacDonald, J. D., & Mitchell, B. (2002). *Communicate with your child: 15 ways to become a communicator.* Ashland, OH: BookMasters.

MacDonald, R., Clark, M., Garrigan, E., & Vangala, M. (2005). Using video modeling to teach pretend play to children with autism. *Behavioral Interventions, 20,* 225– 238.

MacDonald, R. P. F., Dube, W. V., Klein, J. L., Roberts, S. N., Smaby, K., & Wheeler, E. (2006, May). *Analysis and treatment of joint attention in young children with autism.* Paper presented at the 32nd Annual Convention of the Association for Behavior Analysis, International. Atlanta, Georgia.

MacDonald, R., Sacramone, S., Mansfield, R., Wiltz, K., & Ahearn, W. H. (2009). Using video modeling to teach reciprocal pretend play to children with autism. *Journal of Applied Behavior Analysis, 42,* 43–55.

MacDuff, G. S., Krantz, P. J., & McClannahan, L. E. (2001). Prompts and prompt-fading strategies for people with autism. In C. Maurice, G. Green, & R. M. Foxx (Eds.), *Making a difference: Behavioral intervention in autism* (pp. 37–50). Austin, TX: Pro-Ed.

Madrigal, S., & Winner, M.G. (2008). *Superflex: A superhero social thinking curriculum.* San Jose, CA: Social Thinking Publishing.

Mager, R. F. (1997). *Preparing instructional objectives.* Atlanta, GA: CEP Press.

Mahoney, G., Kim, J. M., & Lin, C. (2007). Pivotal behavior model of developmental learning. *Infants & Young Children, 20,* 311–325.

Mahoney, G., & MacDonald, J. (2005). *Responsive teaching: Parent-mediated developmental intervention.* Cleveland, OH: Case Western Reserve University.

Mahoney, G., & MacDonald, J. (2007). *Autism and developmental delays in young children: The responsive teaching curriculum for parents and professionals.* Austin, TX: Pro-ed.

Mahoney, G., & Perales, F. (2003). Using relationship-focused intervention to enhance the social-emotional functioning of young children with autism spectrum disorders. *Topics in Early Childhood Special Education, 23*(2), 77–89.

Mahoney, G., & Perales, F. (2005). Relationship-focused early intervention with children with pervasive developmental disorders and other disabilities: A comparative study. *Journal of Developmental and Behavioral Pediatrics, 26*(2), 77–85.

Makarushka, M. (1991, October). The words they can't say. *New York Times Magazine,* 35–36, 70.

Mancina, C., Tankersley, M., Kamps, D., Kravits, T., & Parrett, J. (2000). Brief report: Reduction of inappropriate vocalizations for a child with autism using a self-management treatment program. *Journal of Autism and Developmental Disorders, 30*(6), 599–606.

Mandelberg, J., Laugeson, E. A., Frankel, F., Gantman, A., Cunningham, T., & Bates, S. (2011). Long-term outcomes of a parent-assisted social skills intervention for adolescents with autism: The UCLA PEERS program. Poster presented at the 10th International Meeting for Autism Research, May, San Diego, CA.

Manolson, A. (1992). *It takes two to talk.* Toronto, Canada: The Hanen Centre.

Marcus, L. M., Kunce, L. J., & Schopler, E. (2005). Working with families. In F. Volkmar, R. Paul, A. Klin, & D. Cohen (Eds.), *Handbook of autism and pervasive developmental disorders* (pp. 1055–1085) Somerset, NJ: Wiley.

Marcus, L., Lansing M., Andrews, C., & Schopler, E. (1978). Improvement of teaching effectiveness in parents of autistic children. *Journal of the American Academy of Child Psychiatry, 17,* 625–639.

Martin, C. A., Drasgow, E., Halle, J. W., & Brucker, J. M. (2005). Teaching a child with autism and severe language delays to reject: Direct and indirect effects of functional communication training. *Educational Psychology, 25,* 287–304.

Martin, J. E., & Marshall, L. H. (1995). ChoiceMaker: A comprehensive self-determination transition program. *Intervention in School and Clinic, 30,* 147–156.

Martin, J. E., Marshall, L. H., Maxson, L. M., & Jerman, P. L. (1996). *The self-directed IEP.* Longmont, CO: Sopris West.

Martinez, K. (2011). Employment of people with disabilities: Federal efforts to increase job placements. *Autism Advocate, 61*(2), 12–16).

Mason, S. A., Mcgee, G. G., Farmer-Dougan, V., & Risley, T. R. (1989). A practical strategy for reinforcer assessment. *Journal of Applied Behavior Analysis, 22,* 171–179.

Matson, J. L., Benavidez, D. A., Compton, L. S., Paclawskyj, T., & Baglio, C. (1996). Behavioral treatment of autistic persons: A review of research from 1980 to the present. *Research in Developmental Disabilities, 17*(6), 433–465.

Mauk, J. E., Reber, M., & Batshaw, M. L. (1997). Autism. In M. L. Batshaw (Ed.), *Children with disabilities* (pp. 425–433) Baltimore, MD: Brookes.

Maurice, C. (1993). *Let me hear your voice.* New York: Knopf.

Maurice, C., Green, G., & Luce, S. (1996). *Behavioral intervention for young children with autism: A manual for parents and professionals.* Austin, TX: Pro-ed.

Mayer, G. R., Sulzer-Azaroff, B., & Wallace, M. (2012). *Behavior analysis for lasting change.* Cornwall-on-Hudson, NY: Sloan Publishing.

McAfee, J. (2002). Navigating the social world. Arlington, TX: Future Horizons.

McClannahan, L. E. (2005, February). *Disseminating autism intervention technology: Don't go froth and mortify.* Invited address: California Association of Applied Behavior Analysis, Dana Point, CA.

McClannahan, L. E., & Krantz, P. J. (1993). On systems analysis in autism intervention programs. *Journal of Applied Behavior Analysis, 26,* 589–596.

McClannahan, L. E., & Krantz, P. J. (1999). *Activity schedules for children with autism: Teaching independent behavior.* Bethesda, MD: Woodbine.

McClannahan, L. E., & Krantz, P. J. (2001). Behavior analysis and intervention for preschoolers at the Princeton Child Development Institute. In J. S. Handleman and S. L. Harris, (Eds.), *Preschool education programs for children with autism* (pp. 191–213). Austin, TX: Pro-ed.

McClannahan, L. E., & Krantz, P. J. (2004). Some guidelines for evaluating behavioral intervention programs for children with autism. In H. E. Briggs & T. L. Rzepnicki (Eds.), *Using evidence in social work practice: Behavioral perspectives* (pp. 92–103). Chicago: Lyceum Books.

McClannahan, L. E., & Krantz, P. J. (2005). *Teaching conversation to children with autism: Scripts and script fading.* Bethesda, MD: Woodbine.

McClannahan, L. E., & Krantz, P. J. (2006). Behavior analysis and

intervention for school-age children at the Princeton Child Development Institute. In J. S. Handleman & S. L. Harris (Eds.), *School-age education programs for children with autism* (pp. 143–162). Austin, TX: Pro-ed.

McClannahan, L. E., & Krantz, P. J. (2010). *Activity schedules for children with autism: Teaching independent behavior.* Bethesda, MD: Woodbine.

McClannahan, L. E., Krantz, P. J., & McGee, G. G. (1982). Parents as therapists for autistic children: A model for effective parent training. *Analysis and Intervention in Developmental Disabilities, 2,* 223–252.

McClannahan, L. E., MacDuff, G. S., & Krantz, P. J. (2002). Behavior analysis and intervention for adults with autism. *Behavior Modification, 26*(1), 9–26.

McCollum, J., & Hemmeter, M. L. (1997). Parent-child intervention when children have disabilities. In M. J. Guralnick (Ed.), *The effectiveness of early intervention* (pp. 549–576. Baltimore, MD: Brookes.

McConachie, H., Randle, V., Hammal, D., & Le Couteur, A. (2005). A controlled trial of a training course for parents of children with suspected autism spectrum disorder. *Journal of Pediatrics, 147,* 335–340.

McCormick, K. M., & Brennan, S. (2001). Mentoring the new professional in interdisciplinary early childhood education: The Kentucky teacher internship program. *Topics in Early Childhood Special Education, 21*(3), 131–144.

McCoy, K., & Hermansen, E. (2007). Video modeling for individuals with autism: A review of model types and effects. *Education and Treatment of Children, 30,* 183–213.

McCracken, J. T. (2011). Pharmacotherapy for autism spectrum disorders. In D. G. Amaral, G. Dawson, & D. H. Geschwind (Eds.), *Autism spectrum disorders* (pp. 1309–1322). New York: Oxford University Press.

McEachin, J., & Leaf, R. (1999). The autism partnership curriculum for discrete trial teaching with autistic children. In R. Leaf & J. McEachin

(Eds). *A work in progress: Behavior management strategies and a curriculum for intensive behavioral treatment of autism.* New York: DRL Books.

McEachin, J. J., Smith, T., & Lovaas, O. I. (1993). Long-term outcome for children with autism who received early intensive behavioral treatment. *American Journal on Mental Retardation, 97,* 359–372.

McEvoy, M. A., Nordquist, V. M., Twardosz, S., Heckaman, K. A., Wehby, J. H., & Denny, R. K. (1988). Promoting autistic children's peer interaction in an integrated early childhood setting using affection activities. *Journal of Applied Behavior Analysis, 21,* 193–200.

McGee, G. G., Almeida, M. C., Sulzer-Azaroff, B. & Feldman, R. S. (1992). Promoting reciprocal interactions via peer incidental teaching. *Journal of Applied Behavior Analysis, 25,* 117–126.

McGee, G., & Daly, T. (1999). Prevention of problem behaviors in preschool children. In A. C. Repp & R. H. Horner (Eds.), *Functional analysis of problem behavior: From effective assessment to effective support* (pp. 171–196). Belmont, CA: Wadsworth.

McGee, G. G., Feldman, R. S. & Chernin, L. (1991). A comparison of emotional facial display by children with autism and typical preschoolers. *Journal of Early Intervention, 15*(3), 237–245.

McGee, G. G., Krantz, P. J., Mason, D., & McClannahan, L. (1983). A modified incidental- teaching procedure for autistic youth: Acquisition and generalization of receptive object labels. *Journal of Applied Behavior Analysis, 16,* 329–338.

McGee, G. G., Krantz, P. J., & McClannahan, L. (1984). Conversational skills for autistic adolescents: Teaching assertiveness in natural game settings. *Journal of Autism and Developmental Disorders, 14*(3), 319–330.

McGee, G. G., Krantz, P. J., & McClannahan, L. (1985). The facilitative effects of incidental teaching on preposition use by autistic children. *Journal of Applied Behavior Analysis, 18,* 17–31.

McGee, G. G., & Morrier, M. J. (2005). Preparation of autism specialists. In F. Volkmar, R. Paul, A. Klin, & D. Cohen (Eds.), *Handbook of autism and pervasive developmental disorders* (pp. 1123–1160). Somerset, NJ: Wiley.

McGee, G. G., Morrier, M. J., & Daly, T. (1999). An incidental teaching approach to early intervention for toddlers with autism. *Journal of the Association of Persons with Severe Handicaps, 24,* 133–146.

McGee, G. G., Morrier, M. J., & Daly, T. (2001). The Walden early childhood programs. In J. S. Handleman & S. L. Harris (Eds.). *Preschool education programs for children with autism* (157–190). Austin, TX: Pro-Ed.

McHugh, R. K., & Barlow, D. H. Geschwind (2010). The dissemination and implementation of evidence-based psychological treatments. *American Psychologist, 65,* 73–84.

Meadan, H., Ostrosky, M. M., Zaghlawan, H. Y., & Yu, S. Y. (2009). Promoting the social and communicative behavior of young children with autism spectrum disorders: A review of parent-implemented intervention studies. *Topics in Early Childhood Special Education, 29,* 90–104.

Mehring, T. A., & Dow, M. J. (2001). Preparing future teachers for students with autistic spectrum disorders. In T. Wahlberg, F. Obiakor, S. Burkhardt, & A. F. Rotatori (Eds.), *Autism spectrum disorders: Educational and clinical interventions* (pp. 69–88). Oxford, England: Elsevier Science.

Meltzoff, A., & Moore, M. K. (1989). Imitation in newborn infants: Exploring the range of gestures imitated and the underlying mechanisms. *Developmental Psychology, 25,* 954–962.

Mesibov, G. B. (1984). Social skills training with verbal autistic adolescents and adults: A program model. *Journal of Autism and Developmental Disorders, 14,* 395–404.

Mesibov, G., & Howley, M. (2003). *Accessing the curriculum for pupils with autistic spectrum disorders.* London: David Fulton.

Mesibov, G. B., Schopler, E., & Hearsey, K. A. (1994). Structured teaching. In E. Schopler & G. B. Mesibov (Eds.) *Behavioral issues in autism* (pp. 195–207). New York: Plenum Press.

Mesibov, G. B., Schopler, E., Schaffer, B., & Landrus, R. (1988). *Adolescent and Adult Psychoeducational Profile (AAPEP): Volume IV.* Austin, TX: Pro-ed.

Mesibov, G. B., & Shea, V. (1996). Full inclusion and students with autism. *Journal of Autism and Developmental Disorders, 26*(3), 337–346.

Mesibov, G. B., Shea, V., & Adams, L. W. (2001). *Understanding Asperger syndrome and high-functioning autism.* New York: Kluwer Academic/Plenum Press.

Mesibov, G. B., Shea, V., & Schopler, E. (2004). *The TEACCH approach to autism spectrum disorders.* New York: Springer.

Meyer, L. S., Taylor, B. A., Cerino, K. E., Fisher, J. R., Moran, L., & Richard, E. (2006). Alpine learning group. In J. S. Handleman, & S. L. Harris (Eds.), *School-age education programs for children with autism* (pp. 19–47). Austin TX: Pro-ed.

Michael, J. (2007). Motivating operations. In J. Cooper, T. Heron, & W. Heward (2007). *Applied behavior analysis* (2nd ed., pp. 374–391). Columbus, OH: Pearson Education.

Miller-Kuhaneck, H. (2004). *Autism: A comprehensive occupational therapy approach* (2nd ed.). Bethesda, MD: Aota Press.

Millward, C., Ferriter, M., Calver, S., Connell-Jones, G., et al. (2004). Gluten- and casein-free diets for autistic spectrum disorder. *Cochrane Database Syst Rev.:* CD003498.

Minchew, N. J., Scherf, K. S., Behrmann, M., Humphreys, K. (2011). Autism as a developmental neurobiological disorder: New insights from functional neuroimaging. In D. G. Amaral, G. Dawson, & D. H. Geschwind (Eds.), *Autism spectrum disorders* (pp. 632–650). New York: Oxford University Press.

Minchew, N. J., Sweeney, J. A., Bauman, M. L., & Webb, S. J. (2005). Neurological aspects of autism. In F. Volkmar, R. Paul, A. Klin, & D. Cohen (Eds.), *Handbook of autism and pervasive developmental disorders* (pp. 473–514). Somerset, NJ: Wiley.

Minjarez, M.B., Williams, S. E., Mercier, E. M., & Hardan, A. Y. (2011). Pivotal response group treatment program for parents of children with autism. *Journal of Autism and Developmental Disorders, 41,* 92–101.

Mirenda, P. (2001). Autism, augmentative communication, and assistive technology: What do we really know? *Focus on Autism and Other Developmental Disabilities, 16*(3), 141–151.

Mirenda, P., & Bopp, K. D. (2003). "Playing the game": Strategic competence in AAC. In J. Light, D. Beukelman, & J. Reichle (Eds.), *Communicative competence for individuals who use AAC: From research to effective practice* (pp. 401–437). Baltimore, MD: Brookes.

Mirenda, P., & Erickson, K. A. (2000). Augmentative communication and literacy. In A. M. Wetherby & B. M. Prizant (Eds.), *Autism spectrum disorders: A transactional developmental perspective* (pp. 333–367). Baltimore, MD: Brookes.

Moes, D. R. (1998). Integrating choice-making opportunities within teacher-assigned academic tasks to facilitate the performance of children with autism. *Journal of the Association for Persons with Severe Handicaps, 23*(4), 319–328.

Moes, D. R., & Frea, W. D. (2000). Using family context to inform intervention planning for the treatment of a child with autism. *Journal of Positive Intervention, 2*(1), 40–46.

Mollica, B. M. (2003). Representational competence. In J. Light, D. Beukelman, & J. Reichle (Eds.), *Communicative competence for individuals who use AAC: From research to effective practice* (pp. 107–146). Baltimore, MD: Brookes.

Moody, E. J., & McIntosh, D. N. (2006). Mimicry and autism: Bases and consequences of rapid, automatic matching behavior. In S. J. Rogers &

J. S. G. Williams (Eds.), *Imitation and the social mind: Autism and typical development* (pp. 71–95). New York: Guilford Press.

Moreland, J. R., Schwebel, A. T., Beck, S., & Wells, R. (1982). Parents as therapists: A review of the behavior therapy parent training literature—1975–1981. *Behavior Modification, 6*, 250–276.

Morrison, R. S., Sainato, D. M., Benchaaban, D., & Endo, S. (2002). Increasing play skills of children with autism using activity schedules and correspondence training. *Journal of Early Intervention, 25*, 58–72.

Morrow, R. M., & Walsh, C. A. (2011). Isolate populations and rare variation in autism spectrum disorders. In D. G. Amaral, G. Dawson, & D. H. Geschwind (Eds.), *Autism spectrum disorders* (pp. 766–775). New York: Oxford University Press.

Mullen, E. M. (1995). *Mullen Scales of Early Learning.* Torrance, CA: Western Psychological Services.

Mullen, K. B., & Frea, W. D. (1996). A parent-professional consultation model for functional analysis. In R. L. Koegel & L. K. Koegel (Eds). *Teaching children with autism: Strategies for initiating positive interactions and improving learning opportunities* (pp. 175–188). Baltimore, MD: Brookes.

Mundy, P., Sigman, M., Ungerer, J., & Sherman, T. (1986). Defining the social deficits of autism: The contribution of non-verbal communication measures. *Journal of Child Psychology and Psychiatry, 27*(5), 657–669.

Murdick, N. L., Gartin, B. C., & Crabtree, T. (2007). *Special education law* (2nd ed.). Upper Saddle River, NJ: Pearson Education.

Myles, B. S., Hagiwara, T., Dunn, W., Rinner, L., Reese, M., Huggins, A., & Becker, S. (2004). Sensory issues in children with Asperger syndrome and autism. *Education and Training in Developmental Disabilities, 39*(4), 283–290.

Myles, B. S., & Simpson, R. L. (1998a). *Asperger syndrome: A guide for educators and parents.* Austin, TX: Pro-ed.

Myles, B. S., & Simpson, R. L. (1998b). Inclusion of students with autism in general education classrooms: The autism inclusion collaboration model. In R. L. Simpson & B. S. Myles (Eds). *Educating children and youth with autism* (pp. 241–256). Austin, TX: Pro-ed.

Myles, B. & Simpson, R. (2001). Effective practices for students with Asperger syndrome. *Focus on Exceptional Children, 34*(3), 1–14.

National Autism Center. (2009a). Evidence-based practice and autism in the schools. Cape Cod, MA: Author.

National Autism Center. (2009b). National standards project: Findings and conclusions. Cape Cod, MA: Author.

National Longitudinal Transition Study-2 (NLTS2) (2007). Wave 3-2005: Parent/youth survey.

National Professional Development Center on Autism Spectrum Disorders – autismpdc.fpg.unc.edu/contents/briefs

National Research Council. (2001). *Educating children with autism.* Committee on Educational Interventions for Children with Autism. Division of Behavioral and Social Sciences and Education. Washington, DC: National Academy Press.

Neisworth, J. T., Bagnato, S. J., Salvia, J., & Hunt, F. M. (1999). *TABS Manual for the Temperament and Atypical Behavior Scale.* Baltimore, MD: Brookes.

Nelson, C., & Huefner, D. S. (2003). Young children with autism: Judicial responses to the Lovaas and discrete trial teaching debates. *Journal of Early Intervention, 26*, 1–19.

Neuhring, M. L. & Sitlington, P. L. (2003). Transition as a vehicle. *Journal of Disability Policy Studies, 14*(1), 23–35.

New York State Department of Health (1999). *The guideline technical report: Autism/pervasive developmental disorders.* New York: Department of Health Early Intervention Program.

Newman, B., Buffington, D. M., Hemmes, N. S. (1996). Self-reinforcement used to increase the appropriate conversations of autistic teenagers. *Education & Training in Mental Retardation & Developmental Disabilities, 31*, 304–309.

Newman, B., Reinecke, D. R., & Meinberg, D. L. (2000). Self-management of varied responding in three students with autism. *Behavioral Interventions, 15*, 145–151.

Newman, B., Tuntigian, L., Ryan, C. S., & Reinecke, D. R. (1997). Self-management of a DRO procedure by three students with autism. *Behavioral Interventions, 12*(3), 149–156.

Nikopoulos, C., & Keenan, M. (2006). *Video modeling and behaviour analysis: A guide for teaching social skills to children with autism.* London: Jessica Kingsley.

Northup, J., Wacker, D. P., Berg, W. K., Kelly, L., Sasso, G., & DeRaad, A. (1994). The treatment of severe behavior problems in school settings using a technical assistance model. *Journal of Applied Behavior Analysis, 27*, 33–47.

Oatley, K., & Jenkins, J. M. (1996). *Understanding emotions.* Oxford, England: Blackwell.

Obiakor, F. E. (2002). Developing self-empowerment in African American learners with special problems. In F. E. Obiakor & B. A. Ford (Eds). *Creating successful learning environments for African American learners with exceptionalities* (pp. 119–132). Thousand Oaks, CA: Corwin.

O'Connor, A. (2004, March 6). Researchers retract a study linking autism to vaccination. New York Times. Retrieved October 26, 2007, from *http://qery.mytimes.com.*

O'Connor, M. J., Frankel, F., Paley, B., Schonfeld, A. M., Carpenter, E., Laugeson, E. A, & Marquardt, R. (2007). A controlled social skills training for children with fetal alcohol spectrum disorders. *Journal of Consulting and Clinical Psychology, 74*, 639–648.

O'Connor, T. (1999). *Teacher perspectives of facilitated play in integrated play groups.* Masters thesis, San Francisco State University.

Odom, S. L., Boyd, B. A., Hall, L. J., & Hume, K. A. (2010). Evaluation of comprehensive treatment models for individuals with autism spectrum disorders. *Journal of Autism and Developmental Disorders., 40*, 425–437.

Odom, S. L., Brantlinger, E., Gersten, R., Horner, R. D., Thompson, B., & Harris, K. (2005). Research in special education: Scientific methods and evidence-based practices. *Exceptional Children, 71*, 137–148.

Odom, S. L., Collet-Klingenberg, L., Rogers, S. J., & Hatton, D. D. (2010). Evidence- based practices in interventions for children and youth with autism spectrum disorders. *Preventing School Failure, 54*, 275–282.

Odom, S. L., & Strain, P. S. (1986). A comparison of peer-initiation and teacher- antecedent interventions for promoting reciprocal social interaction of autistic preschoolers. *Journal of Applied Behavior Analysis, 19*, 59–71.

Ogletree, B. T., & Oren, T. (2006). *How to use augmentative and alternative communication.* Austin, TX: Pro-Ed.

Oke, N. J., & Schreibman, L. (1990). Training social initiations to a high-functioning autistic child: Assessment of collateral behavior change and generalization in a case study. *Journal of Autism and Developmental Disorders, 20*, 479–497.

O'Neill, R. E., Horner, R. H., Albin, R. W., Sprague, J. R., Storey, K., & Newton, J. S. (1997). *Functional assessment and program development for problem behavior: A practical handbook.* Pacific Grove, CA: Brookes/Cole.

O'Neill, M., & Jones, R. S. P. (1997). Sensory-perceptual abnormalities in autism: A case for more research. *Journal of Autism and Developmental Disorders, 27*(3), 283–293.

Oosterling, I., Visser, J., Swinkels, S., Rommelse, N., Donders, R., Woudenberg, T., Roos, S., Jan van der Gaag, R., & Buitelaar, J. (2010). Randomized tontrolled trial of the focus parent training for toddlers with autism: 1-year outcome. *Journal of Autism and Developmental Disorders, 40*, 1147–1158.

Osterling, J. A., & Dawson, G. (1994). Early recognition of children with autism: A study of first birthday home videotapes. *Journal of Autism and Developmental Disorders, 24*, 247–257.

Ottenbacher, K. J., Tickle-Degnen, L., & Hasselkus, B. R. (2002). Therapists awake! The challenge of evidence-based occupational therapy, *American Journal of Occupational Therapy, 56*(3), 247–249.

Overton, T. (2012). *Assessing learners with special needs: An applied approach.* Upper Saddle River, NJ: Pearson Education.

Owens, R. E. (1996). *Language development: An introduction* (4th ed.). Boston, MA: Allyn & Bacon.

Ozonoff, S., & Cathcart, K. (1998). Effectiveness of a home program intervention for young children with autism. *Journal of Autism and Developmental Disorders, 28*(1), 25–32.

Ozonoff, S., Heung, K., & Thompson, M. (2011). Regression and other patterns of onset. In D. G. Amaral, G. Dawson, & D. H. Geschwind (Eds.), *Autism spectrum disorders* (pp. 60–74). New York: Oxford University Press.

Ozonoff, S., Iosif, A. M., Baguio, F., Cook, I. C., Hill, M. M., Hutman, T., Rogers, S. J., Rozga, A., Sangha, S., Sigman, M., Steinfeld, M. B., & Young, G. (2010). *American Academy of Child & Adolescent Psychiatry, 49*, 256–266.

Ozonoff, S., South, M., & Provencal, S. (2005). Executive functions. In F. Volkmar, R. Paul, A. Klin, & D. Cohen (Eds.), *Handbook of autism and pervasive developmental disorders* (pp. 606–627). Somerset, NJ: Wiley.

Panerai, S., Ferrante, L., Caputo, V., & Impellizzeri, C. (1998). Use of structured teaching for treatment of children with autism and severe and profound mental retardation. *Education and Training in Mental Retardation and Developmental Disabilities,33*(4), 367–374.

Panerai, S. Ferrante, L., & Zingale, M. (2002). Benefits of the Treatment of Education of Autistic and Communication Handicapped Children (TEACCH) programme as compared with a non-specific approach. *Journal of Intellectual Disability Research, 46*, 318–327.

Panerai, S., Zingale, M., Trubia, G., Finocchiaro, M., Zuccarello, R., Ferri, R., & Elia, M. (2009). Special education versus inclusive education: The role of the TEACCH program. *Journal of Autism and Developmental Disorders, 39*, 874–882.

Pangborn, J., & Baker, S. M. (2005). *Autism: Effective biomedical treatments.* San Diego, CA: Autism Research Institute.

Parette, P., Chuang, S. L., & Huer, M. B. (2004). First-generation Chinese American families' attitudes regarding disabilities and educational interventions. *Focus on Autism and Other Developmental Disabilities, 19*, 114–123.

Parks, S. Furono, S., O'Reilly, K., Inatsuka, T., Hoska, C. M., & Zeisloft-Falbey, B. (1994). *HELP at home (birth to 3).* Palo Alto, CA: Vort.

Partington, J. W. (2006). *The assessment of basic language and learning skills (ABLLS-R Protocol): An assessment, curriculum guide, and skills tracking system for children with autism and other developmental disabilities.* Pleasant Hill, CA: Behavior Analysts.

Partington, J. W., & Sundberg, M. A. (1998). *The Assessment of Basic Language and Learning Skills (The ABLLS): An assessment, curriculum guide, and skills tracking system for children with autism and other language delays (version 2.3).* Pleasant Hill, CA: Behavior Analysts.

Patti, P. J., & Lupinetti, L. (1993). Brief report: Implications of hyperlexia in an autistic savant. *Journal of Autism and Developmental Disorders, 23*(2), 397–405.

Paul, R., & Sutherland, D. (2005). Enhancing early language in children with autism spectrum disorders. In F. Volkmar, R. Paul, A. Klin, & D. Cohen (Eds.), *Handbook of autism and pervasive developmental disorders* (pp. 946–976.) Somerset, NJ: Wiley.

Pavone, L., & Ruggieri, M. (2005). The problem of alternative therapies in autism. In M. Coleman (Ed.), *The neurology of autism* (pp. 173–200). New York: Oxford University Press.

Pearpoint, J., O'Brien, J. & Forest, M. (1993). *Path: A workbook for planning* possible positive futures: Planning alternative tomorrows with hope for schools, organizations, businesses, families. Toronto: Inclusion Press.

Peyton, R. T., Lindauer, S. E., & Richman, D. M. (2005). The effects of directive and nondirective prompts on noncompliant vocal behavior of a child with autism. *Journal of Applied Behavior Analysis, 38,* 251–255.

Piaget, J. (1950). *The psychology of intelligence.* London: Broadway House.

Piaget, J. (1973). Piaget's developmental theory: Memory and intelligence. [Video]

Pierce, K., Carter, C., Weinfeld, M., Desmond, J., Hazin, R., Bjork, R., & Gallagher, N. (2011). Detecting, studying, and treating autism early: The one-year well-baby check-up approach. *Journal of Pediatrics, 159*(3), 458–465.

Pierce, K., & Schreibman, L. (1995). Increasing complex behaviors in children with autism: Effects of peer-implemented Pivotal Response Training. *Journal of Applied Behavior Analysis, 28,* 285–295.

Pierson, M. R., & Glaeser, B. C. (2005). Extension of research on social skills training using comic strip conversations to students without autism. *Education and Training in Developmental Disabilities, 40,* 279–284.

Pierson, M. R., & Glaeser, B. C. (2007). Using comic strip conversations to increase social satisfaction and decrease loneliness in students with autism spectrum disorder. *Education and Training in Developmental Disabilities, 42,* 460–466.

Powers, M. D., Palmieri, M. J., D'Eramo, K. S., & Powers, K. M. (2011). Evidence-based treatment of behavioral excesses and deficits for individuals with autism spectrum disorders. In B. Reichow, P. Doehring, D. V. Cicchetti, & F. R. Volkmar (Eds.), *Evidence-based practices and treatments for children with autism* (pp. 55–92). New York: Springer.

Prater, L. P. (2002). African American families: Equal partners in general and special education. In F. E. Obiakor & B. A. Ford (Eds), *Creating successful learning environments for African American learners with exceptionalities* (pp. 145–158). Thousand Oaks, CA: Corwin.

Prelock, P. A., Paul, R., & Allen, E. M. (2011). Evidence-based treatments in communication for children with autism spectrum disorders. In B. Reichow, P. Doehring, D. V. Cicchetti, & F. R. Volkmar, F.R. (Eds.) *Evidence-based practices and treatments for children with autism* (pp. 93–169). New York: Springer.

Pretti-Frontczak, K., & Bricker, D. (2004). *An activity-based approach to early intervention.* Baltimore, MD: Brookes.

Prizant, B. M., & Rydell, P. J. (1984). Analysis of the functions of delayed echolalia in autistic children. *Journal of Speech and Hearing Research, 27,* 183–192.

Prizant, B. M., & Rydell, P. J. (1993). Assessment and intervention strategies for unconventional verbal behavior. In J. Reichle & D. Wacker (Vol. Eds.), *Communicative approaches to challenging behavior: Integrating functional assessment and intervention strategies* (pp. 263–297). Baltimore, MD: Brookes.

Prizant, B. M., Wetherby, A. M., Rubin, E., Laurent, A. C., & Rydell, P. J. (2006a). *The SCERTS model: A comprehensive educational approach for children with autism spectrum disorders: Volume 1 Assessment.* Baltimore, MD: Brookes.

Prizant, B. M., Wetherby, A. M., Rubin, E., Laurent, A. C., & Rydell, P. J. (2006b). *The SCERTS model: A comprehensive educational approach for children with autism spectrum disorders: Volume 2 Program planning and intervention.* Baltimore, MD: Brookes.

Quill, K.A. (2000). *Do-watch-listen-say: Social and communication intervention for children with autism.* Baltimore, MD: Brookes.

Quill, K. A., Bracken, K. N., & Fair, M. E. (2000). Assessment of social and communication skills for children with autism. In K. A. Quill (Ed.), *DO-WATCH-LISTEN-SAY: Social and communication intervention for children with autism* (pp. 53–69). Baltimore, MD: Brookes.

Quirmbach, L. M., Lincoln, A. J., Feinberg-Gizzo, M. J., Ingersoll, B. R., & Andrews, S. M. (2009). Social stories: Mechanisms of effectiveness in increasing game play skills in children diagnosed with autism spectrum disorder using a pretest posttest repeated measures randomized control group design. *Journal of Autism and Developmental Disorders, 39,* 299–321.

Rao, P. A., Beidel, D. C., & Murray, M. J. (2008). Social skills interventions for children with Asperger's syndrome or high-functioning autism: A review and recommendations. *Journal of Autism and Developmental Disorders, 38,* 353–361.

Reagon, K. A., Higbee, T. S., & Endicott, K. (2006). Teaching pretend play skills to a student with autism using video modeling with a sibling as model and play partner. *Education and Treatment of Children, 29*(3), 1–12.

Reichle, J., Cooley Hidecker, M. J., Brady, N. C., & Terry, N. (2003). Intervention strategies for communication: Using aided augmentative communication systems. In J. Light, D. Beukelman, & J. Reichle (Eds.), *Communicative competence for individuals who use AAC: From research to effective practice* (pp. 441–478). Baltimore, MD: Brookes.

Reichler, R. J., & Lee, E. M. C. (1989). Overview of biomedical issues in autism. In E. Schopler & G. B. Mesibov (Eds.), *Neurological issues in autism* (pp. 13–41). New York: Plenum Press.

Reichow, B., Barton, E. E., Neely-Sewell, J., Good, L., & Wolery, M. (2010). Effects of weighted vests on children with developmental delays and autism. *Focus on Autism and Other Developmental Disabilities, 25,* 3–11.

Reichow, B., Volkmar, F. R., & Cicchetti, D. V. (2008). Development of the evaluation method for evaluating and determining evidence-based practices in autism. *Journal of Autism and Developmental Disorders, 38,* 1311–1319.

Reichow, B., & Wolery, M. (2009). Comprehensive synthesis of early intensive behavioral interventions for young children with autism based on the UCLA young autism project model. *Journal of Autism and Developmental Disorders, 39,* 23–41.

Reinecke, D. R., Newman, B., & Meinberg, D. L. (1999). Self-management of sharing in three pre-schoolers with autism. *Education and Training in Mental Retardation and Developmental Disabilities, 34,* 312–317.

Remington, B., Hastings, R. P., Kovshoff, H., Espinosa, F. D., Jahr, E., Brown, T., . . . & Ward, N. (2007). Early intensive behavioral intervention: Outcomes for children with autism and their parents after two years. *American Journal of Mental Retardation, 112,* 418–438.

Renzaglia, A., Karvonen, M., Drasgow, E., & Stoxen, C. C. (2003). Promoting a lifetime of inclusion. *Focus on Autism and Other Developmental Disabilities, 18*(3), 140– 149.

Repp, A. (1994). Comments on functional analysis procedures for school-based behavior problems. *Journal of Applied Behavior Analysis, 27*(2), 409–411.

Revell, G., & Miller, L. A. (2009). Education and transition planning. In P. Wehman, M. D. Smith, & C. Schall (Eds.), *Autism and the transition to adulthood: Success beyond the classroom* (pp. 139–161). Baltimore: Brookes.

Rice, C. (2009). Prevalence of autism spectrum disorders—Autism and developmental disabilities monitoring network, United States, 2006. *Morbidity and Morality Weekly Report Surveillance Summary 2009, 58,* 1–14.

Rice, M. L. (1993). "Don't talk to him; he's weird": A social consequences account of language and social interactions (pp. 139–158). In A. Kaiser & D. Gray (Eds.), *Enhancing Children's Communication: Research Foundations for Intervention.* Baltimore, MD: Brookes.

Ring, H. A. (1999). Cerebral correlates of preserved cognitive skills in autism: A functional MRI study of embedded figures task performance. *Brain: A Journal of Neurology, 122,* 1305–1315.

Risley, T. (1996). Get a life! Positive behavioral intervention for challenging behavior through life arrangement and life coaching. In L. K. Koegel, R. L. Keogel, & G. Dunlap (Eds.), *Positive behavioral support: Including people with difficult behavior in the community* (pp. 425–437). Baltimore, MD: Brookes.

Ritvo, E. R., Freeman, B. J., Mason-Brothers, A., Mo, A., & Ritvo, A. M. (1985). Concordance for the syndrome of autism in 40 pairs of afflicted twins. *American Journal of Psychiatry, 142*(1), 74–81.

Robins, D. L., Fein, D., & Barton, M. L. (1999). *The modified checklist for autism in toddlers.* Authors.

Robins, D.L., Fein, D., Barton, M. L., & Green, J. A. (2001). The Modified Checklist for Autism in Toddlers: An initial study investigating the early detection of autism and pervasive developmental disorders. *Journal of Autism and Developmental Disorders, 31,* 131–144.

Rodier, P. M. (2011). Environmental exposures that increase the risk of autism spectrum disorders. In D. G. Amaral, G. Dawson, & D. H. Geschwind (Eds.), *Autism spectrum disorders* (pp. 863–874). New York: Oxford University Press.

Rogan, P., Grossi, T. A., & Gajewski, R. (2002). Vocational and career assessment. In C. L. Sax & C. A. Thoma (Eds.), *Transition assessment: Wise practices for quality lives* (pp. 103–117). Baltimore, MD: Brookes.

Rogers, S. J., (2000, February). The Denver Model: A comprehensive educational approach for young children with autism and their families [unpublished presentation].

Rogers, S. J. (2006). Studies in imitation in early infancy: Findings and theories. In S. J. Rogers & J. S. G. Williams (Eds.), *Imitation and the social mind: Autism and typical development* (pp. 3–26). New York: Guilford Press.

Rogers, S. J., & Bennetto, L. (2000). Intersubjectivity in autism: The roles on imitation and executive function. In A. Wetherby & B. Prizant (Eds), *Autism spectrum disorders: A transactional developmental perspective* (pp. 79–108). Baltimore, MD: Brookes.

Rogers, S. J., & Dawson, G. (2010a). *Early Start Denver Model curriculum checklist for young children with autism.* New York: Guilford Press.

Rogers, S. J., & Dawson, G. (2010b). *Early Start Denver Model for young children with autism: Promoting language, learning and engagement.* New York: Guilford Press.

Rogers, S. J., & Di Lalla, D. L. (1991). A comparative study of the effects of a developmentally based instructional model on young children with autism and young children with other disorders of behavior and development. *Topics in Early Childhood Special Education, 11*(2), 29–47.

Rogers, S. J., Hall, T., Osaki, D., Reaven, J., & Herbison, J. (2001). The Denver model: A comprehensive, integrated educational approach to young children with autism and their families. In J. S. Handleman & S. L. Harris (Eds.), *Preschool education programs for children with autism* (pp. 95–133). Austin, TX: PRO-ED.

Rogers, S. J., Herbison, J. M., Lewis, H. C., Pantone, J., & Reis, K. (1986). An approach for enhancing the symbolic, communicative, and interpersonal functioning of young children with autism or severe emotional handicaps. *Journal of the Division for Early Childhood, 10*(2), 135–148.

Rogers, S. J., & Lewis, H. (1989). An effective day treatment model for young children with pervasive developmental disorders. *American Academy of Child and Adolescent Psychiatry, 28*(2), 207–214.

Rogers, S. J., Lewis, H. C., & Reis, K. (1987). An effective procedure for training early special education teams to implement a model program. *Journal of the Division for Early Childhood, 11,* 180–188.

Rogers S. J., & Ozonoff, S. (2005). Annotaton: What do we know about sensory dysfunction in autism? A critical review of the empirical evidence. *Journal of Child Psychology and Psychiatry, 46,* 1255–1268.

Rogers, S. J., & Vismara, L. A. (2008). Evidence-based comprehensive treatments for early autism. *Journal of Clinical Child and Adolescent Psychology, 37,* 8–38.

Rogers, S. J., & Wallace, K .S. (2011). Intervention for infants and toddlers with autism spectrum disorders. In D. G. Amaral, G. Dawson, & D. H. Geschwind (Eds.), *Autism spectrum disorders* (pp. 1081–1094). New York: Oxford University Press.

Rogers, S. J., & Williams, J. H. G. (2006). Imitation in autism: Findings and controversies. In S. J. Rogers & J. S. G. Williams (Eds.), *Imitation and the social mind: Autism and typical development* (pp. 277–309). New York: Guilford Press.

Rogers-Adkinson, D., Ochoa, T. A., & Delgado, B. (2003). Developing cross-cultural competence: Serving families of children with significant developmental needs. *Focus on Autism and Developmental Disabilities, 18,* 4–8.

Rogoff, B. (1990). *Apprenticeship in thinking: Cognitive development in social context.* New York: Oxford University Press.

Romoser, M. (2000). Malemployment in autism. *Focus on Autism and Other Developmental Disabilities, 15(4),* 246–247.

Rosenblatt, J., Bloom, P., & Koegel, R. L. (1995). Overselective responding. In R. L. Koegel & L. K. Koegel (Eds.), *Teaching children with autism* (pp. 33–51). Baltimore, MD: Brookes.

Rosinski, R. R. (1977). *The development of visual perception.* Santa Monica, CA: Goodyear.

Ross, D. E. (2002). Replacing faulty conversational exchanges for children with autism by establishing a functionally equivalent alternative response. *Education and Training in Mental Retardation and Developmental Disabilities, 37(4),* 343–362.

Rowland, C., & Schweigert, P. (1993). *Analyzing the communication environment: An inventory of ways to encourage communication in functional activities* [Manual and videotape].

Tucson, AZ: Communication Skill Builders.

Rowland, C., & Schweigert, P. (2000). Tangible symbols, tangible outcomes. *AAC Augmentative and Alternative Communication, 16,* 61–78.

Rozga, A., Hutman, T., Young, G. S., Rogers, S. J., Ozonoff, S., Dapretto, M., & Sigman, M. (2011). Behavioral profiles of affected and unaffected siblings of children with autism: Contribution of measures of mother-infant interaction and nonverbal communication. *Journal of Autism and Developmental Disorder, 41,* 287–301.

Rutter, M. (2005). Genetic influences and autism. In F. Volkmar, R. Paul, A. Klin, & D. 452). Somerset, NJ: Wiley.

Ryan, J. B., Katsiyannis, A., Peterson, R., & Chmelar, R. (2007). IDEA 2004 and disciplining students with disabilities. *NASSP Bulletin, 91,* 130–140.

Ryndak, D. L., & Billingsley, F. (2004). Access to the general education curriculum. In C. H. Kennedy & E. M. Horn (Eds.), *Including students with severe disabilities.* (pp. 33–53). New York: Pearson Education.

Salazar, M. J. (2010). Defining a role for parents and professionals: Providing family-centered early intervention for young children with autism spectrum disorders. In H. H. Schertz, C. Wong, & S. L. Odom (Eds), *Young exceptional children (Monograph Series No. 12) Supporting young children with autism spectrum disorders and their families* (pp. 97–106). Missoula, MT: Division of Early Childhood of the Council for Exceptional Children.

Sallows, G. O., & Graupner, T. D. (2005). Intensive behavioral treatment for children with autism: Four-year outcome and predictors. *American Journal on Mental Retardation, 110,* 417–438.

Sameroff, A., & Chandler, M. (1975). Reproductive risk and the continuum of caretaking causality. In F. Horowitz (Ed.), *Review of child development research. Vol. 4.* (pp. 187–244). Chicago: University of Chicago Press.

Sandall, S., Hemmeter, M. L., Smith, B. J., & McLean, M. E. (2005). *DEC recommended practices: A comprehensive guide for practical application in early intervention/early childhood special education.* Longmont, CO: Sopris West.

Sandall, S. R., & Schwartz, I. S. (2002). *Building blocks for teaching preschoolers with special needs.* Baltimore, MD: Brookes.

Sandler, A. D., & Bodfish, J. W. (2000). Placebo effects in autism: Lessons from secretin. *Developmental and Behavioral Pediatrics, 21(5),* 347–350.

Sarokoff, R. A., Taylor, B. A., & Poulson, C. L. (2001). Teaching children with autism to engage in conversational exchanges: Script fading with embedded textual stimuli. *Journal of Applied Behavior Analysis, 34,* 81–84.

Sautter, R. A., & LeBlanc, L. A. (2006). Empirical applications of Skinner's analysis of verbal behavior. *Analysis of Verbal Behavior, 22,* 35–48.

Sax, C. (2002). Person-centered planning: More than a strategy. In C. L. Sax & C. A. Thoma (Eds.), *Transition assessment: Wise practices for quality lives* (pp. 13–24). Baltimore, MD: Brookes.

Schaaf, R. C. (2011). Interventions that address sensory dysfunction for individuals with autism spectrum disorders: Preliminary evidence for the superiority of sensory integration compared to other sensory approaches. In B. Reichow, P. Doehring, D. V. Cicchetti, & F. R. Volkmar (Eds.), *Evidence-based practices and treatments for children with autism* (pp. 245–273). New York: Springer Science+Business Media.

Schall, C. & Wehman, P. (2009). Understanding the transition from school to adulthood for students with autism. In P. Wehman, M. D. Smith, & C. Schall (Eds.), *Autism and the transition to adulthood: Success beyond the classroom* (pp. 1–14). Baltimore: Brookes.

Schalock. R. L. (2000). Three decades of quality of life. *Focus on Autism and Other Developmental Disabilities, 15(2),* 116–127.

Schepis, M. M., Reid, D. H., Fitzgerald, J. R., Faw, G. D., Van Den Pol, R. A., & Welty, P. (1982). A program for increasing manual signing by autistic and profoundly retarded youth within the daily environment. *Journal of Applied Behavior Analysis, 15,* 363–379.

Scheuermann, B., & Hall, J. A. (2012). *Positive behavioral supports for the classroom.* Upper Saddle River, NJ: Pearson Education.

Scheuermann, B., & Webber, J. (2002). *Autism: Teaching does make a difference.* Belmont, CA: Wasdworth/Cengage Learning.

Schilling, D. L., & Schwartz, I. S. (2004). Alternative seating for young children with autism spectrum disorder: Effects on classroom behavior. *Journal of Autism and Developmental Disorders, 34,* 423–432.

Schlosser, R. W., Sigafoos, J., & Koul, R. K. (2009). Speech output and speech-generating devices in autism spectrum disorders. In P. Mirenda & T. Iacono (Eds.), *Autism spectrum disorders and AAC* (pp. 141–169). Baltimore, MD: Brookes.

Schneider, N., & Goldstein, H. (2010). Using social stories and visual schedules to improve socially appropriate behaviors in children with autism. *Journal of Positive Behavior Interventions, 12,* 149–160.

Schopler, E., Brehm, S. S., Kinsbourne, M., & Reichler, R. J. (1971). Effect of treatment structure on development in autistic children. *Archives in General Psychiatry, 24,* 415–421.

Schopler, E., Lansing, M. D., Reichler, R., & Marcus, L. M. (2005). Psychoeducational profile (3rd ed.) (PEP-3): TEACCH individualized psychoeducational assessment for children with autism spectrum disorders. Austin, TX: Pro-ed.

Schopler, E., Mesibov, G., & Baker, A. (1982). Evaluation of treatment for autistic *children and their parents. Journal of the American Academy of Child Psychiatry, 21,* 262–267.

Schopler, E., Mesibov, G., DeVellis, R., & Short, A. (1981). Treatment outcome for autistic children and their families. In P. Mittler (Ed.), *Frontiers of knowledge in mental retardation. Vol. I. Social, educational, and behavioral aspects* (pp. 293–301). Baltimore, MD: University Park.

Schopler, E., Mesibov, G. B., & Hearsey, K. (1995). Structured teaching in the TEACCH system. In E. Schopler & G. B. Mesibov (Eds.), *Learning and Cognition in Autism* (pp. 243–268). New York: Plenum Press.

Schopler, E., Mesibov, G. B., & Kunce, L. J. (Eds.). (1998). *Asperger syndrome or high-functioning autism?* New York: Plenum Press.

Schopler, E., & Reichler, R. J. (1971). Parents as cotherapists in the treatment of psychotic children. *Journal of Autism and Childhood Schizophrenia, 1*(1), 87–102.

Schopler, E., Reichler, R. J., Bashford, A., Lansing, M. D., & Marcus, L. M. (1990). *Individualized assessment and treatment for autistic and developmentally disabled children. Vol. 1. Psychoeducational Profile Revised (PEP-R).* Austin, TX: Pro-ed.

Schopler, E., Reichler, R., & Renner, B. R. (1988). *The Childhood Autism Rating Scale (CARS).* Los Angeles: Western Psychological Services.

Schopler, E., Van Bourgondien, M. E., Wellman, G. J., & Love, S. R. (2010). *Childhood Autism Rating Scale—CARS2: Manual* (2nd ed.). Los Angeles: Western Psychological Services.

Schreibman, L. (2005). *The science and fiction of autism.* Cambridge, MA: Harvard University Press.

Schreibman, L., & Carr, E. G. (1978). Elimination of echolalic responding to questions through the training of generalized verbal response. *Journal of Applied Behavior Analysis, 11,* 453–463.

Schreibman, L., & Ingersoll, B. (2011). Naturalistic approaches to early behavioral intervention. In D. G. Amaral, G. Dawson, & D. H. Geschwind (Eds.), *Autism spectrum disorders* (pp. 1056–1067). New York: Oxford University Press.

Schreibman, L., Kaneko, W. M., & Koegel, R. L. (1991). Positive affect of parents of autistic children: A comparison across two teaching techniques, *Behavior Therapy, 22,* 479–490.

Schreibman, L., & Lovaas, I. O. (1973). Overselective response to social stimuli by autistic children. *Journal of Abnormal Child Psychology, 1,* 152–168.

Schreibman, L., Stahmer, A. C., & Pierce, K. L. (1996). Alternative applications of pivotal response training: Teaching symbolic play and social interaction skills. In L. K. Koegel, R. L. Koegel, & G. Dunlap (Eds.). *Positive behavioral support: Including people with difficult behavior in the community* (pp. 353–371). Baltimore, MD: Brookes.

Schreibman, L., Whalen, C., & Stahmer, A. C. (2000). The use of video priming to reduce disruptive transition behavior in children with autism. *Journal of Positive Behavior Interventions, 2,* 3–11.

Schuler, A. L. (1980). Aspects of communication. In W. H. Fay & A. L. Schuler: *Emerging language in autistic children* (pp. 87–111). Baltimore, MD: University Park Press.

Schuler, A., & Wolfberg, P. J. (2000). Promoting peer play and socialization: The art of scaffolding. In A. Wetherby & B. Prizant (Eds.), *Autism spectrum disorders: A transactional developmental perspective* (pp. 251–278). Baltimore, MD: Brookes.

Schultz, R. T., & Robins, D. L. (2005). Functional neuroimaging studies of autism spectrum disorders. In F. Volkmar, R. Paul, A. Klin, & D. Cohen (Eds.), *Handbook of autism and pervasive developmental disorders,* (pp. 515–533). Somerset, NJ: Wiley.

Schwartz, I. S., & Garfinkle, A. N. (1998). The Picture Exchange Communication System: Communication outcomes for young children with disabilities. *Topics in Early Childhood Special Education, 18,* 144–160.

Scott, F. J., Baron-Cohen, S., Bolton, P., & Brayne, C. (2002). Brief report: Prevalence of autism conditions in children 5–11years in Cambridgeshire, UK. *Autism, 6,* 231–237.

Scott, T. M., Liaupsin, C., Nelson, M., & McIntyre, J. (2005). Team-based functional behavior assessment as a proactive public school process: A descriptive analysis of current barriers. *Journal of Behavioral Education, 14,* 57–71.

Sell, J. (2011). Presume competence, presume employment: Improving integrated employment outcomes. *Autism Advocate, 61*(2), 7–10.

Seroussi, K. (2000). *Unraveling the mystery of Autism and Pervasive Developmental Disorder: A mother's story of research and recovery.* New York: Simon and Schuster.

Shabani, D. B., Katz, R. C., Wilder, D. A., Beauchamp, K., Taylor, C. R., & Fischer, K. J. (2002). Increasing social initiations in children with autism: Effects of a tactile prompt. *Journal of Applied Behavior Analysis, 35,* 79–83.

Shafer, M. S., Egel, A. L., & Neef, N. A. (1984). Training mildly handicapped peers to facilitate changes in social interaction skills of autistic children. *Journal of Applied Behavior Analysis, 17,* 461–476.

Shapiro, E. S., & Elliott, S. N. (1999). Curriculum-based assessment and other performance-based assessment strategies. In C. R. Reynolds & T. B. Gutkin (Eds.), *The handbook of school psychology* (3d ed., pp. 383–402). New York: Wiley.

Shattock, P., & Whiteley, P. (2000, April). *The Sunderland protocol: A logical sequencing of biomedical interventions for the treatment of autism and related disorders.* Conference Proceedings from the University of Durham.

Shattuck, P. T., Durkin, M., Maenner, M., Newschaeffer, C., Mandell, D. S., Wiggins, L., & Cuniff, C. (2009). Timing of identification among children with an autism spectrum disorder: Findings from a population-based surveillance study. *Journal of the American Academy of Child & Adolescent Psychiatry, 48,* 474–483.

Shaw, S. R. (2002, October). A school psychologist investigates sensory integration therapies: Promise, possibility, and the art of placebo. *NASP Communique,* National Association of School Psychologists, Retrieved February 25, 2005, from *http//www.nsponlin.org/publications.*

Sheinkopf, S. J., & Siegel, B. (1998). Home-based behavioral treatment of young children with autism. *Journal of Autism and Developmental Disorders, 28*(1), 15–23.

Sherer, M., Pierce, K. L., Paredes, S., Kisackv, K. L., Ingersoll, B., & Schreibman, L. (2001). Enhancing conversation skills in children with autism via video technology: Which is better, "self" or "other" as a model? *Behavior Modification, 25,* 140–158.

Sherer, M., R., & Schreibman, L. (2005). Individual behavioral profiles and predictors of treatment effectiveness for children with autism. *Journal of Consulting and Clinical Psychology, 73,* 525–538.

Shinn, M. R., & Bamonto, S. (1998). Advanced applications of curriculum-based measurement: "Big ideas" and avoiding confusion. In M. R. Shinn (Ed), *Advanced applications of curriculum-based measurement* (pp. 1–31). New York: The Guilford Press.

Shook, G. L., & Favell, J. E. (1996). Identifying qualified professionals in behavior analysis. In C. Maurice, G. Green, & S. Luce (Eds.), *Behavioral intervention for young children with autism: A manual for parents and professionals* (pp. 221–229). Austin, TX: Pro-ed.

Sicile-Kira, C. (2004). *Autism spectrum disorders: The complete guide to understanding autism, Asperger's syndrome, pervasive developmental disorder, and other ASDs.* New York: Berkley Publishing Group.

Sicile-Kira, C. (2006). *Adolescents on the autism spectrum: A parent's guide to the cognitive, social, physical, and transition needs of teenagers with autism spectrum disorders.* New York: A Perigree Book.

Sidener, T. M., Carr, J. E., & Firth, A. M. (2005). Superimposition and withholding of edible consequences as treatment for automatically reinforced stereotypy. *Journal of Applied Behavior Analysis, 38,* 121–124.

Siegel Causey, E., & Guess, D. (1989). *Enhancing nonsymbolic communication interactions among learners with severe disabilities.* Baltimore, MD: Brookes.

Sigafoos, J., O'Reilly, M., & Cannella, H. (2005). Computer-presented video prompting for teaching microwave oven use to three adults with developmental disabilities. *Education and Training in Developmental Disabilities, 39,* 240–252.

Sigafoos, J., O'Reilly, M. F., & Lancioni, G. E. (2009). Functional communication training and choice-making interventions for treatment of problem behavior in *Spectrum disorders and AAC.* In P. Mirenda & T. Iacono (Eds.), *Autism Spectrum disorders and AAC* (pp. 333–353). Baltimore, MD: Brookes.

Sigman, M., & Mundy, P. (1989). Social attachments in autistic children. *Journal of the American Academy of Child & Adolescent Psychiatry, 28*(1), 74–81.

Sigman, M., & Mundy, P., Sherman, T., Ungerer, J. (1986). Social interaction of autistic, mentally retarded and normal children and their caregivers. *Journal of Child Psychology and Psychiatry, 27*(5), 647–656.

Sigman, M., & Ruskin, E. (1999). Continuity and change in the social competence of children with autism, Down syndrome and developmental delays. *Monographs of the Society for Research in Child Development, 64*(1), 1–114.

Sigman, M., Spence, S. J., & Wang, A. T. (2006). Autism from developmental and neuropsychological perspectives. *Annual Review of Clinical Psychology, 2,* 327–355.

Sigman, M., & Ungerer, J. A. (1984). Cognitive and language skills in autistic, mentally retarded, and normal children. *Developmental Psychology, 20,* 293–302.

Simpson, R. L. (1994). School reform and children and youth with autism. *Focus on Autistic Behavior, 9*(2), 9–15.

Simpson, R. L. (2005). *Autism spectrum disorders: Interventions and treatments for children and youth.* Thousand Oaks, CA: Corwin.

Simpson, R. L., de Boer-Ott, S. R., & Smith-Myles, B. (2003). Inclusion of learners with autism spectrum disorders in general education settings. *Topics in Language Disorders, 23*(2), 116–133.

Simpson, R. L., & Myles, B. S. (1998). Controversial therapies and interventions with children and youth with autism. In R. L. Simpson & B. S. Myles (Eds.), *Educating children and youth with autism* (pp. 315–331). Austin, TX: Pro-ed.

Skinner, B. F. (1938). *The behavior of organisms: An experimental analysis.* New York: Appleton-Century Crofts.

Skinner, B. F. (1957). *Verbal behavior.* New York: Appleton-Century Crofts.

Skinner, B. F. (1974). *About behaviorism.* New York: Alfred A. Knopf.

Smith, B. J., McLean, M. E., Sandall, S., Snyder, P., & Ramsey, B. (2005). DEC Recommended practices: The procedures and evidence base used to establish them. In S. Sandall, M. L. Hemmeter, B. J. Smith , & M. E., McLean & (Eds) *DEC Recommended practices in early intervention/early childhood special education: A comprehensive guide for practical application.* (pp. 27–39). Longmont, CO: Sopris West.

Smith, L. E., Hong, J., Seltzer, M. M., Greenberg, J.S., Ameida, D. M., & Bishop, S. L. (2010). Daily experiences among mothers of adolescents and adults with autism spectrum disorder, *Journal of Autism and Developmental Disorder, 40,* 167–178.

Smith, L., Seltzer, M. M., Tager-Flusberg, H., Greenberg, J. S., & Carter, A. S. (2008). A comparative analysis of well-being and coping among mothers of toddlers and mothers of adolescents with ASD. *Journal of Autism and Developmental Disorders, 38,* 876–889.

Smith, M. D., & Belcher, R. G. (1993). Brief report: Facilitated communication with adults with autism. *Journal of Autism and Developmental Disabilities, 23*(1), 175–183.

Smith, M. D., Belcher, R. G., & Juhrs, P. D. (1995). *A guide to successful employment for individuals with autism.* Baltimore, MD: Brookes.

Smith, M. D., & Targett, P. S. (2009). Critical life skills. In P. Wehman,

M. D. Smith, & C. Schall (Eds.), *Autism and the transition to adulthood: Success beyond the classroom* (pp. 209–231). Baltimore: Brookes.

Smith, T., & Antolovich, M. (2000). Parental perceptions of supplemental interventions received by young children with autism in intensive behavior analytic treatment. *Behavioral Interventions, 15,* 83–97.

Smith, T., Groen, A. D., & Wynne, J. W. (2000). Randomized trial of intensive early intervention for children with pervasive developmental disorder. *American Journal on Mental Retardation, 105*(4), 269–285.

Smith, T., Parker, T., Taubman, M., & Lovaas, O. I. (1992). Transfer of staff training from workshops to group homes: A failure to generalize across settings. *Research in Developmental Disabilities, 13,* 57–71.

Snyder-Mclean, L. K., & Mclean, J. E. (1978). Verbal information gathering strategies: The child's use of language to acquire language. *Journal of Speech and Hearing Disorders, 43,* 306–325.

Snyder-McLean, L. K., Solomonson, B., McLean, J. E., & Sack, S. (1984). Structuring joint action routines: A strategy for facilitating communication and language development in the classroom. *Seminars in Speech and Language, 5*(3), 213–228.

Sofronoff, K., Attwood, T., Hinton, S., & Levin, I. (2007). A randomized controlled trial of a cognitive behavioral intervention for anger management in children diagnosed with Asperger syndrome. *Journal of Autism and Developmental Disorders, 37,* 1203–1214.

Sofronoff, K., & Beaumont, R. (2009). The challenges of working with young people diagnosed with Asperger syndrome. In D. McKay & E. A. Storch (Eds.), *Cognitive-behavior therapy for children* (pp. 421–443). New York: Springer.

Solomon, R., Necheles, J., Ferch, C., & Bruckman, D. (2007). Pilot study of a parent training program for young children with autism: The PLAY project home consultation program. *Autism, 11,* 205–224.

Sparks, D. (2004). Focusing staff development on improving the learning of all students. In G. Cawalti (Ed.), *Handbook of research on improving student achievement* (pp. 245–255). Arlington, VA: Educational Research Service.

Sparrow, S. S., Balla, D. A., & Cicchetti, D. V. (1984). *The Vineland Adaptive Behavior Scales.* Circle Pines, MN: American Guidance Service.

Sparrow, S. S., Balla, D. A., & Cicchetti, D. V. (1994*). Vineland Adaptive Behavior Scales (Survey Form).* Circle Pines, MN: American Guidance Service.

Sparrow, S. S., Balla, D. A., & Cicchetti, D. V. (1998). *Vineland Social-Emotional Early Childhood Scales.* Circle Pines, MN: American Guidance Service.

Squires, J., Bricker, D., & Twombly, E. (2002). *The ASQ: SE user's guide for the Ages and Stages Questionnaires: Social-Emotional.* Baltimore, MD: Brookes.

Sroufe, L. A. (1995). *Emotional development: The organization of emotional life in the early years.* New York: Cambridge Press.

Stagnitti, K., Raison, R., & Ryan, P. (1999). Sensory defensiveness syndrome: A pediatric perspective and case study. *Australian Occupational Therapy Journal, 46,* 175–187.

Stahmer, A. C. (1995). Teaching symbolic play skills to children with autism using pivotal response training. *Journal of Autism and Developmental Disorders, 25,* 123–141.

Stahmer, A. C., & Gist, K. (2001). The effects of an accelerated parent education program and mastery of child outcome. *Journal of Positive Behavior Interventions, 3,* 75–82.

Stahmer, A. C., & Ingersoll, B. (2004). Inclusive programming for toddlers with autism spectrum disorders: Outcomes from the Children's Toddler School. *Journal of Positive Behavior Interventions, 6,* 67–82.

Stahmer, A. C., Ingersoll, B., & Carter, C. (2003). Using point-of-view video modeling to teach play to preschoolers with autism. *Topics in Early Childhood Special Education.*

*Special issue: Special Issue on Play,* 7(4), 401–413.

Stahmer, A. C., & Schreibman, L. (1992). Teaching children with autism appropriate play in unsupervised environments using a self-management treatment package. *Journal of Applied Behavior Analysis,* 25, 447–459.

Stahmer, A. C., Suhrheinrich, J., Reed, S., Bolduc, C., & Schreibman, L. (2011). *Classroom pivotal response teaching: A guide to effective implementation.* New York: Guilford Press.

State of the Art Productions, Inc. (2004). *Autism is a world.* DVD Documentary Short Subject: CNN and State of the Art Productions, Inc.

Steffenburg, S., Gillberg, C., Hellgren, L., Anderson, L., Gillberg, I. C., Jakobsson, G., et al. (1989). A twin study of autism in Denmark, Finland, Iceland, Norway and Sweden. *Journal of Child Psychology and Psychiatry,* 30, 405–416.

Stern, D. N. (1985). *The interpersonal world of the infant: A view from psychoanalysis and developmental psychology.* New York: Basic Books.

Stevens, M., Washington, A., Rice, C., Jenner, W., Ottolino, J., Clancy, K., Whitney, J., & Hentz, J. (2007). *Prevalence of the autism spectrum disorders (ASDs) in multiple areas of the United States, 2000 and 2002.* Atlanta, GA: Centers for Disease Control and Prevention.

Stichter, J. P. (2001). Functional analysis: The use of analogues in applied settings. *Focus on Autism and Other Developmental Disabilities,* 16(4), 232–239.

Stichter, J. P., & Conroy, M. A. (2006). *How to teach social skills for and plan for peer social interaction.* Austin, TX: Pro-ed.

Stichter, J. P., Shellady, S., Sealander, K. A., & Eigenberger, M. E. (2000). Teaching what we do know: Preservice training and functional behavioral assessment, *Preventing School Failure,* 44, 142–146.

Stoel-Gammon, C. (1998). Role of babbling and phonology in early linguistic development. In A. M. Wetherby, S. F. Warren, & J. Reichle (Eds.) *Transitions in prelinguistic*

*communication,* (pp.87–110). Baltimore, MD: Brookes.

Stokes, T. F., & Baer, D. M., (1977). An implicit technology of generalization. *Journal of Applied Behavior Analysis,* 10, 349–367.

Stone, W. L., Coonrod, E. E., Turner, L. M., & Pozdol, S. L. (2004). Psychometric properties of the STAT for early autism screening. *Journal of Autism and Developmental Disorders,* 34, 691–701.

Stoner, J. B., Beck, A. R., Bock, S. J., Hickey, K., Kosuwan, K., & Thompson, J. R. (2006). The effectiveness of the Picture Exchange Communication System with nonspeaking adults. *Remedial and Special Education,* 27, 154–165.

Strain, P. S., & Bovey, E. H. (2011). Randomized controlled trial of the LEAP model of early intervention for young children with autism spectrum disorders. *Topics in Early Childhood Special Education,* 31, 133–154

Strain, P. S., Kerr, M. M., & Ragland, E. U. (1979). Effects of peer-mediated social interactions and prompting/ reinforcement procedures on the social behavior of autistic children. *Journal of Autism and Developmental Disorders,* 9, 41–54.

Strain, P. S., Schwartz, I. S., & Bovey, E. H. (2008). Social competence interventions for young children with autism. In W. H. Brown, S. L. Odom, & S. R. Mconnell (Eds.), *Social competence of young children: Risk, disability and intervention* (pp. 253–272). Baltimore, MD: Brookes.

Sugai, G., & White, W. J. (1986). Effects of using object self-stimulation as a reinforcer on the prevocational work rates of an autistic child. *Journal of Autism and Developmental Disorders,* 16, 459–471.

Sussman, F. (1999). *More than words: Helping parents promote communication and social skills in children with autism spectrum disorder.* Montreal, Canada: A Hanen Centre Publication.

Swinkels, H.N., Dietz, C., van Daalen, E., Kerkhof, H. G. M., van Engeland, H., & Buitelaar, J. K. (2006).

Screening for autistic spectrum in children aged 14 and 15 months. I. The development of the Early Screening of Autistic Traits (ESAT) questionnaire. *Journal of Autism and Developmental Disorders,* 36, 723–732.

Sze, K. M., & Koegel, R. L. (2006). Ecocultural theory and cultural diversity in intervention programs. In R. L. Koegel, & L. K. Koegel (Eds). *Pivotal response treatments for autism: Communication, social, and academic development* (pp. 117–127). Baltimore, MD: Brookes.

Szempruch, J., & Jacobson, J. W. (1993). Evaluating facilitated communications of people with developmental disabilities. *Research in Developmental Disabilities,* 14, 253–264.

Tager-Flusberg, H., Edelson, L., & Luyster, R. (2011). Language and communication in autism spectrum disorders. In D. G. Amaral, G. Dawson, & D. H. Geschwind (Eds.), *Autism spectrum disorders* (pp. 172–185). New York: Oxford University Press.

Tarbox, R. S., & Najdowski, A. C. (2008). Discrete trial training as a teaching paradigm. In J. K. Luiselli, D. C. Russo, W. P. Christian, & S. M. Wilczynski (Eds.), *Effective practices for children with autism: Educational and behavioral support interventions that work* (pp. 181–194). New York: Oxford University Press.

Tardif, T. (1996). Nouns are not always learned before verbs: Evidence from Mandarin speakers' early vocabularies. *Developmental Psychology,* 32, 492–504.

Taubman, M. (2008). Data can and should be your friend! In R. Leaf, M. Taubman, & J. McEachin (Eds.), *It's time for school: Building quality ABA educational programs for students with autism spectrum disorders* (pp. 137–151). New York: DRL Books.

Taubman, M., Leaf, R., & McEachin, J. (2011). Crafting connections: Contemporary applied behavior analysis for enriching the social lives of persons with autism spectrum disorders. New York: DRL Books.

Taylor, B., & Harris, B. A. (1995). Teaching children with autism to seek information: Acquisition of novel information and generalization of responding. *Journal of Applied Behavior Analysis, 28*, 3–14.

Taylor, B. A., & Jasper, S. (2001). Teaching programs to increase peer interaction. In C. Maurice, G. Green, & R. Foxx (Eds.), *Making a difference: Behavioral intervention for autism* (pp. 97–162). Austin, TX: PRO-ED.

Taylor, B. A., Levin, L., & Jasper, S. (1999). Increasing play-related statements in children with autism toward their siblings: Effects of video modeling. *Journal of Developmental and Physical Disabilities, 11*, 253–264.

Taylor, B. A., & McDonough, K. A. (1996). Selecting teaching programs. In C. Maurice, G. Green, & S. Luce (Eds.), *Behavioral intervention for young children with autism: A manual for parents and professionals* (pp. 63–177) Austin, TX: Pro-ed.

Test, D., Mason, C., Hughes, C., & Konrad, M. (2004). Student involvement in individualized education program meetings. *Exceptional Children, 70*, 391–407.

Test, D. W., Maxxotti, V. L., Mustian, A. L., Fowler, C. H., Kortering, L., & Kohler, P. (2009). Evidence-based secondary transition predictors for improving postschool outcomes for students with disabilities. *Career Development for Exceptional Individuals, 32*, 160–181.

Test, D. W., Richter, S., Knight, V., & Spooner, F. (2011). A comprehensive review and meta-analysis of the social stories literature. *Focus on Autism and Other Developmental Disabilities, 26*(1), 49–62.

The Help Group. (2011). *Social skills group for young adults with autism spectrum disorders: Program for the education and enrichment of relational skills (PEERS).* Los Angeles, CA: Autism Research Alliance.

Thiemann, K. S., & Goldstein, H. (2001). Social stories, written text cues and video feedback: Effects on social communication of children with autism. *Journal of*

*Applied Behavior Analysis, 34*, 425–446.

Thompson, G. L. (2004). *Through ebony eyes: What teachers need to know but are afraid to ask about African American students.* San Francisco: Jossey-Bass.

Thorp, D. M., Stahmer, A. C., & Schreibman, L. (1995). Effects of sociodramatic play training on children with autism. *Journal of Autism and Developmental Disorders, 25*(3), 265–282.

Tincani, M. (2004). Comparing the Picture Exchange Communication System and sign language training for children with autism. *Focus on Autism and Other Developmental Disabilities, 19*, 152–163.

Towbin, K. E., Mauk, J. E., & Batshaw, M. L. (2002). Pervasive developmental disorders. In M. L. Batshaw (Ed.), *Children with disabilities* (5th ed., pp. 365–387). Baltimore, MD: Brookes.

Tsang, S. K. M., Shek, D. T. L., Lam, L. L., Yang, F. L., & Cheung, P. M. P (2007). Brief report. Application of the TEACCH program on Chinese children with autism—Does culture make a difference? *Journal of Autism and Developmental Disorders. 37*, 390–396.

Tuchman, R. (2011). Epilepsy and electroencephalography in autism spectrum disorders. In D. G. Amaral, G. Dawson, & D. H. Geschwind (Eds.), *Autism spectrum disorders* (pp. 381–394). New York: Oxford University Press.

Turan, Y., & Halle, J. (2006, May). *Are social interactions for children with autism spectrum disorders reinforcing?* Paper presented at the 32nd Annual Convention of the Association for Behavior Analysis, International. Atlanta, GA.

Turnbull, A., Turnbull, R., Erwin, E., Soodak, L., & Shogren, K. A. (2011). *Families, professionals, and exceptionality: Positive outcomes through partnership and trust* (6th ed.). Upper Saddle River, NJ: Pearson Education.

Turnbull, A. P., Zuna, N., Turnbull, H. R., Poston, D., & Summers, J. A. (2007). Families as partners in educational decision making. In S. L.

Odom, R. H. Horner, M.E. Snell, & J. Blacher (Eds). *Handbook of Developmental Disabilities* (pp. 570–587). New York: Guilford Press.

US Code of Federal Regulations (CFR) 34 Part 303.18(b)

U.S. Office of Special Education Programs (2005). *FACTS from OSEP's national longitudinal studies.* Washington, DC: Author.

Utley C. A., & Obiakor, F. E. (2001). Multicultural education and special education: Infusion for better schooling. In C. A. Utley & F. E. Obiakor (Eds.), *Special education, multicultural education, and school reform* (pp. 3–29). Springfield, IL: Charles C. Thomas.

Van Bourgondien, M. E., Reichle, N. C., & Schopler, E. (2003). Effects of a model treatment approach on adults with autism. *Journal of Autism and Developmental Disorders, 33*(2), 131–140.

Vandercook, T., York, J., & Forest, M. (1989). The McGill Action Planning System (MAPS): A strategy for building the vision. *Journal of the Association for Persons with Severe Handicaps, 14*(3), 205–215.

van Kleeck, A. (1994). Potential cultural bias in training parents as conversational partners with their children who have delays in language development. *American Journal of Speech-Language Pathology, 31*, 67–78.

Van Reusen, A. K., & Bos, C. S. (1994). Facilitating student participation in individualized education programs through motivation strategy instruction. *Exceptional Children, 60*, 466–475.

Van Reusen, A. K., Bos, C., Schumaker, J. B., & Deshler, D. D. (1994). *Self-advocacy strategy for education and transition planning.* Lawrence, KS: Edge Enterprises.

Venter, A., Lord, C., & Schopler, E. (1992). A follow up study of high-functioning autistic children. *Journal of Child Psychology and Psychiatry, 33*, 489–508.

Vernon, D. S., Schumaker, J. B., & Deshler, D. D. (1995). Development and validation of an instrument to measure social processes and intervention effects within mainstream class environments, USDE, H023C10135-92, final report.

Vihman, M. M., & McCune, L. (1994). When is a word a word? *Journal of Child Language, 21,* 517–542.

Vismara, L.A., Colombi, C., & Rogers, S. J. (2009). Can one hour per week of therapy lead to lasting changes in young children with autism? *Autism, 13,* 93–115.

Vismara, L. A., & Lyons, G. L. (2007). Using perseverative interests to elicit joint attention behaviors in young children with autism: Theoretical and clinical implications for understanding motivation. *Journal of Positive Behavior Interventions, 9,* 214–228.

Vismara, L. A., & Rogers, S. J. (2008). The Early Start Denver Model: A case study of an innovative practice. *Journal of Early Intervention, 31,* 91–108.

Vismara, L. A., Young, G. S., Stahmer, A. C., Griffith, E. M., & Rogers, S. J. (2009). Dissemination of evidence-based practice: Can we train therapists from a distance? *Journal of Autism and Developmental Disorders, 39,* 1636–1651.

Vort Corporation. (1995). *HELP for preschoolers.* Palo Alto, CA: Author.

Vygotsky, L. S. (1978). *Mind in society: The development of higher psychological processes.* Cambridge, MA: Harvard University Press.

Wagner, S. (1999). *Inclusive programming for elementary students with autism.* Arlington, TX: Future Horizons.

Wagner, S. (2002). *Inclusive programming for middle school students with autism/Asperger's syndrome.* Arlington, TX: Future Horizons.

Wakeford, L., & Baranek, G. T. (2011). Occupational therapy. In D. G. Amaral, G. Dawson, & D. H. Geschwind (Eds.), *Autism spectrum disorders* (pp. 1113–1128). New York: Oxford University Press.

Walden, T. A. (1993). Communicating the meaning of events through social referencing. In A. Kaiser & D. Gray (Eds.), *Enhancing children's communication: Research foundations for intervention* (pp. 187–200). Baltimore, MD: Brookes.

Walden, T., Knieps, L., & Baxter, A. (1991). Contingent provision of social referential information by parents of normally developing and delayed children. *American Journal on Mental Retardation, 96,* 177–187.

Walker-Hirsch, L., & Champagne, M. P. (1991). The circles concept: Social competence in special education. *Educational Leadership, September,* 65–67.

Warren, S. F., Yoder, P. J., & Leew, S. V. (2002). Promoting social-communicative development in infants and toddlers. In H. Goldstein, L. Kaczmarek, & K. English (Eds.), *Promoting social communication* (pp. 121–150). Baltimore, MD: Brookes.

Watson, N. P. (1976). A theoretical and empirical study of empathy and sex role differentiation. *Abstracts International, 37*(5-B), 2533–2534.

Webb, B. J., Miller, S. P., Pierce, T. B., Strawser, S., & Jones, W. P. (2004). Effects of social skill instruction for high-functioning adolescents with autism spectrum disorders. *Focus on Autism and Other Developmental Disabilities, 19,* 53–62.

Webber, J., & Scheuermann, B. (2008). *Educating students with autism: A quick start manual.* Austin, TX: Pro-ed.

Weeks, S. J., & Hobson R. P. (1987). The salience of facial expression for autistic children. *Journal of Child Psychology and Psychiatry, 28*(1), 137–151.

Wehman, P., Smith, M. D., & Schall, C. (2009). *Autism and the transition to adulthood: Success beyond the classroom.* Baltimore: Brookes.

Wehmeyer, M. L. (2002). Self-determined assessment. In C. L. Sax & C. A. Thoma (Eds.), *Transition assessment: Wise practices for quality lives* (pp. 25–38). Baltimore, MD: Brookes.

Wehmeyer, M. L. (2005). Self-determination and individuals with severe disabilities: Reexamining meanings and misinterpretations. *Research and Practice in Severe Disabilities, 30,* 113–120.

Wehmeyer, M. L., & Kelchner, K. (1995). *The Arc's Self-Determination Scale.* Arlington, TX: The ARC National Headquarters.

Wehmeyer, M. L., & Schalock, R. L. (2001). Self-determination and quality of life: Implications for special education services and supports. *Focus on Exceptional Children, 33*(8), 1–16.

Wehmeyer, M. L., Shogren, K. A., Smith, T. E. C., Zager, D., & Simpson, R. (2010). Research-based principles and practices for educating students with autism: Self-determination and social interaction. *Education and Training in Autism and Developmental Disabilities, 45,* 475–486

Weiss, M. J. (1999). Differential rates of skill acquisition and outcomes of early intensive behavioral intervention for autism. *Behavioral Intervention, 14,* 3–22.

Weiss, M. J., & Harris, S. L. (2001). *Reaching out, joining in: Teaching social skills to young children with autism.* Bethesda, MD: Woodbine House.

Wendt, O. (2009). Research on the use of manual signs and graphic symbols in autism spectrum disorders. In P. Mirenda & T. Iacono (Eds.), *Autism spectrum disorders and AAC* (pp. 83–139). Baltimore, MD: Brookes.

Wert, B. Y., & Neisworth, J. T. (2003). Effects of video self-modeling on spontaneous requesting in children with autism. *Journal of Positive Behavior Interventions, 5,* 30–34.

Wetherby, A. M., Alexander, D. G., & Prizant, B. M. (1998). The ontogeny and role of repair strategies. In A. M. Wetherby, S. F. Warren, & J. Reichle (Eds.), *Transitions in prelinguistic comunication* (pp.135–159). Baltimore, MD: Brookes.

Wetherby, A., Cain. D., Yonclas, D., & Walker, V. (1988). Analysis of intentional communication of normal children from the prelinguistic to the multi-word stage. *Journal of Speech and Hearing Research, 31,* 240–252.

Wetherby, A. M., & Prizant, B. M. (2000). *Autism spectrum disorders: A transactional developmental perspective.* Baltimore, MD: Brookes.

Wetherby, A., & Prizant, B. (2002). Communication and Social Behavior Scales Developmental Profile—Infant-Toddler Checklist. In A. M.

Wetherby & B. M. Prizant, *CSBS DP^{TM}* (manual, p. 171). Baltimore, MD: Brookes.

Wetherby, A., & Prutting, C. (1984). Profiles of communicative and cognitive-social abilities in autistic children. *Journal of Speech and Hearing Research, 27,* 364–377.

Wetherby, A. M., Reichle, J., & Pierce, P. L. (1998). The transition to symbolic communication. In A. M. Wetherby, S. F. Warren, & J. Reichle (Eds.) *Transitions in prelinguistic communication* (pp.197–232). Baltimore, MD: Brookes.

Whalen, C., & Schreibman, L. (2003). Joint attention training for children with autism using behavior modification procedures. *Journal of Child Psychology and Psychiatry, 44,* 456–468.

Wheeler, D. L., Jacobson, J. W., Paglieri, R. A., & Schwartz, A. A. (1993). An experimental assessment of facilitated communication. *Mental Retardation, 31*(1), 49–60.

Wheeler, A. J., Miller, R. A., Springer, B. M., Pittard, N. C., Phillips, J. F., & Myers, A. M. (1997). *Murdoch Center program library. Volume II.* Butner, NC: Murdoch Center Foundation.

Wilbarger, P. (1995, June). The sensory diet: Activity programs based on sensory processing theory. *Sensory Integration Newsletter, 18*(2), 1–4.

Wilbarger, P., & Wilbarger, J. (1991). *Sensory defensiveness in children age 2–12: An intervention guide for parents and other caretakers.* Denver, CO: Avanti Educational Programs.

Wilcox, M. J., & Shannon, M. S. (1998). Facilitating the transition from prelinguistic to linguistic communication. In A. Wetherby, S. Warren, & J. Reichle (Eds.), *Transitions in prelinguistic communication* (pp. 385–416). Baltimore, MD: Brookes.

Wilder, L. K., Dyches, T. T., Obiakor, F. E., & Algozzine, B. (2004). Multicultural perspectives on teaching students with autism. *Focus on Autism and Other Developmental Disabilities, 19,* 105–113.

Williams, K. E., & Foxx, R. M. (2007). *Treating eating problems of children with autism spectrum disorders and developmental disabilities.* Austin, TX: PRO-ED.

Wilson, K. E. (1998). Centers for independent living in support of transition. *Focus on Autism and Other Developmental Disabilities, 13,* 246–252.

Wing, L., & Gould, J. (1978). Systematic recording of behaviours and skills of retarded and psychotic children. *Journal of Autism and Childhood Schizophrenia, 8,* 79–97.

Wing, L., Leekam, S. R., Libby, S. J., Gould, J., & Larcombe, M. (2002). The Diagnostic Interview for Social and Communication Disorders: Background, inter-rater reliability and clinical use. *Journal of Child Psychology and Psychiatry, 43*(3), 307–325.

Winner, M. G. (2002). Assessment of social skills for students with Asperger syndrome and high-functioning autism. *Assessment for Effective Intervention, 27,* 73–80.

Winner, M. G. (2007). *Thinking about you, thinking about me: Teaching perspective taking and social thinking to persons with social cognitive learning challenges.* San Jose, CA: Social Thinking Publishing.

Winner, M. G. (2008).*Think social! A social thinking curriculum for school-age students.* San Jose, CA: Social Thinking Publishing.

Winner, M. G., & Crooke, P. (2009). *Socially curious and curiously social: A social thinking guidebook for teens & young adults with Asperger's, ADHD, PDD_NOS, NVLD, or other murky undiagnosed social learning issues.* San Jose, CA: Social Thinking Publishing.

Wolery, M. (2004). Monitoring children's progress and intervention implementation. In M. McLean, M. Wolery, & D. B. Bailey (Eds.), *Assessing infants and preschoolers* with special needs (3rd ed., pp. 545–584). Columbus, OH: Pearson Education.

Wolery, M., Barton, E. E., & Hine, J. F. (2005). Evolution of applied behavior analysis in the treatment of individuals with autism. *Exceptionality, 13*(1), 11–23.

Wolf, M. (2003, February). *Application of operant conditioning procedures to the behavior problems of an autistic child: A 25-year follow-up.* Paper presented at the meeting of the 21st Annual Western Regional Conference of the California Association for Behavior Analysis, Newport Beach, CA.

Wolf, M. M., Risley, T. R., & Mees, H. (1964). Application of operant conditioning procedures to the behavior problems of an autistic child. *Behavior Research and Therapy, 1,* 305–312.

Wolfberg, P. J. (1999). *Play & imagination in children with autism.* New York: Teachers College Press.

Wolfberg, P. J. (2003). *Peer play and the autism spectrum: The art of guiding children's socialization and imagination.* Shawnee Mission, KS: Autism Asperger Publishing.

Wolfberg, P. J., & Schuler, A. L. (1993). Integrated play groups: A model for promoting the social and cognitive dimensions of play in children with autism. *Journal of Autism and Developmental Disorders, 23*(3), 467–489.

Wood, J. J., Drahota, A., Sze, K., Har, K., Chiu, A., & Langer, D. A. (2009). Cognitive behavior therapy for anxiety in children with autism spectrum disorders: A randomized, controlled trial. *Journal of Child Psychology and Psychiatry, 50,* 224–234.

Wood, J. J., Fujii, C., & Renno, P. (2011). Cognitive behavior therapy in high-functioning autism: Review and recommendations for treatment development. In B. Reichow, P. Doehring, D. V. Cicchetti, & F. R. Volkmar (Eds.), *Evidence-based practices and treatments for children with autism* (pp. 197–230). New York: Springer.

World Health Organization. (1992). *International classification of diseases: Classification of mental and behavioural disorders.* London: Author.

Wrobel, M. (2003). *Taking care of myself: A hygiene, puberty and personal curriculum for young people with autism.* Arlington, TX: Future Horizons.

Yang, T. R., Wolfberg, P. J., Wu, S. C., & Hwu, P. Y. (2003). Supporting children on the autism spectrum in peer play at home and school:

Piloting the integrated play groups model in Taiwan. *Autism, 7,* 437–453.

Yeargin-Allsopp, M., Rice, C., Karapurkar, T., Doernberg, N., Boyle, C., & Murphy, C. (2003). Prevalence of autism in a US metropolitan area. *Journal of the American Medical Association, 289,* 49–55.

Yell, M. L. (2012). *The law and special education* (3d ed.). Upper Saddle River, NJ: Pearson Education.

Yell, M. L., & Dragsow, E. (2005). *No child left behind: A guide for professionals.* Upper Saddle River, NJ: Pearson Education.

Yell, M. L., Drasgow, E., & Lowrey, A. K. (2005). No child left behind and students with autism spectrum disorders. *Focus on Autism and Other Developmental Disabilities, 20*(3), 130–139.

Yi, J. I., Christian, L., Vittimberga, G., & Lowenkron, B. (2006). Generalized negatively reinforced manding in children with autism. *Analysis of Verbal Behavior, 22,* 21–33.

Yoder, P. J., & Davies, B. (1992). Do children with developmental delays use more frequent and diverse language verbal routines? *American Journal of Mental Retardation, 97*(2), 197–208.

Yoder, P. J., & Stone, W. L. (2006). Randomized comparison of two communication interventions for preschoolers with autism spectrum

disorders. *Journal of Consulting and Clinical Psychology, 74,* 426–435.

Yoder, P., Stone, W. L., Walden, T., & Malesa, E. (2009). Predicting social impairment and ASD diagnosis in younger siblings of children with autism spectrum disorder. *Journal of Autism and Developmental Disorders, 39,* 1381–1391.

Yoder, P. J., & Warren, S. F. (1993*).* Can developmentally delayed children's language development be enhanced through prelinguistic intervention? In A. P. Kaiser & D. B. Gray (Eds.), *Enhancing children's communication: Research foundations for intervention (pp. 35–61).* Baltimore, MD: Brookes.

Yoder, P. J., Warren, S. F., McCathren, R., & Leew, S. V. (1998). Does adult responsivity to child behavior facilitate communication development? In A. M. Wetherby, S. F. Warren, & J. Reichle (Eds.) *Transitions in prelinguistic communication,* (pp. 39–58). Baltimore, MD: Brookes.

York, S. (2006). *Roots and wings: Affirming culture in early childhood programs.* Upper Saddle River, NJ: Pearson Education.

Young, B., & Simpson, R. L. (1997). An examination of paraprofessional involvement in supporting inclusion of students with autism. *Focus on Autism & Other Developmental Disabilities, 12*(1), 31–40.

Zager, D. (2005). *Autism spectrum disorders: Identification, education, and*

*treatment.* Mahway, NJ: Lawrence Erlbaum.

Zanolli, K., Daggett, J., & Adams, T. (1996). Teaching preschool age autistic children to make spontaneous initiations to peers using priming. *Journal of Autism and Developmental Disorders, 26*(4), 407–422.

Zercher, C., Hunt, P., Schuler, A. L., & Webster, J. (2001). Increasing joint attention, play and language through peer supported play. *Autism: The International Journal of Research and Practice, 5,* 374–398.

Zionts, L. T., Zionts, P., Harrison, S., & Bellinger, O. (2003). Urban African American families' perceptions of cultural sensitivity within the special education system. *Focus on Autism and Other Developmental Disorders, 18*(1), 41–50.

Zuniga, M. E. (2004). Families with Latino roots. In E. W. Lynch & M. H. Hanson (Eds.), *Developing cross-cultural competence: A guide for working with children and their families* (pp. 179–218). Baltimore, MD: Brookes.

Zwaigenbaum, L. (2011). Screening, risk, and early identification of autism spectrum disorders. In D. G. Amaral, G. Dawson, & D. H. Geschwind (Eds.), *Autism spectrum disorders* (pp. 75–89). New York: Oxford University Press.

# Name Index

Abraham, L. M., 198
Abrahams, B. S., 6
Adams, L. W., 2, 229
Adams, T., 201
Adamson, L. B., 126, 127, 171, 174,
    193, 194
Addison, L., 49
Ahearn, W. H., 95
Akshoomoff, N., 28, 29, 59
Alaimo, D. F., 170, 188
Alberto, P., 60, 66, 74, 81, 85, 94, 104,
    105, 106, 107, 114, 117, 118, 119
Albin, R. W., 107, 110
Alcantara, P. R., 95
Alexander, D. G., 172
Alfred, C., 178
Algozzine, B., 163
Allen, E. M., 174
Allen, J., 174, 195
Allen, K. D., 136
Almeida, M. C., 202
Almond, P. J., 29
American Psychiatric Association
    (APA), 2, 3, 4, 41, 195
American Speech-Language-Hearing
    Association (ASHA), 44
Amerine-Dickens, M., 98
Anderson, J. L., 49, 64
Anderson, S., 202
Anderson, S. R., 85, 91
Andrews, C., 156
Andrews, S. M., 214
Antolovich, M., 11, 16
Anzalone, M. E., 13, 14, 15
APA. see American Psychiatric
    Association
Apple, A. L., 118
Arbesman, M., 14
Arias, M. B., 161
Arick, J. R., 29
Arnold, K. B., 198
Arnold, N., 69
ASHA. see American Speech-
    Language-Hearing Association

Ashbaugh, K., 207
Asher, S. R., 195
Asmus, J. M., 110
Asperger, H., 2
Aspy, R., 35
Association for Children's Mental
    Health, 56
Attermeier, S. M., 33
Attwood, T., 195, 207, 215
Autism Research Institute, 11, 12
Autism Speaks, 234, 235, 236
Ayllon, T., 79
Ayres, A. J., 14
Ayres, K. M., 94, 210, 233

Baer, D. M., 74, 75, 83, 85, 88
Baglio, C., 75, 101
Bagnato, S. J., 33, 132
Bailey, A., 6, 23
Bailey, J., 97
Baird, G., 21
Bakeman, R., 193
Baker, A., 151
Baker, S. K., 32
Baker, S. M., 11
Baker-Ericzen, M. J., 93
Balla, D. A., 29, 132, 157
Bambara, L. M., 116
Bamonto, S., 32
Banda, D. R., 82
Bandura, A., 123, 126
Baraneck, G. T., 13, 14, 15, 16, 132
Barlow, D. H., 48
Baron-Cohen, S., 21, 23, 174, 195
Barouski, K., 175
Barrera, I., 159, 160, 161, 162, 164
Barron, S., 206, 216, 230
Barry, L. M., 120, 121
Barthelemy, C., 157
Barton, E. E., 14, 101
Barton, M. L., 21, 22
Bashford, A., 157
Bates, E., 170
Batshaw, M. L., 4, 59

Bauman, K. E., 103
Bauman, M. L., 6
Baumgartner, P., 196
Bauminger, N., 206, 208
Baxter, A., 197
Beattie, J., 224
Beaumont, R., 207, 208
Beck, A. R., 187
Beck, A. T., 207
Beck, S., 96
Becker, R. L., 225
Behrmann, M., 8
Beidel, D. C., 208
Beisler, J. M., 181
Belcher, R. G., 69, 229
Bellinger, O., 58
Bellini, S., 10
Ben, K. R., 110
Ben-Arieh, J., 65, 66
Benavidez, D. A., 75, 101
Benchaaban, D., 202
Benito, N., 112
Bennett, A., 10
Bennetto, L., 193, 195
Bergstrom, M. K., 113
Bertotti, D., 189
Berument, S. K., 23
Betancur, C., 6, 8, 9
Bettelheim, B., 5–6
Betz, A., 202
Beukelman, D. R., 55
Bijou, S., 74
Biklen, Douglas, 68, 69
Billingsley, F., 60, 118
Billsted, E., 235
Birnbrauer, J. S., 59, 76
Bishop, M. R., 81, 93
Bishop, S. L., 24
Blackwelder-Williams, S., 236
Blair, K. C., 114
Blankenship, K., 10, 11
Blase, K. A., 41
Bligh, S., 175
Blockberger, S., 180

# Subject Index